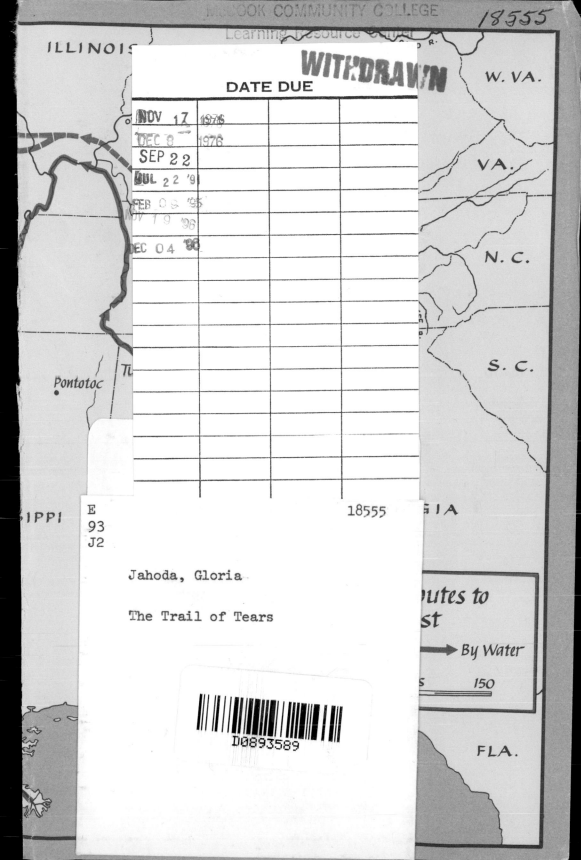

The TRAIL OF TEARS

OTHER BOOKS BY GLORIA JAHODA

NONFICTION

River of the Golden Ibis
The Other Florida
The Road to Samarkand:
Frederick Delius and His Music

FICTION

Annie
Delilah's Mountain

The
TRAIL
OF
TEARS

GLORIA JAHODA

HOLT, RINEHART AND WINSTON
NEW YORK

Library of Congress Cataloging in Publication Data

Jahoda, Gloria.
    The trail of tears.

    Bibliography: p.
    1.   Indians of North America—Land transfers.
2.   Indians of North America—Government relations—
1789–1869.   I.   Title.
E93.J2   813'.5'4   75–5470
ISBN 0–03–014871–5

First Edition

PRINTED IN THE UNITED STATES OF AMERICA
10   9   8   7   6   5   4   3   2

To the memory of my Great-Grandfather, Anders Larsson, of Torstuna and Österunda, Västmanland, Sweden, and Chicago, Illinois: historian of the new world in the language of the old.

And to the Creek Nation East of the Mississippi, Inc., especially Sakim.

Contents

LIST OF ILLUSTRATIONS   viii

Foreword   ix

Introduction: Holy Ground   1

1. Tahlonteskee Goes West and Quitewepea Brings an Invitation   19
2. Jacksa Chula Harjo Makes a Law   37
3. "Drunk, Sober, or Sick, We Will Move Them Along"   57
4. "Under the Pressure of Hunger"   73
5. The Lost Prince   89
6. Ma-ka-tai-me-she-kia-kiak Goes to War   109
7. A Gathering of Vultures   143
8. The Road to Clear Boggy   161
9. The Life and Death of Ma-to-toh-pe   173
10. Apostle to the People of Fire   189
11. White Bird's Last Stand   209
12. Asi-Yaholo Makes a Promise   243
13. Pascofa Takes the Cup   263
14. Prayers for the White Chief   279
15. The Munificent Mr. Manypenny   287
16. Sir St. George Gore Goes Hunting   301

REFERENCES   313

Notes   314

Bibliography   323

Appendix: Selected Government Documents on Indian Removal   339

INDEX   341

List of Illustrations

INTRODUCTION
Jacksa Chula Harjo and Red Eagle   10

CHAPTER 1
Quitewepea   28

CHAPTER 4
Pushmataha   76
Greenwood LeFlore   81
Moshulatubbee   83

CHAPTER 5
Eleazer Williams   91

CHAPTER 6
Wabokeshiek   114
Black Hawk   141

CHAPTER 7
Opothleyaholo   152
William McIntosh   157

CHAPTER 9
Ma-to-toh-pe ("Four Bears")   175

CHAPTER 10
Shabbona   199

CHAPTER 11
The Ridge   213
John Ridge   218
John Ross   222

CHAPTER 12
Osceola   250

Foreword

"We are going with Washington.
Which boat do we get in?"
  —SEMINOLE *Removal Song*

"The many moons and sunny days we have lived here
will long be remembered by us. The Great Spirit has
smiled upon us and made us glad. But we have agreed
to go.

"We go to a country we know little of. Our home will
be beyond a great river on the way to the setting sun. We
will build our wigwams there in another land. . . . In
peace we bid you good-bye. . . . If you come to see us,
we will gladly welcome you."

  —KEOKUK, SAC

In 1950, WHEN I WAS A GRADUATE STUDENT IN ANTHROPOLOGY AT the University of Wisconsin, I was awarded an academic fellowship which (I was told) demanded a keen research mind. I soon found out just what sort of keenness was required. Universities were innocent of copying machines in those days. I was given sets of historical documents; whenever I saw the word "Potawatomi" I was to copy it down in its context. The professor for whom I was working was trying to plot out the villages in Illinois and Wisconsin and Michigan and Indiana where the Potawatomis had once lived; he was establishing an ethnohistorical file on midwestern Indians. Somehow I kept my sanity, for I was only transcribing the word "Potawatomi" in its context for four hours a day. Others were doing it for eight. "At night I forget with ouzo," confided a fellow student with a taste for Greek liquor.

The Potawatomi project taught me how America had forcibly removed her Indian tribes originally located east of the Mississippi. These were, for the most part, people already advanced in their accommodation to whites. They were set down in a western wilderness surrounded by hostile warriors, where they were given a pittance and turned loose to fend for themselves. The Potawatomis had called their journey the "Trail of Death." But the term used by southeastern tribes wrenched from farms and plantations became the general one. Because the Creeks and Cherokees and Choctaws had wept, they called it the "Trail of Tears."

Today, some members of the removed tribes have returned. The ancestors of others never left because they were mixed-bloods who looked white and could pass. Where I now live in north Florida, the Muskogee Creek Nation East of the Mississippi, Inc., is an active member tribe of the Coalition of Eastern Native Americans. Once more the Creeks are dancing in the pinewoods; their strong voices reverberate in southern groves as they sing old songs; many of their children are attending classes in the language spoken by their forebears. The Creeks are gathering together the surviving fragments of their ancient civilization and building it anew. My own journey into

American Indian civilization began in the University of Wisconsin library, where in autumn from the window of my carrel I could see the rain of golden maple leaves falling to wood-smoke-scented earth. It was—and is—beautiful country, and another race before mine loved it. My journey has continued, especially among the Creeks of Florida. This is not an impartial book. Historians stronger than I will have to resist the temptation of passing judgment on an enormity.

It seemed neither necessary nor desirable to burden the reader with a quantity of footnotes. However, principal sources have been cited, and a bibliography is appended. All dialogue is fact; the words quoted were spoken by the persons named. In the case of several well-known figures whose words appear in a variety of sources, I have not named a specific reference; this applies to Osceola, John Ross, Tenskwatawa, Black Hawk, Keokuk, Neamathla, and Opothleyaholo.

No study of Indian removal is possible without a great debt to the University of Oklahoma's Civilization of the American Indian series, in particular Grant Foreman's *Indian Removal*. His *Last Trek of the Indians*, published by the University of Chicago Press, has also been valuable. I am, in addition, under obligation to the following: Pace Barnes, who suggested the idea; the Creek Indian Nation East of the Mississippi, Inc., in particular to Sakim, medicine man to the Creeks; to Margaret Coit for material on Andrew Jackson; to Henry M. Althoen for the gift of several tribal histories; to Charles Miller, director, for his staunch support at the Florida State University library; to the State Library of Florida, under the direction of Cecil Beach; and especially to my husband, Gerald Jahoda, Professor of Library Science at Florida State University, for his expertise in the use of government documents, which made *The Trail of Tears* possible in the first place.

GLORIA JAHODA
Tallahassee, Fla.

Introduction: Holy Ground

"Away back in that time—in 1492—there was a man by
the name of Columbus came from across the great ocean,
and he discovered the country for the white man. . . .
What did he find when he first arrived here? Did he
find a white man standing on the continent then? . . .
I stood here first, and Columbus first discovered me."
—Chitto Harjo, Creek

In the North the scarlet council fires burned long and high on frost-touched nights in the spring of 1813. It was the Moon of the Running Sap, and the United States and Britain were at war. Tecumtha of the Shawnees of Ohio was urging America's Indians to declare for the British and push out of Indian land forever the rude settlers who appeared to think they were the only Americans who mattered. The Prophet Tenskwatawa, Tecumtha's brother, was traveling from tribe to tribe exhorting their clans to rebellion as the acrid flames crackled in the dark: "O Shawnee braves! O Potawatomi men! O Miami panthers! O Ottawa foxes! O Miami lynxes! O Kickapoo beavers! O Winnebago wolves! Lift up your hatchets; raise your knives; sight your rifles! Have no fears—your lives are charmed! Stand up to the foe; he is a weakling and a coward! O red brothers, fall upon him! Wound, rend, tear, and flay, scalp, and leave him to the wolves and buzzards! O Shawnee braves! O Potawatomi men!" Had not the Great Spirit first made the Shawnees before he made the French and English out of his breast, the Dutch out of his feet, and the American Long Knives out of his hands? "All these inferior races of man he made white and placed them beyond the Stinking Lake," Tenskwatawa shouted as black smoke vanished upward into a blacker sky where stars glittered crisp and blue-white. Now it was time to drive the inferior races back across the Stinking Lake. The British must be used to help exterminate the Americans; afterward, the united Indians could deal similarly with the British.

Many of America's original settlers listened spellbound to the compelling oratory of Tecumtha and Tenskwatawa as it echoed through their ebony forests. Soon exhortations to vengeance were dividing tribes into hostile factions of moderates and fanatics, none more bitterly than the southern Creeks. The Creeks, so called by the whites because most of the sub-tribes that comprised the nation lived on rivers and streams, owned sprawling fertile lands in Georgia and Alabama. Rivers that flowed red with Georgia clay, the Flint and Chattahoochee and Ocmulgee, and Alabama streams whose slower brown waters moved under high canopies of longleaf pines and moss-draped liveoaks, the Coosa, Tallapoosa, Tombigbee, and Alabama, belonged by tradition to the Creeks. Farther south lived a scattering of Spaniards in west Florida, whose capital, Pensacola, was a boisterous town full of an assortment of outlaws, pirates between expeditions, petty Spanish officialdom, and dark-eyed señoritas who welcomed the visiting British army and navy with enthusiasm. The British Indian trading firm of Panton Leslie and Company was based in Pensacola too. In the 321 years since Columbus had begun exterminating the Tainos of the West Indies, America's Indians had become dependent on the goods traders sold them: muzzle-loading rifles, keen-honed knives, osnaburg cloth, flannel and calico and sturdy blankets, brightly colored glass beads, and also potent whiskey.

No tribe relied on traders more than the Creeks; they took to the white man's ways so readily that they were considered a "civilized tribe."[1] Parties of Creeks regularly journeyed from Georgia and Alabama to exchange skins and furs at Pensacola; many Creek women had married traders. Names like McGillivray, Farquharson, Weatherford, and McIntosh were common in the war towns and peace towns which lined ferny southern riverbanks. The Creeks had appropriated white customs that suited them—cloth dress, hunting weapons and ammunition, the keeping of peach orchards and livestock. But in most of their minds there was no doubt that their lands were theirs forever. "They are our life and breath," said one of their chiefs, Yahola Micco. "If we part with them we part with our blood."[2]

The Creeks, though not as drastically as Tecumtha's Shawnees, had already felt the pressure of white expansion into their country. They watched horrified as American frontiersmen killed game not only for food but for fun. The Creeks had taken a long step into the nineteenth century, at the same time that they had also been pushed back from the Atlantic Coast they had once known. Some were fatalists: what would be, would be. But some were not.

When Tecumtha's Religion of the Dancing Lakes came to

young Creek braves, they were ready to believe in it. As they gyrated, leaders of the dance carried red sticks that Tecumtha's followers said would show the direction from which the whites were coming. Any Indian who bore a red stick could not be injured. Soon council fires were also burning in the heavy, humid nights of the South. In the Creek war town of Tuckabatchee, five thousand people crowded the main square to watch Red Stick dancers whirl naked except for breechclouts and eagle feathers. As the hard, hammering music of rattles and the wails of reed flutes rose and fell in the perfumed darkness, the Red Stick men undulated into the *chofoka*, the town meetinghouse, while sweat poured down their burnished faces. In ringing tones, they prophesied miracles. Soon afterward, in rapid succession, came a comet, a meteor shower, and a mild earthquake. Could anyone doubt Tecumtha when he said that the earth would tremble when he stamped his foot upon it? The hotheaded warriors of the Creeks did not. But Lumhe Chati, Red Eagle, had misgivings.[3] The whites he knew in southern Alabama had been friendly. Why could the two peoples not live together?

Red Eagle was born Bill Weatherford, son of a white trader and a Creek mother whose maiden name had been Tait. The lands he knew best were the pinewoods and swamps where the Tombigbee and the Alabama rivers joined, a few miles north of the site of the ancient Indian town of Mabila. The Mabila Indians, obliterated by conflict and disease, had already passed into history, along with the Natchez and Timucuas and Calusas and Apalachees. Now Mabila (the French, when they had owned it, had called it Mobile) belonged to the Creeks. The path between Mobile and Pensacola was well worn with Creek footprints as it wound among light-speckled forests and sluggish coastal rivers, past broad bays full of marsh grasses shining darkly in the southern sunlight. The place of pilgrimage in Pensacola was the store of Panton Leslie and Company. Also in Pensacola, as American frontiersmen knew, British soldiers, with the compliance of the Spanish, were training bands of Creek Indians in organized warfare. These particular Creeks had left their old lands in Georgia and Alabama to become Siminoli, wanderers. The main body of the tribe had severed its ties with them. A Creek in Tuckabatchee was as much like a Seminole of steaming Florida as an urban Yankee merchant who carried a gold-headed cane was like a squatter in the hinterlands who lived on deer, opossum, and raccoon meat. The Creeks considered their Siminoli brothers "wild men."[4] Red Eagle, like so many of his nation, admired the efficiency of white civilization. He found the Religion of the Dancing Lakes excessive, the flight of the Siminoli futile, and the belief in the invincibility of those who carried red sticks grotesque.

During the Summer Moon, in July 1813, ninety Alabama Creek warriors set out for Pensacola with laden packhorses. Their leader was the half-breed Peter McQueen, chief of the Tallassee band. They made their way slowly through the dank heat. Frequently, they paused to rest in the shade of high pines along sepia streamlets where there was fresh water to drink. To the whites of the Alabama frontier settlements, the group of traveling Indians was frightening. The British fleet had been seen off Pensacola, and it was common knowledge that the British and Spanish were inciting Indians and selling them ammunition. From cabin to farflung cabin word was passed that the Creeks, urged on by Red Stick braves, were planning a massacre. Alabama Colonel James Caller called out a ragtag territorial militia and crossed the Tombigbee to Sisemore's Ferry on the Alabama. There, on the river's western bank, he bivouacked for the night. His recruits listened to the calling of owls and the thumping of marsh rabbits, wondering if the noises came from animal or human throats.

The militia had passed through the town of Jackson, named for the American major-general who had written such stirring recruiting notices in Tennessee: "VOLUNTEERS TO ARMS! . . . Are we the titled slaves of George the Third? The military conscripts of Napoleon? Or the frozen peasants of the Russian Czar? No—we are the freeborn sons of the only republick now existing in the world."[5] Andrew Jackson, who had known the Indian wars of the Appalachians as a boy, knew there were no

republics among Indians. Most red men understood his contempt for their race. The man whose name was an inspiration to
Colonel Caller was Jacksa Chula Harjo to the Creeks—"Jackson, old and fierce." Some said he was mad. Neighboring Choctaws called him, more succinctly, The Devil.

On the morning of July 26, Caller started the laborious crossing to the east side of the Alabama. Horses swam by the side of
long dugout canoes; it took most of the morning to get the animals across. At noon, Caller's party halted at the cowpens of a
frontiersman, where they were reinforced by a company under
the command of Dixon Bailey, a mixed-blood Creek who had
been educated in Philadelphia at white expense. Bailey's men
carried the same mixture of rifles and shotguns as Caller's; they
were as ready to fight, and their frontier horses were as sturdy.
They wanted their pay, however, more than they wanted glory.

By July 27, Peter McQueen's Creeks were returning from
Pensacola with their purchases: rifles and shotguns like those
the Long Knives carried, the bright cloth Creek wives fancied,
metal fishing hooks, sharp hunting knives, and the British-
made cookware that had replaced Creek pottery. The morning
was torrid. Before noon, McQueen's party stopped by a tiny
rivulet named Burnt Corn Creek where they cooked and ate
the game they had caught. The smoke of their fire rose slowly
into the pinetops of the little barren where they were resting.

Without warning, the Americans fell on them with shrill
yells, forcing them to plunge into the river. Soon the Americans
were loosing Creek packhorses and plundering the wares of
Panton Leslie and Company. Only a few bothered to pursue
the Indians swimming down the Alabama. Then Colonel Caller
ordered a retreat to a nearby hill in order to consolidate his
position. But the greediest of his followers held onto their
booty as they drove their horses before them, while the remaining Indians disappeared into a nearby swamp. The militiamen
clung to their new possessions thinking themselves victorious,
while Caller and Bailey tried to rally them. But the Indians
rushed out from the swamp brandishing the guns they had
never relinquished. From the swamp they ran to a bed of tall

reeds, where they began shooting at the whites in the open woodland. This was more than Caller's militia could endure. Two-thirds of them fled into the surrounding forest. Caller himself, who had marked no trail, became lost in a labyrinth of pond and hammock land and saw-palmetto thickets. When he was found fifteen days later he was "starved almost to death and bereft of his senses," babbling idiocies in his verdant hell. For him the war of the United States of America versus the Creek Indian nation had had an inglorious beginning.[6]

The prosperous mixed-bloods of southern Alabama were frightened. The white settlers were more so. The Battle of Burnt Corn would surely be avenged by the Indians. Again the council fires began spiraling over the Creek towns: Hoithlewaula, Sawanogee, Mooklausa, Woccocau, Fooschatchge, Eufaula, Hookchoioochee. Again chanting echoed through velvet summer midnights, and the whites and mixed-bloods heard it as they tossed sleepless on their cots. They knew they had to take shelter.

A mile east of the Alabama on cypress-studded Lake Tensaw lived Samuel Mims, who had built himself a rambling frame house and large storage sheds. He had plenty of fresh water from nearby springs. Here the settlers quickly erected a stockade around an acre of sandy Alabama earth; they left five hundred portholes in the fence, each one three and a half feet from the ground. They put up two unwieldy gates, one on the east and one on the west. Within the fort they hewed out temporary cabins, and at the southwest corner they started a blockhouse. To the south was a potato field, dotted by a few ramshackle slave cabins. Between the fence and Lake Tensaw tall slash pines flashed high needles in the sun; on the north were dense cane swamps, on the east trackless marshes. Fort Mims was possibly the most vulnerably situated outpost in the history of the American frontier. Men might hide undetected on any side of it.

The settlers did not wait for the blockhouse to be finished. They poured in with their featherbeds and cookpots, spinning wheels and axes and dogs and rations of dried meat. When

Major Daniel Beasley arrived to take charge, he found two of the youngest men in what passed for command. The picketing needed to be strengthened, the blockhouse to be completed and two more built and scouts sent out to tell any friendly Indians that if they were hungry there was food for them at Fort Mims. Possibly Beasley himself believed that there were friendly Indians even after the unprovoked attack at Burnt Corn Creek. By this time there were 553 people jostling each other in the fort: civilians, whites, half-bloods, officers and re-cruits, black slaves, and bedraggled women in faded calico who nursed the inevitable sick in the Alabama swamp country in high summer. Malaria and dysentery claimed fresh victims daily; within the stockade the stench of their suffering was undiluted by wind. Inland Alabama has no summer winds. In the swamps the water shimmered darkly and the slow snouts of alligators made semicircular ripples as they moved forward; water moccasins were curled over looping branches. The smell of sulfurous marsh gas drifted over the stockade to mix with the smell of disease and spoiling food. And thus Fort Mims waited.

Meanwhile Peter McQueen, the literate leader of the fateful expedition to Pensacola, received an interesting communica-tion from British and Spanish agents in Pensacola who had heard of Burnt Corn Creek. "Fight the Americans," they urged him. "If they prove too hard for you, send your women and children to Pensacola and we will send them to Havana; and if you should be compelled to fly yourselves, and the Americans should prove too hard for both of us, there are vessels enough to take us all off together."[7] The advice was bitterly debated in long *chofoka* councils. During these debates the young Chief Red Eagle sat pondering, his eyes flashing restlessly over his gathered tribesmen, his lips compressed. In his long blue-black hair he wore two eagle feathers. Red Eagle's father had been a white Georgian, his mother, a mixture of Creek and Scottish and French. He himself had elected his Creek identity. His brother, John Weatherford, had taken the white man's way. He had not felt the same strong bonds to Creek earth and to the mystical Creek religion which taught the identity of man and nature under Isakita Immissi, the Master of Breath.

Red Eagle knew that so far the Creek War had really been a civil war. His half-brother David Tait was a Red Stick dancer; a sister and all her sons were also in the war party, while her husband, McNac, had fled to Fort Mims. When Red Eagle spoke at last in the *chofoka* it was to say tersely: "Do not avenge Burnt Corn. Civil War will only weaken us."[8] In Fort Mims the Creeks had many relatives, and there were white and black women and children there as innocent as the red women and children of the Creek villages. Red Eagle was listened to, for he was trusted as a man of honor, but the Red Stick warriors outvoted him. They then asked him to lead them on a Fort Mims expedition. No one had a better reputation than Red Eagle as a fighter and a commander of men. For the sake of his honor he consented; his loyalty was with his nation. The fort would be shut tight; the battle could be turned into a token charge against an impregnable target, and such a token would surely satisfy the families of the warriors killed by the whites at Burnt Corn.

On August 29 two young blacks were ordered to mind some Fort Mims cattle in a nearby field. Not long after they passed through the gate they came running back with the news that they had seen twenty-four Indians in war paint. Hurriedly, an officer rode to the spot with the blacks and a detachment of horses. There was not a sign of the enemy. The officer and his horsemen were disgusted. At sunset the blacks were dragged back to Fort Mims. One of them was tied to the stockade and beaten until his dark back was striped red with blood. The owner of the other refused to let his slave be punished for lying and was ordered by Major Beasley to leave the fort by ten o'clock on the morning of August 30. By then the slave who had been flogged left the fort again to tend the cattle. Once more he saw a large group of Indians in the nearby forest. But this time, his back swollen with lashes, he fled to a distant settlement where he might be believed. In the meantime, the other slave's owner had abandoned his defense. The hapless

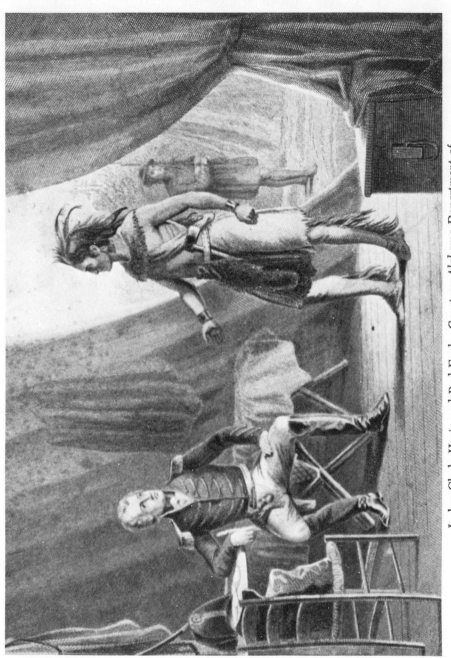

Jacksa Chula Harjo and Red Eagle. *Courtesy Alabama Department of Archives and History, Montgomery.*

black was tied to the stockade in the hot sun where he waited to be beaten. Some of the soldiers sprawled on the ground laughed at him; others indifferently played cards. A group of teenagers danced by the open gate, while nearly a hundred small children frolicked among the tents and, giggling, hid from each other behind the cabins. Inside, the sick moaned fitfully.

Red Eagle and his men—a thousand Red Sticks—waited in the swamps, their view of the fort obscured by thick cane. Their faces were painted black and their arms and legs yellow, for they had taken the path of war. They carried medicine bundles, the red sticks of invincibility, and their tomahawks, and they also carried rifles and guns from Panton Leslie and Company. At noon they heard the fort's drum summoning the officers and soldiers to lunch. For a breathless moment longer they waited. Then, with a massive whoop, they sprang forward. Only then was Red Eagle close enough to see, to his horror, that the fort gate stood wide. His warriors rushed ahead. Beasley hurried to the gate and tried to shut it, but it was banked in Alabama soil and wouldn't move. In a single blow Red Sticks felled Beasley, then left him to crawl behind the gate where he died of his gashes. Five designated prophets began dancing Red Stick dances; some of the soldiers managed to get to their weapons and shot them down. Red Eagle was shouting, trying to hold his men back. See! he roared out, the Red Stick prophets weren't invincible! But there was no stopping the Indians. They killed soldiers, settlers, blacks, women, and children. Outside the pickets another group of prophets had gathered to dance and shriek their incantations.

When the Indians set fire to the main building as well as the sheds, the flames fanned into a sunburst, and their smoke stifled the people of Fort Mims. "Oh, God, I am a dead man!" cried the father of Samuel Mims as his scalp was lifted from the pulp of his head. Somebody shouted, "To the bastion! To the bastion!" A Spaniard from Pensacola knelt with sandspurs digging into his knees, crossing himself. A black slave exultantly delivered a white child to one of the Red Sticks. Fort

Mims burned on, and its stench now was that of a charnel house. Five hours later the Indians collected the booty that was left and melted away to spend the night in the forest, its stolid trunks interlaced against the hectic light from the burning cotton gin. Not until midnight did the flames subside. By then the Red Sticks slept by their small camp fires. But Red Eagle did not sleep.

In the fetid fog of early morning, he ordered his braves to bury the Fort Mims dead. Quietly they began laying them between rows of potatoes, covering them with loose dirt and thickly clustered potato leaves. But there were too many corpses, and the Indian wounded were moaning in pain, begging to be returned to their villages. Some were put into palmetto canoes on the Alabama; others left on foot. A party of them staggered to Burnt Corn Creek where they died. In the forest, terrified dogs ran and yelped. Also in the forest a Red Stick warrior named Sanota hid. In Fort Mims he had found a woman who had once befriended him. He had hurried away with the woman and her children, explaining to his fellows that he wanted them as slaves. For weeks he hunted game for the little family; eventually, when they were strong enough, he guided them to a white settlement and then faded back into the wilderness from which he had come. At Fort Mims, a party of militia arrived to bury the dead. A young captain swallowed hard: "It is a promiscuous ruin."⁹

Early in September, at an inn in Nashville, Tennessee, Jacksa Chula Harjo lay dying. The blood from a dueling wound was soaking through the two mattresses underneath him. All the frock-coated physicians of Nashville were gathered gravely at his bedside, sure the end was near. His left shoulder had been shattered by one bullet, and another had imbedded itself in the upper bone of his left arm. All but one of the doctors agreed on amputation. Jackson was only half-conscious, but as he heard the rising and falling of their voices he began to realize what was being said. "I'll keep my arm," he rasped.

On September 12 he was still alive and convalescing at the Hermitage, his Nashville plantation. He was in bed when the news of the Fort Mims massacre came to him. "By the Eternal, these people must be saved!" His voice grew stronger as he raised himself on feather pillows and cried vengeance for the whites of the Alabama frontier. Soon he was sitting up and announcing to the men of his regiment: "The health of your general is restored. He will command in person!"

Shortly thereafter he swung onto a tall horse to ride against Red Eagle and the Red Sticks in their Moon of Roasting Ears. Fastidious politicians in Washington hadn't liked Andrew Jackson when he had represented his district in Congress. "A tall, lanky, uncouth-looking personage," they had sniffed. "Queue down his back tied with an eel skin . . . Dress singular . . . Manners those of a rough backwoodsman." But backwoodsmen were better at dealing with rebellious Indian chiefs than perfumed dandies were. In Winchester, Virginia, another "rough backwoodsman" prepared with his regiment to march against the Creeks. His name was David Crockett.

Driving hard into Alabama, where Choctaw Chief Push-mataha joined them (Choctaws and Creeks were traditional enemies), Jackson's forces descended on Black Warriors' Town, a Creek settlement on the Black Warrior River, where they sacked what they could and then razed the place. The Creeks had fled before them. Then Jackson turned south, establishing forts as he went. By early November he was camped at Ten Islands, near present-day Gadsden, from where he sent out his subordinate John Coffee to destroy the nearby Creek town of Tallussahatchee. Just after sunrise Coffee's men rushed up to the doors of the Creeks' houses; in a matter of minutes they had killed every warrior in the town, though "the enemy fought with savage fury." The surprised Red Sticks, Coffee noted, "met [death], with all its horrours, without shrinking or complaining. Not one asked to be spared, but fought as long as they could stand or sit." Coffee's troops were not satisfied with killing the 186 warriors of Tallussahatchee. For good measure they shot down women and babies until the ground ran vermilion. They went from house to house slashing and firing. Tallussahatchee had been a peaceful little town without any defenses whatever. One of the Indian women "had at least twenty balls blown through her," David Crockett noted. Afterward he added, "we shot them like dogs." The avenging of Fort Mims was crueler than the original massacre since it involved a place utterly without fortifications. Fort Mims, Red Eagle had assumed, would have protection. Not a warrior escaped from Tallussahatchee. One of the Creek houses had forty-five people inside it when Coffee's men put the torch to it. The Indians' screams didn't bother the soldiers; they spent the next day "eating potatoes from the cellar stewed in the oil of the Indians we had burned up the day before which had run down on them."[10]

A few days later Jackson led his troops into Talladega. "We shall repeat Tallussahatchee," he said confidently. But his ranks broke; veteran army men blamed it on draftees. Later the draftees started to mutiny. Jackson held them at bay with his rifle resting on the neck of his horse; his left arm was still useless. "I'll shoot dead the first man who makes a move to leave!" he thundered. That ended the mutiny.

The warriors of eight Creek towns gathered in Artussee on the east bank of the Tallapoosa River, at the mouth of Calebee Creek. It was a place sacred to the Red Sticks, "beloved ground" which had been reserved for Creek war councils. Surely the magic sticks, the incantations, and the Dance of the Lakes would protect them here. But the Red Sticks hadn't reckoned on the bizarre reinforcements which arrived to swell Jackson's ranks. Four hundred friendly Indians, mostly Choctaws but some Creeks who opposed the Red Sticks, arrived in the care of a Jewish trader named Abraham Mordecai. Mordecai had a reputation as "a queer fellow" among the Creeks. He traded his wares for ginseng root, hickory nut oil, and pelts. What the Indians didn't know was that hickory nut oil was considered a delicacy by French epicures in New Orleans; Mordecai sold it there for many times more than what he had paid for it. Sometimes Mordecai was "amorous." He had been charmed by a Creek squaw, wife of a Red Stick warrior, and emerged from this intrigue with a thrashing that had left him unconscious and his trading post a heap of ashes. The Red Sticks recognized Mordecai only too well when they saw him. They also recognized many of their brother Creeks who, with Jackson's soldiers, put the torch to Artussee's houses. This time two hundred Creek Indians were burned alive; four hundred of their wooden houses and outbuildings went up in smoke, and women and children and infants perished in a second avenging of Fort Mims. When the news reached Red Eagle, he led his warriors to Ecunchate, the most holy ground of all, where they believed they would truly be unconquerable. Not only would red sticks protect them, but stout fencing and a location atop a river bluff. Ecunchate symbolized the relationship of the Creeks to the earth. Its sacredness represented the sacredness of every other inch of Creek soil where Creeks hunted or tilled.

In marched the troops of Jacksa Chula Harjo. The Creeks hastily evacuated their wives and children into the sanctuary of surrounding swamps across the river. Most of the Red Sticks also were able to escape when Jackson's cavalry failed to understand orders and charge. But the soldiers were exultant; they had the destroyer of Fort Mims, Red Eagle himself, at bay. Red Eagle, however, was too quick for them. He leaped onto his gray horse and began a wild ride along the banks of the Alabama. With Jackson's cavalry in pursuit, horse and man flew against the wind until they reached a high bluff fifteen feet above the river. Red Eagle hesitated only a moment. Then "with a mighty bound" he and his horse pitched over the bluff to the river below, where they disappeared beneath the waves. Incredulous, Jackson's horsemen watched horse and man rise again. Red Eagle held his horse's mane with one hand and his rifle with the other. Ecunchate, the Holy Ground, had been reduced to smoldering ruins, but Red Eagle survived.

The winter of 1814 passed with Jackson on an elusive Red Eagle's trail, while Jackson's troops laid waste Creek towns. Now Red Eagle was determined never to give up. Jackson had turned Indian against Indian in his determination to subjugate every red man in the United States. At the Horseshoe Bend of the Tallapoosa River, Red Eagle gathered his Red Sticks to build a breastwork of logs; assailants would be exposed to cross fire. Into the Horseshoe Bend poured the militant braves of Hillabee Town, Ocfuske, Oakchoie, Eufaulahatchee, Yauca, Hickory Ground, and the Fish Pond Town, all of them waiting for Andrew Jackson who had been joined by a regiment of Cherokees from north Georgia and the Carolinas. These Cherokees believed that in the Red Sticks they were fighting renegade outlaws and that Jackson cherished their loyalty and would reward them well. It was the Cherokees who captured the Red Sticks' canoes by stealth and took them to the other side of the river, where they were soon filled with Choctaws, Cherokees, and Americans who paddled furiously across to throw torches into the warriors' midst at Horseshoe Bend. The breastwork went up in smoke. The defenses of the Red Sticks crumbled. The Indians died at knife- and gunpoint, red sticks clutched in their charred hands. Most of the warriors who tried to escape by plunging into the Alabama were caught by Jackson's men and drowned, their heads wrenched by hostile hands under the brown water. After it was all over, gunsmoke drifted above the Tallapoosa while mockingbirds sang obliviously and sunlight streamed through the vapor onto the corpses. Only ten Red Sticks had escaped. But one of them was Red Eagle, and at the junction of the Coosa and Tallapoosa he tried heartening the other nine. It was no use. This, too, was Beloved Ground, but the demoralized Creek warriors had lost their faith in the Religion of the Dancing Lakes, in Tecumtha's prophecies and red sticks and the blood-tingling music of war. They left Red Eagle to muse at the Beloved Ground alone.

One evening, in front of his quarters, Jackson was "accosted by an unarmed, light-colored Indian" who wore buckskin breeches and tattered moccasins.

"General Jackson?"

"Yes?"

"I am Bill Weatherford."

Inside, Red Eagle explained why he had come to surrender to his antagonist. "I can oppose you no longer. I have done you much injury. I should have done you more, but my warriors are killed. I am in your power. Dispose of me as you please."

"You are not in my power," Andrew Jackson answered slowly. "I had ordered you brought to me in chains, but you have come of your own accord. You see my camp. You see my arms. You know my object. If you think you can contend against me in battle go and head your warriors."

"Ah!" Red Eagle's smile was dry. "Well may such language be addressed to me now. There was a time"—he paused—"a time when I could have answered you. I could animate my fighters to battle, but I cannot animate the dead. General Jackson, I have nothing to request for myself, but I beg you to send for the women and children of the war party who have been driven to the woods without an ear of corn. They never did any harm. Kill me instead, if the white people want it done."

Wordlessly Jackson offered Red Eagle a glass of brandy. The warrior drank it. "Save the wives and children of the Creeks, and I will persuade to peace any Red Sticks remaining in my nation," he said. Deliberately, Jackson nodded. Then he extended his hand. Red Eagle took it, looked at his adversary's craggy features for a long moment and then, bowing, departed.[11]

With that handshake, the two principal architects of the ultimate fate of the American Indian had sealed a bargain. Red Eagle's leadership in war had angered America. It had also convinced Andrew Jackson that America's frontiers would always be frontiers while there were Indians to annoy the settlers. The Indians must go. They couldn't be exterminated wholesale because of world opinion. But they could be uprooted and packed off to some remote corner of the country where they wouldn't be in the way. This haven would belong to them, they would be told in the traditional language of America's Indian treaties, "as long as the green grass grows and the water flows," provided they began hiking en masse with a military escort to get there. At the Horseshoe Bend of the Tallapoosa River in Alabama, Andrew Jackson silently pledged himself to the policy of Indian Removal which in his presidency was to become law. It would be a simple law: any Indian who remained on his ancestral lands affirming his Indian identity would be a criminal. The Indians would be relocated somewhere on the West's Great Plains. It didn't matter that the Great Plains already had Indian inhabitants who could hardly be expected to welcome red refugees. But the government would tout as a mecca the grasslands and forested river bottoms near the Red and Arkansas and Verdigris rivers, in Red Eagle's time an all but uncharted mystery. Not until five decades had passed did the Choctaw Indian Allen Wright give it a name—perhaps not without irony. The Choctaw word for red was *houma; okla* meant people. Oklahoma was Indian destiny before it graced a single map. Not an Indian alive, except those who already inhabited it, considered it Holy Ground. East of the Mississippi, Ecunchate was lost land, a lost dream, and the road that led out of it forever became the Trail of Tears.

1

Tahlonteskee Goes West and Quitewepea Brings an Invitation

"It all meant nothing but 'Move a little farther. You are too near me.' "

—Speckled Snake, Cherokee

THE IDEA OF AN INDIAN TERRITORY WAS OLDER THAN THE LOUISI-
ana Purchase of 1803, which marked the beginnings of the
American quest for an empire stretching from ocean to rock-
bound ocean. It was older, too, than Meriwether Lewis and
William Clark, who had toiled over high emerald mountains
and across scorched infinities where grasses murmured a perpetual litany. The land Lewis and Clark penetrated was known
only to Indian tribes who lived on the buffalo and by the horse.
The Indian woman Sacajawea had been the expedition's guide;
by the beginning of the nineteenth century, red men were
courteously arranging their own doom. The first indication of
the white man's dream of settling the continent's original inhabitants somewhere far from the fertile lands that in the East
white farmers coveted had come in a treaty made with the
Delaware Indians in 1778. The treaty provided that the Delawares, with the approval of the Continental Congress, might
enter the union of former British colonies and eventually head
a state composed of all other tribes subject to the Delawares.
It sounded splendid from the mouths of interpreters, and the
Delawares made their marks on the parchment. They were to
be the rulers of something or other someday; because of this
promise, they fought with the Americans in the Revolution.
After the peace, they had not the slightest idea of how to go
about starting their state, and the Long Knives were less than
eager to tell them.

Not quite ten years later, in a treaty with the Cherokees of
Georgia and the Carolinas, the government promised Indians
"the right to send a deputy of their choice whenever they think
fit to Congress."[1] On paper it looked impressive, but nobody
bothered to tell the Cherokees the clause meant anything other
than an Indian agent to represent their interests and see that
they were not cheated by traders. The Creeks had dallied with
the concept of an Indian state under their shrewd eighteenth-
century chief, Alexander McGillivray, who had promised land-
hungry Georgians that he would grant them Creek lands on
the Oconee if they would permit his tribe to claim all Georgian
land south of the Altamaha. The suggestion came to nothing. A

generation later a dashing and glib adventurer named William Augustus Bowles declared himself director-general of the Muskogee Creeks and attempted to form an empire of his own. He cut an imposing swath through the South, pillaged the warehouses of Panton Leslie and Company and threw lighted faggots into them, was captured, escaped, and then was captured again to die in prison, his visions of grandeur faded forever, and his world a patch of blue sky beyond glinting gunmetal bars.[2]

With the Louisiana Purchase, suggestions came thick and fast to Thomas Jefferson as to how he could most quickly get rid of the Indians. One suggestion was to colonize the western part of the Louisiana lands with them. Where before there had been only the idea of putting them somewhere, there was now the somewhere to put them. From the surf-etched shores of the Atlantic to the meandering, muddy width of the Mississippi, the Long Knives were breaking the country with their moldboard plows. They hotly resented the Indians living beside them. What rights did the Indians have?

Occupancy? [asked a settler of Pennsylvania] A wild Indian, with his skin painted red, and a feather through his nose, has set his foot on the broad continent of North and South America; a second wild Indian with his ears cut out in ringlets or his nose slit like a swine or a malefactor also sets his foot on the same extensive tract of soil. . . . What use do these ringed, streaked, spotty and speckled cattle make of the soil? Do they till it? Revelation said to man, "Thou shalt till the ground." This alone is human life. . . . What would you think of . . . addressing yourself to a great buffalo to grant you land?[3]

But such an argument could cut two ways. James Madison, planter in the Virginia which had once belonged to Powhatan and his allies, was by 1817 President of the United States, and confided his misgivings to his friend James Monroe.

The *unqualified* right [he pronounced in italics] of a civilized people to claim land used by people in the hunter-state, on the principle that the earth was intended for those who would make it most conducive to the sustenance and increase of the human race, might imply a right in a people cultivating it with the Spade to say to one using the Plough, either adopt our mode or let us substitute it ourselves. It might also not be easy to repel the claims of those without land in other countries, if not in our own, to vacant lands within the U.S. likely to remain for a *long* period unproductive of human food.

If a French peasant wanted a farm, could he not ask for a stretch on the Arkansas River because nobody else was growing any crop there? To Madison it was not a comforting thought. The more conscientious of the Indian agents had doubts of their own. America was marching westward ever faster to the merry tune of Yankee Doodle. "Nothing will repress them this side of the Pacific. The snowy heights of the Rocky Mountains are already scaled."[4] Would western settlers forget Red Eagle and Fort Mims? Would they suddenly become kind to people they hated with self-righteous fury? And if they didn't want Indian land themselves, wouldn't their children want it after them? Some of the Indian agents, who had lived long enough with their tribes to have formed deep friendships with Indian men and liaisons or marriages with Indian women, thought the whole idea of an Indian territory unrealistic. They knew their countrymen would want the last acre of the continent that wasn't pure desert. And if you were justifying the idea of an Indian territory on humanitarian grounds, it wouldn't look quite right to the rest of the world to put the Indians on such a desert. There was also an additional problem with the trans-Mississippi west: Indians already lived there.

Some of the Cherokees realized what would happen, even before Jackson had vanquished Red Eagle at Horseshoe Bend. The Carolinas and Georgia were swiftly, inexorably filling with stern Scotch-Irish and tough plebeian English who wanted better lives than the old country had given them. One of the sternest of the Scotch-Irish was Andrew Jackson himself. The Cherokee Chief Tahlonteskee, who had witnessed the slaughter at Horseshoe Bend, decided to leave eastern America before he was dispossessed of everything he had. Nervously, William Clark, now a general and the Indian superintendent based in St. Louis, gathered together some Osage chiefs living in the vicinity of the Arkansas River and asked them whether they would mind sharing their lands with Tahlonteskee's followers. Pots, pans, cloth, beads, and shining knives were lavishly distributed to the Osages. They were also sold whiskey by attendant traders. Before long they had signed away what was to become most of Arkansas and a large chunk of Missouri. This, Clark reasoned, could become the new land of Tahlonteskee's people. Tahlonteskee set out from the East to explore it with three hundred of his band—seventy of them warriors—and across the Mississippi he discovered a country like none he had ever seen before. At first, as a man of the Appalachian Mountains, he did not know what to make of it.

It was a world of high grasses that sang in the wind, of riverbanks thick with willows and cottonwoods, of the eroded oak-filled Ozark Mountains. On the uplands scurried prairie chickens. From south to north, in summer, ranged the great buffalo herds which had already disappeared from Tahlonteskee's country in the East. Ruddy rivers became choked with them as they swam across. In the mud of buffalo wallows they rubbed their hides free of insects and vermin. Their calves fattened on the abundance of forage. Their meat fed the Osages and Blackfeet and Piegans and Mandans and Hidatsas and a host of other tribes. But there was surely enough for all, Tahlonteskee reasoned. He watched river hackberries shimmering in the sunlight; he heard the beating wings of golden eagles and the jumping of catfish. Magpies and crows shouted to each other. At night Nahquisi, the evening star, hung low, and coyotes howled. It was a good country, Tahlonteskee argued with himself. The rivers flowed as bright as the brocades that rich white planters' wives wore back home. Wild turkeys

ran in the buffalo and grama grasses, and at twilight the whip-
poorwills called softly. The smells were those of blossoming
violet prairie clover and black earth and the bluestem grasses
that were so tough they could exhaust a man walking through
them. The sweetish smell of gypsum-rich river water was borne
on long wind swells that combed the prairies and mountain
maples and rippled the waters. Elk herds moved slowly as far
south as the river the Long Knives called the Red. There were
deer and jackrabbits and prairie dogs, squirrels and cottontails.
In autumn the migrating geese arrived, their silhouettes swift
against orange moons. Here the Cherokees could follow the
chase unimpeded. Had not the Osages agreed to sign part of
this place away? It was an expanse whispering with its own
abundance. By 1819 Tahlonteskee's Cherokees had ceded
much of their territory east of the Mississippi, and his band
had begun the long trek toward the sun-dappled wilderness
where Osages rode with the wind and now regretted their bargain with William Clark. But the rest of the Cherokees clung
on to their Appalachian villages. To them, the devil they knew,
the white man, was better than the devil they didn't know, the
Osages, who were a storied scourge to other prairie tribes. Yet
Tahlonteskee feared the Long Knives more.

Soon he was writing, "I am here settled, fond of my situation, loving my present house and field." But he began to see
disturbing things. White hunters came into the grasslands
every summer and began a wholesale extermination:

> They do not destroy less than five thousand buffaloes every
> summer for no other profit but for the tallow. We are far from
> having any objection to any persons killing game, provided they
> take it away, but a thousand weight of meat is thrown away for
> no other profit than perhaps 20 pounds tallow. This is a thing
> which will render game shortly scarce and we must then see our
> children suffer.[5]

The Osages grew restless, both at the presence of the hunters
and of Tahlonteskee's Cherokees. Under their Chief Pahuska,

White Hair, they raided the Cherokee settlements, stealing weapons and horses and plows and often murdering Cherokee families. A frightened Indian agent, Major William Lovely, begged Washington for troops. The Osage chiefs Clermont and Tallai traveled to Prairie du Chien, on the Mississippi, to receive their customary presents—government bribes for peace. When they received an unusually meagre handout they were incensed, and on their return across the tallgrass they were surprised by vengeance-seeking Cherokees who shot ten of the party. Clermont and Tallai escaped, but reported to Major Lovely: "We have received no present. We should be glad if you would appoint some person close to us that could see our conduct towards our brothers the whites and that could see our presents brought to our village."[6] As Lovely studied the sprawling script of a literate Osage amanuensis, he foresaw a holocaust; then he called together representatives of the rival nations at the mouth of the Verdigris River.

The two tribes were a sharp contrast. The Cherokees farmed, lived in well-built houses, and most wore the same clothing white men wore. The great Sequoyah had not yet catapulted his people into literacy in their native tongue, but they had readily taken to the technology of the Long Knives. The Osages were horsemen who wandered the plains. Their vegetable plots were small. Their heads were resplendent with eagle feathers. The buffalo and grass and sky were their universe. Buffalo furnished home, clothing, food, warm bedding, and tack. When the first frosts came, the Osages followed the buffaloes after the harvest of their crops until spring planting time, and they believed they had enough hunting rivalries with other tribes of the plains without permitting eastern refugees to settle close at hand.

Major Lovely's proposition to the Osages was that the federal government would pay all the fines they had incurred on raids of the Cherokees if they would cede the country which lay between the Cherokee villages and the Verdigris River. This could become the Cherokees' hunting grounds. On its southern frontier ran the Arkansas, bordered by rich oak bottoms and full of catfish and pike. At the council the Osages reluctantly agreed, but not until one of them had neatly stolen Major Lovely's horse and disappeared.

The government now became enchanted with the idea that it could get rid of all the Cherokees left in the East. The Secretary of War appointed commissioners to treat with them, and one of the commissioners was Andrew Jackson. Jackson rounded up all the Cherokees he could at Calhoun, Tennessee, and also received a delegation from Arkansas. When he asked the Indians to give up all their lands east of the Mississippi they were at first incredulous. Were they not good neighbors and farmers? The eastern Cherokees swore they would not give up their homes; then Jackson found two half-breeds who were corruptible. Grandly they signed a treaty Jackson quickly forwarded to Washington; since the signers were from the Arkansas country, they had nothing to lose. "We were compelled," Jackson reported,

> to promise to John D. Chisholm the sum of one thousand dollars to stop his mouth and obtain his consent . . . without this we could not have gotten the national relinquishment. In the course of the conference we were obliged to promise the chiefs from the Arkansas one hundred dollars each for their expenses in coming here—and to three other influential chiefs the sum of one hundred dollars.[7]

Under the presidency of James Monroe, Indian Removal turned gradually from scheme to policy. Monroe had long bouts with his conscience. By 1819 there were six thousand Cherokees on the Arkansas, and traders who traveled the frontier marveled that their settlements "look like those of white people." At first Monroe considered it "too absurd" to herd the Indians into a corner of the West, but Andrew Jackson did not. Incensed by the reports he heard of British agents lingering on in Spanish Florida, he rode south with an army of rifle-toting backwoodsmen to exterminate the Seminoles who were flirting with the British crown. Soon America was involved in a Florida war, which ended with Jackson's capture of Pensacola and the death of two Englishmen at Fort St. Marks, near Apalachee Bay. Jackson decided, although he had no evidence, that the Englishmen had been plotting with the natives with whom one of them, Alexander Arbuthnot, had been trading.

The United States negotiated with a weakened Spain for the purchase of Florida, and while official Washington expressed horror at Jackson's high-handedness, the rank and file of the Long Knives loved him for it. Old Hickory was a hero, the darling of the small farmers and tradespeople who made up the bulk of the nation. The Seminole War was as great a triumph as Horseshoe Bend had been. All this the Cherokees watched. The treaty most had opposed was now law.

In 1821 a test case, *Johnson v. McIntosh*, found its way to the Supreme Court, and Justice John Marshall delivered an opinion that was a profound shock to the Long Knives. Indians, he pronounced, not only owned land but had a right to do with it as they thought fit. Congress had no more reason to steal their land than the land of white people. The defense attorney for the Indians involved in the case had been crusty constitutional lawyer Daniel Webster, who felt the triumph of an avenging angel at the case's conclusion. Jackson grimly understood he would have to bide his time. Daniel Webster and John Marshall said they wanted to save the redskins from "degradation and extinction."

Support for the removal policy came from an unexpected quarter: a band of Shawnees. Quitewepea was a chief under whom the Shawnees had handed over much of their land in Ohio. What Quitewepea had gotten out of the arrangement was a large tract of property and the empty title "colonel." But most of the Shawnees soon regretted their decision to leave the soft green Ohio forests where deer abounded and thrushes sang. Quitewepea, sensing his unpopularity, moved west to his new estate, and a faithful group joined him. The rest, remembering Tecumtha's great days, stubbornly remained in Ohio and refused to budge. Long before the advent of the Long Knives, the Shawnees had crossed the western sea from Asia on

Quitewepea. Portrait by C.B. King. *Courtesy Smithsonian Institution, Washington, D.C.*

the back of Great Turtle. It was they who had found America, not the Long Knives. But Quitewepea still cherished plans for further power and began ingratiating himself with William Clark.[8]

In 1823, in a Cherokee village in Arkansas, members of several tribes gathered in council. The Cherokees and Shawnees were not the only peoples who had fled the Long Knives in the East. The West was beginning to fill with Delawares, Weas, Kickapoos, Piankeshaws, and Peorias. By this time Tahlonteskee was dead. The new Cherokee leader, Takatoka, was old and respected. John Jolly, a mixed blood and Tahlonteskee's brother, was also influential. Jolly feared whites less than the others, perhaps because he had grown up in Tennessee with a rangy white boy who had loved hunting and forest life: Sam Houston. Once Houston had struck him, but Jolly had forgotten their quarrel and remained steadfastly loyal. They were kindred spirits, and Sam Houston had been eager to learn Indian ways with nature, game, and endurance. Still, not all white men were Sam Houstons, so Jolly had followed Tahlonteskee and Takatoka west.

On the Arkansas campground the spectacle was impressive. The eastern Indians had covered their tents with bearskins, while those of the upper Missouri had used tanned buffalo robes. The women were stylish in buckskins and ornaments that caught the harsh southern light when they moved. Over open fires, dogs were roasted on branch spits. Children shouted, and the men laughed and gambled with each other in Indian games with bone counters. The odor of woodsmoke was pungent. Solemnly the chiefs gathered in the lodge to debate. When they emerged, it was with the decision that Quitewepea should send an invitation to the tribes east of the Mississippi to come and join their brethren in the West. Far from white communities, the Indians could establish a civilization of their own. To the Shawnees in Ohio, Quitewepea was to carry a ceremonial string of white wampum as a mark of respect. On the way east he stopped to visit William Clark, now two decades removed from the conquest of the Rockies with Meriwether Lewis. Sacajawea was for Clark a steadily dimming memory.

"We are surrounded in Ohio, Indiana and New York by a dense white population," Quitewepea told him. "We have few lands left to hunt on. There is too much whiskey. We want our own laws, and to receive teachers of husbandry among us, so that we may enjoy the blessings of agriculture and industry." Clark was impressed. Quitewepea and the Monroe administration obviously saw eye to eye. To Secretary of War John C. Calhoun, Chief Jolly sent a similar message: "Father you must not think that by removing we shall return to the savage life, you have learned us to be herdsmen and cultivators, and to spin and weave. Our women will raise the cotton and the Indigo and spin and weave cloth to cloath our children."[9] The Mother Hubbard was about to cross the Mississippi. By now Sequoyah had invented his Cherokee syllabary, and his people were asking for the Preacher Book. It was only, thought Jolly, a matter of time until they would intermarry so thoroughly with the whites that as a nation they would cease to exist. Meanwhile, they would have elbow room in the West.

Takatoka was visiting tribes southwest of the Arkansas Cherokees to put forth Quitewepea's plans and assure the hunters of the plains that the newcomers would kill little game but grow many crops. Several times the Osages went on the warpath, and Takatoka had to lead his delegation against them. At last he was able to set out to join Quitewepea; the Cherokees had commissioned him as their Beloved Man to represent them among the Shawnees, Ottawas, Wyandots, Tuscaroras, and Miamis at their Wapakoneta council ground in Ohio.

But the weary Takatoka got no farther than Kaskaskia, Illinois. There he was felled by a fever. On his sickbed he pleaded with his men to continue the mission without him. The future of America's Indians, he told them, depended on it. After delirium-filled hours he was placed in an unadorned grave near the Mississippi, and his cohort of seventeen silently turned their thin horses toward the East. While they traveled, President Monroe delivered a speech to Congress:

> It would promote essentially the security and happiness of the tribes within our limits if they could be prevailed on to retire west and north of our States and Territories on lands to be procured for them by the United States in exchange for those on which they now reside. Surrounded as they are, and pressed as they will be on every side by the white population, it will be difficult if not impossible for them with their kind of government to sustain order among them. Their interior will be exposed to frequent disturbances, to remedy which the interposition of the United States will be indispensable, and thus their government will gradually lose its authority until it is annihilated. In this process the moral character of the tribes will also be lost. . . . All these evils may be avoided if these tribes will consent to remove beyond the limits of our present States and Territories. Lands equally good and perhaps more fertile may be procured for them in those quarters. The relations between the United States and such Indians would still be the same.[10]

How the Indians had survived so far with their system of social control in the presence of white settlers was not specified. The tribes had had nearly three hundred years in which to fall apart. Neither did Monroe explain the exact way in which moral character might be lost east of the Mississippi but preserved west of it when whites were already settling there. Veteran Indian agents smiled thinly. Did President Monroe really believe that if the Indians were given fertile lands in the West no Americans would go there and want them? What of peoples like the remote Pawnees, who sang to their Morning Star and murmured on their own Holy Ground:

> *Remember, remember the sacredness of things,*
> *Running streams and dwellings,*
> *The young within the nest,*
> *A hearth for sacred fire,*
> *The holy flame . . .*[11]

Would the moral character of the Pawnees be improved by the coming of rivals to their sacred earth?

Secretary Calhoun suggested that immediate cessions be sought from the Osage and Kansa Indians and that the eastern tribes be collected to live on these relinquished acres. It seemed most fitting to Calhoun to remove the Cherokees first, because they had already begun the transplant from the Appalachians to Arkansas, then the Piankeshaws and Weas and Shawnees and Kickapoos and Delawares who had also begun drifting, dispossessed, into Arkansas and Missouri. Ohio and Indiana could then be swept clear of the Wyandots, Senecas, Miamis, and Eel River Indians, and the Illini and related tribes could be shoved out of Illinois. It would be very tidy; Mr. Calhoun was an orderly man. When a delegation of Cherokees and Shawnees arrived in Washington, Mr. Calhoun's joy was great. The Indians agreed with him! The visitors were dined, but not often wined, at stately Washington dinner tables under sparkling chandeliers for a pleasant month and then sent back to join their brethren at the Wapakoneta Council grounds. They left laden with gifts of top hats and spats. Calhoun also sent Lewis Cass, a representative of the War Department, to Wapakoneta.[12] When Cass arrived, he found that the Ohio Shawnees were not impressed with the invitation of Quitewepea to join him in the West. Most of the Shawnees flatly refused to be dislodged, though a few Shawnees and Senecas, unhappy with their Ohio chiefs, went over to Quitewepea's side after he had made an impressive speech. Then Quitewepea rode west to meet again with William Clark to whom one of the Cherokees gave a less than truthful picture of how matters stood: "This wampum is from the Mingoes, this the Wyandots, this the Delawares, this the Senecas, this the Oneidas, this the Ontarios, and this from the women begging us to pursue our undertaking and not give it up." Quitewepea added: "We have a large party of Shawnees and Senecas with us. We will make our fires for the present and enter the swamps near the Mississippi and try to sustain ourselves until we hear from you. I hope you will take pity on us and afford us some aid in corn, lead, and powder this winter."[13] The bitter saga of charity had begun. Quitewepea also deplored the intransigence of Tecumtha's surviving brother Tenskwatawa. The Prophet had "learned no sense" since the days of his exhortations during the War of 1812.

Senator Benton of Missouri grew alarmed. He and his people didn't relish the idea of having the red men dumped on *them!* The exiles must be shipped still farther west, he warned. White civilization "threatened to swallow" red. The morals of the Indians must be preserved by sending them to the northern half of what was to become Oklahoma. Kansas, too, ought to be cleared of them, except for the white Osage descendants of the powerful Chouteau fur-trading dynasty based in St. Louis. To the Indians back east the situation was increasingly bewildering. A few more decided to cast their lots with Quitewepea after all, while some vehemently vowed that nothing but death would banish them. Councils reverberated with shrill arguments. Straggling parties of refugees began passing through small Indiana and Ohio towns. The Indians' belongings were strapped to their horses and piled in rickety wooden wagons. Even Tenskwatawa had a change of heart. But when he reached his new domain he didn't think much of it, and he was given property on the Kansas River which he would have to share with the South Wind People for whom the river was named.

Christian missionaries also played a part in the first stages of the epic of removal. The Reverend Jedidiah Morse, reporting to the War Department, told them what they wanted to hear. The Indians'

independence, their rights, their title to the soil which they occupy are all *imperfect* in their kind. . . . The *jurisdiction* of the whole country they inhabit, according to the established law of nations, appertains to the Government of the United States, and the right of disposing of the *soil* attaches to the power that holds the jurisdiction. . . . The *complete* title to their lands rests in the Government of the United States.[14]

Through the person of the Reverend Mr. Morse, it was possible for the War Department to "get right with God," in the evangelists' phrase.

But even the Reverend had some qualms. "Arkansas must be called sickly. Every newcomer without exception has been sick. The sickness here is fever and ague: a slow bilious fever. Very few deaths occur by disease, but people remain weak and fit for nothing for a long time." Arkansas was full of swamps and mosquitoes. "Back from the water streams the land is quite indifferent."

Morse tried mediating quarrels between Osages and Cherokees. The Cherokees were "very decent in their deportment," and the Osages "knew nothing of the use of money." Morse was torn by his own ambivalence. Something in him was stirred when he came to a great Osage village, its warriors and chiefs massed on horseback to greet him before its oven-shaped earth lodges. At night the braves danced for the missionary; they had a God, Wakontah, to whom they chanted prayers every morning for an hour. The Osages were "the only Indians with a religion,"[15] Morse decided. Had they not given him eight horses?

The Reverend Isaac McCoy, a Baptist, found the condition of the Ottawas of the Great Lakes less impressive. Wagonloads of whiskey were being driven from village to village by eager snarling traders, their faces thick with stubble. Whole bands of hopeless Ottawas lay drunk for days at a time under the tall firs of their rocky domain. In his diary McCoy noted that no matter what missions he established, he would be driven out if other whites lived nearby. "No band of Indians has ever thrived when crowded by white population." While he was camping beside a rushing northern brook, McCoy had an inspiration. Why not an Indian Canaan, a Promised Land? It was "a supernatural revelation." He would herd his charges away from temptation. Stirred by his project, McCoy traveled to Washington, where he confessed he "found little pleasure in sitting on fine sofas in ceiled houses." He missed the clean winds and fragrant forests of the Ottawas. But Secretary of

War Calhoun was friendly. The Monroe administration found McCoy's plan acceptable, though it didn't care if the Indians turned Baptist or not. McCoy believed he would have to pass through a region of "irreclaimable sterility" to reach his paradise. The Indians to whom he had been talking had told him the West was full of serpents and man-devouring snakes. But he persevered:

> We are going to look for a home for a homeless people who were once lords of all the Continent of America, and whose just claims have never been acknowledged by others nor conveyed away by themselves. . . . We are limited to the regions west of Arkansas Territory and Missouri state. Should the inhospitableness of that country deny them a place there, they will be left destitute.[16]

The Ottawas saw the proposed journey differently:

> *The hawks turn their heads nimbly round;*
> *They turn to look back on their flight.*
> *The spirits of the sun place have whispered them words.*
> *They fly with their messages swift:*
> *They look as they fearfully go.*
> *They look to the furthermost end of the world,*
> *Their eyes glancing light and their beaks boding harm.*

For the hawks knew the Ottawas' fate.

Everyone who advocated removal had a reason. Some, like Isaac McCoy, were idealists. Some, like Quitewepea, wanted to secure a personal fortune. Other Indians wanted to flee Long Knife factories. But there were still those who maintained the lands of their birth were sacred. How could men buy and sell earth, air, water, and trees? When the United States created the Bureau of Indian Affairs in 1824, as a division of the War Department, the bureau's official business was described as the making of treaties to expedite exile. And when the Cherokees adopted a formal constitution in Georgia three years later, Georgians were gleeful. This was a violation of Article 4 of the U.S. Constitution, they argued, which provided that "no new

State shall be formed or erected within the jurisdiction of any other state . . . without the consent of the Legislatures of the States concerned as well as of the Congress." Swiftly Georgia annexed the Cherokee lands within her domain and declared the Indians were subject not to their own laws and constitution but to Georgia's.[17] The operative Washington word was still usually "emigration," but Georgians especially knew what emigration meant. When Monroe stepped down from office in 1825 and John Quincy Adams succeeded him, people who had ruefully watched the legal triumph of Daniel Webster in the Supreme Court were encouraged. Adams himself had fought Webster and had contempt for Monroe's hesitations.

All the while James Fenimore Cooper was creating fictional Indians of tall stature and impressive character. Some of his readers wondered whether all of Uncas's race were wild animals—especially those readers who had not seen Indians gorged with the liquor white profiteers sold them. But John Quincy Adams, "Old Man Eloquent," knew Cooper's prose was nonsense. Indians were savages, and Justice Marshall was a fool. During 1825 and 1826 Adams initiated treaties with the Dakotas, Osages, Kansas, Chippewas, Sacs, Foxes, Winnebagoes, Miamis, Ottawas, and Potawatomis by which the tribes agreed, under the influence of rotgut moonshine, to emigrate west. The Shawnees of Ohio watched them start on their way knowing their own days in the high hickory forests near Wapakoneta were numbered. Everywhere chiefs were being created by the Long Knives and then made to sign their marks for a price. Other chiefs, like McIntosh of the Creeks, were recognized as leaders of their tribes but they still proved human in the face of pressure. And perhaps the Delawares were remembering some stanzas from the Walum Olum, their tribal epic, as they prepared for the journey west:

> Large and long was the east land.
> Rich and good was the east land.
> Shall we be free and happy then in the new land?
> We want rest, and peace, and wisdom.

~ 2 ~

Jacksa Chula Harjo Makes a Law

"I cannot believe that the United States Government will
still continue to pursue the lukewarm system of policy,
in her relations with the Indians, as has hitherto been
adopted, to effect the purpose of removing nation after
nation of them from the lands of their fathers into
the remote wilderness."
                                    —JOHN ROSS, CHEROKEE, 1822

"An Indian tribe is sovereign to the
extent that the U.S. permits it to
be sovereign."
      —FEDERAL DISTRICT JUDGE
         RUSSELL SMITH, 1973

"Father, as to the plan of removing to some other
part of the country, and leaving our present
habitations, we have no idea of it, and are at
present determined to remain here."
                          —CAPTAIN POLLARD, SENECA, 1819

THE SEEDS OF THE CONFLICT HAD BEEN SOWN, OF COURSE, EVEN before the Pilgrim Fathers had asked Squanto for help and learned to fertilize their corn with pungently dead New England pollack and cod. A short way inland from grassy maritime dunes and thickets of beach plums, they had found out how to stay alive. Subsequently, France and Britain had for centuries played one North American tribe against the other. The new and rambunctious United States had used the Indians in the same way, as counters in a deadly and inexorable game of expansion, which the explorations of Lewis and Clark had shown the perceptive would end only on the rocky shores of the Pacific. California and Oregon territories were to be the end of the road. If things weren't good in the stony hills and valleys of Pennsylvania, reasoned other whites, why not try the level black earth of Illinois? And, in Georgia, why let the red men work their prosperous plantations under the pines and publish their newspaper, the *Cherokee Phoenix*? Their copper-colored soil might be made to yield for whites.

If the Indians of America had been unified, John Quincy Adams and Andrew Jackson might have encountered more difficulty. But the Indians were not. Their political confederations were loose, their technology secondary to their philosophical concepts of man in union with his land, of individual heroism, and of eternal recurrence in nature. The Reverend Jedidiah Morse had seen the implications of Indian disunity a decade before Jacksa Chula Harjo's succession to John Quincy Adams in the White House:

A part are for removing and a part for remaining. . . . To remove Indians far away from their present homes, from "the bones of their fathers" into a wilderness, among strangers, possibly hostile, to live as their new neighbors live, by hunting, a state to which they have not lately been accustomed, and which is incompatible with civilization, can hardly be reconciled with the professed views and objects of the Government in civilizing them.[1]

The reasoning of the Long Knives was tortuous. Indians only "infested" the land; they were hunters and did not farm it. (When one saw corn and cotton and squash and beans and peach trees and cattle in Indian towns, one turned the other way.) The hunters must be removed for go-getting farmers. On the other hand, the officially nonexistent Indians who were becoming go-getting farmers themselves were competing with white Americans. Therefore, they must be turned into hunters again, and hunters could not be civilized so they would have to go. The Indians were damned if they hunted and damned if they didn't. The more agricultural the tribes became, the more of an autonomous threat they were. During the administration of John Quincy Adams, treaty after treaty obtained large chunks of Indian land. Thirty-seven cents an acre was the going price. And when Andrew Jackson ran for the presidency he made Indian Removal, which he called frankly by its correct name, a campaign issue. It was no longer arguable, he said. In 1829, when "the Devil became President of the United States," as the Choctaws of Mississippi phrased it, the Indian Removal Bill went from the realm of possibility into near certainty.

As bills go, it was forthrightly phrased:

> *Be it enacted by the Senate and the House of Representatives of the United States of America, in Congress assembled,* That it shall and may be lawful for the President of the United States to cause so much of any territory belonging to the United States, west of the river Mississippi, not included in any state or organized territory, and to which the Indian title has been extinguished, as he may judge necessary, to be divided into a suitable number of districts for the reception of such tribes or nations of Indians as may choose to exchange the lands where they now reside, and remove there; and to cause each of said districts to be so described by natural or artificial marks, as to be easily distinguished from every other.

> *Section 2. And be it further enacted,* That it shall and may be lawful for the President to exchange any or all of such

districts, so to be laid off and described, with any tribe or nation of Indians now residing within the limits of any of the states or territories and with which the United States have existing treaties, for the whole or any part or portion of the territory claimed and occupied by such tribe or nation, within the bounds of any one or more of the states or territories, where the land claimed and occupied by the Indians is owned by the United States, or the United States are bound to the state within which it lies to extinguish the Indian claims thereto.

Section 3. And be it further enacted, That in the making of any such exchange or exchanges, it shall and may be lawful for the President solemnly to assure the tribe or nation with which the exchange is made, that the United States will forever secure and guaranty to them, and their heirs or successors, the country so exchanged with them; and, if they prefer it, that the United States will cause a patent or grant to be made and executed to them for the same; *Provided always*, That such lands shall revert to the United States if the Indians become extinct or abandon the same.

Section 4. And be it further enacted, That if, upon any of the lands now occupied by the Indians, and to be exchanged for, there should be such improvements as add value to the land claimed by any individual or individuals of such tribes or nations, it shall and may be lawful for the President to cause such value to be ascertained by appraisement or otherwise, and to cause such ascertained value to be paid to the person or persons rightfully claiming such improvements. And upon the payment of such valuation, the improvements so valued and paid for, shall pass to the United States, and possession shall not afterwards be permitted to any of the same tribe.

Section 5. And be it further enacted, That upon the making of any such exchange as is contemplated by this Act, it shall and may be lawful for the President to cause such aid and assistance to be furnished to the emigrants as may be necessary and proper to enable them to remove to, and settle in, the country for which they may have exchanged; and also, to give them such aid and assistance as may be necessary for their support and subsistence for the first year after their removal.

Section 6. And be it further enacted, That it shall and may be lawful for the President to cause such tribe or nation to be protected, at their new residence, against all interruption or disturbance from any other tribe or nation of Indians, or from any other person or persons whatever.

Section 7. And be it further enacted, That it shall and may be lawful for the President to have the same superintendance and care over any tribe or nation in the country to which they may remove, as contemplated by this Act, that he is now authorized to have over them at their present place of residence: *Provided,* That nothing in this Act contained shall be construed as authorizing or directing the violation of any existing treaty between the United States and any of the Indian tribes.

Section 8. And be it further enacted, That for the purpose of giving effect to the provisions of this Act, the sum of five hundred thousand dollars is hereby appropriated, to be paid out of any money in the Treasury not otherwise appropriated.

What the Removal Bill did not do was as significant as what it did. It did not define precisely the constitutional rights of any tribe that had been removed. It did not make mandatory the allocation of funds for tribal assistance if Congress wanted the money for anything else. It specified no machinery for carrying out the removal. Also, it made no mention that in 1828 gold had been discovered on Cherokee land at Dahlonega, Georgia, and it drew no lines between state or federal rights. Was Georgia sovereign? Did states' rights apply to her? America was taking another lurch toward the Civil War that would rend her in thirty years and the Cherokees with her. Meanwhile, Long Knives who wanted to operate gold mines in north Georgia could not be expected to be patient with legal niceties.

The battle lines were quickly drawn. Lewis Cass, a stolid veteran of treaty negotiations with Michigan's beleaguered Chippewas, quickly allied himself with Jackson. Like Jackson, he believed in the march of civilization, of which there could be only one kind. "It would be miserable affectation to regret

progress and improvement, the triumph of industry and art,"
he pronounced. The prodigal Indians "satisfied the wants of
today with no thought for the morrow." All the Cherokee
strides toward self-development agriculturally, technologically,
and literarily were a flash in the pan. It was all "a moral problem involved in much obscurity," to be sure, but the world had
had "enough of romantic description." James Fenimore Cooper
and the Frenchman Rousseau, who had published balderdash
in the eighteenth century about noble savages, were lunatic
dreamers. Cass had his own ideas on Indians:

> It is difficult to conceive that any branch of the human family
> can be less provident in arrangement, less frugal in enjoyment,
> less industrious in acquiring, more implacable in their resent-
> ments, more ungovernable in their passions, with fewer princi-
> ples to guide them, with few obligations to restrain them, and
> with less knowledge to improve and instruct them. We speak of
> them as they are.[2]

For Indians drank. The Puritan ethic and the despair of a people under constant threat of dispossession had met head-on.
Lewis Cass had decided for the Puritan ethic.

Jackson was especially anxious to defend his pronouncement
that the Supreme Court had no right to grant the Cherokees
sovereignty in Georgia. Scornfully, his white mane drawn back
from his deeply carved face, he put impassioned rhetorical
questions to the rank and file who idolized him as one of their
own. Didn't Georgia and Alabama own their own land? Would
Maine be made to tolerate an independent state set up, say, by
the Penobscot Indians? Would New York have to yield to what
was left of the Iroquois within her borders if they wrote a
constitution? Could Indians calmly establish "separate republics in Ohio" if the notion struck them? No, vowed the man
who had fought Red Eagle at Horseshoe Bend, they could not.
By the Eternal, they could not. The Indians should be made to
go—"voluntarily." Voluntarily, for instance, from Dahlonega,
Georgia, where raw prospectors, their gimlet eyes reflecting

visions of glory, were pouring into the Cherokee nation
equipped with picks, pans, axes, and stout rifles. The Indians
didn't own Dahlonega just because they had "seen it from the
mountain or passed it in the chase," said Andrew Jackson. Dahlonega's gold was white America's.

Georgia had meanwhile passed a law of her own. "Any ordinances, regulations, and orders" passed by the Cherokee Indians were null and void. Indians who discouraged their fellow
Cherokees from removing were guilty of a "high misdemeanor"
and could be jailed. "And be it further enacted, That no Indian
or descendant of any Indian, residing within the Creek or
Cherokee nations of Indians, shall be deemed a competent witness in any court of this state to which a white person may be a
party." Jim Eagle was preparing the way for Jim Crow.

Thomas McKenney, superintendant of the Bureau of Indian
Affairs, immediately called Jackson's Removal Bill "a mockery."
Jackson had given Georgia and other states a mandate to
"harass, persecute, and force out their Indian populations."
McKenney hurried to the White House to protest. "Sir," Jackson fixed him with a pale eye, "the Sovereignty of the States
must be preserved." It was a paradoxical echo of states' rights
advocate John C. Calhoun's famous banquet toast: "The Union,
next to our liberty, most dear." As Georgia's streams began to
yield up their share of gold, states' rights became expedient for
Jackson. When Thomas McKenney was in Philadelphia to see
the publisher of his forthcoming *History of the North American Indians* he received a letter from the chief clerk of the War
Department. Mr. McKenney's services, after October 1, would
no longer be required in the Indian Bureau. Back in Washington, McKenney strode into the chief clerk's office without
ceremony.

"What are the grounds of my dismissal?" he demanded.

"Why, sir!" the chief clerk smiled dryly. "Everybody knows
your qualifications for the place, but General Jackson has been
long satisfied that you are not in harmony with him in his
views in regard to the Indians." And McKenney knew that the
verdict had "closed his connection with the government" as

surely as if he had been guilty of a high crime and misdemeanor himself.[3]

All during the winter of 1830 the Removal Bill was hotly debated. It violated United States treaties with the Indians, declared bespectacled lawyers. The peaceful Society of Friends officially repudiated it; Quaker meetinghouses echoed that year with speeches charged with the emotions of personal revelation. Jackson partisans countered with the assertion that the Removal Bill was really philanthropy in disguise. The Indians were "doomed to perish from the face of the earth," but meanwhile they must be given new hunting grounds. Also, they were catching white diseases back east; the West would endow them with health and resistance. Diseases, presumably, did not cross the Mississippi River.

In Congress, the Indians had an eloquent champion in the angular, aristocratic senator from New Jersey. Theodore Frelinghuysen's family of patroons was as distinguished as was his intellect. For six hours he took the Senate floor in a defense of the Cherokees which was reprinted in every newspaper in the land and made him famous. The abolitionist William Lloyd Garrison wrote a poem to him and declared that henceforth Frelinghuysen should be known by the title of "Christian statesman." The senator moved adroitly from irony to outrage. To the president of the Senate he said:

I believe, Sir, it is not now seriously denied that the Indians are men, endowed with kindred faculties and powers with ourselves; that they have a place in human sympathy, and are justly entitled to a share in the common bounties of a benignant Providence. And, with this conceded, I ask in what code of the law of nations, or by what process of abstract deductions, their rights have been extinguished? . . . How can Georgia . . . desire or attempt, and how can we quietly permit her, to invade and disturb the property, rights, and liberty of the Indians? . . . How can we tamely suffer these States to make laws, not only not founded in justice and humanity "for preventing wrongs being done to the Indians" but for the avowed purpose of inflicting the gross and wanton injustice of breaking up their government, of abrogating their long-cherished customs, and of annihilating their existence as a distinct people?

The first Frelinghuysen patriarch had undoubtedly had mixed thoughts about the Delaware Indians of New Jersey, but his descendant Theodore was a man of conscience. So was Senator Sprague of Maine, who rose to support Frelinghuysen and voice his own denunciation of the bill. From volatile Edward Everett, in the House, came a presentation of petitions from "Sundry citizens of Massachusetts, praying that the Indian Tribes may be protected in the rights secured to them by the laws." It was not the last time Massachusetts was to act as America's moral watchdog. "Whoever heard of such a thing before?" shouted Everett, his handsome face alive with indignation. Admirers called him "Apollo in politics."

> Whoever read of such a project? Ten or fifteen thousand families, to be rooted up, and carried a hundred, aye, a thousand miles into the wilderness! There is not such a thing in the annals of mankind. . . . To remove them against their will, by thousands, to a distant and different country, where they must lead a new life, and form other habits, and encounter the perils and hardships of a wilderness: Sir, I never heard of such a thing! . . . They are not barbarians; they are essentially a civilized people. . . . They are planters and farmers, they are tradespeople and mechanics, they have cornfields and orchards, looms and workshops, schools and churches, and orderly institutions!

Jacksa Chula Harjo's champion in the House was Representative Wilson Lumpkin of Georgia, a self-made man with bitter memories. The memories included "the death of Arthur Lot and his son, murdered by the Creek Indians, in the path which I had but recently traveled." They included the recital of the Fort Mims Massacre, but not the battle of Burnt Corn Creek, and personal experience of the Creeks as "unaccommodating, stubborn, and insolent." Some of the insolence may have been due to the fact that strips of Creek skin from Alabama corpses had been used to make bridle reins for Jacksa Chula Harjo's cavalry, and that serviceable footwear had been provided for soldiers when dead Indians had been "skinned from the hips down for boot legs."[4] On December 7, 1829, Wilson Lumpkin had taken his seat in the House of Representatives and had been immediately appointed a member of the Committee on Indian Affairs "to which was referred that part of the President's message connected with Indian Affairs." The opposition tried to suppress the committee's report favoring removal, but "Mr. Buchanan, of Pennsylvania, moved the printing of 10,000 copies" and the report was circulated throughout the states. James Buchanan, the Scotch-Irish future fifteenth President, was firm on the side of the seventh, his ethnic kinsman.

Mr. Lumpkin of Georgia believed in oratory. "Words fitly spoken," he was fond of saying, "are like apples of gold in pictures of silver." As he stood in the House to present his case, he was aware that he had a national audience the size of which was bound to secure him immortality. Mr. Lumpkin pointed out the legal chaos in Georgia which had resulted from the self-declared existence of the Cherokee Nation:

Why, Sir, the United States law prohibits peddling in the Nation, or selling merchandise at any other than the place designated by the agent, and annexes its fines and forfeitures for a violation of the law. The Cherokee law authorizes any citizen to peddle or trade where they please in the Nation, on paying twelve dollars a year to the Treasurer of the Nation, and one dollar to the officer issuing the license. The laws of Georgia admit of no peddling without first obtaining a license, for which the applicant pays one hundred dollars a year, which entitles him to peddle and vend his goods anywhere within the limits of the state.

The distribution among the Cherokees of needles, combs, and hand mirrors by pack-laden itinerants was clearly causing grave constitutional crises daily. "This state of things cannot exist," opined Mr. Lumpkin. Never had he felt "such a solemn sense of responsibility." The Quakers, he had no doubt, would soon see reason. But there were *"canting fanatics, Sir,"* who had denounced Georgians as *"Atheists, Deists, Infidels, and Sabbath-Breakers* laboring under the curse of slavery," and these fanatics had "placed themselves behind the bulwark of their religion" in their opposition to removal. How could anyone doubt the humanitarian motives of General Jackson?

> If any President of the United States has deserved the appellation *friend and father* to the Indians it is he who is now at the helm. Having been the instrument of the Government to chastise them in times that are gone by, so far as to bring them to a knowledge of their true condition and duty, he is the better qualified to sympathize with them in all their afflictions . . . I trust in God. . . . The opposition reminds me of Jonah's gourd which sprung up in a night and perished in a day. It could bear the light and heat of but a single day, because there was a canker at the root. The present opposition cannot stand before the light of truth, reason and sound policy. It will soon pass away.[5]

But it did not, and Representative Lumpkin was forced to rise several more times to challenge it. Among his earliest recollections, he elaborated, were the walls of an old fort which had "sheltered women and children from the tomahawk and scalping knife." But even so, some of his best friends were Cherokees: "I blame not the Indians; I commiserate their case. . . . To me they are in many respects an interesting people. If the wicked influence of designing men, veiled in the garb of philanthropy and Christian benevolence, should excite the Cherokees to a course that will end in their speedy destruction I now call upon Congress and the whole American people not to charge Georgia with this sin." The trouble came from outside agitators. "Sir, my State stands charged before this House, before the nation, and before the whole world, with cruelty and oppression towards the Indians. I deny the charge, and I demand proof from those who make it." Cherokee Chief John Ross was seven-eighths white but, like Red Eagle of the Creeks, he had elected the physical and spiritual destiny of his Indian heritage. To Ross, Jacksa Chula Harjo was even more explicit than Mr. Lumpkin when Ross came to Washington.

"You cannot remain where you are, Mr. Ross. . . . You cannot drive back the laws of Georgia." States' rights could not be violated. "I will not go to war for you, John Ross. There will be no civil war in America." And when Ross attempted an answer, Jackson's mouth was grim. "It's too damned late," he told him.[6]

In mid-May 1830, the bill for the removal of the Indians passed Congress by a vote of 102–97; on May 28, Jacksa Chula Harjo signed it into law. Dazed because they had counted on the American national conscience to prevent this, the Cherokees met at their Georgia capital of New Echota and framed a trenchant memorial. They had kept every treaty they had ever made, they declared. Among the declarers were John Ross, Joseph Vann, the rich Cherokee planter, Slim Fellow, and Deer-in-the-Water and White Path and Sleeping Rabbit who could remember the splendor of Tecumtha and the chaos of Horseshoe Bend. Even with "every treaty without exception favorable to the whites," the treaties had not been violated by any Cherokee. Now Jacksa Chula Harjo spoke of emigration as voluntary. Would it be voluntary when it was pressed by the rifle and the bayonet? Would any Cherokees not want to emigrate "voluntarily" when they knew that to say they opposed the law would mean spending six years in a Georgia prison? Would Cherokees elect to stay in a state where they could sign no contracts and enter no courts of justice?

We wish to remain on the land of our fathers. We have a perfect and original right to remain without interruption or molestation. The treaties with us, and the laws of the United States made in pursuance of treaties, guarantee our residence and our privileges, and secure us against intruders. Our only request is that these treaties may be fulfilled and these laws executed. If we are compelled to leave our country, we see nothing but ruin before us. The country west of the Arkansas territory is unknown to us. All the inviting parts of it are occupied by various Indian nations to which it has been assigned. They would look upon us as intruders. The far greater part of that region is, beyond all controversy, badly supplied with wood and water, and no Indian tribe can live as agriculturists without these articles . . . . Were the country to which we are urged much better than it is represented to be, and were it free from the objections which we have made to it, still it is not the land of our birth, nor of our affections. It contains neither the scenes of our childhood nor the graves of our fathers. . . . What must be the circumstances of a removal when a whole community embracing persons of all classes and every description, from the infant to the man of extreme old age, the sick, the blind, the lame, the improvident, the reckless, the desperate, as well as the prudent, the considerate, the industrious, are compelled to remove by odious and intolerable vexations and persecutions brought upon them in the forms of law?

When a group of missionaries among the Cherokees cast their lot with the Indians, Georgia retaliated by revoking the missionaries' licenses. Undaunted, the clergymen resolved to stay on unlicensed, and by the spring of 1831, when Georgia dogwoods were blooming and wild azaleas flamed orange in the Cherokee hills, the Georgia Guard was hauling the missionaries off to jail.

Soon a new actor entered the drama. Sam Houston, as a youngster in Blount County, Tennessee, had had frequent quarrels with his mother. When he was fifteen he had run away to join Chief John Jolly's Cherokees, who had not yet removed with Tahlonteskee to Arkansas. The Indians christened Houston "Blackbird." When one of the Cherokee agents attempted to rape Chief Jolly's small daughter, it was Blackbird who reported it to the authorities. The Jolly family never forgot. For three years Blackbird stayed with them, until the chief told him to return to his home "to avoid arrest and persecution" from the surrounding white community. Later, Blackbird had fought against the Creeks beside the Cherokees loyal to Jacksa

Chula Harjo. Jackson and Houston, strong-boned sons of the American interior and the Scotch-Irish people, had met in the Creek War and had become friends. In 1817 Blackbird, who often wore Indian buckskins and feathers, was appointed a subagent to help supervise the removal of the Tennessee Cherokees to Arkansas. Tahlonteskee and Takatoka were his venerable intimates. On a trip to Washington, Blackbird paid a call on Secretary of War Calhoun, who stared frostily at his visitor's Cherokee leggings. Blackbird's speedy resignation was engineered by the scandalized Mr. Calhoun, and a chastened Blackbird returned to Tennessee to become a lawyer. In 1827, as an ardent supporter of his war comrade Andrew Jackson, he was elected governor of Tennessee. Blackbird knew Jacksa Chula Harjo would listen to his advice, and he believed he could serve the Cherokees' interests. Then he fell in love.

Eliza Allen, fair-haired, ringleted, and blue-eyed, was only a child when Houston had begun visiting her father at his Tennessee plantation on the twisting Cumberland River. But the child grew up into a full-fledged southern belle, with the charming skittishness of her kind, and Houston became determined to marry her. Eliza had already "given her heart to another," but when Sam Houston became the governor of the state, her family decided she was incapable of acting in her own best interests. There were hurried councils on the Cumberland, and soon eighteen-year-old Eliza's engagement to the governor was announced. At blue twilight on a January day in 1829 Colonel Allen led his daughter, robed in clouds of tulle and silk, down the curving staircase of his manor house to waiting Governor Houston. The wedding ceremony was performed by a stylish Presbyterian minister popular in Nashville drawing rooms. Afterward the honeymooners moved into the Nashville Inn, where the other guests decided they must be much in love because they "hardly ever went about." By April Houston, with Jackson's endorsement, was campaigning for reelection, mounting sweetgum stumps to make speeches, and receiving political cronies afterward in "high spirits." After a rally one of the cronies rode to the Nashville Inn.

"Have you heard the news, Sir?" asked the clerk at the desk breathlessly. "Governor Houston and his wife have separated and she has gone to her father's house!"

The rumor was that Houston had "wronged" his bride. How, no one quite knew. There seemed to be no other woman in the case. But "a lady's honor" was at stake.

"You must explain this sad occurrence, else you will sacrifice your friends and yourself," Houston's supporters warned him.

He shook his head. "I can make no explanation. I exonerate this lady freely, and I do not justify myself. I am a ruined man. I will exile myself. And now I ask you to take my resignation to the Secretary of State."[7]

The gossip swirled through Nashville town houses and the plantations of the rich. Eliza's family declared their outrage; she had been dishonored, though none of the Allens specified the exact nature of the crime.

"Remember," Houston said, "that whatever may be said by the lady or her friends, it is no part of the conduct of a gallant or a generous man to take up arms against a woman. If my character cannot stand the shock let me lose it."

By the time Blackbird began his flight west to the family of Chief Jolly of the Cherokees—for the Cherokees were home—his brain was clouded in an alcoholic haze. With bemused regret the Arkansas Cherokees changed Blackbird's name to Ootsetee Ardeetahskee, which meant Big Drunk. When Big Drunk was in his cups, which was most of the time, a small band of Cherokees followed him around to see that he didn't get into trouble. Once, one of them seconded him in a duel at the local trading post from which Big Drunk emerged victorious. At night, in the spacious cabins of the Arkansas plantation Chief Jolly had carved from the wilderness, the chiefs of the clans met to smoke with Ootsetee Ardeetahskee. The Jolly household consisted of Jolly's family and a dozen servants; the chief was in the habit of ordering a beef to be slaughtered each week for his table. Ootsetee Ardeetahskee shaved his face, braided his shining chestnut hair, put a white doeskin shirt dazzling with beaded embroidery over his broad chest, and

donned a long pair of yellow leggings. His head was encircled
by eagle feathers, and over his shoulder he wore a blanket. Soon
he acquired an Indian mistress with her family's blessing; Tiana
Rogers filled the gap Eliza Allen had left, and she asked no
questions. She was dark and slim and withdrawn, and she loved
Sam Houston with quiet intensity. Soon, memorials from the
Arkansas Cherokees began coming to Washington in Sam
Houston's handwriting.[8]

In 1830 Jackson sent him a letter of sympathy about his
divorce from Eliza or, rather, Eliza's divorce from him. The
letter said nothing about Houston's pleas for justice for the
Cherokees in Arkansas and Georgia. Houston immediately
rode east to Washington, where he and two Cherokee chieftains quickly obtained an audience with Jackson and asked for
the dismissal of racketeering Arkansas traders. Jacksa Chula
Harjo listened, nodded, and then fired four of the worst from
their posts as Indian agents. But he would not plunge America
into a civil war over the Georgia Cherokees. His ears were deaf
even to Sam Houston; it was more comforting to listen to the
perorations of the Honorable Wilson Lumpkin, who, upon his
retirement from Congress, had been elected governor of
Georgia and now controlled the fate of the Cherokee Nation
more directly. One of his first acts in office was to divide up the
nation's territory and distribute shares of it to white Georgians
in a state lottery. Lumpkin also railed against Justice John
Marshall and the Supreme Court. The Court had dared to
interfere in the internal affairs of Georgia; the Marshall Court
was, in the governor's opinion, treasonous. He must protest
against the "unjust and unconstitutional encroachment of the
federal judiciary."[9]

Jackson's dismissal of the corrupt Arkansas agents provoked
a volley of protests. Sam Houston, still clad in Cherokee trappings as he reverted slowly from Ootsetee Ardeetahskee back
to Blackbird, traveled with his Cherokee companions to the
great cities of the eastern seaboard to rally support for the
Jackson dismissals. He stormed Baltimore, the red brick pro-

priety of Philadelphia, the bustle and filth and vein-tingling excitement of New York City, where Old World emigrants were arriving daily resolved to seek fortunes in the Golden West, and the chilly gray fastnesses of Boston, where abolitionist eyebrows were raised at Houston's Tennessean exuberance and accouterments but where women flocked to hear this exotic defend Indians as victims of oppression.

Inwardly Houston was divided. Had not Tahlonteskee and Takatoka and his own "friend and Father" John Jolly removed to Arkansas and found prosperity? Couldn't the Georgia Cherokees do the same? Blackbird's own ambivalence tormented him. He could see the constitutional question of states' rights. He understood why Jackson, his old battle captain, did not want to "go to war for Mr. Ross," and he even began to think that if he acted as agent for the Cherokees and Creeks in their westward migrations he could prevent their being cheated. Jackson's political opponents heard about Houston representing Indians and denounced it as evidence of Houston's profiteering self-interest and Jackson's lack of principle. The fired traders were promptly rehired. Houston was aghast. But now his phrases were stirring no longer. The ladies of the East decided this outlander who stood six feet six and carried an Indian blanket around with him was a mountebank. In frustration, Houston retired to Arkansas and the consolations of Tiana Rogers and began writing reams to his old commander. The reams remained unanswered. Jackson pushed ahead with the removal plan, and Blackbird understood that nothing, not even the claims of friendship or mercy, would stop him. Jacksa Chula Harjo talked on about voluntary emigration, and Wilson Lumpkin gazed with satisfaction at the Dahlonega gold fields when he visited them. Blackbird now realized there was only one course of action left; he wrote to John Ross advising him to start a suit to restrain Georgia from enforcing her confiscations.[10]

By this time John Quincy Adams was a member of the House, his truculent presidency behind him. In his study, one

winter evening when he could hear snow winds sweeping outside, he took up his goose quill and wrote in his diary:

> The Resolutions of the Legislature of Georgia setting at defiance
> the Supreme Court of the United States are published and ap-
> proved in the Telegraph, the Administration newspaper at this
> place. . . . The Constitution, the laws and treaties of the United
> States are prostrate in the state of Georgia. Is there any remedy
> for this state of things? None. Because the Executive of the
> United States is in League with the State of Georgia. . . . This
> example . . . will be imitated by other states, and with regard to
> other national interests—perhaps the tariff. . . . The Union is in
> the most imminent danger of dissolution. . . . The ship is about
> to founder.[11]

"I've been in Hell," Sam Houston said simply. "By God,
here's my chance to rise out of it and be a man once more."
What he rose into was the beginning of years of litigation.

That summer, in the far reaches of the Arkansas Territory, a
youthful white traveler named Washington Irving stood in the
warm auburn glow of a July afternoon and beheld the prairie
tallgrass, a carpet of green "enamelled with a thousand flowers." He heard the whirring of grouse and watched the deer
bounding over the grass to come to rest in thickets of wildflowers from which they gazed "wildly and fearfully." In the distance he could make out the silhouette of a vagabond wolf
stalking the deer and waiting for darkness. Then he looked up
to a distant green hill as the final bronze rays of the sun played
over it. There he saw "a solitary Indian mounted upon a horse,
and standing statue-like." The youth drew in his breath. He
had seen the desperate besotted Indians of the frontier towns,
but never one who soberly surveyed his own soil. The Indian
did not move at the exploring party's approach. He gave no
sign at all to acknowledge the visitors' existence. Seated on his
chestnut horse, he continued to measure the distance. Later
the travelers learned that he was a Shawnee who had been the
friend of Tecumtha.[12] The new land was not his own after all.

He was not a romantic denizen of undiscovered country but a survivor. More Shawnees were leaving Ohio every year because shining axes were felling their forests. The Shawnees had heard the crash of mighty maples, hickories, oaks, and iron-woods into the dense brush below. They had watched the bulging arm muscles of white newcomers swell as those arms chopped, razed, swept away, and then built new habitations. They had watched the green-gold forest parakeets disappear and had seen the rush of gray passenger pigeon flocks against flaming sunsets in retreat from Long Knife guns. The Shawnees had heard for the last time the sound of crystal rain on their fathers' resting places. Now there was a law. Removal was no longer a choice.

Yet the Shawnees were luckier than some other tribes. They had the legend of Tecumtha to sustain them as the "voluntary" emigration of the American Indian westward began to the music of coins in Georgia counting houses, saws in Ohio forests, machetes breaking the dense cane stands of south Georgia and Alabama, and fort bells ringing in turgid Florida swamps. The memory of Tecumtha was all there was to drown out not only the soft falls of Shawnee moccasins but also the tramp of booted military feet. Among the Indians the victory of Jacksa Chula Harjo was challenged by the ghost of their unfulfilled savior, but ghosts cannot repeal the statutes of a land and its living people. They can only keep the past alive in the heart while it prepares to endure a hostile future.

⌒ 3 ⌒

"Drunk, Sober, or Sick, We Will Move Them Along"

"I am about to leave you, and when I am gone and my warning shall no longer be heard or regarded, the craft and avarice of the white man will prevail. Many winters I have breasted the storm, but I am an aged tree, and can stand no longer. My leaves are fallen, my branches are withered, and I am shaken by every breeze. Soon my aged trunk will be prostrated, and the foot of the exulting foe of the Indian may be placed upon it with safety; for I leave none who will be able to avenge such an injury. Think not I mourn for myself. I go to join the spirits of my fathers, where age cannot come; but my heart fails when I think of my people, who are soon to be scattered and forgotten."

          —RED JACKET, SENECA

"Father—You know it's hard to be hungry, and if you do not know it we poor Indians know it. . . . We did not think the Big Man would tell us things that was not true."

        —THE DELAWARE CHIEFS
         TO THE INDIAN DEPARTMENT

Piqua, Wapakoneta, Chillicothe, Upper and Lower Sandusky . . . in Ohio, by 1830, the Indian council grounds and towns were fast ceasing to exist. Ohio had long been crowded with red refugees from lands farther east: Senecas and dwindling Delawares and once-formidable Wyandots. Shawnees had come up from the South; Ottawas had fled the advancing tidal wave of homesteaders in Michigan. All these nations had begun to mingle with one another; tribal identities were fading. Now the government decided it was time to clear Ohio of Indians for good. The mandate from the President's Removal Law was clear.

Already those of the restless Delawares who had listened to the siren song of Quitewepea the Shawnee had migrated west of the Mississippi. But, near the hunting grounds of the Osages, things were working out no better for the Ohio Delawares than they had for the Tennessee Cherokees. Not only were the Delawares subject to frequent and devastating Osage raids, but the land itself was hardly utopian. To their Father in Washington, some Delaware chiefs sent a message:

> Last summer a number of our people died just for the want of something to live on. . . . We have got in a country where we do not find all as stated to us when we was asked to swap lands with you and we do not get as much as was promised us. . . . We have found a poor hilly stony country and the worst of all no game to be found on it to live on. Last summer our corn looked very well until a heavy rain come on for 3 or 4 days and raised the waters so high that we could just see the tops of our corn in some of the fields and it destroyed the greatest part of our corn, punkins and beans and a great many more of our people coming on and we had to divide our little stock with them. Last summer there was a few deere here and we had a few hogs but we was obliged to kill all of them and some that was not our own but this summer there are no game and no hogs and our old people and children must suffer. . . . Father, if we go a great ways off we may find some deere but if we do that we cannot make any corn and we must still suffer. Father, we are obliged to call on you onst more for assistance in the name of God. . . . Father, we expect a great many more of our people here this spring. . . .

The game animals of Arkansas were rapidly being depleted; on the Osage grounds, where quarry were left, alien hunters would be inviting murder by their presence.

Nevertheless, the representatives of the United States War Department in Ohio were keen to get on with the business of concluding treaties and carrying forward "voluntary departures." Some of the Senecas were unaware of what was happening to their Delaware brethren in Arkansas, and they told government ambassadors they were actually eager to get out of Ohio because their children were learning bad habits from the whites. In February 1831 Senecas put their marks to a treaty of cession drawn up by James B. Gardiner, a specially appointed real estate commissioner from the Indian office. The government contracted for the Senecas' trek "in a convenient and suitable manner" to territory north of the country of the western Cherokees and east of the Neosho River. For a sizable portion of Ohio, the Senecas were to receive 100 rifles and 400 blankets as well as 50 ploughs, 50 hoes, and 50 axes. Chiefs Cornstalk, Small Cloud Spicer, Seneca Steel, and Hard Hickory made their X's in the presence of a subagent, Henry Brish, and the Senecas prepared to migrate. They thanked their Father for "the great things he has done for the Senecas," and then Mr. Brish began auctioning off the Senecas' Ohio effects. The worldly goods of Small Cloud Spicer brought $298.50:[1]

1 lantern	1 set cups and saucers
1 cleaver	6 acres of corn, growing
1 small stew kettle	6 ditto of wheat, shocked
1 frying pan	Lot of rye in the stack
1 iron pot	Ditto of oats in shock
1 ditto	1 cow and a calf
1 brass kettle	20 hogs, first choice
1 auger	20 hogs, second choice
1 log chain	11 hogs, last choice
1 shovel	1 squaw axe
1 table	1 old sled
1 bureau	1 wagon and harness
1 plough	

The treasures of the Widow Blue Jacket were more modest, and came to $29.36:

1 copper kettle	6 shoats
1 brass ditto	2 hoes
1 skillet	2 old tin cups
1 cow	Lot old iron
1 heifer	Lot squaw corn
3 hogs	

If the Widow Blue Jacket regretted the loss of her tin cups at three cents for the pair, her rusty and wrinkled face did not show it. She heard Mr. Brish tell her people that there awaited in the land of the setting sun "good rich country west of the State of Missouri, designated for all Indians and guaranteed never to fall within any territory or state of the United States. Here are buffalo, elk, and deer in abundance. The Indians may live without working in such a country."

Two of Ohio's Wyandot chiefs, regaled with the same arguments, merely smiled. These particular chiefs were "preachers of the Methodist Society" and more sophisticated than some of their unlettered fellows. "We have been able to find no fault with the overtures of the Government as such," they said, "but we express a *distrust* of the *sincerity* of the President in making them, and a *disbelief* that the Country to which we are invited to remove is such as has been represented." The Wyandots wanted to send scouts west to see for themselves what was there. Agents Gardiner and Brish therefore retreated from the Wyandot strongholds and stepped up their efforts with the trusting Senecas. If the Wyandots preferred to stay on in Ohio "until we are *pushed off* by our Great Father," the Senecas did not. So, at least, they told the agents.

They promised to be prepared in the spring of 1831. But, as they saw the fragrant white blossoming of their pear and cherry orchards in Ohio and as they smelled the sharpness of warmer earth and heard southwest winds humming over their ancestors' graves, their resolution began to fail. They planted a corn crop and promised to go west after the Moon of Roasting Ears, August. But when the Moon of Roasting Ears succeeded the Summer Moon, several Seneca chiefs in Ohio felt they must return one last time to the Senecas remaining in the state of New York; the New York Senecas were managing, astonishingly, to hold on to their land and to get along with white residents already well established in their country. Codes of behavior in New York had been agreed upon. The whites were not newcomers but entrenched citizens, and they noted among themselves that their local Senecas were acting like entrenched citizens too. Some of the Indians had turned respectably Episcopalian, and New York State whites hesitated to ship any member of a socially stylish denomination to the western wilderness. But the Ohio Senecas had no such props to support them. They had never opted for the English of Archbishop Cranmer and the Book of Common Prayer. So the visiting Ohio chiefs surrendered to the New York chiefs a symbolic belt of wampum which had bound the two peoples together. From now on, the Ohio Senecas would be on their own.

In the Harvest Moon, October, Ohio Senecas began loading their ponies with traveling equipment: cooking pots and pemmican, water flasks and blankets and flintlock muskets. Doubtfully, the tribe lined up to be vaccinated for smallpox. By now the women were weeping. Mothers and children embraced individual trees and rocks. Some of the husbands wanted to retreat to New York; others thought of Canada where they would be safe from Jacksa Chula Harjo forever. Impatiently, Henry Brish urged them ahead. At last, in the Moon of Falling Leaves, when November-bare branches scraped each other overhead, the Senecas began the first stage of their journey. V's of geese had preceded them; now the sky was empty of all but clouds. As they rode toward Dayton, steely gray rain glanced against their faces. At night the sodden ground where they slept turned hard with frost. Mud bogged their wagons down by day and forced them to a pace of four miles every twelve hours. In Dayton, Henry Brish bought wagons and teams for the overland part of the trip ahead, for which he would be the conductor. The coughing and chilled Senecas were herded onto canal boats in which they traveled down the Miami River to Cincinnati between shores of ice where coated branches glittered with immobile droplets like diamonds. Many Indians were now tottering with influenza. As the canal boats passed Hamilton, Ohio, the editor of the *Hamilton Intelligencer* stared at the cavalcade: "Would to God that the dark blot fixed on the page of our history by the injustice which the Indians have suffered at our hands could be effaced from it. We envy not the cold, selfish and ignoble feelings of the men who can justify the cruel and tyrannical proceedings of our government toward these people." At Cincinnati, the Miami's end, there was no time for sleep or warmth. On the day of their arrival most of the Senecas were prodded aboard the steamboat *Ben Franklin* for St. Louis. But 110 Senecas, and 58 Delawares traveling with them who were related by ties of village and kinship, mounted tired nags to make the overland journey. The Indians had heard the shrill whistle of the *Ben Franklin* screaming at the wharf and would not trust themselves to a monster which emitted such cacophonies. Henry Brish let them go on to Indiana. Later, unfortunately, he had to pay a settler there $23.25 "for taking care of a Seneca Indian Jim found frostbitten in the night." Brish was not totally without a heart; he furnished his charges with scalping knives out of his own pocket money because he had a feeling they would need them on the edge of Osage territory where they were going.

Six days after leaving Cincinnati the *Ben Franklin* docked at the wide levees of St. Louis and Brish, bracing himself against river gales and subfreezing temperatures, hurried to Superintendent William Clark. The Indians camped seven miles outside the city limits under tents made of sheets. Their baggage, Superintendent Clark saw with disapproval when he came with Brish to the wharf, filled nearly two warehouse rooms: tools, bags of beans and corn, sacks of peach and pear and cherry seeds. But the blankets promised to the Senecas had not yet arrived, and Brish begged Clark for help. After one look at the Indian camp, Clark requisitioned a blanket and a pair of shoes for each Indian; at government expense. "It is an appalling spectacle," said Superintendent Clark shaking his head. The wagons and teams authorized by the Indian Department were already obviously insufficient; there would not be enough of them to transport the Senecas' old and sick. In the Seneca camp beyond St. Louis, the gunmetal rains of winter continued to fall, and the Indians' flimsy makeshift tents were oozing with water. Brish also asked Clark for money with which to pay three white assistants—necessary, said Mr. Brish, to protect his person against the "extremely dissipated habits and blood-thirsty disposition of so many of the Senecas under my guidance."

Early in the Hunting Moon, December, the Senecas took up their journey once more. Long ago they had been a stalwart member tribe of the formidable Iroquois confederation of the Six Nations; they had been *Ongweh Howeh*, Men of Men. They had also been Keepers of the Western Door of Iroquois territory. Had they not been created by Earth Holder, Chief of the Gods, whose wife Yagentji, the Great Mother, had plummeted from heaven to earth when she had, in curiosity, looked too far down over the celestial precipice? On earth she had borne two sons, the Light One of Good Mind and the Dark One of Evil Mind.[2] Through trials of strength and faith, the Light One had sought his father, and when he had found him on a mountaintop Earth Holder had told him, "I am the Sun." To be good-minded, the Senecas believed, one must labor. As seeds die giving life to plants, so through trials of endurance men find their father in heaven. But no myth of the universe, no religious or moral system had ever prepared the Senecas for what was happening to them now. They no longer kept the Western Door. They were no longer the Men of Men, no longer *Ongweh Howeh.* Instead they had been reduced to wanderers trying to hold back tears. Now they traveled on foot, on horseback, and in cumbersome wagons which jolted with every turn of the wheel. Beyond St. Louis it began to snow; leaden skies suddenly poured forth whirling gusts of white, prairie winds keened, and pallid mountains of powder drifted over the road ahead. By the time the party had reached St. Charles for the crossing of the Missouri River, fourteen Senecas were too feeble to go on, and one of the old women died, her face soon frozen both by cold and rigor mortis. Two more Indians died on the way to Troy, Missouri, in Lincoln County, and the entire group was racked by fever. Several children and teamsters had their hands and feet frozen. Camped at night under their tents while blizzards raged around them, the Indians huddled under their single blankets and slept in their new shoes, but neither blankets nor shoes were enough to keep out the anaesthetizing cold. Henry Brish realized he could drag his charges no farther. He set up a winter camp on Missouri's Cuivre River. Then an epidemic of measles broke out among the Indians. Brish sent requests for more money to Superintendent Clark in St. Louis. After all, there now were coffins to be paid for, and two Missouri doctors, English and Woolfolk, who were trying to save what lives they could in the ice-locked camp. Two of the white members of the party were also felled by sickness, contractors who had sold the Senecas traveling provisions at prices reflecting a seller's market.

The overland party which had separated from the Senecas to go through Indiana also had to come to terms with a midwestern winter, its cold billowing ruthlessly down from the Arctic over the Canadian tundra blanketing Indiana as well as Missouri in snow. The agent who was to have brought the Indiana party to St. Louis suddenly decided his health was poor and left the Indians in the charge of their interpreter, all of them blinded by a world of white. Horses began dying. Whippingstick lost his youngest child at St. Mary's, Indiana, and the eldest son of Cayuga Jim perished at Muncietown. At Muncietown a band of roaming Delawares under their aged chief, Captain Pipe, joined the Seneca party. Seneca chiefs marooned at Muncietown sent messengers to Superintendent Clark begging for mercy in the form of food or at least money to pay for it. "Persons acting under the government" had withheld promised funds. The Indians' interpreter, Martin Lane, could not stand any more; he took $150 of his own money—all he had—and bought food for his charges. Then he started soliciting funds in Indiana towns. When word of the plight of the Indians at Muncietown reached the Senecas in their camp on the Cuivre in Missouri, Brish became alarmed. What if the Muncietown Senecas began returning to Ohio? How would Ohio obliterate the red men then, especially since newspapers already carried word of the Indians' misery, and some white citizens were beginning to protest? What made matters worse was the circulation of a speech by the Honorable David Crockett, U.S. Representative from the state of Tennessee:

> I have a settlement to make at the bar of God, and what my conscience dictates to be just and right I will do. . . . I have always viewed the native Indian tribes of this country as a sovereign people. . . . Often I am forcibly reminded of the remark of the famous Red Jacket, in the capital rotunda, when he was first shown the panel which represented in sculpture the first landing of the Pilgrims, with an Indian chief presenting to them an ear of corn in token of friendly welcome. The aged Indian said, "That was good." The Indian said he knew that they came from the Great Spirit, and he was willing to share the soil with his brothers from over the great water. But when he turned round to another panel representing Penn's peace treaty, he said, "Ah! All's gone now."

When Indians were asked to remove, continued Mr. Crockett, many said, "No! We will take death here at our homes. Let them come and tomahawk us here at home. We are willing to die, but never to remove." He, David Crockett, had himself heard these words. By defending the Indians,

> I will have the consolation of my conscience. I will obey that power, and glory in the deed. I care not for popularity. . . . I have been told I don't understand English grammar. This is very true. I was never six months at school in my life. I raised myself up by the labor of my own hands. But I don't on that account yield up my privilege as the representative of free men.[3]

There were those in America who decided that Mr. Crockett's grammar was serving him very well indeed; Andrew Jackson, however, was not among them.

When the Indian Department received news of the plight of the Senecas in Muncietown, the new commissioner, Elbert Herring, reacted by firing Henry Brish because he hadn't forced the reluctant Senecas to travel on the steamboat. An infuriated Brish, to whom a Missouri winter had given a severe case of rheumatism, fired off a letter to Lewis Cass, Secretary of War, in Washington. Cass was impressed with Brish's conscientious recital of his trials with the Senecas and made Herring reinstate him. While letters flew between Missouri and the District of Columbia, four Muncietown Senecas died. The terrible winter wore on in clouds of snow until at last the deathly silence was broken by the boom of cracking ice on the rivers. Brish himself went back to Muncietown to inspect the damage. There he persuaded a contingent of Indians to return with him to St. Louis; when they arrived at the Indians' camp on the Cuivre, Brish found more than a hundred of the Senecas sick. But the procession had to be resumed. Spring was coming. Soon it would be time for the Indians to plant corn in their new home if they were to eat during the following winter. Brish piled Senecas and Delawares into wagons pell-mell and urged on his teamsters. As the expedition continued, the sick in the wagons began dying. Soon there were wagons which held the sick, the dying, and the dead. Six ailing Indians had been left on the Cuivre because Brish had had no doubt that they would die.

With the blustery, wet approach of spring came rampant and swollen rivers. Torrents turned the roads into muddy quagmires. Floods swept down from the hills to overflow the Missouri and the Grand and southwestern Missouri's Marais des Cygnes. The Marsh of the Swans was empty of swans when the Indians reached it—the birds, happier than they, were wintering under soft southern sunlight—but the Marsh's raging waters were churning, and there were no boats available. The party camped again; the hammering of teamsters building

bridges over which the Indians might cross the Marais des
Cygnes echoed while their wagons were floated into the flood.
Their goods were saturated. At night other hammering echoed
through the camp—that of coffins being assembled. After the
crossing of the Marais des Cygnes had been accomplished the
Indians came to waterlogged prairies. All of the wagon teams
had to be attached to half of the wagons at a time. When the
rains finally passed, flies appeared which savaged the hides of
horses and oxen and the skin of human beings and forced the
party to travel only at night. By day the Senecas and Delawares slept if they could and moaned in pain if they couldn't,
while the bites of the flies festered on their arms and legs. The
conductor of the teams was worried; the animals, he said,
might be "unfit for further service" after such an ordeal. Again
the measles broke out, this time among the children. Nine new
graves were dug. Inconveniently, the Christians among the Indians wanted to perform funeral rites, and when the pagans
found this out they demanded the time to perform rites of their
own. It was all very regrettable, thought Henry Brish, and he
hated to hurry his charges on, but "such are the terms of my
employment."

By the time the Seneca and Delaware Indians of Ohio
reached their new lands on the Elk River on July 4, 1832, thirty
more Indians had died and forty-eight were expected to die
soon. In the cities and especially the small towns of America,
bronze bells were gaily clanging from red brick and clap-
boarded white church towers. Aged veterans of the War for
Independence were gathering in town squares, families were
churning ice cream on their porches, and bands were tootling
in dusty streets. Mayors, sweating uncomfortably in their frock
coats, were preparing to deliver patriotic orations, and the
Ladies' Auxiliaries of the Methodists, Baptists, Presbyterians,
and Episcopalians were making lemonade to quench patriotic
thirst. Freedom was ringing in the East, if not the West. On the
empty Elk River, in the first Indian settlement of what would
one day be Oklahoma, the Senecas and Delawares moved as if
in a dream. Somehow, without corn, they would have to make

it through to the next spring. The first of the Indian Removals was over, and Henry Brish wrote to William Clark, conqueror of the Rockies and beneficiary of the guiding services of Sacajawea:

> I charge myself with cruelty in forcing these unfortunate people on at a time when a few days' delay might have prevented some deaths, and rendered the sickness of others more light, and have to regret this part of my duty, which together with the extreme exposure to which I have been subjected and the sickness consequent on it, has made the task of removing the Senecas excessively unpleasant to me.

It had been excessively unpleasant, all things considered, for the Senecas too.

But there were still Indians left in Ohio. A mixed band of Senecas and Shawnees lived at Lewistown; Shawnees still clung to their lodges at Hog Creek and Wapakoneta, and there were Ottawas at Blanchard's Fork and the village of Oquanoxa. All of them were scheduled for a "voluntary" exit in the spring of 1832. Agent James Gardiner, the treaty expert, looked forward to packing his charges off to Kansas. When spring came, and Ohio's woods were clouded in a mist of new green, the Indians began asking Gardiner when they were to leave. Should they plant? Would they have to travel in winter? Gardiner wrote his chief, Elbert Herring, in the Indian Department in Washington, and Mr. Herring replied that technicalities of treaty ratification made it impossible for him to give an answer at that time. The treaties would not be ratified until June. When Gardiner visited the Indian villages he found that several heads of households had not planted corn; some of the families had sold all their cattle and hogs. "You must practice the utmost economy and prudence," he told the Indians somberly. "You must also restrain your young men from yielding to the temptations offered by merchants and traders to fleece them of their money." Whether or not he also gave free advice to the tempting merchants and traders is not recorded.

The Shawnees were firm on one point: they would not travel

by water. They were not used to boats, they had heard that people got sick on boats, and boats were dangerous. To his superior Gardiner reported:

> They are more allied to their ancient customs than any other people on earth. They scarcely ever change a *trail*, when once made, however crooked or circuitous. And now they wish to travel "in the manner of *their fathers*." They know nothing about Steamboats. They do not wish to "move by fire," nor to be scalded, *"like the white man cleans his hog."* Some of their little children might be drowned. Their native modesty revolts at the use of the only convenience on board a boat to obey the calls of Nature. They have many horses, too, from which they could not be induced to part, for any consideration whatever. These, and many other arguments, they use in the most forcible and importunate manner, in favor of selecting the route by land.

Gardiner promised the Indians in his charge that they might travel that way.

When Jacksa Chula Harjo heard about Gardiner's promise, he was furious. By the Eternal, those Indians were going the way he told them to go, and that was by steamboat! He refused to believe they were afraid of drowning. They were just being troublesome as usual, and the law must be laid down to them.

Gardiner tried. An old woman of the Shawnees tottered to her feet.

> We will not go in steamboats, nor will we go in wagons, but we will go on horseback—it is the most agreeable manner for us. And if we are not allowed to go so we can, and will, remain here and die and be buried with our relatives. It will be a short time before we leave this world at any rate. Let us avert our heads from as much unnecessary pain and sorrow as possible. On the steamboats there is cholera. We do not want to catch the cholera.

Cholera was a fact of river life.

On the second day of the Moon of Rains, September 1832, the Shawnees began celebrating the ritual of the Feast of

Death. They leveled the graves of their parents and then covered them with green branches. They knew they must not leave a single trace to be desecrated by the Long Knives. As they mourned aloud for last year's dead, the mourning turned from ritual into reality. They were being wrenched from their soil like diseased roots, and their tears flowed down to that soil; the Shawnees knew they would not pass that way again. Two weeks later, they began their hegira. Men, women, and children were mounted on ponies, their little bags of personal possessions strapped to the saddles. Babies rode on the backs of their mothers. Some of the women were over a hundred years old; they were permitted to ride in government wagons, and from their open backs the great-great-grandmothers stared dumbly at the trail behind them, their eyes glazed and their furrowed throats slack. Along the road white curiosity-seekers had gathered. The wagons rumbled slowly by behind the long procession of ponies. Shawnees, Senecas, Ottawas—Ohio was being drained of her discoverers. Only in spirit would they haunt her now.

At night, in camp, the Indians drank, and the camps reeked with their vomit. By day they were hung over; at night they drank once more, their supplies of whiskey gleefully replenished by attendant white traders whom Gardiner could not restrain. To Lewis Cass he wrote wearily:

The Shawnees . . . have almost exhausted our patience. They forfeited their promises and abused every kindness. It seemed impossible to get them to make the least movement. . . . Nature has sunk under their beastly intemperance. . . . Many are sick; some are wounded . . . and all that can are still drinking whiskey, women as well as men, half-crazy and enfuriated. . . . The whites beset us with their barrels and kegs of whiskey, *hide out in the woods*, and three days were consumed in almost fruitless efforts to remedy the serious evil inflicted by our own citizens. . . . I would to God I could say we were away from these miserable, mean wretches who, for a paltry gain, carry disorder, mutiny, and distraction into our ranks as we pass along the road, and into our camps at midnight. No human vigilance can guard against them. . . . Even in *this* moral and enlightened community, composed principally of members of the Society of Friends, wretches are found to waylay the miserable Indian with a keg or jug, prostrate him by the roadside or in the street, and filch away his last penny. . . . We fail if we *stop three days between this and the Mississippi.*[4]

Gardiner's next letter announced the first deaths, "mostly children." He complained that the Shawnee, Seneca, and Ottawa chiefs were "utterly regardless of the expenses incurred by the Government!" If they could they would halt all their people and "frolic and hunt until spring." But Gardiner kept his Indians going: eighty-five miles of them strung along the main street of mid-America, the National Road. When the procession passed through Indianapolis, the citizens turned out to gawk and sell whiskey. Gardiner and his team of assistants shouted and commanded, and the dejected Indians pushed on toward the Wabash River. There already had been the "few deaths from bad colds, cholera infantum, etc., but there was an equal number of births." The squaws perversely kept wanting to stop to wash their clothes and blankets in the streams they passed. Gardiner hurried them across Indiana into the windswept flats of Illinois, now mushy underfoot with equinoctial rains. But his pace wasn't fast enough for Secretary of War Lewis Cass, who sent out from Washington a hard disciplinarian named Colonel John J. Abert, late of the Topographical Engineers. Abert's instructions were to get the Indians to their destination before winter. Abert assumed charge, much to Gardiner's chagrin. Abert shoved the mounted Indians through St. Louis and an audience with Superintendent Clark into Columbia, Missouri, where the *Missouri Intelligencer* reported that there were two Shawnee women, one 102 and the other 112, who had come all the way from Ohio on their ponies, disdaining the wagons where the other centenarians were riding. "Many of the men of the forest exhibit a fantastic appearance, their clothing and ornaments being of every color and description."

"You would laugh to see how we are received on the road," Colonel Abert wrote one of his friends. Missouri whites feared the Indians might bring in a cholera epidemic.

Doors are slammed in our faces, yet some are bold enough to peep at us through the windows. However, as long as they do not stop our progress, we don't care; and yet some of these whites will continue to sell whiskey to our Indians. About twenty of our Ottaways were as drunk as David's sow yesterday. When sober, they are by far the most orderly and manageable of the whole detachment. But drunk, sober, or sick, we will move them along."[5]

November 18 found Abert and his charges camped on the Missouri River. A violent storm changed rapidly from cutting rain, to hail, to sleet and gales, and then to a blizzard. Prairie winds roared through flimsy leantos; the poor devils inside, Abert noted, were suffering considerably from fever and dysentery, "but I can not help it." He had not made the weather; God had. "I should not be surprised if some of the Shawnees were found frozen to death tomorrow . . . they are a sort of overgrown children, and require continual care. . . . Ah! This weather, this weather! They should have been at their homes before this, and would have been if the business had been properly managed from the start."[6] It did not occur to Colonel Abert to wonder exactly what homes were waiting.

On the last day of November, the sopping, fever-wracked, and half-drunk Indians from Ohio passed through the Missouri town of Independence and kept going until they reached the new Shawnee territory twenty miles to the west. The Ottawa tract was forty miles farther, but the Ottawas refused to go. The Shawnees with whom they had traveled had asked them to stay. The Indians had few tools—the government had not kept its promises of issuing implements with which to build houses. But the Ottawas had ten felling axes, and the Shawnees had two cross-cut saws, and there were still men among both tribes who were healthy enough to start building cabins in which to shelter the old and sick and the children before they were killed by the elements. Between the western boundary of Missouri and the eastern boundary of Chief Jolly's Cherokees, there was a resting place. For a while.

⤳ 4 ⤳

"Under the Pressure of Hunger"

"It has been a great many years since our white brethren
came across the big waters and a great many of them
has not got civilized yet; therefore we wish to be indulged
in our savage state of life until we can have the same time
to get civilized. . . . There is some of our white brethren
as much savage as the Indian."
—SHULLUSHOMA, CHICKASAW

"Brother: When you were young, we were strong; we
fought by your side; but our arms are now broken. You
have grown large; my people have become small. . . .
My voice is weak; you can scarcely hear me; it is not the
shout of a warrior but the wail of an infant. I have lost it
in mourning over the misfortunes of my people. These
are their graves, and in those aged pines you hear the
ghosts of the departed. Their ashes are here and we have
been left to protect them. . . . Here are our dead. Shall we
go, and give their bones to the wolves?"
—CHIEF COBB, CHOCTAW

THE CHOCTAWS OF MISSISSIPPI, BY 1832, WERE ALSO ON THE ROAD west, their faces set grimly against the wind. There were, as usual, miles of Indians on horseback, on foot, and in wagons, with an escort of shouting "conductors" in army blue. Not all of the wagons had been easily come by. "Two have been allowed to every hundred persons," protested a Choctaw chief. "There are many among us who are young, and many who are old and infirm, none of whom can walk, and they have not horses. They all have implements of husbandry. How are they to be got along? And how are these people to live without them in the west?"[1] Reluctantly, the Great Father produced additional wagons, and the Choctaws began their exodus.

It was one more upheaval in a tribal history of tumult which had had its beginning when the Choctaws had migrated from the Place Where the Sun Falls into the Water, the Pacific Ocean, eastward and southward to the Gulf of Mexico.[2] In those ancient and dateless days, they had faithfully followed their leader and his multicolored sacred pole which guided them. When they had come to a huge brown river they stopped in wonder. Never had they seen inland water so wide. "Surely," said one of their medicine men,

> it must be very old and therefore very wise. We cannot pause here, for our pole still beckons us to the sunrise. Let us give to this river a name to mark it as our resting place. In the coming years all may know that our people crossed this great water on their long trail. No man can know the story of the river—it belongs to the time when there were no men upon the earth. Therefore, I give it the name of Misha Sipokni—"beyond the ages, the father of all its kind."

Then, on sturdily constructed rafts, the Choctaws crossed the Mississippi River for the first time. Beyond it they found the holy hill, Nanih Waya, and among gentle green swells of Mississippi earth they began hunting, farming, and building their terraced temples to the sovereign sun.

In 1540 Chief Tuskalusa faced Hernando de Soto and his

conquistadores; the Spaniards left in their wake thousands of Choctaws dead and mutilated—the Spanish favored the cutting off of noses—and whole Indian communities in charred ruins. For two centuries after that, the Choctaws fought to regain their numbers and thus to survive. They were courteous to the first French and Spanish settlers and even showed them how to make gumbo with *filé*, the powder of sassafras leaves which gave it texture. Eventually the Choctaws separated into divisions: the Tall People, the People of the Other Side who lived across Alabama's Tombigbee River, and the central group, the Kunsha, which produced Chief Pushmataha. It was "General Push" who had marched into battle beside Jacksa Chula Harjo at Horseshoe Bend believing American promises that loyal Choctaws might remain on Choctaw land in the shadow of Nanih Waya, the holy hill.

But as much as they loved the soil they tilled, the Choctaws loved politics, and this love was their undoing. They prized eloquence in their councils, and throughout the troubled years of United States emergence, their chiefs vied with one another in intrigue. More than one leader seized power and went on to enjoy it at a predecessor's expense. In the opening years of the nineteenth century, Choctaw headmen had begun signing treaties of cession (usually when drunk) and pocketing personal rewards as they listened to the enticements of the Long Knives. When the Long Knives built a highway from Natchez to Nashville, it bisected the soft hills and dark pines of Choctaw territory. By 1816 the tribe had sold all of its land east of the Tombigbee. Their dealings had brought them various compensations: $2,000, 3 sets of blacksmith's tools, 15 pieces of strouds (a coarse woolen cloth), 3 rifles, 150 blankets, 250 rounds of powder, 250 pounds of lead, one bridle, one saddle, and a black silk handkerchief. District Chiefs Apukshunnubbee, Pushmataha, and Moshulatubbee were granted salaries of $150 a year while they were in office, and afterward $500 each "in consideration of their past services to the Choctaw nation."[3] It was not that the chiefs were deliberately betraying their people; their acceptance of special favors as the due of

Pushmataha. Portrait by C.B. King. *Courtesy Smithsonian Institution, Washington, D.C.*

their rank showed they were only human. They did not understand treaties they could not read.

Among the Choctaws several intermarried whites had given their loyalties and abilities to their adopted people, and their descendants became tribal powers. From South Carolina had come the Folsom brothers. John Pitchlynn, an Englishman's son, had grown up in Mississippi. From the icy rigors of French Canada had come the LeFlore brothers, Michael and Louis. Many of these mixed-bloods kept inns since white people frequently traveled Choctaw trails on their way from Tennessee to Louisiana and back. Pitchlynn's Place was famous for its hospitality and its sweeping view of the russet Tombigbee. A Folsom estimated that there were hardly five days in the year when his tavern didn't have guests, and sometimes he had seventy or eighty at once.

The traveling whites were one thing, but as more and more sedentary whites settled among the Choctaws, some of the chiefs became apprehensive. Would the Choctaws die as a people? At the Treaty of Doak's Stand in 1820, Moshulatubbee signed away the southwestern portion of his holdings in exchange for a wilderness between the Red River on the south and the Canadian River on the north. Here the Choctaws would be not far from Chief Jolly's Cherokees. The Long Knives promised the Choctaws a blacksmith and an Indian agent, and a group of Choctaws prepared to make a willing pilgrimage to southwestern Arkansas. Yet, before they could start they learned that Long Knives had already staked claims in their promised land. The white pioneers, said the federal government, could not be dislodged. Therefore the Choctaws had better cede the new land also, the land they had not even had time to occupy before it was wrested from them. Alarmed, a solemn delegation set out for the White House: Apukshunnubbee, Moshulatubbee, a Pitchlynn, a Folsom, and old Pushmataha himself, whom white Americans regarded as a great show in his high silk hat and his medals. Apukshunnubbee never reached the capital; he died in a brawl in Kentucky. His colleagues continued on, and in Washington they were delighted by the enthusiastic hospitality of their Great Father, whose bills were considerable. The Great Father paid out $2,029 for lodgings, $350 for fresh oysters, and $1,134.74 for new suits of clothes for the chiefs. The bar tariff came to $2,149.50. Officialdom systematically got the Choctaws so befuddled that they touched the goose quill to anything with which they were presented. For General Push it was all too much; after a strenuous bout with oysters and *oka humma* he collapsed and died. The Great Father buried him with full military honors and offered more *oka humma* to his colleagues. Before the chiefs had left Washington they had ceded, in trusting euphoria, everything east of the modern boundary between Arkansas and Oklahoma.[4] For this, in addition to the expenses of their trip, they were rewarded with $6,000 a year apiece for sixteen years and an added yearly sum of $6,320. The chiefs thought the Great Father very generous; the Great Father in turn realized that it was not a bad price to pay for rich Mississippi, Louisiana, and Arkansas land where planters were already making fortunes and sparkling rivers were freighted with sternwheelers carrying cotton, pitch, and grain to hungry markets.[5]

By 1830 Mississippians were getting impatient. The Choctaws still remained by the graves of their dead, still worshiped on Nanih Waya, still farmed their land and built stout frame houses and mills, and still sent their children to mission schools. The state, to speed things up, granted the Choctaws what it magnanimously called citizenship. Under citizenship, the tribal government of the Choctaws was abolished. Anybody who "should exercise the office of chief, mingo, head man, or other post of power established by the tribal statutes, ordinances or customs of the said Indians" was liable to prison and heavy fines.

At first, Chief Moshulatubbee was aghast. Then he had an idea. Why not run for Congress? Dark-skinned, clad in flowing robes, silver belt, and enormous silver gorget, wielding his leadership symbols of eagle feathers and long clay pipe, the stocky Moshulatubbee took to the campaign trails of Mississippi followed by a reporter from the national newspaper *Niles's Weekly Register.* "Fellow citizens!" Moshulatubbee addressed what he hoped would be his constituency:

> I have fought for you, I have been by your own act made a citizen of your state; I am a freeholder, nature my parent. . . . While in a state of nature my ambition was alone in the shade— my hopes to be interred in the mounds of my ancestors. But you have awakened new hopes; your laws have for me brightened my prospects. . . . I have been told by my white brethren that the pen of history is impartial. . . . This, fellow citizens, is plain talk. Listen, for I have spoken in candor. According to your laws I think that I am qualified to a seat in the councils of a mighty republic. . . . I have no animosity against any of my white brethren who enter the list against me, but with Indian sincerity I wish you would elect me a member of the next Congress of the United States.[6]

Mississippians could not believe what they saw and heard. As the realization dawned that this savage actually thought he could act like a citizen as well as call himself one, Mississippians began to laugh. The laughter rang through the Choctaws' lofty forests and in their taverns. It echoed in newspapers and in the pulpits of churches. If the presumption of Moshulatubbee had not been so funny it would have been outrageous. He might be comic relief, but even so he would have to go west with his tribe. The land the Choctaws were on was matchless, and white Mississippi wanted it.

The campaign of Moshulatubbee, who naturally lost the election, precipitated a civil war among the Choctaws as devastating as the one that had racked the Creeks in Red Eagle's time. Mississippi threw the Choctaw country open to liquor traffic, and rivers of whiskey flowed in Choctaw villages. The Methodist missionaries among the Choctaws were powerless to stop the commerce. These missionaries, as well as the rest of Mississippi, wanted the Choctaws out, although the missionaries' motives were more humanitarian, at least in part. They felt the Indians must be gotten away from the corrupting influence of Christian civilization, and if they saw a paradox in this resolve they gave no sign of it. They promptly enlisted the help of one of their most important converts. Greenwood LeFlore, chief of the Upper Towns, not only prayed the prayers of the Wesleys and Bishop Asbury, he also had personal ambitions. Why couldn't he put the other Choctaw chiefs out of business permanently and lead his people, like a veritable contemporary Moses, into the sunlit prairies himself? There he could live like the king he would be, courtesy of the Reverend John Wesley and a keen instinct for survival.

LeFlore called together a council of men he was sure would support him: David Folsom, chief of the Lower Towns, and John Garland, chief of the Six Towns. Folsom and Garland, afraid that Mississippi would fine them and throw them into jail for holding tribal office, resigned in LeFlore's favor, willing to let him brave the Long Knives. LeFlore, however, had no intention of defying the state of Mississippi. His destiny, he thought, lay in the country of the Red and Canadian and Arkansas rivers. As chief of the Choctaw Nation, he gave a public speech in favor of removal. The treaty he proffered was in the handwriting of a Methodist minister named Talley, and it was carried to Washington by another Methodist named Haley.[7]

The U.S. Senate was at first appalled. The treaty was far too generous to the Choctaws, in particular to Greenwood LeFlore. At the same time, the Senate had long since committed itself to Jacksa Chula Harjo's Removal Act. Then Congress had an inspiration. Why not persuade President Jackson to visit the Choctaws in person and negotiate a better treaty himself? Jacksa Chula Harjo agreed, and invited the Choctaws to meet him at Franklin, Tennessee, where he would try to explain away government penny-pinching and would also unfold further the "benevolent purposes" of his administration in removing Mississippi's original citizens to a West where they might live "with none to interrupt" them.

Greenwood LeFlore. *Courtesy Oklahoma Historical Society, Tulsa.*

Jackson arrived in Franklin in the company of John Coffee, the stalwart veteran of Horseshoe Bend. Curious citizens staring at their President saw a tall, stooped, white-faced man whose air of infinite tiredness was belied only by the fierce light in his eyes. Unfortunately, the Choctaws were not waiting for him, and Jackson departed for Washington in a fury. Coffee learned that the Choctaws were not being deliberately contemptuous; they were torn by acid civil strife. Their young braves were fasting, dreaming and talking of taking the path of war against Choctaw opponents. Choctaw full-bloods had no use for Le-Flores and Pitchlynns and Folsoms. Under the banner of Moshulatubbee, whom they elected chief of the Lower Towns in defiance of Mississippi law, and Pushmataha's nephew Nitakechi, whom they made chief of the Six Towns to succeed John Garland, they rallied to form what they christened the Republican Party. Christianity was anathema to the full-blooded Republicans, their hands clasped tightly on their ceremonial eagle feathers. Had not the Republicans dubbed LeFlore's cohorts, who had been trying to crown him Choctaw king, the Despots? The Presbyterian missionaries came to the uncomfortable conclusion that the Republicans who opposed removal were right about wanting to stay in Mississippi, if not in opposing Christianity. By the time the tribe had gathered to receive its customary federal annuities and baubles, the tension was so great that Moshulatubbee and Nitakechi arrived with more than a hundred followers carrying rifles and tomahawks. The armed warriors tried to prevent LeFlore's party from shar-ing in the bounty, and a battle was about to explode when amiable George Gaines, who ran a trading post noted for its honesty, intervened. The Choctaws respected Gaines's integ-rity and forgave his pale face. Nitakechi promised to "walk straight," and Moshulatubbee said he would resign and let a successor be elected. Greenwood LeFlore, satisfied with the surrender, returned to the plantation home he had named Malmaison after Josephine Bonaparte's suburban Parisian villa. As soon as LeFlore was out of the way at Malmaison, Moshu-

Moshulatubbee. Portrait by George Catlin. *Courtesy Oklahoma
Historical Society, Tulsa.*

latubbee discreetly took up the reins of tribal government once more. LeFlore waited for his resignation in vain.[8]

Into this unsettled atmosphere stepped the federal commissioners who came to draw up the new removal treaty Jacksa Chula Harjo had been unable to push through earlier. The commissioners arrived at Dancing Rabbit Creek laden with presents. "Supplies" amounted to $570 and "entertainment" came to $150 for food alone. Nearly $1,500 was expended on calico, razors, soap, and handsome colored quilts. Prominent Choctaws were promised large land grants in the West, and the commissioners constantly reminded them—in the intervals between present-giving, banquets, and toasts—that the Choctaws were powerless against a hostile Mississippi and that the United States Government would never intervene to save the Indian Nation. Moshulatubbee listened with his eyes closed in meditation. On the banks of Dancing Rabbit Creek, its night waters bright with reflected lanterns, he knew he was hearing the call to exile. He was also hearing the alarums of his tribe's disorganization. When he signed the new treaty he knew he had no alternative and that there were Christian Choctaws who wanted to murder him.[9] He asked the commissioners for protection, while his detractors began making bitter speeches about Jacksa Chula Harjo: "The man who said that he would plant a stake and draw a line around us that never should be passed was the first to say he could not guard the line, and he drew up the stake and wiped out all traces of the line." To Secretary of War Lewis Cass, called Big Belly by his red charges, Choctaw interpreter Peter Pitchlynn wrote with ironic courtesy:

> I beg, Sir, that for a whole nation to give up their whole country, and remove to a distant, wild and uncultivated land, more for the benefit of the Government than the Choctaws, is a consideration which I hope the Government will always cherish with the liveliest sensibility. The privations of a whole nation before setting out, their turmoil and losses . . . and settling their homes in a wild world are all calculated to embitter the human heart.[10]

As for Greenwood LeFlore, in the elegance of Malmaison with his slaves tilling his fertile cotton fields, he decided to cease being a Choctaw altogether and to become a citizen of Mississippi by renouncing his tribe. Now it was too late to be a king in the western territory; he had too many enemies. He refused even to join the exploring party bound for the Red River.

When the explorers reached the West, they were met by savage winds and the iron eyes of a Shawnee who noted the presence of storekeeper George Gaines with the delegation. "You are a white man. I hoped never to see the face of another white man."

"And what is your reason for such a hope?" Gaines asked her.

"My husband and several members of my family were killed by the whites. The remnants of my relations were compelled to leave their homes and we traveled to this country where we hoped to live in peace."

"We could not help killing the Shawnees," Gaines answered. Like many other whites, Gaines believed the original fault had been Tecumtha's.[11]

The exploring group, despite the ordeal of western autumnal weather, were impressed by what they saw: fertile stream bottoms, productive grain land, high stands of cane, and evidence of buffalo and wild turkeys. They also understood their approval was academic; the Choctaws would have to make the best of the Red River country, whether it was good or not. They would also have to make the best of the Osages.

Their removal began in the fall of 1831. Removals always began in the fall, after harvest in the old land and before planting in the new. The Choctaw Nation looked on Nanih Waya for the last time. As they prepared for their journey, sheriffs and constables descended on them with fraudulent writs of confiscation for their goods. The additional outrage rankled in Choctaw hearts.

Nearly four thousand Choctaws left Mississippi in the first wave. As winter closed its grip on the exiles, their story became that of the Senecas and Delawares and Shawnees before them.

Greenwood LeFlore's nephew, a product of missionary schools and loyal to his people, kept a record of the march:

> Two hundred fifty head of horses have died on the road. We have had very bad weather. Since we landed at this place about twenty . . . have died, and still they are continuing to die. We are about 200 miles from . . . Red River. It will be some time in February before we get to where we want to settle. . . . We are compelled to travel slow, as there are so many sick people. I am afraid that a great many will die before we get home.[12]

In Louisiana, a white citizen, Joseph Kerr, watched the procession as it passed. There were

> two large deep streams that must be crossed in a boat or on a raft, and one other nearly impassable in any way. This they had to perform or perish, there being no provision made for them on the way. This, too, was to be done in the worst time of weather I have ever seen in any country—a heavy sleet having broken and bowed down all the small and much of the large timber. And this was to be performed under the pressure of hunger, by old women and young children, without any covering for their feet, legs, or body except a cotton underdress. . . . In passing, before they reached the place of getting rations here, I gave a party leave to enter a small field in which pumpkins were. They would not enter without leave, though starving. These they ate raw with the greatest avidity.[13]

From 1831 into 1832 the wagon trains inched westward. Then, after a series of storms and floods, they were ravaged by cholera. "The sick all got up," noted a conductor with satisfaction one winter morning. But the sick didn't stay up. They began dropping dead. In one Arkansas swamp a party spent seven days toiling through waist-high water under leafless cypresses. This did not build resistance to cholera or much else. When they emerged with fresh cholera cases, influenza, and pneumonia into a white setlement there was not a doctor who would treat them. Lieutenant Jefferson Van Horne, accompanying his charges through the mire, fell ill himself in the cabin of a settler named Morris:

> The symptoms increased on me until near midnight, when the constant purging and vomiting, and terrible cramps and pain in my stomach and bowels, induced me to take 20 grains of calomel and a large pill of opium. These I threw up. While vomiting through the floor (from which Morris had torn up a plank) and bent double with pain, I was repeating the dose. I was ordered to leave the house. Morris said he had a large family, and that their lives and his own were at stake, that I had imposed on him in coming there in that condition and that I must quit the house. The ground was already covered with frost and was freezing severely. I rolled myself in my blanket, after begging in vain to remain, and walked three fourths of a mile to my tent.[14]

The Choctaws had not been as lucky as Van Horne, who survived his ordeal. They had had no cabins to shelter them even briefly. The camp resounded with their screams of pain. "Death," said Army Major Armstrong who was urging Moshulatubbee onward with smart military orders, "is hourly among us. The road is lined with the sick. Fortunately they are a people that will walk to the last, or I do now know how we could get on."

"Not a family but more or less sick," reported another witness. "The Choctaws are dying to an alarming extent . . . 100 have died within five weeks. The mortality of these people . . . as far as ascertained, amounts to one fifth of the whole number. The cause of so many deaths probably arises from the change of climate, the overflow of the Arkansas River, and having no physician among them except their own doctors, who are conjurors." So the government of the United States under Andrew Jackson was less culpable than a handful of medicine men whose knowledge of herbs was powerless in the crisis.[15]

The cholera, of course, was not due to the flooding of the Arkansas; it was due to the water's pollution with animal carcasses and human wastes, but no one yet understood the origins of the plague which yearly ravaged most of the world and for which there was no cure. Before the cholera epidemic among the Choctaws ended, one-third of the tribe of eighteen thousand souls were dead. Some perished in the coma of acidosis brought on by the disease; others, before they loosed their tenuous grip on life, swelled grotesquely with uremic poisoning.

Cholera was not the only hazard to the Choctaws as they passed through on their way to the Red River. Enterprising whites sold the Indians high-priced groceries and whiskey. But still the Choctaws plodded on. "The women and children have been from 4 to 6 days without anything to eat; anything." Some began chewing acorn meal, and others were issued rotten pork full of trichinosis organisms. When the Indians complained, the escorts told them not to act like "misguided creatures."

Their destination was the portion of the Arkansas River that flows through Oklahoma, bounded on the south by the Red. When they reached it, they cleared the land of wiry post oaks and tough grasses and tangled roots, and planted their first corn. They built houses. Once more the Arkansas overflowed its banks. This time it swept away the Choctaws' green corn shoots and every trace of their shelters until the Indians wandered disoriented, trying to find the places where their new houses had stood.

"All the people who lived upon the river have been ruined," said Major Armstrong tersely. The river's banks were covered with slimy mud, quicksand, and the corpses of "dead animals destroyed by the water."[16] The cholera returned. Moshulatubbee's freedom came finally with his death, while Greenwood LeFlore, Mississippian and cotton planter, his Gallic eyes bland above high Choctaw cheekbones, lived on in his parody of Napoleonic splendor at Malmaison. Greenwood LeFlore was a long way from the hell to which he had urged his brothers. Nanih Waya, the holy hill he had repudiated forever, was not far from his hearth. But those who had loved Nanih Waya and sung its song in stately tribal ceremonies would never see its substance again.

～ 5 ～

The Lost Prince

"Are my looks not fine? See, is this the face of
a savage? How much Indian blood is there? We will
see, in time, whether the Indian or the white man
prevails in this face."
—ELEAZER WILLIAMS, MOHAWK

"The Great Spirit, when He made the earth, never
intended that it should be made merchandise."
—SOSEHAWA, SENECA

In New York—"the Empire State, as you love to call it," a Cayuga chief noted with a faint smile—the power of the formidable League of the Iroquois had long since been broken. To the confederated Mohawks, Onondagas, Senecas, Oneidas, Cayugas, and Tuscaroras of the Long House, white Americans were "Destroyers of Villages." The first term of Andrew Jackson's presidency found the Iroquois watching the cholera-cursed migration of the Choctaws and reflecting bitterly that New York

> was once laced by our trails from Albany to Buffalo—trails that we had trod for centuries, trails worn so deep by the feet of the Iroquois that they became your roads of travel, as your possessions gradually ate into ours. Your roads still traverse those same lines of communication which bound one part of the Long House to the other. Have we, the first holders of this prosperous region, no longer a share in your history? Glad were your fathers to sit down upon the threshold of the Long House. Had our forefathers spurned you from it, when the French were thundering at the opposite side to get a passage through and drive you to the sea, whatever has been the fate of other Indians the Iroquois might still have been a nation.

Two of the six Iroquois tribes were dispersing. The weakened Ohio Senecas had already been shunted along on their march into sweeping tallgrass plains where there was nothing but buffalo and sky, though Senecas remained in New York. Now the Oneidas, the Granite People, were leaving New York for the Green Bay in Wisconsin, led by a Mohawk who called himself their deliverer. Eleazer Williams, product of a missionary school and the descendant of a Massachusetts clergyman whose daughter had been captured by Mohawks, saw himself in grandiose dimensions. For a while the Oneidas saw him that way too. And the removal saga of the Oneidas had beginnings as tortuous as those of Williams himself, who acknowledged his Mohawk ancestry, but never elaborated on his early life.

Years before the rise of Williams, David A. Ogden, a New York land speculator, had bought out a listless company which had had "preemptive rights" to the Indian reservations of up-

Eleazer Williams. Portrait by George Catlin. *Courtesy State
Historical Society of Wisconsin, Madison.*

state New York. Mr. Ogden was able to put up the fifty cents an acre to preempt them, but the business of acquisition had proved slow. The Iroquois tribes were shrewd. Many of their people had been to white schools and knew a smattering of law. On their rocky, river-laced sanctuaries at Cattaraugus, Allegany, Tonawanda, Tuscarora, and Buffalo, they had clung to what was left of their stake in New York and had refused to budge. Then Ogden had conceived the plan of offering them a happy home in the West. The happy home under discussion was to be carved out of the holdings of tribes in remote Wisconsin. The War Department, when Ogden approached it, was enthusiastic. It took to giving away fat tracts belonging to the Menominees and Winnebagoes and Chippewas.[1]

At first the Indians of Wisconsin were blissfully unaware of these transactions. Not until the 1830s were they confronted with significant numbers of new arrivals from New York. Earlier they had willingly given asylum to a handful of Stockbridge Indians from Massachusetts and had said they would welcome New York Indians too. They had even signed a paper because they were told their marks on it would bring them a windfall of fifteen hundred American dollars. Still, in the wild rice lakes of the North Woods where high firs shivered and white birches flashed silvery leaves under pale summer suns, the Menominees and Chippewas and Winnebagoes had gone on paddling their bark canoes, fishing for arching muskellunge and for walleyed pike and perch. They had kept sacred the ceremonies of their Grand Medicine Societies. Their women, disdainful of trumpery trade beads, had continued embroidering buckskins with dyed porcupine quills. Patriarchs told dark-eyed youngsters rollicking tales of Nanabozho the Prankster and, in more serious moments, prepared them for the vision quest of early adolescence. Every aspiring brave sought his Guardian Spirit by fasting in the densely clustered forests of the western Great Lakes. The Sacs and the Foxes, original possessors of the Green Bay on sungold Lake Michigan, had been driven down to Illinois. The Menominees and the Chippewas still ruled eastern Wisconsin in the early 1830s as the Winnebagoes ruled the western part near the Mississippi River, which was crowned with hard stone bluffs decorated with their pictographs. The tribes' memories of the Jesuit Black Robes who had once come to them from French Canada were dimming. But the fur trade was still profitable: John Jacob Astor's American Fur Company bought from them in quantity. The Menominees and Chippewas and Winnebagoes, as Andrew Jackson came to power in Washington, still sang the old songs and worshiped the old spirits who inhabited their rocks and glades and needle-strewn woods. The buffalo had retreated, but lynxes and beavers and badgers and deer remained. It was a whispering, resiny fastness where rivers leaped and gushed and shining otters splashed in their runs. The refuge looked irresistible to New York Indians, and especially to the Mohawk mixed-blood Eleazer Williams. Williams and the Oneidas longed for room for expansion. "Surely," one of their chiefs said, "in emigration westward lies our escape from grog shops."

In former times Oneidas had put their crops into the ground during days of prayer at the Planting Festival. After the harvest, at the New Year, they had always sacrificed a white dog to the Great Spirit, and their Keepers of the Faith had prayed:

> We return thanks to our mother, the earth, which sustains us. . . . We return thanks to the rivers and streams. . . . We return thanks to all the herbs and plants of the earth. . . . We return thanks to the bushes and the trees which provide us with fruit. . . . We return thanks to the winds, which, moving, have banished disease. . . . We return thanks to the moon and the stars, which give us light when the sun has gone to his rest. . . . We return thanks for the World of Spirits. We thank Thee, our Creator and Ruler, that thou hast provided so many agencies for our good and happiness.

But whiskey had changed the ancient rhythms forever. Among the Senecas a sachem named Handsome Lake had begun having messianic visions. His converts related his revelations:

> At one time Handsome Lake was translated to the regions
> above. He looked down upon the earth and saw a great assembly. Out of it came a man. His garments were torn, tattered and
> filthy. His whole appearance indicated great misery. . . . He had
> taken the fire-water. Then Handsome Lake looked again and
> saw streams of blood. The Messengers of the Great Spirit said,
> "Thus will the earth be if the fire-water is not put from among
> you. Brother will kill brother, and friend friend." Again they
> told him to look towards the east. He obeyed, and as far as his
> vision reached he saw the increasing smoke of distilleries arising
> and shutting out the light of the sun. . . . Many will be burned,
> and others will be drowned, while under the influence of the fire-
> water.[2]

The Oneidas, however, were not impressed by Handsome
Lake, who died prematurely. He had taught that the Oneidas
were merely children to be guided by their wiser elder brothers, the Senecas. A pair of Church of England missionaries
passing through Oneida settlements had had a different tale: in
the sight of the Great Spirit all men were equal, Oneidas included.

Eleazer Williams was a powerful orator and a self-appointed
preacher in his native Mohawk (Mohawks and Oneidas could
understand each other's dialects). He preached a pleasant
Christianity of redemption and rewards as the emissaries of the
Church of England had done. The Catholic Church took notice
of him; he might do great things among the Oneidas. Dark-
skinned and well-padded, Williams was fond of gazing at himself in his shaving mirror. As he gazed, he decided that Protestants offered greener fields than did Catholics. There were
already Episcopalian Senecas. Williams, who was full of homilies on the fervent desire of the Oneidas to become Episcopalians, paid a short visit to the Right Reverend Doctor John
Henry Hobart, Bishop of New York. To be technical, the
Oneidas were not yet Episcopalians, said Williams, but he

could lead the entire tribe to the sacraments of baptism and confirmation, the liturgies of Tudor England, and, by implication, the theological improvisations of a Henry the Eighth lusting for Anne Boleyn. Bishop Hobart, looking into the earnest eyes before him, decided that the Mohawk was a messenger straight from God. The bishop longed to send delegates to go and teach all nations, especially those at his doorstep. He gave Williams the title of Catechist and Lay Reader to the Oneidas, and Williams triumphantly returned to upstate New York. He was somebody of importance now, not a charity boarder in a mission school.

Williams was undismayed when he found Presbyterians among the Oneidas. Presbyterians were not popular among the Iroquois. Moreover, when the Right Reverend Dr. Hobart had defended the authority of bishops, Presbyterians had pronounced his views "of such deep-toned horror as may well make one's hair stand up like quills upon the fretful porcupine and freeze the warm blood at the fountain." Williams read church magazines and was sure Bishop Hobart wouldn't object to an ouster of the Presbyterians' Reverend Mr. Jenkins, a spiritual heir of John Calvin who was offering the Oneidas predestination and infant damnation. The Oneidas didn't much like either. Also, Jenkins stammered. Williams grandly summoned the tribe to a meeting and explained: "It is a mistake to let in this order of Christians." Bishop Hobart announced that he wanted to build them a church, and Episcopalianism promised a stately heaven. Oneida leaders made laborious marks on the document Williams proffered, which signified their consent to join Bishop Hobart's religion. When a group of holdouts hesitated, Williams asked them: "Can any of you refute the Gospels? The Protestant Episcopal Church is the true faith." Indians could not refute gospels they could not read. Besides, Preacher Williams had the ear of rich churchmen who wanted to dispense gifts. When Williams went to Albany he petitioned the governor of New York for a land grant on which to erect his house of worship. The governor was pleased to give Williams room for a wooden chapel thirty-six by fifty feet. Back on the reservation Williams supervised its construction and specified "a small tower, tastefully painted." A beaming Bishop Hobart arrived in Episcopal robes to consecrate the building and confirm fifty willing Oneidas who had looked forward to the ceremony. Though not yet ordained, catechist and Lay Reader Williams became the Oneidas' first resident clergyman. Newspapers carried columns about Williams, bringing him "to great notice and a dizzy height."[3]

Yet, after a while he realized something was wrong. How far could he get in the world as an obscure minister, a half-breed at that? He wanted a larger theater. The cure of fifteen hundred Oneida souls wasn't challenging enough. The name of the Ogden Land Company reverberated in his dreams. It could offer in Wisconsin fresh fields of endeavor blessed by the enthusiasm of the War Department. Williams could offer the company Oneida lands to be vacated by the trek west. In "the neighborhood of Green Bay" he would unite his Oneidas, the refugee Stockbridges, and parties of Munsees and Brothertons who had fled New England for the Great Lakes. Who knew what other tribes would want to enroll under his banner? He would weld them all "into one grand confederacy of cantons, but all under one Federal Head: the government to be a mixture of civil, military, and ecclesiastic, the latter to be preeminent." The design of the new government would be "grand, imposing, and fascinating in the extreme." The federal head would of course be Eleazer Williams, who would train his Episcopalian charges in the arts of law and war. If Bishop Hobart, when he heard the first rumblings from upstate about the proposed hegira, was concerned about the possibility of Protestant Episcopalians going on the warpath in faces streaked with red ochre, he made no comment. Probably the thought was too painful, especially if his co-religionists had any plan of locking horns with the midwestern Baptist legions of Isaac McCoy. The bishop left Williams to his own devices, and soon hypnotized Oneidas were streaming out of the Empire State into the territory of the Menominees, Chippewas, and Winnebagoes. As they carried the cross of Jesus, Williams carried the burden of his ambition. He planned to establish a new country and become its dictator, the peer of presidents and kings.

The Menominees and Chippewas and Winnebagoes were at first unaware of the impending state. When the government summoned them to the Green Bay to receive the promised fifteen hundred dollars, they made a festival of it. Five thousand Indians and several hundred half-breeds gathered to share the bounty of thirty cents apiece. The spectacle especially dazzled Eleazer Williams: the Menominees in their quillwork vests, Sioux-speaking Winnebagoes with Jesuit-bestowed silver crosses and high scalp roaches black with bear grease, Chippewas with thunderbird-crested amulets and deer-hides and long birch canoes. Wizened old men and sinewy boys mingled with the young Wisconsin warriors, black-eyed Indian women in long calico skirts and buckskin shifts, and drowsy papooses strapped into the cradle boards their mothers carried on their backs. Amid trembling North Woods firs and Norway pines, the assembled Indians danced to the music of their drummers. The shrill voices of the Winnebago women rose high above the rest. An enormous ring of spectators circled the performers. The pungent, gamy odor of dogs and deer being roasted on wooden spits blended with the smell of the northern forests. In huge kettles soups made from sunflower seeds, corn-meal, and pumpkins were steaming; cranberries simmered in baths of maple sugar, and frolicking children roasted apples on spindly twigs. A. G. Ellis, a young government representative who observed the crowd, noted the "perfectly formed" bodies of the dancers, their muscles bulging under taut flesh. The nagging music with its irresistible rhythms filled him "with admiration and terror." Sandwiched in between the present giving and the revelry were speeches by white officials on the benefits to the Menominees and Chippewas and Winnebagoes of receiving "their grandfathers the New York Indians" and the Reverend Eleazer Williams, Mohawk man of God. But when the tribes gathered in council, Winnebago and Chippewa spokesmen made it clear that the grandfathers from the Empire State need expect no further cessions. What they had been given was enough. The Menominees, however, several of whose chiefs were absent, were induced to part with most of the shoreline of the Fox River and to extend "the right in common" of the New Yorkers to all Menominee lands. Green Bay traders and settlers who had become friends with individual Menominees were horrified when they heard the news. The tribe would no longer be able to conduct its affairs or to make treaties on its own. They would be overrun by Iroquois immigrants. The truth raced through the smoky tents of the Menominees until half the tribe reconvened to announce they regretted a bargain they had not considered for a long enough time. The other half of the tribe clung doggedly to its belief in portly, smiling Mr. Williams and in the Great Father in Washington, D.C. A pall of gloom hung over the festival now, and the Winnebagoes and Chippewas congratulated themselves for having stood their ground. By the time the Wisconsin tribes returned to their far-flung villages, the Menominees were vitriolically divided; it was a pattern that satisfied American expansionists were becoming adept at introducing.[4]

The Great Father Andrew Jackson sent news that he was unhappy. Weren't the Oneidas already in Wisconsin? How could the Menominees repudiate them? Two white commissioners were sent to the Green Bay, and once more the Menominees were summoned. This time they held a council for eight days, in the course of which they were harangued with official speeches. Finally, the tribe's impatient senior chief, Oshkosh, told the commissioners to desist. Sharp-eyed Oshkosh carried himself with dignity in spite of his small stature and his girth, and he denied all knowledge of the treaty favoring the Oneidas. He had never signed it. Why should the Indians of New York claim Menominee land? As long as the Oneidas were there, they could stay "during good behavior." But they were tenants at the beck and call of Oshkosh and his people; in no sense were they "owners and controllers of the soil." The gathering broke up inconclusively. High on his horse, wearing a black stovepipe hat and a Hudson's Bay blanket, Oshkosh looked contemptuously down at the luckless underlings who had surrendered their lands, their lives, and their souls. Then, his expression fixed and his posture on his mount rigid, he rode home.

When a new American agent, Thomas Stambaugh, was assigned to Green Bay, he met with several Menominee leaders and became as convinced as Oshkosh of the treaty's injustice. The Menominees had been robbed. But Stambaugh was also faithful in his fashion to the Great Father, "No other tribe of Indians is so poor as you are," he told the Menominees.

> You have a wide waste of lands entirely useless to you and not a dollar of annuity, while many of your neighbors are annually receiving twenty to fifty thousand dollars. Happily for you, I have been sent among you just in time to save you from the rapacity of Indian and white sharpers from New York. Now in place of giving away your country to the New Yorkers you can sell a small portion of it to the United States and have heavy annuities for all time to come.

That the "small portion" would be succeeded by other small portions was inevitable. But the Menominees cheered Stambaugh and announced that they wanted to leave immediately for Washington to discuss real estate with the Great Father. So, naturally, did Eleazer Williams.

The Menominee and Oneida chiefs and Williams met with Andrew Jackson in the White House. They were surprised at his frail appearance and his stoop. The chief of the Stockbridge tribe was also present, as was David Ogden of the Ogden Land Company, who said he was protecting the rights of the New York Indians in Wisconsin. Kaush-kaw-no-niew of the Menominees, the Grizzly Bear, began the conference with conventional polite respects to the Great Father and then got to the point. The Menominees wanted to sell land for annuities. To Jackson the event was wearying in its similarity to thousands of other such events. He promised the Grizzly Bear "every attention" and then withdrew.

Jackson had taken what he could for his country. Sometimes, though, he must have thought back to Red Eagle of the Creeks. The Indians he saw these days came to plead. Red Eagle, at Horseshoe Bend, had come to Jackson's camp not to beg but to bargain, if necessary with his life. Red Eagle was dead now, having spent his last days as a flourishing Alabama farmer whose white friends belonged to historical societies. The Menominees looked down-at-heel to Andrew Jackson.

A shocked Eleazer Williams read the revised government treaty when it arrived. In it the New York Indians were given five hundred thousand acres on the west side of the Fox River. That was all. If the New Yorkers refused

> to accept the provision made for their benefit and to remove upon the lands set apart for them, on the west side of Fox river, then the President will direct their immediate removal from the Menominee country; but if they agree to accept the liberal offer made to them by the parties to this compact, then the Menominee tribe, as dutiful children of their Great Father, the President, will take them by the hand as brothers and settle down with them in peace and friendship.

This time Chief Oshkosh found the treaty to his liking. Five hundred thousand acres were a fraction of Menominee holdings. In the slow scratching of pens Eleazer Williams heard the death rasps of his project of dictatorship. There would be no Indian kingdom now for him to rule. The Wisconsin land which had been fobbed off on the immigrant Oneidas was hunting land. Its stones and gullies made it nearly impossible to farm. And if the Oneidas didn't settle the unappealing tract within three years, they would lose it altogether. David Ogden was as depressed as Williams, and Ogden was not a man to hesitate. He immediately contacted his senators and various New York State politicians, who wrote letters to their friends. When the revised Menominee-Oneida treaty came up for ratification in the Senate it was defeated, and as an added fillip agent Thomas Stambaugh was fired. Jackson, his orders defied, made Stambaugh a "special agent" to the Menominees, but the chief executive was weary of the whole Wisconsin wrangle. During the following session of Congress clauses were added to the treaty providing for the Stockbridges and for Brotherton and Munsee refugees as well as the Oneidas. But the acreage granted for the Oneidas was not increased. It stood at five hundred thousand, though some indifferent parcels were exchanged for potential farmland.

The Oneidas, still in New York, declared their intention to stay put. They felt more than justified when the government offered the Wisconsin Oneidas land in Missouri in exchange for their Great Lakes allotment. The Oneidas' Wisconsin claims were slowly eroded into a piece of land eight miles wide and twelve miles long near Green Bay; the news was broken to the tribe by their interpreter John Sundown. Eleazer Williams retired to the tiny cottage he had built himself at Kaukaulin. He frequently traveled to eastern cities to raise money for his "self-sacrificing missionary laborers," as he described them to fascinated matrons in parlors full of horsehair furniture and lace doilies. The self-sacrificing missionary was very pot-bellied, his hostesses noted, but they pitied him when he told them how his hard work for God had wrecked his physique.

"Tea or coffee, Mr. Williams?"

"Neither, dear lady. My health does not admit of taking tea or coffee."

Some milk, perhaps? No, he could not digest milk. He might try a very, very small glass of warm water. When he was pressed to choose a main course he modestly asked for "just a piece of dry toast." He discreetly nibbled and sipped while the hostesses made mental notes about increasing the size of their gifts to him. Fortunately, they were unaware that when he left them he would return to his hotel and "with a hearty Indian chuckle" order four pounds of cold ham and assorted vegetables—in sauce. "He is the hungriest Indian I ever saw!" exclaimed a bemused waiter.[5]

For the exiled Oneidas of Green Bay, the constant junketings of their missionary was exasperating. He had promised them a

nation and hadn't given it to them. He had promised to save
their souls, and now that they wanted them saved, he had lost
interest in the project. He was taking his pay from tribal missionary funds and doing no work. His aggressively Episcopalian converts drew up a petition to the Church begging the
Right Reverend bishops to rid them of a millstone. In the
words of Chief Daniel Bread, Williams had led them into a
waste and then had abandoned them. They had no schools, no
churches, no religious services. They didn't even have the
money sent them by eastern charities; Williams was feasting
on it. The Oneidas knew, in short, that they had been had.
They sent copies of their denunciation to the governor of New
York, the Secretary of War, and to Bishop Hobart's successor, the Right Reverend Henry Onderdonk, bishop of New
York. Bishop Onderdonk was the formidable descendant of
Dutch patroons. Officially he declined to act; Mr. Williams was
now under the jurisdiction of Missionary Bishop Jackson
Kemper, he said. Kemper's far-flung territory included Wisconsin. Salty and worldly wise, the missionary bishop extricated
himself by saying that Williams held a commission from New
York sources and, therefore, ecclesiastical discipline was not up
to himself. Episcopalians didn't like scandals that might get
into the papers. Privately, both bishops told Williams to get
out and stay out. Again he retired to Kaukaulin, this time "an-
nihilated and disgraced." But Williams basically was an opti-
mist. He couldn't hate the whole human race for long.

One morning America was gripped by the revelation that the
Lost Dauphin of France, Louis XVII, son of Marie Antoinette
and the last of the royal Capets, had been found living in Wisconsin. Miraculously His Majesty had escaped the guillotine; a
substitute had died in his place. Faithful retainers had spirited
him to the states. The Dauphin's name? With suitable fanfare,
Putnam's Magazine announced it to a breathless public on the
Atlantic coast: Eleazer Williams. The repudiated savior of the
removed Oneidas had found himself another set of gullible
Episcopalians.

On a trip to New York, Williams had succeeded in impressing the Reverend Dr. Hawkes with the story that his French servants had deposited him with the Mohawk Indians, believing he would never be found there by the antiroyalist citizenry back home. He showed Dr. Hawkes several scars on his arms and legs—the result of terrible beatings in the Tower of the Temple in Paris. His skin had darkened as a result of overexposure to the sun during his residence with the Mohawks. The shock of his imprisonment and escape had been so great, he continued as he warmed to his role of Louis XVII, that he had completely lost his memory of childhood. It stayed lost until he was sent to school by Mohawk benefactors at Lake George where, while playing on the shore, he had fallen and hit his head on a rock and toppled over into the water. The strenuousness of his efforts not to drown had instantly cleared his recollection. Naturally, he had kept silent, first from fear of discovery by Danton and Robespierre, and later because he wanted to save the souls of the Oneidas; he was a religious man, and he had wished to serve God in humble obscurity. Duty to France, however, now called. When a friend of Dr. Hawkes wrote Williams a letter addressed to the Dauphin, Williams graciously replied with the royal cipher "L.C." (for Louis Charles Capet) and told his correspondent: "I wish to maintain the dignity of my Family by manifesting at all times in my conduct that sense of honor which becomes my royal race." He also issued a Royal Manifesto stating that he would govern France as justly as had "my ancestors."

Dr. Hawkes was bowled over, as were some congressmen he knew, but Dr. Hawkes was no writer. The Reverend John H. Hanson, another trusting Episcopalian, was. Williams soon transferred his attentions from Dr. Hawkes to the Reverend Mr. Hanson, and it was Hanson who fascinated the United States with the news that the Lost Dauphin had been found. So greatly did the sensation increase the circulation of *Putnam's Magazine*, that Mr. Hanson expanded his original article into a book, titled simply and movingly *The Lost Prince*. Whether the bishop of New York had retired to a darkened room with cold cloths upon his forehead is not recorded. The book was a sensation, though not in the environs of Green Bay, Wisconsin, whose citizens knew Eleazer Williams at first hand. Lewis Cass, Jackson's Secretary of War, threw back his head and roared with laughter. Mr. Hanson raked in royalties at a smart pace, while the editors of *Putnam's* continued to rejoice.

They rejoiced less when an article was submitted to them by a gentleman in Montreal who had lived in Caughnawaga, the small Canadian town where Williams had been raised by the Mohawks. Williams the Dauphin? It was ludicrous, according to the writer. *Putnam's* turned it down, but promised to run a synopsis of it and "have it published entire" by a New York daily newspaper. Neither synopsis nor publication was forthcoming. Mr. Hanson was not disturbed; he still believed in Williams. But the *New York World* got wind of the controversy and sent its reporters to Caughnawaga where they found an ancient Mohawk woman named Marie Anne Kenewatsenri. They collected an affidavit from her and sent it south to Manhattan. Mrs. Kenewatsenri described a Mohawk named Williams who "was very poor; he had a large family":

> He had a son named Lazare. She knew the said Lazare at the age of three or four years; so soon as he was able to run about the streets, which he then used to do with nothing but a shirt on him, and bare-footed and bare-legged. As Lazare grew up and was able, he did little chores for different people in the village, such as carrying water and going for the cows, which he would do for a piece of bread or something else to eat. . . . The deponent remembers well when Lazare left Caughnawaga to go to the United States. . . . Deponent further says that Lazare's body and limbs may be full of scars from running among rocks, stumps, and thorn-bushes, he seldom having sufficient clothes in his youth to protect himself.[6]

Mrs. Kenewatsenri's affidavit was not the only one collected by the *New York World*. There was one from Charles Soskonharowane, who had played with Lazare Williams as a boy and had been visited by the grown-up Lazare. Little Lazare was often "running about the village in the most inclement season, bare-footed and bare-legged, the blood running down his legs from scratches caused by cold, wet and wind. . . . There are innumerable other incidents connected with Lazare's days of youth that deponent could relate . . . which would remove him from the thought of his being the son of the great *Anonthica*." Anonthica was the Mohawks' name for the King of France.

More damaging still, the *New York World* found Lazare's mother Mary Anne, who thought she might be in her eighties but did not know. What she did know was that she was the mother of Lazare who had changed his name to the American Puritan Eleazer. In her affidavit Mary Anne put it on record

> that she is the natural mother of Rev. Eleazer Williams, and that she is aware of his pretensions to be the son of Louis XVI and knows them to be false . . . When he was about nine years old some of his father's friends from the States came to Caughnawaga and took him and a younger brother away to send them to school. . . . Some time after, he returned home and had a sore leg that made him lame.[7]

The Dauphin's scars were looking less French every minute.

Mr. Hanson, to save his profits, sent a man named Phineas Atwater to Caughnawaga. Atwater's instructions were to find Mary Anne Williams and have her repudiate her affidavit. No doubt the resident Catholic priest at Caughnawaga had made her give it, Hanson told himself. Everybody knew what tyrants Catholic priests were. That they generally supported Catholic kings Mr. Hanson chose to ignore. Sure enough, Mary Anne was "surrounded by Roman Catholic Indians," Atwater reported, and when he importuned her to deliver another affidavit for Mr. Hanson, the assembled Indians "embarrassed the examination." But Atwater persevered—how he never explained—and emerged with a document in which Mary Anne said she had been coerced by the local priest to make the first declaration: "It is not true . . . that my *adopted* son had a sore leg when he returned from school the first time to us. I remember that my husband had a medal which he ordered Charles and Jarvis to pawn to a merchant for him. The names of my children were Peter, Catherine, Ignatius, Thomas, Eleazer (adopted), Louisa, John, Hanna, Rhoda, Charles and Jarvis."

But people who had known Lazare Williams, later Eleazer, began to come forward. The Masonic Lodge at Green Bay found a membership application from Williams that said forthrightly, "I was born at Sault St. Louis." Colonel H.E. Eastman of Green Bay recalled his own acquaintance with Eleazer after Williams had come to Wisconsin with the Oneidas in tow. Eastman and Williams had had business dealings. In his leisure, Eastman enjoyed reading French history and had gone so far as to outline a romantic novel based on the imaginary escape of the Dauphin. He had had a brainstorm: why not make the Lost Prince of his novel an Indian and base him on the Mohawk cleric? Williams had asked to see the outline and had said that he was "amused and flattered." "Busy times came on," explained Eastman, "and I thought no more of my romance. . . . You were none of you so much astonished as I when I went into Burley Follett's book store at Green Bay one day . . . and bought a number of Putnam's Magazine containing the startling discovery of the mislaid Dauphin, in my own language. . . . My facts were drawn entirely from imagination." Williams must have had the outline copied, added Colonel Eastman, and it must have been "several years in his hands before he got the courage . . . of claiming my fictions as his facts; when Mr. Hanson builded his book . . . he had my model before him, of which he adopted something more than the name and the theory. . . . I shall be willing to forego the *glory* of the monstrous conception, if it is not already too late to be saved the mortification of having been so monstrously absurd."

The bubble had burst, shocking Eleazer Williams into a belated honesty. On a trip to Baltimore (Williams was always traveling, and his share of Hanson's royalties had helped pay his way) he met an old Green Bay friend, a Mr. Robinson.

"Have you seen Hanson's work?" Williams asked him.

"Oh yes, and I have read it with a great deal of interest."

"What do you think of it, Mr. Robinson?"

"It is admirably written, far better than I could have done it, but I don't believe there is a word of truth in it."

Williams burst into a good-natured guffaw. "Nor do I either, Mr. Robinson. Nor do I either!"

He remained cheerful even when the money ran out and he couldn't think of any more angles.

"Uncle Eleazer," a small nephew asked him once, "how old are you?"

"If I am Williams," he told the boy, "I am old." And with a jaunty grin he finished: "But if I am the Dauphin, I am older."

Ma-ka-tai-me-she-kia-kiak Goes to War

"You have asked, Who is Black Hawk? I am a Sac; my
forefather was a Sac, and all the nations call me Sac.
Black Hawk is satisfied with the lands the Great Spirit
has given him. Why then should he leave them? We have
never sold our country. We never received any annuities
from our American father. And we are determined to
hold on to our village."

—BLACK HAWK, SAC

"Father, we were told that the Americans were determined
shortly to lay hands on all our males, both old and young,
and deprive them of those parts which are said to be
essential to courage. . . . We assure you, Father, that this
has had a great Influence on the minds of All."

—TAI-MAH, FOX

"The President is very sorry to be put to the trouble and
expense of sending a large body of soldiers here."

—MAJOR GENERAL EDMUND PENDLETON GAINES

BETWEEN THE MISSISSIPPI AND THE ROCK RIVERS, IN ILLINOIS, LAY more than three thousand acres of rich black soil. To New Englanders back east struggling with unyielding stones on meager hillsides, to the small farmers of the South who watched rain leach their sandy fields year after year, the fertility of Illinois was already a taunting legend by the time of Lewis and Clark's expedition in 1803. Illinois was, according to a popular ballad, "the Garden Adam played in as a boy." When Andrew Jackson became President, the rush for paradise was on. But the newcomers with their hunted looks and squeaky wagons in which sat pallid wives were not the first to make the pilgrimage to the peninsula between the Mississippi and the Rock. The Sac Indians, allied since the middle of the seventeenth century with the Foxes, had originally lived in upper Michigan. The expansion of the Iroquois and the French had forced the Sacs south to Green Bay and the thickly forested country of Wisconsin. The Foxes were being harassed by neighboring Chippewas on the shores of Lake Superior. When the French threatened to exterminate the Foxes because they were interfering with French traders, the Sacs and the Foxes joined forces against their common enemies. The united tribes swept south to the nation of the Illiniwek and seized the Rock Island which lay between rushing rivers whose waters spilled a bounty of northern topsoil on Illinois earth. The Illiniwek retreated, and the conquerors planted corn, beans, pumpkins, squashes, and tobacco. Gradually the ancestral fields of the Illiniwek assumed in Sac and Fox eyes the sacredness of a fatherland. On the north bank of the Rock the Sacs built a city and called it Saukenuk. The confederated tribes prospered at Saukenuk until they inhabited the largest settlement between the Allegheny Mountains of the east and the umber Mississippi in the west. Under golden summer suns Saukenuk lay shining, the striated bark roofs of its lodges reflecting back the prairie's light. In winter Saukenuk stood alabaster and silent, its ghost-bare trees weighted down with ice and snow. The Indians hunted then; each spring, in their laden canoes, they returned to Saukenuk at the foot of the Rock River's rapids where wild roses and lilies

bloomed on green banks dense with grass. In spring, said the
Sacs, the Rock's rapids laughed for joy. So did the chattering
Indian women, tenders of future crops. High on the bluffs that
guarded the Mississippi the Sacs and Foxes lived, worshiped,
and watched for adversaries. They had seized their Eden, and
they knew there were men who waited to seize it from them
in turn. Saukenuk sheltered eleven thousand people. If they
had taken their country by force, they had built their capital by
diligence. Saukenuk, they believed, was theirs because they had
created it.[1]

The city was laid out regularly in lots. Its streets and alleys
rang with the cries of children, most of them Sacs. The Foxes
were clustered in small towns across the Mississippi. In the
center of Saukenuk there was an esplanade where Sac tribal
dignitaries gathered to smoke, pray, parade, and gossip. Saukenuk had no wigwams or tepees. Several families shared log
houses which ranged from thirty to a hundred feet in length
and sixteen to forty feet in width. These were made of saplings
carefully graded in size and lashed together with vines. Inside,
the fur of bears, panthers, and lynxes, and the hides of deer
served as beds that rested on flexible poles supported by cross-
pieces.

Early white travelers marveled at Saukenuk. Europeans ex-
pecting to find the rudest of savages living in hovels and attacking strangers found instead a metropolis fragrant with the
woodsmoke of lodge cooking fires, where visitors could report:
"No people are more hospitable, kind, and free than these Indians. They will readily share with any of their own tribe the
last part of their provisions, and even with those of a different
nation if they chance to come in when they are eating." Another observer added: "They are so hospitable, kind-hearted
and free they would share the last part of their own provisions,
even to a single ear of corn. . . . An open, generous temper is a
standing virtue among them; to be narrow-hearted, especially
to those in want or to any of their own family, is accounted a
great crime and to reflect scandal on the rest of the tribe. Such
wretched misers they brand with bad characters."[2] Sac and

Fox braves were also gallant to their women, for the women had the power to depose leaders and to elect successors. This process was called "knocking the horns from the head of the chief," and the politically oriented wives and daughters of Saukenuk enjoyed showing their power. The Sacs and Foxes loved oratory; their councils enforced tribal laws through a trial system where lawyers on opposing sides appeared before a judge who was considered the wisest, and was sometimes the oldest, among the headmen of the city.

All around Saukenuk the land was enchanting and, the Indians believed, enchanted. The spirits of their forefathers hovered over thickets of Illinois briar, high deciduous forests, and the bluffs that served as watchtowers. Saukenuk had its counterpart in a world of shadows: Chippionnock, the silent City of the Dead, spreading to the edges of river bottomlands thick with wild cherries, ironwoods, broad-leaved sycamores, walnuts, and beeches. There was no need for survivors to mark the graves on the cleared land of the City of the Dead itself. Every Sac and Fox clan knew where their honored ones slept.

The Sacs and Foxes did not fear English and French and white Americans as much as they feared Osages and Sioux who preyed on their hunting parties in the west. To the south lived the Cherokees; it was a Cherokee raider who had killed a Sac chief in the closing years of the eighteenth century. The chief left a son who had been born in 1767: Ma-ka-tai-me-she-kia-kiak, the Black Sparrow Hawk. The whites of the frontier settlements shortened the name until Black Sparrow Hawk began using the abbreviation Black Hawk himself.

When Andrew Jackson arrived in Washington with his buck-skin-clad admirers in 1829, Black Hawk was sixty-two. His brown face was seamed with wrinkles, but he carried his head with an upward tilt that accentuated the hard curve of his nose and the depth of his enigmatic eyes, which were the color of bloodstones. On his otherwise shaved head he wore a bushy scalplock, and around his neck hung a silver medal of His late British Majesty, King George III. Black Hawk prized the medal, which had been presented to him by British agents who had invited him to their post at Fort Malden, in Canada, across from Detroit, and had offered him their protection. On forays into Cherokee and Osage and Sioux country, Black Hawk had earned his war chieftaincy. He was pleased when a European monarch honored him as what he thought was an equal.

Black Hawk lived with his wife Asshewequa, Singing Bird. Both Sacs and Foxes were polygamous, but Black Hawk never wanted another mate. He and Singing Bird had several children. All of the boys, on entering their teens, had retired for a period to the forests beyond Saukenuk to fast and wait for a vision from the Great Spirit. Black Hawk, too, believed in visions: his own, and those of a half-Sac, half-Winnebago medicine man named Wabokeshiek. Wabokeshiek had his own village farther up the Rock, where he presided over a motley crew of Sac, Fox, and Winnebago renegades. Most of his followers were exiled violators of tribal ordinances. But if Wabokeshiek, the White Cloud, led a gang of desperadoes, he also dreamed of power, and when he spoke his Indian hearers listened transfixed. Wabokeshiek had eyes that burned when he was inspired. He was a big man, fatter and taller than Black Hawk and wore a sacred feather as well as a moustache. He was more than twenty years younger than Black Hawk, but he had a reputation of making true predictions and of reading the minds of distant rival Osages and Cherokees.

The Sacs and Foxes owned ore mines on the Mississippi; the Foxes were traditionally the tribal smelters. After the spring mining, Fox and Sac men returned to Saukenuk. The job of planting seeds and of performing the three or four hoe cultivations necessary before harvest fell to their women. Crops were hardy on the Rock and the Mississippi and were planted thickly enough to discourage weeds but not too thickly to crowd each other. When the harvest was over, chiefs allotted hunting grounds for the coming winter and bought equipment from the traders Farnham and Davenport, local agents of the American Fur Company. The purchases were traps, powder, guns, knives, axes, and stewpans, all obtained on credit. Farnham and Davenport knew their customers would return

Wabokeshiek. Drawing by Peter Rindisbacher. *Courtesy State Historical Society of Wisconsin, Madison.*

weighted down with furs. When Lewis and Clark had entered the Sac and Fox nation on their way west, they had seen what they estimated was ten thousand dollars' worth of beaver, muskrat, and racoon pelts. Farnham and Davenport had almost no competitors. They invested capital of between thirty and sixty thousand dollars a year in the Sac and Fox tribes on behalf of the Astors. The traders knew, if the Indians did not, that their goods had become indispensable. Sac women preferred metal cookware to aboriginal hot stones; squaws also liked bright calicoes, glass beads, and heavy blankets for chilly nights in their log houses. Farnham and Davenport knew, too, that if the Indians failed to bring them enough pelts or enough money, there were other ways in which debts might be collected. One was by land cession. The Sacs and Foxes wanted rifles and knives for the coming season; a scrap of land yielded here and there for white occupancy in twenty years' time seemed less real than the arrival of *Pe-boan*, Old Man Winter. Messrs. Farnham and Davenport also encouraged the Indians to buy playing cards and mirrors.

The United States Indian agents at Rock Island watched the trade prosper; and they kept an eye on the Sacs and Foxes, because they knew of Black Hawk's pride in his British medal. As American settlements began moving closer to Saukenuk, it was left to American agents to keep the peace between white men and red. Cattle rustling, horse stealing, drinking bouts, and riots were not the monopoly of either people, and all such incidents had to be arbitrated.

During his presidency, Thomas Jefferson had ordered his agents to get influential chiefs as deeply in debt as possible. "We observe," said Jefferson, "that when these debts get beyond what the individuals can pay, they become willing to lop them off by a cession of lands."[3] During Jefferson's period in office, Black Hawk was not the only chief to get into debt. Keokuk, the Watchful Fox, was a Sac peace chief who had drawn heavily on Farnham and Davenport for hunting paraphernalia. The Panther, Outchequaka the Sun Fish, Hashe-quarhiqua the Bear, and Quashquame the Jumping Fish were also in hock. By 1804 they all were getting liberal and enthusiastic advice from their Great Father on exactly how to erase their deficits.

When a solitary Sac brave who had killed three whites near St. Louis was captured, the Great Father announced that the brave could be released only in return for a land cession. The indebted Sac chiefs, wanting their comrade back home again, agreed to surrender tracts both west and east of the Mississippi. As soon as the chiefs the Great Father had filled with whiskey had made their marks on the treaty, the young warrior was released and shot in the head when only a few feet from his friends. The official American version of the murder was that the Indian had been caught in a prison break. Ironically, a pardon from the President had been on the way; Thomas Jefferson did not want to anger the native inhabitants of his newly purchased domains and had decided on a show of mercy.

Flamboyant General James Wilkinson, whose talents included espionage for the Spanish, arrived too late with the pardon. When Wilkinson addressed the combined Sacs and Foxes, he told them piously that the Sac warrior's pardon was late because of "the will of the Great Spirit that he should suffer for spilling the blood of his white brethren without provocation." Wilkinson then handed the useless pardon to the slain Indian's brother. "Receive it," said the general, "and carefully preserve it as a warning against bad deeds." He smoothly explained to the two nations that they had relinquished a large part of their lands and now were expected to move on.[4]

The Sacs and Foxes were incredulous. The chiefs who had made their marks on a paper had done this to "oblige" the Americans since the authorities obviously had wanted this before they would give up their red prisoner. Now the Indians learned that "we have given away a great country for a little thing." The treaty had a curious feature: Article VII stated that the Sacs and Foxes could stay on their native soil and hunt there "as long as the lands which are now ceded to the United States remain your property." In other words, until white men wanted it. The Panther, Outchequaka the Sun Fish, Hashe-quarhiqua the Bear, and Quashquame the Jumping Fish, had delivered up Saukenuk for a motive of compassion and were told the treaty could not be annulled.

During the War of 1812 the Sacs and Foxes sided with the British. Black Hawk, in particular, wanted revenge against the Americans, whom his dialect transformed into Chemokemons. "I have not discovered one good trait in their character," he said. "They make fair promises but never fulfilled them. The British made but few—but we can always rely on their word." Why had the Great Spirit ever sent the Chemokemons "to drive us from our homes and introduce among us poisonous liquors, disease, and death?"

But not even the combined forces of Sacs, Foxes, Potawatomis, Ottawas, and Winnebagoes had been enough to stop the headlong Chemokemon rush to possess a continent. After their victory, the Chemokemons built Fort Armstrong at Rock Island, the better to observe Saukenuk. Soon the Indians noticed something disturbing: the swan-winged Spirit of the Rock Island, ten times the size of a man, no longer appeared in Indian fasting visions. The noise of the Chemokemon army had driven Swan Wings away. The army also regularly denuded the countryside of fruits: wild strawberries, blackberries, gooseberries, plums, apples, and nuts. Some of the soldiers explained the Christian religion to the Sacs and Foxes. "If I have been correctly informed," said Black Hawk, "the whites may do bad all their lives and then if they are sorry for it when about to die, *all is well*! But with us it is different; we must continue throughout our lives to do what we conceive to be good."[5]

Despite Fort Armstrong, life at Saukenuk went on. Each spring Sac and Fox hunters returned to the city bearing pelts from the prairies and woods of their hunting grounds. Then they held their annual medicine feast, which began with the honoring of Sac and Fox dead. Bereaved relatives gave away everything they owned to show the Great Spirit they were humbled by sorrow. The men of the tribes repaired lodges and fenced cornfields, and the women planted the summer's crops.

Afterward, the Sacs and Foxes danced the Crane Dance of courtship and, in the great square at Saukenuk, performed the National Dance. Youngsters swept the square clean; chiefs and old warriors filed in to take their places on grass mats. Drummers and singers followed, and braves and women formed rows on the square's sides. A musician pounded his drum in a rising crescendo as a brave pantomimed the adventures of war: approaching the enemy, striking him, and killing him. Tribal legends were told like the story of how corn came to the Sacs and Foxes. A beautiful woman had descended from the clouds and found two Sac hunters roasting venison. When they offered her some, she thanked them and told them to come back in twelve months to the ground she was sitting on. Then she ascended into heaven. Next year the Indians returned to find corn growing where her right hand had touched the ground, beans where her left hand had rested, and tobacco where she had been seated.

When it was time for the yearly lacrosse game, Sac and Fox players gathered by the hundreds to compete for horses, guns, blankets, and anything else they owned. After the contest there were horse races and hunting dances. But often Black Hawk left the crowd to climb a high limestone bluff over the Mississippi. In his retreat he sat and smoked peacefully, watching the play of the sun's rays on the water and its rippling reflections on treetrunks. He bitterly regretted the defeat of the British in the War of 1812; they had been kind to him as Chemokemons never had. But the Chemokemons were friendly toward Keokuk, the Watchful Fox. Was Keokuk a rival? Black Hawk wondered. He wondered, too, how long his people could maintain Saukenuk and the very fabric of their lives.

When Keokuk accepted an invitation to Washington, Black Hawk knew his fears were justified. Keokuk and his party returned full of awe at what they had seen—teeming cities like red-brick Baltimore and Philadelphia, resonant on Sundays with church bells, the belching steamboat that had taken the Indians to New York, festive Castle Garden and marble-halled museums, and a frenetic circus. An astounded Black

Hawk learned that the Chemokemons also danced a National Dance at a place called West Point, "where the old warriors recount to their young men what they have done, to stimulate them to go and do likewise. . . . I did not think that the whites understood our way of making braves." On his journey Keokuk had realized something else which Black Hawk, who had stayed at home, had not: The nature-worshiping red men had little chance against the technological power of America. And so Keokuk had signed another treaty of cession with his mark, this one for Sac and Fox lands west of the Mississippi and a tract in Illinois which Keokuk believed to be safely north of Saukenuk. The Treaty of 1804 had been reinforced, and the dancers of the American National Dance rejoiced.

Until 1829 these treaties gave the Sacs and Foxes no serious worries. But that year Chemokemons began to settle lands purchased legally from the government. Sac and Fox delegations protested to their agent at Rock Island, Thomas Forsyth, who told them curtly that they had given up their terrain years ago. Now they must leave. Not only did this edict apply to the truculent Black Hawk, but even to friendly Keokuk, who wanted to stay with friends in Illinois to harvest the corn he had planted. Angry Rock Island Chemokemons sent memorials to the Governor of Illinois. The Indians had been ordered to remove, yet they were tearing down white men's fences; they were horse thieves and were even threatening murder. The pioneers of northern Illinois expressed a righteous horror of Black Hawk. William Clark, in St. Louis, shook his graying head. He knew he had no influence with Black Hawk, the war chief "who had always looked to Canada." And on the outskirts of Saukenuk, a newcomer named Joshua Vandruff set himself up in the whiskey business. It was not long before he had plenty of Sac and Fox customers.

Keokuk and his band docilely withdrew to the Iowa River, as did most of the Foxes. Black Hawk stayed on at Saukenuk, declaring coldly that only death could make him leave it. Major-General Edmund Pendleton Gaines of the Western Department of the United States Army, brother of George Gaines, the Choctaw trader in Mississippi, took a particular interest in the war chief; letters flew between Washington and Rock Island, where an irate Black Hawk rounded up a party of braves and visited peddler Joshua Vandruff. Black Hawk ordered Vandruff to close down his liquor store; Vandruff refused. Since he paid twenty-five cents for a gallon of "sure-fire liquid pop," and sold it for twenty dollars, he was getting rich on Indian benders.

Black Hawk and his men strode into Vandruff's shanty and rolled Vandruff's barrels of red-eye outside where they hacked at them with tomahawks. This outrage, fumed the settlers, was a violation of Vandruff's sacred property rights. On the Indian side, young men of what was now known as the "Black Hawk band"—or the "British band"—urged wholesale eviction of the Chemokemons. One of Black Hawk's warriors, Neapope, came from a long line of chieftains himself; his claim to aristocracy was even more ancient than Black Hawk's. He filled Black Hawk daily with heady dreams of conquest and with hatred of the groveling Keokuk. Neapope urged the assassination of Keokuk as well as of the Indian agent Forsyth, the trader Davenport, and even William Clark in St. Louis. When the Chemokemons heard of these plans they panicked. In Washington, President Jackson was outraged. "British band" indeed! His hatred of the British had never waned. He was prepared to back the squatters of Illinois in their fight for farmland.

Black Hawk bent young saplings and blazed high trunks in Illinois and Michigan woodlands as he set out over the Great Sac Trail to Fort Malden. His heart was high with hopes of help from his British Father. But the British wanted no more Indian wars. They would only bring destruction to the Sac and Fox nations, the British said. At Vandalia, the capitol of Illinois, state senators and representatives cursed "Injun varmints" and the governor, John Reynolds, asked for power to call out the state militia. Squatters moved into the Fox mines. Agent Thomas Forsyth wrote indignantly to William Clark: "You must know what will be the consequences when [the Indians] are informed that their mineral land is occupied by the whites, and permitted to remain so. . . . This, in my opinion, is the moment for the Government to show its affection toward the Sac and Fox Indians."[6]

William Clark showed his disaffection toward Forsyth by removing him summarily from office, while Joshua Vandruff went on selling rotgut, and the Illinois militia began to gather. Andrew Jackson sent General Gaines to the Rock Island, where he called on Governor Reynolds and "discovered the linsey-woolsey excellency coiled upon a truss of tarnished straw" in a buckboard wagon which "looked like a Jersey fish cart." General Gaines was not impressed. Nor were the squatters happy. The militia were shooting their hogs, turning army horses loose in fields of corn and oats, and digging up vegetable gardens: "I have lost all my crop for one year . . . the soldiers doing me ten times as much damage as the Indians ever done."

John Reynolds, governor of Illinois, often enjoyed reminiscing about the joys of his frontier childhood. He had gone about in a wolf-pelt hat and had been fond of "stoning darkies." An uncle had put him through college, and he had had a nervous breakdown there. His doctor had ordered him "never to study again, lest it damage his mind," and he never had. He spent his time with cronies who killed Indians for fun; one such fighter he later called "one of the greatest men that was ever raised in Illinois." His campaign resolution had been, "I must stir or git beat. The people is with me." His opponent had been illiterate, and Reynolds had won handily with the financial help of an amorous Creole widow from Cahokia, an old French settlement opposite St. Louis. The actors in the pageant of the Black Hawk War were all gathering: Black Hawk who loved the soil on which he had been born, The Prophet Wabokeshiek who wanted power, Neapope who saw himself as a red messiah, Keokuk who preferred surrender to bloodshed, and a phalanx of white officialdom mindful that Andrew Jackson hated Indians and didn't care when or how they perished.[7]

Chastened by his British Father, Black Hawk consented reluctantly to meet with General Gaines and Governor Reynolds at Fort Armstrong on Rock Island. The U.S. general and the Illinois governor had drawn up an agreement, without orders from Washington or St. Louis, that they had grandly christened "Articles of Agreement and Capitulation." A humiliated Black Hawk listened to the document's terms. Black Hawk and his British Band were to be governed by Keokuk and were not to take any further trips to Fort Malden. He was to leave immediately for Iowa, and no members of his band were to cross to the eastern shore of the Mississippi again without the permission of President Jackson or Governor Reynolds. When the reading was over, Black Hawk slowly came forward, the sound of his heels echoing on the fort's wooden floor. For a moment he glared at his opponents. Then he made a large cross on the paper with such force that his quill broke. A few days later he crossed the Mississippi, and the white squatters of Saukenuk congratulated themselves that Black Hawk had been "chawed up pretty small." But they had reckoned without Black Hawk's braves, without Neapope, and especially without Wabokeshiek, the White Cloud, known to most of the Sacs and Foxes as The Prophet. And The Prophet dreamed of war.

In Iowa, the Indians gathered to parley in Keokuk's modest village. Black Hawk and Wabokeshiek urged Keokuk's Sacs to take up their tomahawks. In his tent, Keokuk, his broad face grave in a cloud of smoke, listened. Then he spoke slowly to Black Hawk. "You urge us to terrible sacrifice. Your mind has grown weak, and you have lent a willing ear to the whisperings of evil counselors." Keokuk's eyes met Wabokeshiek's. "It is a dark and crooked path. The white soldiers are springing up like grass on the prairies. And they have the talking thunder, which carries death a long way off." Wabokeshiek did not answer; his own eyes were amused and contemptuous.

On April 1, 1832, at the Jefferson Barracks in St. Louis, Brevet Brigadier General Henry Atkinson opened a dispatch from the War Department. He was to go to the Rock Island to prevent an Indian war. In the pitch-black dampness of late night on April 12, Atkinson arrived at Fort Armstrong. To announce his coming, the signal guns of the fort boomed over the water in stunning hollow peals. Black Hawk and his band heard them as they crossed the Mississippi in their canoes. The chief's mind was made up. He would march to the Rock River and there his people would plant their corn as they had always done. His band was hungry. As long as the Indians behaved peacefully, said Wabokeshiek, the Chemokemons would not attack them. Beating their hide drums and singing songs of courage, the Sacs and Foxes began their ascent of the Rock. In this situation Andrew Jackson would probably have shot them all on the spot, but General Atkinson's temperament was different. Atkinson did not want to take risks. He called in local citizens and self-appointed Indian experts, who told him it was obvious that Black Hawk was preparing a full-scale offensive. The general did not take the time to send a messenger to the Sacs under a flag of truce to check whether this was correct. Instead, he started organizing an army. The only Chemokemon to talk to the Indians was a farmer named John Spencer, who forded the Rock to encounter Whirling Thunder, one of Black Hawk's sons whom he knew slightly.

"Where are the Indians going?" Spencer asked bluntly.

"Maybe Saukenuk." Whirling Thunder was vague.

Spencer found Whirling Thunder courteous enough, but when he relayed the information to the trader Davenport, Davenport decided the frontier settlements were in danger of extermination. The Sacs and Foxes would pick up Potawatomi and Winnebago recruits from the north and east and descend, bringing a holocaust that would leave fences crackling, fields smoking, and heads scalpless. Besides, Davenport wanted to recoup the forty thousand dollars he had advanced the Sacs and Foxes in equipment and remembered the Jeffersonian doctrine that indebted Indians were willing to cede land. Davenport already owned 2,652,870 acres of the Rock Valley, which he could resell to incoming Americans.

On April 16, Governor Reynolds petitioned General Atkinson for permission to call up the militia. When he got an obliquely worded but positive reply, his minions posted notices:

> Fellow citizens! Your country requires your services. The Indians have assumed a hostile attitude, and have invaded the State in violation of the treaty of last summer. The British band of Sacs, and other hostile Indians, banded by Black Hawk, are in possession of the Rock river country to the great terror of the frontier inhabitants. . . . No citizen ought to remain inactive when his country is invaded. . . . Provisions for the men and food for the horses will be furnished in abundance.[8]

War! It stirred the dreams of Illinois frontiersmen who knew the legend of Andy Jackson. When a messenger from Governor Reynolds arrived in Denton Offutt's general store at New Salem, in Sangamon County, he delivered the governor's notice to a stringbean clerk with a shock of dark hair and deep-set eyes. The notice represented deliverance to the clerk; Offutt's store was about to "wink out" and he needed a livelihood. He also needed a reputation, for he had announced his candidacy for the Illinois legislature and knew that heroes win elections. Abraham Lincoln was enrolled in the state militia at Richland, near New Salem, on April 21. His friends and neighbors served with him and elected him their captain. His fund of shady stories and his ability to laugh at himself made him popular. But he knew less of military tactics than he did of rail splitting. When he first drilled his troops he would forget the prescribed commands. In order to turn his men endwise he would resourcefully yell: "Halt! This company will break ranks for two minutes and form again on the other side of that gate!"

There were other more experienced members in what Illinois, recently self-christened the Sucker State, called its "people's army." Colonel Zachary Taylor of the infantry was a veteran of the War of 1812 whose active memory reminded him that Black Hawk had spent many hours at Canada's Fort Malden during that war. Taylor was fearless and a stickler for discipline. He once drilled a company that included a German who spoke no English. When Taylor ordered him to stand at attention, the recruit did not understand the command. Taylor was unaware of this, and boxed his ears, whereupon the recruit swiftly knocked Taylor to earth with a single blow. Taylor refused to have the recruit lashed. "Let that man alone," he barked. "He will make a good soldier." To the men serving with him, Taylor was "Old Rough and Ready." To a later generation, he would be a general, the hero of an expansionist American war with Mexico, and finally the twelfth President of the United States.

Lieutenant Albert Sidney Johnston was a native of Kentucky and was also destined to become a general; he would fall at Shiloh before the onslaught of Ulysses S. Grant. Lieutenant Jefferson Davis was stationed at Fort Crawford, near Prairie du Chien, Wisconsin; Black Hawk's defiance necessitated his return from a furlough. The Michigan militia boasted "Uncle Billy" Hamilton, Alexander's son, a dark-haired, fair-skinned, and handsome solitary ex-cattle drover who read Voltaire in French. "He has none of your damned foolish pride," one of his recruits explained. "He would just as soon drive any honest man's hogs over the prairie as his own." Because he had been a fifth son and there had been no money for law school tuition, he hated the human race. Major William Whistler, a veteran of thirty years on frontiers, also served in the "people's army." Long before he had helped build Fort Dearborn on the River of Wild Garlic, the Chicago. His brother George Washington Whistler, a West Pointer, was destined to supervise the construction of a railroad from St. Petersburg to Moscow in Russia, and Mrs. George Washington Whistler was destined to be painted by her son, James Abbott McNeill Whistler.

Thus the war of Ma-ka-tai-me-she-kia-kiak versus the United States contained a cross section of America's political and social history, red and white and black. It was also an uproarious debauch during which at one time or another most of the participants were blind drunk. "Heavy fall of rain," an Illinois volunteer confided to his diary. "Could not sleep. Stood in mud ankle-deep till day. . . . Encampment much infested with rattlesnakes. . . . Took some refreshments. Got merry."[9]

"I found the company about sixty strong full of patriotism mixed with whiskey," a lieutenant reported to his superior. An Illinois recruiter in Pike County had no luck relying on oratory or a military band until he formed the spectators into two lines and sent a bucket of free moonshine down each. Soon he had a hundred volunteers. "Damn the fatback! Where's the whiskey?" Governor Reynolds's volunteers yelled lustily to the counter-point of, "Fall in, gentlemen, fall in! Gentlemen, will you *please* come away from that damned barrel?" Captain Lincoln noted with grim humor that there were plenty of bloody struggles in the war, but most of his own were with mosquitoes; his trousers were habitually too short and the bugs feasted on his shins. On his head he wore an old straw hat several sizes too large. He soon became an institutional jester.

But the comedy quickly faded. Major Isaiah Stillman of Canton in Illinois and Major David Bailey of Pekin patrolled the land between the Rock and the Illinois rivers late in April.[10] The militiamen found themselves on a trackless prairie where the wind raced through tough grasses, and the air smelt faintly of fermenting reeds. When Governor Reynolds paid his militia a visit in the company of an elderly Baptist general named Whiteside, the troops of Stillman and Bailey begged to show "how brave Suckers could end the war." The general forbade impulsive sorties, but Reynolds couldn't find it in his heart to refuse constituents. Early in May he composed an exhortation:

> The troops under the command of Major Stillman, including the battalions of said Major Stillman, and Major Bailey will forth-with proceed with four days' rations to the head of Old Man's Creek, where it is supposed the hostile Sac Indians are assembled, for the purpose of taking all cautious measures to coerce said Indians into submission, and report themselves to this department as soon thereafter as practicable.

With the troops drowning in firewater, it was debatable how cautious any measures would be. But Major Stillman, a Massachusetts Yankee turned prairie peddler, was a brigadier general–elect, and wanted to distinguish himself. On May 13, with something less than three hundred men, Stillman and Bailey set out for Black Hawk's camp on the Kishwaukee River, accompanied by a Conestoga wagon full of five days' worth of rations drawn by two yoke of steaming oxen. The covered wagon also contained two barrels of whiskey. In a driving rain the men swapped stories and sang songs to keep their spirits up, and that night in a frigid mist they drank whiskey as "an anti-fogmatic." The next morning most of them overslept on sodden pallets, and in another kind of fog their commanders barked arousing orders.

Before the militia reached the stream called Hickory Creek they struck a swamp with a quicksand floor. The smell of festering prairie muck in their nostrils, the soldiers watched transfixed as the Conestoga wagon sunk to its axles. They raced to save the precious barrels of whiskey and gulped their contents from hastily filled canteens, then fought their way back to solid ground carrying their provisions. They headed toward the tiny town of White Rock, twelve miles from the mouth of the Kishwaukee, where Black Hawk and a hungry band of Sacs had made their camp.

Black Hawk was not happy. The British had deserted him, even though Neapope had told him that British troops would come from Milwaukee to help despite their refusal to help at Fort Malden. But they had not appeared. Wabokeshiek had prophesied that the Winnebagoes and Potawatomis would rejoice to join their Sac brothers. But they had not come either. One band of Potawatomis summarily ordered the Sacs to leave their camp near the Rock. The Sacs were ravenous, but the Potawatomis would give them no food for fear of offending the Chemokemons.

Black Hawk called a council on the Kishwaukee. Waubonsee and Shabbona, representing Potawatomis to the east, were in-

vited to share a ritual feast of dog meat. Waubonsee and Shabbona were veterans of the War of 1812; Shabbona had fought
with Tecumtha himself. But while Waubonsee still hated
Chemokemons, he feared the power of their generals. Atkinson
was the White Beaver. Waubonsee was filled with hate, but as
the warm odor of roasting dog meat rose to his nostrils and he
reflected on the goodness of life, he knew he didn't want to
leave it. Shabbona no longer even hated. He had known too
many Chemokemons he liked. His white neighbors had made a
pet of him and listened to his stories. He trusted the Chemokemons and was sure they would always let the Potawatomis stay in Illinois. Shabbona also knew about the cities of the
East. What chance did Indians have against Chemokemons
when Indians lived in a rough country of wooded bottomland,
trackless prairie, and thickets of hazel brush, while the whites
built machines and lofty monuments and cruised broad rivers
in fire-breathing monsters?[11]

Black Hawk understood that he was alone. If the White
Beaver pursued him, he would have to turn back. He was still
sitting with Waubonsee and Shabbona when a Sac runner
burst into the camp on the Kishwaukee with the news that a
gigantic army was on the way. With gloomy resignation, Black
Hawk improvised a truce flag out of a white piece of cloth; he
ordered the runner to deliver it to the white commander and
summon him for a parley. Sac and white leaders would meet on
the neutral ground of Potawatomi territory. The runner and
two of Black Hawk's young warriors rode out of the Kishwaukee camp toward White Rock; they were followed by five
braves, whom Black Hawk ordered to report back on the re-
ception the Sac visitors were given.

Stillman's men were cooking suppers of game and beans over
open camp fires when they saw the Indians. With a huge
whoop, a party of Chemokemon infantrymen bounded forward
to seize the Sacs and hurl down the white flag. Then they
dragged the two messengers and the runner into camp and
interrogated them in bastard Sac-English, but not before Captain Abner Eads had spotted the five other Indians. He and his

whole company of undrilled and intoxicated soldiers set off in pursuit of the five braves. Meanwhile the three captured Indians were shot. In the confusion the five other Indians escaped. They had to abandon their mounts, but managed to reach the edge of the woods in which Black Hawk had camped and soon were blurting out before his fire that the Chemokemons had violated a flag of truce.

"Some of our people have been killed. Let us avenge them!" Black Hawk gathered forty of his warriors around him. The moon was shining over the brush and smoke of the Indian camp; in his time Black Hawk had crept along many a war trail in white moonlight. He motioned to his men to be still; they ducked behind a cluster of bushes, from which they could fire first on any advancing troops. When he heard the roaring confusion of Stillman's army, he ordered his men to charge. He believed they would all be killed, but they would die for a matter of honor. In a hazel thicket near the Kishwaukee, Black Hawk, braced for death, watched the astonishing spectacle of four hundred Chemokemons coming face to face with forty Sacs. The whites, yelping and belching with fear, retreated. Stillman's army, in fact, retreated so fast, Black Hawk's braves could hardly keep up with them. His head thrown back with laughter now, Black Hawk summoned a group of followers back to camp with him where they took up their pipes and smoked in thanks to the Great Spirit. Twenty-five Sacs were still chasing Isaiah Stillman's comic opera militia.

"It is unaccountable," said Black Hawk. "It is a different spirit from any I have ever seen before among the palefaces. I expected to see them fight as the Americans did against the British in the last war, but they have no such braves among them."

Stillman's troops kept running until they hit the swamp, where they began losing their guns and canteens in the mud. One of them crouched sobbing before a stump thinking it was a Sac: "Oh, Mr. Indian, I surrender!" Others were begging their cohorts, "For God's sake, don't leave me!"

"Damn it, stop and fight!" yelled a captain. But his men were too full of alcohol. Some of them ran all the way to the town of Galena, where they got more whiskey and swore that they hadn't really seen any Injuns themselves. Soon the news of Stillman's Run was racing along the wide western Illinois frontier. The morale of the White Beaver's army deteriorated disastrously: "There were so many jealousies and irritations, there was such a lack of cohesion," wrote a literate one of them, "and certainly lack of organization and discipline, that men naturally disposed to continue their service lost interest by the contagion of dissatisfaction."[12] In other words, they deserted.

Black Hawk was flabbergasted, but he knew he was still outnumbered. The freak exhibition of Chemokemon cowardice that had happened once might not happen again. Neapope and Wabokeshiek had raved of supplies from the British which never had come and which Black Hawk knew had never been promised by the British. The Great Father at Fort Malden had said, "Stay at peace. War will accomplish nothing but your own ruin." Black Hawk estimated the number of his warriors at about five hundred. (Nine of the braves who had pursued the tipsy Suckers had been lost.) The Chemokemons probably had at least four thousand soldiers. It was inevitable that the whites would soon learn about the true state of affairs.

But the question of safety for the Sac women and children was urgent. Black Hawk decided to try to reach the head of the Rock by way of the Kishwaukee, a tortuous trail the Chemokemons would have difficulty following. At the brushy head of the Kishwaukee he was met by a party of Winnebagoes who offered their services. He organized his augmented forces into war parties and each set out in a different direction. Black Hawk's own contingent had not gone far when a Winnebago came shouting with a fresh white scalp at his belt. Four days later another Winnebago returned with the scalp of the agent who had replaced Thomas Forsyth. The Winnebagoes wanted to dance in celebration, but Black Hawk told them to dance in their own camp. "We have lost young braves," he explained.

Black Hawk called his men together in his quarters. "Now is the time, if any of you wish to come into distinction and be honored with the medicine bag. Now is the time to show your courage and avenge the murder of our braves." Several parties left to forage; in a few days they returned with stolen flour and corn and the news that the Chemokemon army had fallen back to Dixon's Ferry, several miles up the Rock from the village of The Prophet. Black Hawk ordered the preparation of a dog feast, and once more he gathered his band: "Here are the medicine bags of our forefather Muk-a-ta-quet, who was the founder of the Sac nation. They were handed down to the great war chief of our nation, Na-na-ma-kee, who has been at war with all the nations of the lakes and all the nations of the plains. These bags have never been disgraced. I expect you all to protect them." Then the Sacs prayed over their ceremonial fires of roasting canine flesh from which the smoke coiled slowly to merge with the fog of a spring night. Afterward, two hundred Sacs prepared to follow their chief and his inviolate talismans.

The trail of pursuit led to a white fort where, as an American boy raised his head above the pickets of the stockade, the Sacs shot him down. Then they raided outbuildings of flour, food, and horses. They did not set fire to the fort, fearing such an act would provoke an attack by the army. By late June the Sacs were more confident. At Kellogg's Grove, north of the Rock on the trail that led to the Pecatonica River, a Sac band attacked a small detachment of Chemokemons. The air was full of yelling and shooting, but this time the Chemokemon leader, Major Dement, stood his ground. "They are acting like *braves*," Black Hawk said with a grim smile. No sooner had he reached this conclusion than Major Dement's men turned tail and ran. But the major and a handful of stalwarts stayed where they were. Black Hawk ordered his warriors to attack. In the melee of smoking powder and shouts that followed, two Sac chiefs were felled. The rest of the braves wanted to pursue the fleeing army, but Black Hawk didn't want to waste further powder, and let Dement escape. "We have run the bear into his hole," he said. "We will there leave him, and return to our camp."

Raids and reprisals continued over northern Illinois and

southern Wisconsin. Prominent among the Chemokemon pursuers was Colonel Henry Dodge, technically of the Michigan
territorial militia. His headquarters was on the Mississippi, on
Wisconsin land that had once belonged to Michigan. He
owned lead mines near Dubuque, and wanted to own more on
land that the Foxes held. While digging for a fortune in Missouri, Dodge had been indicted for treason. He had been on
the point of joining General James Wilkinson's and the accused
traitor Aaron Burr's grandiose dreams of a trans-Mississippi
empire. Dodge's immediate reaction was to thrash singlehandedly nine of the jurors who had denounced him.

Five Dodge uncles had fallen in Indian wars, and the colonel
had been reared on Indian-hating lore. He had not fought
many Indians himself; he was too busy garnering profits from
mid-western subsoil, but to Colonel Dodge, Indians were
merely vermin. Fired with the prospect of acquiring rich Fox
lodes, he had joined forces with the White Beaver.

A band of disgruntled Kickapoos were added to Black
Hawk's forces even while Shabbona, the Potawatomi—who
liked being called Mr. Shabbona—was riding the countryside
like a red and corpulent Paul Revere to warn white settlers
against the Sacs. In the valleys of the Rock, Fox, and Pecatonica rivers, tiny battlefields rang with Chemokemon cries of
"Charge 'em, boys! Damn 'em! Charge 'em!" Always the
whiskey flowed. On the Pecatonica some of Uncle Billy Hamilton's Michiganders surprised several Kickapoos and promptly
hacked their bodies to pieces, leaving their bones to bleach on
the prairie. By this time Black Hawk had reached Lake Koshkonong, in southern Wisconsin, a watershed of the Rock. Here
in the pungent fullness of summer while tall reeds and bright
wildflowers bent in mild winds beside the sparkling water,
Black Hawk's braves began a hot Valley Forge. They had consumed most of their supplies. Black Hawk had selected the
marshes and swamps of the Koshkonong country, the Trembling Lands, because the Chemokemons wouldn't easily be
able to penetrate it. But in such country there was little game
and the fishing was poor. The Indians were miles from any

white settlement. They took to digging roots and eating bark in order to stay alive. For some of the old Sacs it was too much; aged grandfathers and grandmothers died of hunger, their bellies grotesquely swollen. Then Black Hawk's runners brought him the news that the White Beaver's army was on the move again. Black Hawk began removing his women and children west toward the Mississippi. Guided by five Winnebagoes, he descended the Wisconsin River toward Prairie du Chien and safety for wives and daughters, Singing Bird among them. The Sacs were still hungry, and continued to strip trees of bark. Black Hawk underestimated the White Beaver, who not only realized the significance of the torn bark when he and a detachment came upon it but realized that the Sacs were obligingly leaving their own trail behind them. Once again the Chemokemon army began marching.

By July 21 both Sacs and Chemokemons had left behind the marshes of eastern Wisconsin's lake country. To the west were rolling hills, tall hickory groves, and dry thickets of underbrush to be hacked through. The Sacs pushed determinedly on without acknowledging their retreat for what it was. After all, there were the women to think of. When they were safe there would be time enough to follow the great medicine bags into glory alive or dead. But some of the old Indians could not keep up the pace of the march and were left behind. Black Hawk had no alternative; it was his old people or all his band.

When Dr. Addison Philleo, editor of the Galena, Illinois, newspaper ("Let Us Support the Interest of our own Country and She Will Support Ours"), found his first debilitated Sac crouching famished in a thicket of burr oak, he did not hesitate but "popped him on the spot." To remove the Sac's scalp Dr. Philleo used the Indian's own knife. The knife needed sharpening; it was hard and bloody work to tear the scalp from the skull of its still-living owner. The Sac screamed in agony, while Dr. Philleo laughed. "If you don't like being scalped with a dull knife, why don't you keep a better one?" He left the corpse to decompose and proceeded to scalp two more octogenarians who had faltered on the trail west. One of them Philleo bayoneted to death, and kept bayoneting for some time after death had occurred. Philleo sent the scalps on to Galena by messenger with a statement for his paper: "It is not common for *editors* to fight with weapons more potent than the *quill*! And when they do, it is the duty of the press to note them." He would send along a treatise on Indian killing later, he promised. The frontier settlers of Illinois and Wisconsin, weary of alarums and excursions, delightedly made Dr. Philleo their hero. The Scalping Editor! It had a fine ring to it—finer than that of Stillman's Run.[13]

North and west of the lake and swamp district, the Wisconsin River was full of sandbars. On its surrounding heights were ravines for Indians to hide in. The north bank of the Wisconsin had once been the site of a holy Sac village, abandoned long before Black Hawk's time but commemorated in tribal lore. Here Black Hawk determined to bring his people to a river island; in such a sacred place, the Great Spirit would help him. But the crossing was hardly under way when Neapope, who had been scouting the rear, came riding out of the ravines with the tidings that the White Beaver's army was closing the gap. Black Hawk swiftly decided to take fifty of his braves to a nearby hilltop and fight, leaving the rest to guard the women and children as they crossed the Wisconsin. The old warrior was riding his best horse; the eager attention of his braves pleased him as he exhorted them on. But as he began to form his warriors into ranks, he was attacked by a charge of the White Beaver's front runners. The Chemokemons shot twice into the belly of his horse. Shouting to his warriors to return to the river, he plunged swiftly into a ravine where he rested the horse and tried to stop the flow of its blood from what proved to be flesh wounds. Twilight was falling; the blue darkness would mean deliverance. The White Beaver's troops would not fight at night. By now, he hoped, the women and children were safe. Black Hawk's horse gained its second wind and carried him back to the Wisconsin, while the Chemokemons were bracing in camp for a Sac attack that never came. In the Battle of Wisconsin Heights, the Sacs had lost six men, and their women and children had been saved.

Lieutenant Jefferson Davis, learning of Black Hawk's retreat while Davis was still at Prairie du Chien, pronounced Black Hawk's "the most brilliant exhibition of military tactics I have ever heard of." The Indian women had floated their papooses across the Wisconsin on improvised rafts of bark. That savages could be not only clever but tender came as a surprise to Davis and his men, reared as they had been on the frontier doctrine that "they ain't no game like Injuns. Nossir, no game like Injuns!"

Now the midwestern stage was set for the final scene of Black Hawk's bitter drama. Some of his band, desperate with hunger and fatigue, left him to make their way to the Mississippi on their own. If they could save themselves, he said, let them. But it was not long before a party of soldiers from Prairie du Chien found them. Some the Chemokemons shot, some they threw into the Wisconsin to drown, some they captured, and some they let escape to die of starvation in forests full of scarlet maples and sumacs. For Wisconsin and for the Sacs, autumn was coming. Black Hawk and a small troop of braves began toiling away from the Wisconsin over rugged hills Wisconsin settlers called the Ocooch Mountains toward the Mississippi. The Ocooches were not really mountains, but they were cluttered with pine and brush and made hungry Indians breathless. The Sac leaders decided to head for the mouth of the Bad Axe River, on the Mississippi thirty miles north of Prairie du Chien. There Winnebagoes might give them canoes. Meanwhile, on the Wisconsin, the White Beaver arrived and soon enmeshed himself in red tape: orders, supplies, and directions for the rafts his men were to build. "Doctor Mister General," Lieutenant Albert Sidney Johnston contemptuously called Atkinson in the privacy of his journal. The Illinois soldiers scanned the darkly tufted hills around them and did not like what they saw. They were used to ague-ridden swamps and flat prairies. In Illinois only the river bluffs were high, and they were easily traversed. "Here, hit's the Alps," one of the militia said about the hostile ranges ahead. When the White Beaver searched for signs of Indians he reminded a subordinate of "a baffled city dog looking for a ground squirrel." Compared to the Ocooches, the Trembling Lands began to assume the remembered lineaments of old friends. But the Ocooches were familiar country to Black Hawk now. Most of his people were by this time on foot. Old men and babies were dying by the wayside; there was scarcely time to say prayers over their shrunken bodies. The chief knew that there was no hope of adding glory to the legend of his medicine bags. If he could save his people, he would. It would be enough. When the Sacs finally reached the Mississippi most of them looked like skeletons, "clothed in rags scarcely sufficient to hide their nakedness." Some of the children had starved so long they were "past restoring." As he stood on shore of the great river with the wreckage of his tribe and his dreams, Black Hawk saw an approaching steamboat. Ironically, though he did not know it, it was called the *Warrior*.

"Go," he said to one of the women. "Run and get me the white flag. I will go on board that boat." Turning to his men, he ordered them to, "Put down your guns." As the *Warrior* steamed closer and closer against a backdrop of rugged pale bluffs and dark shoreline conifers, its boilers smoking on the open deck, Black Hawk recognized the red faces of stiffly roached Winnebagoes at the rail. He also saw that the *Warrior* flew the flag of Captain Joseph Throckmorton, an old Mississippi river hand, whom he knew slightly from trading expeditions. Now, to this American, he would surrender. But as he prepared to let himself be captured, and one of his braves paddled a ramshackle canoe out to the steamer with an improvised white flag on a pole, he heard the Winnebagoes shout: "Black Hawk! Run and hide! The whites are going to shoot!"

A volley of fire exploded from the steamer. There was a six-pound cannon in the bow, which "mowed a swath clean" through the Sacs before they had time to reach protecting trees. A roar of musketry followed. The whites on the *Warrior* kept up their barrage until twilight; they managed to kill twenty-three Sacs despite sheltering trunks; only one white was wounded. After this round of sport, the *Warrior* moved on. Once more Black Hawk attempted to lead his people across the Mississippi. A party of scouts from the White Beaver's army emerged from the woods; Black Hawk signaled to them, and several of his braves tried to surrender. The scouts were not interested. They began shooting Indians and the few Indian horses that had not been eaten by starving Sacs. On the tail of the White Beaver's scouts arrived the great man himself, his troops fresh from trampling down the hastily improvised tomb of a Sac chief who had perished on the retreat to the Mississippi and Bad Axe. The Chemokemon army opened fire on the squaws. In the midst of the smoke and screaming, some of the Sac women leaped into the Mississippi with their children on their backs. The soldiers shot most of them. A few escaped the bullets to drown instead. One of the soldiers seized a woman with her child on her back and yelled, "See me kill that damn squaw!" He broke the child's arm and shot the mother in the back. A horrified lieutenant rescued the child only to commit it to the hands of Dr. Addison Philleo, who amputated the arm while the child chewed on a moldy biscuit as an anaesthetic. By this time the troops were "fast getting rid of these demons in human shape"—that is, a band of famine-wracked and feeble Indians trying to surrender themselves. The squaws and children left alive were retching in terror as the volunteers ran through the band shouting and lifting skin from scalps. On the river, strapped to a piece of cottonwood bark, floated a Sac papoose whose mother had drowned. A volunteer shot the baby in the heart while reciting a proverb, "Kill the nits and you'll have no lice." A group of squaws who had attempted to bury themselves in riverbank mud were bayoneted and then scalped; the soldiers found their writhing on the ground funny. Some of the Suckers carried young Sac girls into the woods where they raped them because the militia, an army of crazed Puritans on the loose, had begun "to feel the symptoms of romance." Many of the squaws were naked, their rags ripped from their backs. Rapes were permissible because Indians were not "capable of making any improvement in the natural mind," observed one of the White Beaver's privates. The Battle of Bad Axe turned into a sexual orgy sanctioned by "the Ruler of the Universe, He who takes vengeance on the guilty." The murders and violations went on until Colonel Zachary Taylor arrived and found the proceedings letting up for want of victims. The militia then turned its attention to what it thought was a group of Sacs crouching together on a river island. Zachary Taylor ordered his soldiers to open fire. Not a shot came from the island, but the attackers charged it. What they found on the island was a blanket hanging on a tree, its length pocked with bullet holes. Beside it a fatally wounded Sac baby lay screaming beside its dead mother.

The *Warrior* appeared again in the blistering afternoon, its six-pounder belching shot. It sailed up and down the river islands methodically picking off any Sacs the keen-eyed captain saw. Some of the Indians were ground up in the paddlewheel; crushed arms and legs shot into the air before they fell into the Mississippi. Captain Throckmorton complained of being blinded by the brightness of the grass in the heat of the sun: "I tell you what, Sam," he told a friend, "there is no fun in fighting Injuns." John Fonda, a gunner, saw a group of Suckers scalping fresh victims and then knifing long gashes down the red backs and ripping off the skin. Indian skin made good razor straps, and Fonda made a mental note to ask for one.[14]

After a whiskey break, the militia began shooting again. One Sucker shot a Menominee serving with the White Beaver's army as interpreter; this didn't matter, he reasoned, redskins were redskins. "White man, white man, have mercy on me!" cried wizened Sac patriarchs bleeding to death. Black Hawk's band which had numbered a thousand was down to forty. The White Beaver and Captain Throckmorton had been aided by a Menominee and even some Dakotas who had joined up to shoot their traditional enemies, the Sacs. Fewer than ten whites had fallen. When the White Beaver's men came on an abandoned Sac camp they looted it of beads, bracelets, stew-pans, hides sodden with Indian blood, and anything else they found. A Sac corpse unexpectedly yielded up five hundred dollars in cash. Some of the Sacs were taken on board the *Warrior* as prisoners. One of them amused the Chemokemons by trying to kill himself by beating a rock on his head. When the Battle of Bad Axe was over, the White Beaver congratu-lated his men on their gallant victory. The *Warrior* turned downstream toward Prairie du Chien, its passengers shooting at Sac corpses in the river along the way just to keep their hand in. At Prairie du Chien the *Warrior* was met by a party of friendly Winnebago squaws who offered to sell the still-wet scalps of "corpses four days in the water." It would have been a perfect carnival but for one unfortunate fact: Black Hawk and Wabokeshiek were nowhere to be found. Corpse by corpse the Chemokemons searched for them and did not find them. A few days later, Black Hawk turned up anticlimactically to surrender himself, and this time the Chemokemons let him. He and The Prophet had ridden to the Ottawas and Winnebagoes to get help, which the Ottawas and Winnebagoes had denied them, though some Winnebago squaws proud of their handwork had presented Black Hawk with a white buckskin suit.

With a stoicism reminiscent of ancient Greece, Black Hawk delivered up his cherished medicine bags to a white Winne-bago agent in the barracks of Fort Crawford at Prairie du Chien. "Take them. They are the soul of the Sac nation. They are my life, dearer than life. Give them to the American chief. They have never been dishonored in any battle." Before Black Hawk was handed over to Lieutenant Jefferson Davis for a trip downriver where a ball and chain awaited him at the Jefferson barracks in St. Louis, he made his farewell through an inter-preter to White Beaver Atkinson and Old Rough and Ready Taylor:

> An Indian who is as bad as a white man could not live in our nation; he would be put to death and eaten by the wolves. The white men are bad schoolmasters. They carry false looks and

deal in false actions; they smile in the face of the Indian to cheat him, they shake him by the hand to gain his confidence, to make him drunk, to deceive him, to ruin his wife. We told them to let us alone and keep away from us, but they followed on and beset our paths, and they coiled themselves around us like the snake. They poisoned us by the touch. We are not safe. We live in danger. We are becoming like them. . . .

Black Hawk is a true Indian, and disdains to cry like a woman. He feels for his wife, his children and his friends. But he does not care for himself. He cares for his nation, and the Indians. They will suffer. He laments their fate. The white men . . . poison the heart; it is not pure with them. Black Hawk has done nothing of which an Indian need feel ashamed. He has fought the battles of his country against the white man, who came year after year to cheat his people and take away their lands. You know the cause of our making war. It is known to all white men. They ought to be ashamed of it. The white men despise the Indians and drive them from their homes. But the Indians are not deceitful. . . . Black Hawk is satisfied. He will go to the world of spirits contented. He has done his duty.

Farewell, my nation. . . . He can do no more, he is near his end. His sun is setting, and will rise no more. Farewell to Black Hawk!

But Black Hawk and The Prophet did not remain in prison long. Keokuk successfully petitioned the White Beaver and Jacksa Chula Harjo for clemency. As a reward for loyalty, he was made the Sacs' puppet ruler. In retrospect, the Chemokemons were embarrassed by some of the features of the Battle of Bad Axe. Rapes were not good for public relations. The Chemokemons took Black Hawk east, first to a guardless custody at Fortress Monroe in Virginia and then on a tour to show him Chemokemon wonders such as fireworks and New York City traffic jams. The curious who came to stare at the Sacs on exhibit were disappointed because Black Hawk was "infirm of body." Washington Irving found him and The Prophet, Neapope, and Whirling Thunder "a forlorn crew, emaciated and dejected—the redoubtable chieftain himself a meager old man

Black Hawk. Portrait by Thomas Sully. *Courtesy State Historical Society of Wisconsin, Madison.*

upwards of seventy." Secretary of War Lewis Cass, more than ever the Big Belly, was ready to be "liberal and generous." He gave the captives their freedom and thirty barrels of pork, twelve bushels of salt, and thirty-five beef cattle, all war surplus. Even at this gesture there were Sucker frontiersmen who demurred: "Give 'em lead, not corn."

Eventually Black Hawk came face to face with Andrew Jackson. The Great Father himself was a meager old man, Black Hawk noted with surprise. "Why did you go to war?" the President asked, his eyes burning in a face as white as his hair. Black Hawk met his gaze but did not answer. Perhaps, temporized interpreters, the Sac chief hadn't understood the question. Probably he was becoming senile.

Once more at Rock Island, this time to dictate his memoirs to a half-breed linguist named Antoine Leclair, Black Hawk confirmed his resignation to exile. "Rock River was a beautiful country. I loved my towns, my cornfields, and the home of my people. I fought for it." He turned to American agents standing nearby. "It is now yours. Keep it as we did. It will produce good crops." Then, less genially, he murmured: "Nesso Chemokemon." Leclair knew it meant "the American kills."

When they were alone again Black Hawk told him, "I am done. A few more moons and I must follow my fathers to the shades." Chippionnock, the City of the Dead, was more durable than Saukenuk had been. It could be moved. The road to Chippionnock now led fifty miles west of the Mississippi where prairie winds raked the buffalo grass and gray geese were flying south.

"Black Hawk," Leclair asked, "why didn't you answer the President?"

Black Hawk's mouth formed the suggestion of a smile. "Why I went to war?" He paused. "I was too stunned. He ought, you see, to have known this before."

A Gathering of Vultures

"Murders have already taken place, both by the reds and the whites. We have caused the red men to be brought to justice; the whites go unpunished. We are weak and our words and oaths go for naught; justice we don't expect, nor can we get. We may expect murders to be more frequent. . . . White officers among us take our property from us for debts that were never contracted. . . . We are made subject to laws we have no means of comprehending; we never know when we are doing right."
—TUCKABATCHEE HARJO, CREEK

"Oh, to wander where
The grey moss clings
And south wind sings
Forever low, enchantingly,
Of islands girdled by the sea!
. . . I'll journey back
Some day . . ."
—ALEXANDER LAWRENCE
POSEY, CREEK

In Florida, Georgia, and Alabama, the Creeks who had once marched on Jacksa Chula Harjo under the leadership of Red Eagle were dying, some of them from age and others from hunger. The news of Black Hawk's defeat spread among them like a bleak contagion: the northern Sacs and Foxes had had their own Horseshoe Bend, and Black Hawk, like Red Eagle of the Creeks, had failed against the material might of white America. In northern Florida the Creek Chief Neamathla had been gulled out of seven hills once rich with Creek corn; Neamathla had been made to yield up Tallahassee, the territory of Florida's capital. Tallahassee meant "abandoned fields," but the Creeks had not wanted to abandon them. Yet they had had to because the tribe had no more strength to fight. Everywhere their lands were steadily shrinking, and their forests were being emptied of game by trigger-happy Scotch-Irish who wandered down from the Appalachians to a country of perpetual summer. *Itchee*, the deer, and *coacoochee*, the wildcat, were disappearing before the onslaught.

On March 24, 1832, the Great Father wined and dined several Creek chiefs at Brown's Hotel in Washington and then presented them with a treaty.[1] On the surface, it did not demand Creek removal. It gave each head of a family 320 acres of land. The Indian was now his own guardian, the smiling authorities explained. The Creeks had not really ceded their land at all. Of course, if the heads of families wanted to sell their lands to whites and then go west where Indians were happier, who could prevent them? And while a Creek might enter into a land sale, he was a nonperson before the law and could not testify in an Alabama court. If his lack of reading and writing expertise rendered him liable to fraud, he had no recourse. Now, in the West, where everything was wonderful for Indians, there would be no such problems. If the Creeks stayed on, courting famine in Alabama, they had only themselves to blame.

Yet the appalling condition of the Creek tribe prompted letters to southern newspapers from white readers. One that appeared in the *Milledgeville Recorder* in Georgia said:

To see a whole people destitute of food—the incessant cry of the emaciated creatures being *bread! bread!*—is beyond description distressing. The existence of many of the Indians is prolonged by eating roots and the bark of trees. The berries of the Indian or China tree of last year's growth were eaten by them as long as they lasted—nothing that can afford nourishment is rejected however offensive it may be.[2]

The Indians were even stripping prickly smilax vines of their leaves. A correspondent of the *Arkansas Advocate* reported from Columbus, Georgia: "They beg their food from door to door. . . . It is really painful to me to see the wretched creatures wandering about the streets haggard and naked." The governor of Georgia notified Andrew Jackson that the Creek Nation was "absolutely starving or subsisting on the bark of trees." The famine didn't bother most of the citizens of Mobile County, however. They wrote to their representative in the legislature that they wanted a law passed "to authorize Justices of the Peace etc. to seize any meat found in the possession of Indians who followed hunting for a livelihood." The editor of the *Mobile Commercial Register* denounced the proposal. United States Government officials remained aloof and cited the sacredness of states' rights: what Alabama did was its own business. Fortunately for Creek hunters, the law was not passed.

Although Alabama didn't seize the meat a few fortunate Indians happened to possess, it did smile on whites "including horsethieves and other criminals" who longed to make a fresh start on lands occupied by the Creeks. Eneah Micco, chief of the Lower Towns, watched these renegades carve their initials on his trees. "We expect to be driven from our homes," he told the Creeks' agent, John Crowell. In Alabama the swath of 5,200,000 acres still in Creek hands was at stake. When government agents approached Creek headmen to negotiate, the headmen answered that the Creek Nation had made too many treaties with the United States, "at all times in the belief that the one making is to be the last . . . from the great assurance given us for protection, and the frequent solicitations of our

Great Father, we have frequently given up large tracts of our country. . . . We are now called on for the remnant of our land and for us to remove beyond the Mississippi." Aging Creeks begged not only for bread but for their children's right to stay in their homeland so that, one day, the ashes of parents and children could be mingled in the southern dust. "It would appear," said a subagent, "that the Creek tribe of Indians are not yet prepared to emigrate. They are, however, sufficiently apprised that it is next to impossible, situated as they are, for them to remain a much greater length of time in their present state, and that however fondly they may for a little while continue to linger about the now alienated abode of their forefathers they must at last tear themselves from it."[3]

The process of alienation was being speeded by whiskey traders. "We are surrounded by the whites with their fields and fences, our lives are in jeopardy, we are daily threatened," complained Creek chiefs to Big Belly Cass. "We are prevented from building new houses or clearing new fields." Moreover, they had heard disturbing things about the West where Big Belly wanted them to go. It was not healthy there; many Creeks who had already emigrated had died.

These early migrants had been followers of Chief William McIntosh, who in defiance of the laws of the Creek Nation had obligingly ceded all Creek land in Georgia and several chunks of it in Alabama years before. McIntosh's mark, obtained for a consideration, was hardly dry on United States parchment when he was murdered by a group of tribesmen who had decided execution was the only fitting fate for such a traitor. The tribesmen refused to consider that McIntosh had had honest scruples about the welfare of his people in the East. Terrified, three thousand of McIntosh's band had fled westward.[4] Now, in 1833, those who survived were sending messages to their onetime rivals in the South that refuge in the West was a snare and a delusion. Hang on, they told the Creeks of the South. But it was increasingly difficult to hang on when white settlers attached Creek farms in payment of nonexistent Creek debts the Indians could not go to court to deny. Some of the more

enterprising merchants married Indian women in order to qual-
ify for benefits granted the Creeks by past treaties. Agent John
Crowell's successor deplored these practices, but how, he asked
plaintively, could he "offend the people of Alabama" by "giving
advice to the distracted Indians"?

Creeks had not starved in the past. Many had built flourishing farms which white newcomers now marched in to occupy.
Again, Alabama law offered the Indian no redress. Though
Alabama was steadily grinding her natives under an iron heel
of oppression, there were citizens who still found these natives
terrifying. The Creeks, said a white Alabaman in a letter to
Andrew Jackson, would "take a malignant delight" in destroying white improvements. They were sunk in the "depth of ignorance and barbarism, and their innate and inexorable hate of
the white man." Should Alabama retreat?

> The first token of a general removal of our citizens would be to
> [the Indians] the joyful signal for their savage triumph, and the
> furious burst and ebullition of their unrestrained and demonaic
> feelings. . . . The conflagration of burning dwellings and en-
> closures, the indiscriminate erasure of every trace and sign of
> civilization and refinement, would but add rich zest to their
> barbarian thirst for destruction. . . . No accurate calculation can
> be made of the deep and lasting evil that must of necessity
> ensue.[5]

The old soldier in the White House agreed; the Creeks had to
go soon.

Jackson sent that veteran of removal Colonel John J. Abert
to read his ultimatum to the Creeks. Abert had assisted the
Senecas and Shawnees whether "drunk, sick or sober" out of
Ohio. When the colonel journeyed down to Alabama he found
the Creeks "a people who appear never to think of tomorrow."
Every spot of good hunting ground, "every storm, every triv-
ial accident" would occasion days of delay, he reflected gloom-
ily. "And join to these listless, idle, lounging habits, their love
of drink . . . what can be expected? . . . They need the unceas-

ing exertions of a vigilant and intelligent agent to urge them forward." Who was, naturally, Colonel John J. Abert, this time a counselor rather than a conductor.[6]

He soon found himself in the midst of a scandal. A local squatter named Hardiman Owen, who enjoyed beating Indians weak from hunger, had also taken to killing their hogs and horses.[7] The federal marshal ordered him to stop. He promised he would and even invited the marshal home with him. The marshal consented, adding that he would be delayed briefly. Owen went back to his dwelling, mined it with gunpowder, and when the marshal came to the front door Owen disappeared out the back one. The marshal was about to go in when an Indian urgently motioned him to retreat. When the two were safely in the yard, the house blew up. The vengeful marshal sent out a body of soldiers who killed Owen in the woods when he fired at them. The governor of Alabama subsequently declared that states' rights had been infringed upon and demanded the marshal's removal. Lewis Cass flatly refused. But he and the governor worked out a compromise: the state's charges against the federal officers who had killed Owen would be dropped if white settlers could stay on their Creek claims.

By the summer of 1834, 630 Creeks had signed up for emigration. Colonel Abert had described the western landscape in glowing terms and was disappointed by the small number of the first party. Most were destitute, though Sampson Grayson owned thirty-four slaves and the Widow Stidham twenty-three. The Indians stayed in Alabama long enough to garner what paltry harvests they could and in December bade their kinsmen good-bye. Their conductor, Captain John Page, was "experienced." He had evicted other Indians. First they dragged themselves—the old, the infants, the embittered men and women—with their rickety wagons and skinny horses, to the state capital at Tuscaloosa. The chief of the little band, Eufaula Harjo, visited the House of Representatives to say good-bye. Then they all moved on, out of their country of singing, sunlit pines into the fury of prairie blizzards where "the roads were impassable for all carriages of every description.

Except those employed in the emigration," said one of the soldiers traveling with the Indians, "I do not recollect of meeting
anyone but two or three horse carts, and they gave it up when
they struck the road that we came over, there was nothing but
prying out wagons from morning till night." The superannuated and the sick began to die—as was usual in a "voluntary"
emigration—but Eufaula Harjo and his people were lucky
enough to find abandoned farms near the Verdigris River.
These had been started by McIntosh Creeks who had then
decided they wanted to locate on the banks of the Arkansas,
near present-day Tulsa.[8] Eufaula Harjo and his band came
upon dwellings with roofs and fireplaces, but when they saw
the pale dust clouds whirling in the air on windy days, they
decided that such clouds were the ghosts of past Indians who
had drowned in the Verdigris. It was not unnatural for a people who had long walked the road with death to see it even in
the haven at the road's end.

In Alabama the vultures were gathering. Many Creek heads
of families had recently died of sickness or hunger, and under
Alabama law a white man could administer these estates and
pay himself handsomely with the title to half the land involved.
Flocks of whites began descending to pick Creek bones clean.
They soon developed an efficient modus operandi. The Indians
about to remove were told to deliver the deeds to their property in Alabama and then be paid compensation. Since most of
the tribe knew little English, white "advisers" helped them out
—out, often, of all they owned. Horrified certifying agents
complained to Colonel Abert, but the colonel told them that if
their accusations got to Washington it would "create confusion." The agents persisted until they were informed by Secretary Cass that the frauds "were clearly beyond your reach as
they are beyond the reach of this office." By the spring of 1835
the white advisers and purchasers of Creek real estate were
carrying on as if it were "rather an honor than a dishonor to
defraud the Indian out of his land." The whites organized
themselves into bands; some of them robbed Indians as they
came away from land offices after having received compensa-

tion money. Land purchasers gathered Indians together by the hundreds and fed them; the hungry and innocent Indians made marks on deeds of conveyance whose contents were unknown to them. In the town of Cusseta some whites held a banquet where one of them rose to give a toast: "Here's to the man that can steal the most land tomorrow without being caught at it!" His hearers rocked with laughter.

The white people of Chambers County were revolted; Chambers County was full of former Virginians with traditions of family honor, who were sensitive to the landgrabbers' lack of morals. Defrauding, they wrote Andrew Jackson, was "a regular business not more distinguished from its baseness and corruption than for the boldness with which it was carried into execution." The President was startled; these were white voters. When other white citizens wrote to him in angry protest, he issued an order for Alabama agents to stop certifying land sales and to begin investigating those already approved. But the action was belated. When Eneah Micco and his band wanted to travel to Columbus, Georgia, to complain to the President's representative, General Sanford, agents of the land thieves told them it was a ruse to get them into Georgia where they would be "arrested for old debts" and then packed off to Arkansas. When Eneah Micco asked Sanford to come to the Alabama bank of the Chattahoochee, Sanford refused.

Eneah Micco still would not consider removal, though the chief of the Upper Towns, Opothleyaholo, decided it might not be so bad in Texas. Texas was a part of Mexico, and most Mexicans had Indian origins. But the Creeks of the Lower Towns had kin in Oklahoma, and the letters they were getting told them conditions on the Verdigris and the Arkansas weren't always good. They were told of blizzards in winter and churning floods in spring. Eneah Micco and Opothleyaholo called a grand council of the nation at Setelechee, Alabama, where a government agent informed the Creeks he was giving them their last annuity payment before emigration. When the white speculators present heard this they were dismayed. Most of them had piles of Indian I.O.U.'s, real or manufactured. "There was two jack-legged lawyers on the ground," reported a witness, "threatening to sue if the Indians did not pay the claim they held." The situation was complicated by the appearance of two Cherokees who announced that the Creeks owed the Cherokees five thousand dollars over past land transactions between the tribes. With them was a letter from Big Belly Cass telling the Creeks to pay. One Creek, full of whiskey, lost hope and stabbed another Creek on the council ground in the belief that his victim had Cherokee sympathies. The slain man's relatives seized the drunk and tied him to a tree where they stabbed him to death. Neither the whites present nor the principal Creek chiefs affected to notice the incident. They had troubles of their own.

In September 1835 Opothleyaholo told his people in the Upper Towns of northern Alabama that they were to leave their homes in a month: "We shall at that time take our last black drink in this nation, rub up our tradition plates, and commence our march." Opothleyaholo had "prepared his marching physic."[9] But Opothleyaholo did not march. Alabama lawyers informed him that if he left, the whites would attach his black slaves and those of every other solvent Indian. Poorer Creeks had sold their possessions and now had no tools and no crops to harvest. Bands of the desperate began migrating into Cherokee country in north Georgia. The Cherokees were appalled when the number had swelled to 2,500 starving Creeks. The Cherokees had their own troubles trying to stave off removal. In one incident, the Georgia militia advanced shooting at fifty Creeks clustered along the banks of the Coosa River; several Indians were killed and others were wounded. Then the militia turned its attention to some elderly Indians picking cotton on the Chattahoochee. When the Indians began fighting with the militiamen, the militia general ordered a thousand of his followers to cross the Chattahoochee into Alabama where there were other Creeks to kill. If Georgia was going to make war, she preferred doing it in Alabama. Most of the Creeks were now frantic to get out of Alabama. They couldn't leave, because the frauds against them were being

Opothleyaholo. Portrait by C.B. King. *Courtesy Smithsonian Institution, Washington, D.C.*

"investigated"—very slowly. One resourceful merchant arrested Opothleyaholo himself for a debt that disgusted Creek agents said the Indian was "as much responsible for as he is for the national debt of Great Britain."

Early in May 1836 Creek warriors of the Lower Towns attacked white settlers and burned their property. Once more orange flames shot into the fragrant Alabama dark. From Tuskegee to the shores of the Chattahoochee the Indians left a trail of arson. They burned houses and barns and corncribs and the toll bridge across the Chattahoochee. On May 16 they seized a stagecoach near Tuskegee, set it afire, and tomahawked the passengers. Subsequent investigations revealed that they had been urged on by a white who had wanted to distract attention from investigations of the land frauds.

> The War with the Creeks is all a humbug [editorialized the *Montgomery Advertiser*]. It is a base and diabolical scheme, devised by interested men, to keep an ignorant race of people from maintaining their just rights, and to deprive them of the small remaining pittance placed under their control, through the munificence of the government. We do trust, for the credit of those concerned, that these blood suckers may be ferreted out and their shameful misrepresentations exposed. . . . There is nothing like a system of hostility mediated by the Creeks; their Chiefs are utterly averse to a war fare with the whites; that it is foreign to their intentions to resist . . . that they are now preparing to remove, and will, in a short time, commence emigrating west of the Mississippi.[10]

Creeks had done the scalping, but at the orders of white counselors.

Secretary Cass, inundated with the depressing evidence of white crime, decided the time had come to stop investigating the frauds altogether. The way to get rid of the Creeks was by force. He ordered General Thomas S. Jesup to put an army into the field in Alabama to "subdue and remove" the red men. Ahead of General Jesup were wandering bands of white vigilantes who began driving Creeks into the swamps and burning their towns. The number of whites fighting the Creeks sky-rocketed to eleven thousand. One of them descended on Opothleyaholo, whose recent release from jail had convinced him to obey his oppressors. Opothleyaholo was persuaded by the man's eloquence to offer eighteen hundred of his warriors to General Jesup for putting down Creek rebels. Against Jesup and Opothleyaholo stood a resolute Eneah Micco; but Eneah Micco only had a thousand men. Outnumbered by nearly thirteen to one, Eneah Micco had to face the truth: the struggle to stay in his homeland was doomed. Still, he fought on while he could. His brother, Chief Neamathla of Hitchiti Town on the Hutchechubbee River, fought too; he stole enough stage horses and mules from the whites to lead his band into Florida where the Seminoles were waging battles of their own against the United States Army. Neamathla was very familiar with north Florida; he had been the one to deliver Tallahassee with its verdant fields and dreaming liveoaks over to the whites. Now he was in his eighties, six feet tall and straight, and clear-eyed still. He had told the territorial governor of Florida years before: "This country belongs to the red man, and if I had the number of warriors at my command that this nation once had I would not leave a white man on my lands. I would exterminate the whole." But physical magnificence and the fire of his resentment could not save Neamathla against informers in his own band. For white money, they fell upon him and brought him to General Jesup. Less than a week later his band surrendered. Most of them were dizzy with hunger. Men, women, and children rode in through the stockaded gates of Fort Mitchell, on the upper Chattahoochee. The Indians were scrawnier than their ponies. Babies bawled for nourishment half-dead mothers could not give them. White onlookers marveled at the variety in the Creek faces. Some were white, blond, and blue-eyed, descendants of generations of intermarriage with Scottish traders. Some, like Neamathla himself, were an intriguing mixture, pale-faced and dark-eyed. Others were ruddy full-bloods. With them they brought a handful of black slaves. By the first of July, Jesup's troops, aided by Opothleyaholo's, had captured most of the holdouts. Chief Jim Henry escaped for a short time but was hunted down in the Alabama pinewoods. The war was over. Now it was the blacksmiths' turn to take charge.[11]

Handcuffs had to be made for sixteen hundred prisoners. Sparks flew in sweltering forges, and the environs of Fort Mitchell echoed with the chinking of hammers. The smell was of human sweat and molten metal. When the Creeks had finally been shackled together they were prodded toward Tuskegee, where they were joined by other captured militants. It was all quite tedious for Captain Page. "It is very slow moving them in irons," he complained, "and Montgomery is the nearest point we could take water." The Indians, half-fainting in their manacles, had to march on dry-mouthed. Neamathla was also manacled. "He is 84 years old," said a spectator,

> but his eyes indicate intelligence and fire and his countenance would give the impression that he was a brave and distinguished man. . . . They were all handcuffed and chained together; and in this way they marched to Montgomery, on the Alabama, 90 miles. Old Neamathla marched all the way, handcuffed and chained like the others, and I was informed by Captain Page, the agent for moving the Indians, that he never uttered a complaint.[12]

Captain Page was not without mercy. He let the women and children of the Creeks ride ponies; those who could not walk traveled in covered wagons. In Montgomery an ancient warrior, too weak to totter, nevertheless found the strength to draw a knife and cut his own throat. "To see a remnant of a once-mighty people fettered and chained together forced to depart from the land of their fathers into a country unknown to them is . . . sufficient to move the stoutest heart," said the *Montgomery Advertiser*.[13] But most Alabamans, along with most Americans, believed that the whites were the master race. Civilized men had every right to concentrate their inferiors in camps, just as they had the right to seize new territory from conquered nations until America's spacious skies stretched from sea to shining sea. Meanwhile old Chief Menawa looked toward the far horizon with moist eyes. When darkness fell on the Creek camp he lay restlessly awake. He told his captors in the morning, "Last night I saw the sun set for the last time, and its light shine upon the tree tops, and the land, and the water, that I am never to look upon again." He was bound for a setting sun from which, according to the poem that was the Creeks' migration legend, his people had originally come.

One of the steamboats that carried the Creeks to Mobile was aptly named the *Lewis Cass*. It was so crowded, a correspondent of the *New York Observer* noted, that it would be a miracle if there were no outbreak of disease. The miracle held as far as the Great Water Road, Ukhina, where the Indians tried to wash down the thirst from their salt rations with muddy Mississippi River water and green fruit. Then they began dying. Most of the victims were either very old or very young but a few were "in the prime of life," as the surgeon accompanying them put it.

The Creeks who were already in the West grew increasingly nervous: the Creeks on the way had murdered Chief William McIntosh. The western Creeks held a council and petitioned the governor of Arkansas for ten companies of militia. Catastrophe was averted, however, when a meeting between the western Chief Roley McIntosh and the eastern Neamathla was arranged on the Mississippi. Roley McIntosh stared. Was this the man he had feared, this old exile whose possessions were knotted in the single bundle he carried? Everywhere McIntosh saw handcuffs. In that moment he knew his kinsman Chief William had been right in wanting to remove peaceably before he was dragged.

Late in the autumn a Creek party reached the tough river city of Memphis, where the newspaper commented that "our town and vicinity have been filled and no little annoyed for the past two weeks by the emigrating Creek Indians: 8,000 of them have crossed the Mississippi and 5,000 more are around us. In about two weeks the whole tribe, about 15,000, will be west of

William McIntosh. Portrait by Washington Allston. *Courtesy
Alabama Department of Archives and History, Montgomery.*

the Mississippi. . . . Most of the chiefs opposed taking water, fearing sickness, but their greatest dread was being thrown overboard when dead." The chiefs had their reasons: cholera came to the Creeks along with dysentery, and death was a daily passenger on the ships bound for the swamps of Arkansas. No prayers to the Master of Breath could help them. A marine corps lieutenant saw "a disposition in the Indians among both old and young to remain behind." A party of Upper Town Creeks being marched overland annoyed their conductors by straggling listlessly, with "utter disregard for the future. . . . I threatened them with confinement in irons," the lieutenant said of Opothleyaholo's bands, "and this had a salutary effect."[14] The reason they were yet unconfined was Opothleyaholo's past service with General Jesup; now they were reminded that chains were standard operating procedure. In this particular party the lame, sick, and blind were "left behind dependent on the charity of the country."

It was now winter. Snows swirled and winds keened, and the blind froze to death. The Indians' shoes wore out, and their conductors pushed them barefooted, the men covered only with thin smocklike cotton shirts and flimsy trousers. Bare feet bled while Arctic storms roared out of the north. Some of the Indians went mad. Others, visited in camp by aggressive moonshine salesmen, got drunk. When one company reached Fort Gibson, with its American flag flying high over snow and ice in a halfhearted winter sun, they dictated a letter to their interpreter intended for their wardens:

You have been with us many moons. . . . You have heard the cries of our women and children . . . our road has been a long one . . . and on it we have left the bones of our men, women and children. When we left our homes the great General Jesup told us that we could get to our country as we wanted to. We wanted to gather our crops, and we wanted to go in peace and friendship. Did we? No! We were drove off like wolves . . . lost our crops . . . and our people's feet were bleeding. . . . Tell General Jackson if the white man will let us we will live in peace and friendship. . . . We are men. . . . We have women and children, and why should we come like wild horses?[15]

But General Jackson was nearing the end of his second term. Presently, he would be turning the reins of government over to his hand-picked successor. Martin Van Buren, of Kinderhook, New York, was already known affectionately to Americans as Old Kinderhook; this was soon to be shortened to O.K. Jacksa Chula Harjo's beloved Hermitage plantation near Nashville was waiting to welcome him, and there, almost a decade later, he would die in his bed, content that he had done his work with America's native race. He had torn down one people and raised up another, his own. He had made his nation strong. To the south, in Alabama, mixed-bloods who had escaped imprisonment told their children never to acknowledge their Creek ancestry. No longer might they safely hail their fellows with the traditional Creek greeting: *"Ixchay!"* And thus they, too, were contributors to the Creek nation's near genocide.

But in Oklahoma and Alabama and Georgia and Florida, the chiefs, the lawmakers, the medicine men, and the poets of the Creeks lived on. And privately beside their hearths, if not publicly in the dusty streets of American villages, they remembered.[16]

8

The Road to Clear Boggy

"With the exception of the Creek nation I expect there never has been such frauds imposed on any people as the Chickasaws, but we look with confidence to the President of the United States. . . ."

—James Colbert, Chickasaw

"Have a care over our red children. The white men are cheating them out of their lands and they do not know what to get for it. . . . Let us be robbed of our rights and we will be the poorest miserable people on earth. . . ."

—Ton-e-pia, Chickasaw

"The noise of passing feet
On the prairie—
Is it men or gods
Who come out of the silence?"
—Plains Chippewa Song

THE CHOCTAWS CALLED THE PEOPLE WHO LIVED NORTH OF THEM *chikkih asach*. To Hernando de Soto, their land was the Province of Chicaza. The Chickasaws lived in upper Mississippi and Alabama and southern Tennessee; the Choctaw name for them meant "they left as a tribe not a very great while ago." The Chickasaws, like the Choctaws, had come from the Place Where the Sun Falls into the Water; they too had followed the Choctaw leader with his sacred pole. With the Choctaws they had crossed the Misha Sipokni, the wide river which was the "father of all its kind." They spoke the Muskogee dialect of the Choctaws. The eighteenth-century American naturalist William Bartram found their speech "very agreeable to the ear, courteous, gentle and musical. . . . The women in particular so fine and musical as to represent the singing of birds: and when heard and not seen one might imagine it to be the prattling of young children. The men's speech is . . . more strong and sonorous, but not harsh and in no instance guttural. . . ."

But among the Choctaws there had arisen a dangerous faction: tall, strong-boned young braves who esteemed the arts of war above all other arts. The path to war was dearer to them than the path to plenty. They spent most of their time looking for glory; to their women fell the burden of agriculture. "Such a male bestirs himself only when the devil is at his arse," reported one explorer. "They are the readiest and quickest of all people in going to shed blood." Abruptly the Choctaws severed these braves, called Chickasaws, into a separate nation. After that the Chickasaws exalted war more than ever; into a thousand battles their men carried clan medicine bundles cherished as sacraments because they contained the clans' mystic powers. For days before expeditions the Chickasaws fasted, purging themselves with a decoction of button snakeroot. When the fast was over, the warriors listened to a distinguished old chief who recounted his own battles and triumphs and then told them to imitate his valor. "Go in confidence; be great in manly courage and strong in heart; be watchful and keen in sight; be fleet of foot, attentive in ear and unfailing in endurance. Be cunning as the fox, sleepless as the wolf, and agile as the panther." To propitiate war deities the braves danced in huge circles from which Mississippi and Alabama nights were pierced with high music that shouted of fame and death. Chickasaws danced to the rhythms of terrapin shell knee rattles, flutes and log drums, and hard hand rattles.

Other southeastern tribes feared the Chickasaws for their ruthless dedication. The Chickasaws descended without mercy on the towns of the Creeks and the Choctaws and Cherokees; when they returned to their women it was with scalps and booty and victory hymns. At every new moon, the men and women of the Chickasaw nation gathered on slopes rich with carpets of oak leaves and pine needles to hail the white light of evening while they sang and stretched out their hands. The Chickasaws were a handsome and terrible people, and over them ruled Ababinili, the composite force made up of the Four Beloved Things Above: the Sun, Clouds, Clear Sky, and He That Lives in the Clear Sky. This force, symbolized in each town by a sacred fire, had made men out of the dust of earth. Over the fire a priest stood watch, and from time to time he told his people to take burning embers from it into their lodges to keep their medicine strong. The ghosts of murdered warriors haunted every lodge until they were avenged; without the power of the sacred fire, vengeance was impossible. Inside the lodges infant Chickasaw boys were placed on panther skins in the hope that the skins would impart to them the gifts of strength, cunning, a strong sense of smell, and a quick spring from firm ankles. Infant girls were placed on the skins of fawns or buffalo calves to make them "shy and timorous." It was the men who mattered.

The austerity of the Chickasaws was reinforced early in the eighteenth century when their ranks were augmented by the last of the Natchez Indians, whom the French of Louisiana were bent on exterminating. Too many Natchez braves had killed too many French soldiers in devastating raids. The Natchez brought rigid social distinctions to their Chickasaw hosts. The Natchez chief had been called the Great Sun; next below him were the Suns, then Nobles, then Honored People, and finally the ignominious Stinkards. The Chickasaws did not adopt these names, any more than they adopted the extreme sun-centered worship of the Natchez, but they did make their chief or High Minko equivalent to a king.

Hernando de Soto, the French explorer Robert Cavelier de la Salle, the French noblemen Bienville and Iberville in Louisiana, all had a horror of the High Minko and his exhortations to his braves to seek glory in the taking of Spanish and French lives. When the British began dealing with the Chickasaws, they were careful to send them traders and luxuries on which they became dependent. The British also used Chickasaw warriors in their conflicts with France and Spain. Because they knew how to harness the power of Chickasaw Spartanism, the Chickasaws gave them undying loyalty. French officials noted sourly that "the love they have for their country, their recent successes, and the great number of hostile nations with which they are surrounded will make them remain in their country until the last."[1] Before 1800, no white statesman in his right mind would have thought of trying to evict the Chickasaws by force and marching them across a continent. But what the martial French and Spanish failed to achieve in destroying the tribe, the British accomplished without intending to. Their traders slept with Chickasaw women, and a new class of mixed-bloods skilled at dealing with complex European civilization came into the tribe. James Logan Colbert, a Scotsman, successively married three Chickasaw women and kept 150 slaves to do his bidding. McIntoshes and Stuarts begot babies. The full-blood High Minkos Payamataha and Piomingo tried, in vain, to stop the trend. Chickasaw warriors discovered whiskey; traders dethroned Minko Houma and meddled in tribal politics.

The mixed-bloods stayed with Britain during the American Revolution. During his presidency Thomas Jefferson vigorously applied to the Chickasaws his doctrine of inducing Indians to owe their souls to the company store—in this case the entrepreneur who represented the government-sponsored factory which turned out goods that were the means of red enslavement. The factory system seldom failed. "Establish among the Chickasaws," Jefferson ordered an agent, "a factory for furnishing them all the necessaries and comforts they may wish, spirituous liquors excepted, encouraging them and especially their leading men to run into debt for these beyond their individual means of paying: and whenever in that situation, they will always cede lands to rid themselves of debt."[2] And who could prevent white merchants from opening grog shops? It was a free country, wasn't it?

The American Long Knives also took to giving Chickasaws big parties where they dispensed beef and rum and brandy and flour. It took the Chickasaws a long time to realize that every time they got fed by Mr. Jefferson, Mr. Madison, Mr. Adams, Mr. Monroe, or Mr. Jackson very peculiar things happened to Chickasaw land. It shrank. Jackson managed to pare their holdings down to a corner of northeastern Mississippi and half a million acres in northwestern Alabama. White settlers flocked around them, and soon the once-mighty Chickasaws were fighting for the tribe's life. Missionaries wiped out their gods with Baptist, Methodist, and Presbyterian handouts. The clerics' wrath was swift when an intellectual Indian agent tried to introduce his literate charges to "Paine's *Age of Reason*, Voltaire, Hume, Gibbon, and other infidel writers." Would a drunken and decimated people take to the flowing periods of *The Decline and Fall of the Roman Empire*? Apparently the men of God thought so. The decline and fall of the Chickasaw empire was proceeding at a headlong pace. Red-skinned Colberts, Loves, McIntoshes, McGilverys, and Johnstons acquired slaves even while they took note of the capitulation on treaty paper of the Choctaws to Andrew Jackson in 1830 and the Creeks and Seminoles in 1832. Then Jackson sent Chickasaw Colberts and Loves west with the Choctaws to "explore." When they returned the Chickasaw leaders told him:

> Our opinion is different to that of a portion of our White Brethren who accompanied us on the expedition. . . . They have

represented it was a Country suited to the convenience of Indians and one in which all the wants and necessaries of life could be secured with facility. But of this we are disposed to doubt. . . . The country in which we now live is one that pleases us. . . . We cannot consent to remove to a country destitute of a single corresponding feature of the one in which we at present reside.[3]

The Chickasaws were now a civilized tribe with a vengeance. Levi Colbert, the High Minko, was a man whose Colbert inheritance had supplied him with money and his Chickasaw inheritance with stubbornness. He had no intention of going west. But in 1834 Levi Colbert died, and on January 17, 1837, at Doak's Stand in the Choctaw Nation, dispirited Chickasaw leaders promised to pay the Choctaws half a million dollars in federal money for a portion of the Choctaws' trans-Mississippi sanctuary. Already American surveyors were flourishing on Chickasaw land in the East, and the government busied itself giving out "allottments" to Chickasaw heads of families for "temporary homesteads." By the Treaty of Pontotoc, Mississippi, the Chickasaws delivered up six million acres. When they were paid, the Chickasaws began to live it up. Gold and silver jewelry appeared on the necks and arms of Chickasaw women who no longer tended the fields their slaves now did. "The Chickasaws are a rich people," said one observer. "Allow me to say that it is highly important to the future welfare of the Chickasaws that they be removed west of the Mississippi as soon as possible." American flimflam men stepped up their land buying, and the price of liquor rose to new heights. Mississippi begrudged the Chickasaws every day they occupied their fertile lands. To Mississippians Indian Claims were "an obstruction." In the same way that the Creek obstruction had been razed by fraud in Georgia and Alabama, Chickasaw obstruction was razed in the Magnolia State. But government agents were having a hard time rounding up the Chickasaws since "Indians are slow in their movements and take time. . . .

An average of 50 to 100 are drunk each day."[4] Nobody in Mississippi counted white drunks.

When the first emigrating party of 450 was finally ready to start, it had miles of slaves in its train, whole herds of horses and sleek cattle, wagons piled with personal baggage like clothes, household furniture, and farm tools like plows and harrows and milking buckets. The Chickasaws were a far cry from the Spartan warriors they had been. The men in their gay, multicolored turbans and sashes and the Chickasaw women whose curls were elaborate enough to require the attentions of a hairdresser wanted an easy life.

By July 4, 1837—the significance of the date probably did not escape them—the emigrants had reached the banks of the Mississippi. In vain their civilian conductor, John M. Millard, had begged them to sell their horses. The Chickasaws said flatly they would as soon part with their lives as with their mounts. Nor would they part with any baggage. The journey to the Mississippi had been accomplished baggage, horses, and all. But on July 8, after a heavy summer rain, the Chickasaws' troubles began. Their wagons sank to their axles on what passed for roads in Arkansas. Logs were drenched, and no fires could be made for cooking or drying out clothing. Dysentery and ague appeared in the camps. Women and children wept; why had they had to leave their homes? A party Millard termed "recalcitrants" declared they would travel no farther along the soggy Arkansas River Valley. They struck out, over Millard's protests, for Fort Towson on the Red River, near the Choctaw district. Millard himself herded the sick and old and infants on board a steamer bound for Fort Coffee on the Arkansas. The Indians were wailing and moaning now; they did not want to die by drowning. But Millard was unmoved. When he caught up with the group bound for Fort Towson, he found them using every pretext they could for delay. The Chickasaw men had to spend every morning rounding up the horses that had broken loose in the night, they told Millard. Millard knew that the men were deer hunting. And why did they need deer when the United States Army had sold the Indians salt pork, wheat flour, and salt to the tune of eight and a half cents per head?

The dysentery continued, bringing deaths, which meant funerals, and Millard fumed as the Chickasaws insisted on conducting burial rites. It was not "orderly and efficient." The Indians were being "refractory and ungovernable." At one point Millard asked an aide, Lieutenant Gouverneur Morris, to read an ultimatum to the tribe. Two companies of United States Infantry were going to be requested from Fort Towson; it would take a mere six days for them to come. Then the Chickasaw nation would be marched at bayonet point. Their rations would be reduced. Remembering tales of manacled Creeks, the Indian leaders conferred and finally agreed to make as much haste as they could. The dead would have to be prayed for in absentia.[5]

In Mississippi and Alabama, federal officials were forcing the Chickasaws who remained into camps—four thousand red prisoners, each one to be charged for his expenses in being transported west. Late in October the long train reached Memphis, where they heard a rumor of a boiler explosion on a steamer. One thousand Chickasaws refused after that to go by water into Arkansas. Their leader, civilian A.M.M. Upshaw of Pulaski, Tennessee, fumed at them and threatened to withdraw their victuals. Coolly Konope, spokesman for his group, answered that he doubted if that would be possible since the Chickasaws were footing the bill for their own food. Upshaw was forced to give in, and the thousand Chickasaws began marching across Arkansas. One autumn day they were observed by a traveler who wrote:

> Much money could not compensate for the loss of what I have seen. . . . With all, there was mixed sympathy for the exiles—for they go unwillingly—whether it be for their good or not. . . . I do not think that I have ever been a witness of so remarkable a scene as was formed by this immense column of moving Indians . . . with the train of Govt. waggons, the multi-

tude of horses; it is said three to each Indian and besides at least six dogs and cats to an Indian.

For the Indians had refused to abandon their pets. If the Chickasaws went into banishment, so would their dogs and cats.

> It was a striking scene at night. Multitudes of fires kindled, showed to advantage the whole face of the country covered with the white tents and white covered waggons, with all the interstices . . . filled with a dense mass of animal life . . . the picturesque looking Indian negroes, with dresses belonging to no country but partaking of all, and these changing and mingling with the hundreds of horses hobbled and turned out to feed and the troops of dogs chasing around in search of food . . . then you would hear the whoops of Indians calling their family party together to receive their rations, from another quarter a wild song from the negroes preparing the corn, with the strange chorus that the rest would join in . . . this would set a thousand hounds baying and curs yelping—and then the fires would catch tall dead trees and rushing to the tops throw a strong glare over all this moving scene, deepening the savage traits of the men and softening the features of the women.[6]

Ishtehopa, the High Minko, remained aloof in his tent. His kingship was meaningless now and he knew it.

The newspapers of Mississippi and Alabama were rejoicing. The *Chickasaw Union* of Pontotoc reported: "The presence of an Indian village, but recently the great place of rendezvous for the redmen, is now almost a curiosity. The demoralizing, brutalizing effects of contact between the white man and the savage, which but a few weeks since were most painfully conspicuous in our streets, are now removed, and our town presents the same quiet, orderly appearance which is always to be seen in the inland villages of the Atlantic states." Mississippi admired "law and order," then as now, and hoped the Chickasaws were going the way of the Mohegans.

But not all the Chickasaws had left. There were widows and

orphans who had been assigned white guardians by Alabama and Mississippi courts. The women and children were trapped and being systematically cheated out of everything they had. "Their husbands have died and some persons have been appointed to administer their estates," complained a Chickasaw leader. "It appears their object is to keep the Indians there until all of their property is destroyed."[7] Eventually several Chickasaw chiefs had to return from the Indian Territory to the South to extricate helpless tribal brothers and sisters from the tangle of white corruption. Meanwhile, the long columns toiled through Arkansas toward Oklahoma. The journey was "tranquil," read reports sent to Washington that ignored the deaths and funerals.

In Oklahoma, there were fresh troubles for the arriving Indians. The Chickasaw Nation had been assigned the fertile Washita Valley and there were other nations who resented this —marauding Shawnees and Kickapoos, and the even fiercer Kiowas and Comanches to the immediate west. Chickasaw chiefs declared the western part of the new Chickasaw tract uninhabitable, and did what any prudent pioneer would do— they asked the United States Government to protect them from the Indians. When the Great Father responded, after repeated delays, the stockades of Fort Washita rose to house bluecoated cavalry prepared, if necessary, to ride to the rescue of the Chickasaws, the smart peals of army bugles in their vanguard.

On the Clear Boggy River, 120 miles south of Fort Coffee on the Arkansas, the most daring of the Chickasaw nation established camp. The land was isolated but good; cane was abundant and at intervals in the canebrakes were swards of lush green grass. Oaks grew thickly in the bottoms. There were Chickasaws willing to risk their lives for a stake in Clear Boggy, but they did not dare to begin building houses because of the enemies around them. They clustered instead in a huge camp, their tents lining the Clear Boggy's shore. Soon after dysentery and fever had come to the camps, a smallpox epidemic broke out. The festering rash tormented more than five hundred people and finally killed most of them. Those who survived suffered next from malnutrition; the army was slow in delivering rations, and local contractors fell into the habit of holding back food until the price went up.[8]

When Mr. Upshaw, the conductor, visited the smallpox-stricken camp he found several Indians dying of starvation because of "gross mismanagement on the part of the contractors. . . . There has been corn within forty miles of this place for four or five days without [the army's] moving a peg to relieve the suffering of the people."

> The rations . . . issued . . . consisted of damaged pork, damaged flour, and damaged corn, with salt . . . not regularly issued. The provision was so bad that, on distributing it to the party, many would not receive it. The corn appeared to have been shelled in the green state, and had been mildewed. A part of the corn was weevil-eaten. Some of the corn was so much injured that horses would not eat it. The flour was sour, but occasionally a barrel of it could be used. . . . The pork was so bad that Dr. Walker told me that if the emigrants continued to use it it would kill them all off. It gave those who ate it a diarrhea . . . many of our poor people died in consequence of it.[9]

Enterprising contractors were charging the Chickasaws four dollars a bushel for this corn, and their weights were on the average one-third short. On one occasion, a traveler reported, "where [there was] an issue of corn from some waggons that were on their way to Boggy, the teams had been fed overnight. . . . Indian women came about and picked up the kernels of corn that had been left upon the ground where the horses had been fed."[10]

Inquiries were raised in Congress. The Senate and the House of Representatives listened in their stately chambers to the witnesses of contractor fraud. The War Department ostentatiously sent an "investigator," Major Ethan Allen Hitchcock, west. When he reached Oklahoma, he investigated so thoroughly that the War Department heartily wished he had never been dispatched to the Indians' territory. The army didn't want a real investigation; it wanted a paper one that would look good in the national press. Major Hitchcock doggedly itemized the outrages he found:

> Worn-out oxen and bulls were forced upon the half-starving people at an exorbitant price. Various white men are pointed out as having made $10,000 to $20,000 each in a year in this plunder of the helpless. Bribery, perjury, and forgery were the chief agents in these infamous transactions . . . spoiled rations to the value of $200,000 have been sold to the Chickasaws.

The tribe had been charged with an additional $700,000 for food they never received. The transportation charges, Hitchcock found, were "shockingly high." The air, he said, "is full of scandals. It will certainly appear very extraordinary that the portion of the Indians over whom the Govt. assumed a guardianship should be precisely those fixed upon for a sacrifice."

The major was not happy with the fate of his report. The War Department routed it to the solicitor of the Treasury for an opinion. The solicitor told the War Department not to publish the report under any circumstances. "Indians can be made to say anything," concluded the War Department. When Hitchcock got to Washington he found that the War Department was "avoiding conversation with me." Eventually the report was lost, according to the War Department, in their files.

It took the Chickasaws half a century to obtain a settlement from the government for the food Washington had not sent, the baggage it had lost, and the rotten provisions which had killed so many. Meanwhile, near the Clear Boggy, there was Fort Washita. At sunrise, when red mornings began to the accompanying chorus of mockingbirds and the leaves of oaks shook down droplets of dew in the wind to the sharp-scented grass below, the Chickasaws heard the blowing of reveille, and many of them knew that the army's horses would that day be fed better than any of themselves. Chickasaw princesses no longer needed hairdressers; they needed life.

The Life and Death of Ma-to-toh-pe

Ke - ka   mi - o - wa - te - dos   ki - ka - de - tû

"Raven,
I am going to die.
Fly away."

    —MANDAN *Song to the Raven*

Four Bears, Chief of the Mandans who lived in the rough butte country of the upper Missouri River on the edge of Dakota Sioux Territory, could not reckon his age in years. But by 1837, as Ma-to-toh-pe, he was an acknowledged leader of his nation, who called themselves the Pheasant People. Their lands were broad expanses of plateau and roughly carved rocks which at intervals thrust themselves upward through dry air toward a clear sky the color of precious turquoise. The Missouri River Valley itself was bordered by rich grasses, sunflowers, wild lilies, serviceberry bushes laden with fruit in cool summers, and, everywhere, the bluish-leaved buffalo bushes, which crept into the defiles of the bluffs and as autumn approached were so heavy with red berries that their stems bent down to the ground. Until the Moon of Ripe Corn the berries were bitter; then, when the frosts came down from the north, they turned sweet and juicy. Always, too, in the land of the Pheasant People, were the buffalo, huge and shaggy, moving and bellowing from grassland to grassland and creek to creek, north in the Moon of Flowers, south in the Moon of the Freezing Rivers. The prairie was scarred by their saucer-shaped wallows where they rolled in the earth to free themselves of insects. On the upper Missouri the odor of buffalo dung mingled in the heat with that of wild roses. Russet wrens trilled in the cottonwoods. Winter brought still and ethereal days and cold and empty nights when the Pheasant People heard the lonely howling of timber wolves. But in their sunken earth lodges before glowing embers they were warm, wrapped in the skins of buffalo they had killed on the hunt.

Three days' march to the southwest towered their holy Medicine Rock. In spring the Mandans made a pilgrimage to it, for it told them everything that would happen to them in the following year. It stood on the level top of a high hill, and the trail which led to it was full of the footprints of men and dogs and the marks of travois and horses hooves. The Mandans brought gifts of pipes and cloth. Whenever they went to war against the Arikaras, Crows, Assiniboins, Dakota Sioux, or Blackfeet, they wept there unashamedly in prayer. Then they

Ma-to-toh-pe, "Four Bears." From the drawing by George Catlin.
Courtesy Smithsonian Institution, Washington, D.C.

retired to smoke and sleep. The next morning the priests of the Pheasant People interpreted the markings on the rock's face; these they copied on animal skins and took back to the Mandan villages to show their wisest old men. After this, the braves were ready to set forth. The Mandans were a peaceable people who tilled corn fields and relished the succulent roots of wild Indian turnips that the women gathered. But the Sioux and the Crows and Arikaras were not peaceable, nor were the Minetarees. The Mandans had need of a sacred stone.

Four Bears knew whence his people had come.[1] The Lord of Life had created First Man, who made earth out of mud brought up from the sea's bottom by Pa-to-he, the duck. For many years First Man walked on earth acquainting himself with its animals, until he came face to face with the Lord of Life. They quarrelled over which of them was to be called Father. They decided to sit down, agreeing that the first one to get up should be the Son. The Lord of Life endured patiently. When First Man could bear the cramped sitting no longer, he sprang to his feet; then he acknowledged the Lord of Life as Father, and the two wandered about to remake the earth. From beneath the earth they called up the buffalo and commanded him to fetch grass and wood. When the gods came to the Missouri the Lord of Life took the south side, and First Man the north. The Lord of Life created hills and coulees; First Man made forests. Each carved himself a pipe of ash wood inlaid with stone. Then they placed the two together and the Lord of Life said, "This will be the center, the heart of the world." They met a buffalo who gave them tobacco. They made men, limiting human life to a hundred years so that the country would not be overpopulated. A newly created woman dragged a buffalo to the river's shore, where she ate some of its flesh and as a consequence became pregnant. Her son was the first Mandan chief. He made himself a Sacred Canoe which understood him when he spoke to it. The Mandans had many great chiefs in those days. It was Good Fur Robe who appointed the Corn Priest. Corn Priest purified the corn each year, for it was by corn and buffalo that the Mandans lived. No power in the universe could ever move them from the Missouri. This they knew as surely as they knew heat, cold, hunger, satiation, and love.

All these sacred things, and many others, were part of the existence of Four Bears, who had been named by a tribal elder in honor of a medicine bundle with bear power. His father, Good Boy, a chief before him, had instructed him. Good Boy had also taught him to fast when he was still a small boy. It was through fasting that braves acquired wisdom and could understand Xopini, the power of sacred objects. When Four Bears was older he went to trap eagles with his elders. Someone had to suffer in order that the birds would come to rest on the camouflaged pits the Mandans had dug in the ground. Four Bears himself drove into the ground the stake that would be the instrument of his torture. A long lariat was tied to the stake. Men of his father's clan cut holes in the skin of his chest and put two sticks, each two inches long, through the holes. Then the men left. Four Bears crawled to the edge of the hill where the stake was. There he hung by the rope and the sticks which were tearing at his bloody flesh. When he was rescued he was unconscious, and his wounds were so swollen the sticks could not at first be removed. But he had done well; he had passed the first test of courage.

The religion and the code of honor of the Pheasant People were austere, but there were also much joy and laughter in the life of Four Bears. Always death and life were two facets of the same universe, never far apart. Tears and revels mingled. The grassy roofs of half-submerged Mandan earth lodges were gay with warriors in their robes and eagle feathers, reliving their exploits beneath poles on which the scalps of their enemies were impaled. Just beyond the village stood the scaffolds of the dead, where family patriarchs and matriarchs lay wrapped in consecrated skins until the wood of the scaffolds rotted and the corpses fell to the ground. Then the skulls of the dead were gathered into little circles, where grieving family members might go and talk to the kin they had lost. Sometimes the living cheered up in the act and regaled the dead with jokes.

Once there had been many Mandan villages. Now there were two large ones, Nupta and Mitutak, for the Sioux, the Assiniboins (the Big Bellies), the Arikaras, and other tribes had cut down many of the Pheasant People. The other tribes were more warlike and did not practice the growing of crops. The Mandans were more closely linked with the Hidatsas who did. Often Mandans and Hidatsas danced buffalo dances together. Sometimes rainmakers from both tribes sang to Sun and Moon and the People Above. Drought meant famine. It meant there would be no light hearts in Indian villages, no horse races, ball games, or warm story-telling sessions in smoky lodges, where women ground corn and nursed babies while men spoke of gods and heroes.

The Pheasant People were not killers, but most of the tribes around them were. Because of the Pheasant People's hostile neighbors, war had always been important in Four Bears's life. When he grew to manhood, he began taking many scalps. He painted victory marks on his arms, and with every expedition acquired new rights to wear eagle feathers and narrative insignias on his hide cloak. Many times he fasted and was vouchsafed visions. But the glories of battle were not as central to the life of Four Bears or any Mandan brave as the Okeepa ceremony. To be an Okeepa Maker once brought honor; to be one twice brought enduring fame. Four Bears was ambitious. Even as he prepared for his first ceremony, he knew he would want the ultimate distinction of a second.

The Okeepa time was summer, when the buffalo were near the Mandan settlements and needed to be called ever closer through communion with the spirits of earth and sky. Through a silent village strode the warrior impersonating First Man to announce that Four Bears was to make this year's Okeepa. Women and children were ordered to stay inside their lodges until called. The beginning of the Okeepa was for men. The ceremonial lodge was fragrant with bundles of dried sage as the ritual started. The Sacred Canoe which had belonged to Good Fur Robe rested in its sanctuary. Some of the musicians began beating with long sticks instruments made of buffalo-skin sacks which had been painted to look like Kip-san-de, the tortoise, while others shook gourd rattles. Four Bears, as Okeepa Maker, stood by in silence while the buffalo dancers began their invocations. Carrying their scalp poles, their tall bodies decked with bonnets of eagle feathers and kilts of eagle quills and ermine, they wound out of the lodge into the village's main square and back to the Sacred Canoe. Before them danced Night, his black-coated body dotted with stars, and Day, whose skin was streaked with wavy rain-lines. Snake and Beaver and Grizzly Bear, Rattlesnake and Vulture, all gyrated before the symbol of their universe. Four Bears was waiting, though, for O-ke-hee-de, the Owl, the Evil Spirit whose appearance meant his courage would be put to its ultimate test. The bull dance continued for four days; at last came the dance of O-ke-hee-de, who moved trancelike out of the lodge into the village where summoned women began screaming; then the women chased O-ke-hee-de into the hills with sticks, until one of them managed to grasp his magic wand and break his might. After that the buffalo dance stopped. It was time then for dressing and painting and preparing for the ritual torture, the Pcho-hong, which could make or break the earthly destiny not only of the Okeepa Maker but of any Mandan brave.

The torturers carried large knives that had been hacked with other knives to roughen them. Without great pain, the Okeepa lost its force. Four Bears felt the knife tear into flesh already scarred by his eagle-hunt; then his flesh was rent by splints set above and below his elbow, in his chest and back, and on each leg above and below the knee. In his pain Four Bears sat with a rigid smile as custom dictated. He heard the ripping of his own skin and felt the wash of his own blood and continued to sit serenely. When the medicine men had finished attaching cords to all the splints in his body, they gave him his medicine bag to hold in his left hand. Dried buffalo skulls were attached to his legs so that their weight would prevent him from writhing loose. Then the medicine men handed him his shield. He smiled still as he was raised four feet above the earth to hang by his wounds. But then the rigorous part of the ordeal began, and not even Four Bears could smile.

He felt the scarlet-streaked man below, his hands and feet painted black, begin turning him, slowly, slowly. Four Bears screamed out to the Mandans' gods, but he was not begging to be set free. He cried for strength to endure, and his cries were in the orderly language of ritual. Finally, he fainted. He did not hear the spectators shout the prescribed "Dead, dead!" For twenty minutes he hung lifelessly, his blood spilling with that of his Okeepa subordinates on the floor of the lodge. When he was cut down, no one offered him help. As Okeepa Maker he was beyond help. By his own will he had entrusted himself to the Lord of Life. Now the Lord of Life would save him or not, as He chose.[2]

Four Bears was saved. He was able to crawl to a masked officiant for additional sacrifices to the Lord of Life. Four Bears held out the little finger of his left hand for the priest to sever with a hatchet on a ceremonial buffalo skull. When the severing was over and Four Bears had not cried out, he made the additional sacrifice of the forefinger of his left hand. Dimly, he could hear the crowd gasp. Triumphantly now, his head erect, his eyes open, he held out his right hand for the cutting of its little finger. This was the act of a future chief; he knew the crowd knew it, and in his giddiness he rejoiced.

His ordeal was not over. Still he must do honor to the Sacred Canoe. Half-staggering, he was led outside where his body was coated with red and blue paint and a bunch of willow boughs was thrust into his hand. Then officiants fastened leather straps to his wrists and dragged him, as fast as they could, around the canoe. He could hear the buffalo skulls on his legs clatter in the dirt, and the shrieking of the audience which drowned out his own screams. He knew he must keep running, even though others fainted. The prize of power and the gratitude of the

Mandan Nation came to the man who remained strong. This time Four Bears did not faint. He outlasted his rivals until the weights and skulls and ropes began to drop from his flesh, breaking it so that he would bear for the rest of his life the scars of his accomplishment. He allowed himself to collapse at last. Once more, he trusted himself to the Lord of Life. Ultimately, the onlookers watched him rise, go to his own lodge, and offer his wounds to the women of his clan for dressing. Then he could sleep and, afterward, eat until his strength was restored.

Twice in his life, as he had wished, Four Bears was Okeepa Maker to the Pheasant People. He was, they said, surely invincible. He allowed himself to be admired in all his glory by the men with white faces who came, first from the north, and then from the Hills of the Turtle to the east. These last men had with them a woman of another tribe who introduced herself as Sacajawea. After she had left with her party, other men with white faces came to barter with the Pheasant People for furs and buffalo robes. The whites built a great lodge with a fence and called it Fort Clark. The newcomers brought with them red men from neighboring tribes who could speak the Siouan dialect of the Mandans and who acted as interpreters between the Indians and the American Fur Company. Four Bears was by nature hospitable. He bade the white faces welcome. He marveled at their houses. One of the visitors at Fort Clark said he was a chief in his own land. Prince Maximilian of Neuwied marked a book with a writing stick, and he asked many questions, but there was no thought of admitting him to an Okeepa. No white man was allowed to witness an Okeepa until George Catlin. George Catlin had a terrifying gift. He could put lines and colors on canvas to capture the likeness of the man in front of him. Four Bears heard of the white man's medicine and demanded to see for himself. He came to be painted in full regalia, the bull horns of his chieftaincy atop his war bonnet, his hide robe decorated with his deeds of valor, his eagle-feather staff, buffalo-hide shield, and bone bow. He

smoked red willow bark and sat passive and proud until Catlin
motioned him to come look. To his wonder, there he was! He
saw the faithful rendering of the designs on his robe—the time
he had killed the Sioux brave, the battle with the Cheyennes
and Arikaras, the avenging of his clansman whom the Arikaras
had murdered. Truly George Catlin, he decided, deserved to
see the Okeepa. Four Bears, a spectator this time, could not
understand why the white man cried; it was puzzling in one
who had no part in the ritual. Did Catlin not understand how
braves were made, buffalo herds increased, corn and rain
brought to the Mandans, and their world and their souls linked
in eternal bonds? There were many things Catlin apparently
could not understand, nor could the fur-trader who adminis-
tered Fort Clark, Francis Chardon. Chardon was shocked
when an old woman of the Pheasant People hanged herself. Yet
why not leave this world for the next when one's antique body
became full of pain?

Fire-breathing, bellowing monsters were coming up the river
more often now, and Four Bears grew used to them, though
nothing would have induced him to travel in one. Was it of
these the new and strange marks on the Medicine Rock had
warned that spring? In the Moon of Ripe Chokecherries some
men from the American Fur Company persuaded Four Bears
to come aboard. The monster would not move, they said. He
went, staring curiously at the polished decks and the great
lodge beneath the water where the bunks were. Two of the
steamer's crew were in bed sick. When he returned to his village, Four Bears heard that there were Sioux on all sides of it.
He would have liked to go hunting, but he knew his tribe were
outnumbered and had better stay near their lodges and their
ripening fields. The weather was unusually hot and still.
Through the morning haze, distant bluffs were full of purple
shadows. The river was dark and mysterious, its rippling water
breaking the reflections of the buffalo bushes on its banks. The
air was like smoke when it hit the lungs. At Fort Clark, hunters
Chardon had hired brought him the meat of three bulls; there

would be plenty for the trader in the coming time of frost and blizzard. Sometimes Four Bears heard Mr. Chardon singing to himself:

> *Gentlemen and ladies, I have come to let you know*
> *That Jackson is elected, to jump Jim Crow!*

Jackson had been the Great Father before Van Buren, the trader explained; *Jim Crow* was a popular song. Chardon was an ardent Democrat.

Four Bears went to see Mr. Chardon one very hot summer morning to tell him that a boy had just died in the village. The lad's face had erupted suddenly in repulsive pockmarks, he had gone mad from the great heat within him, and then, writhing and tensing, his body had loosed its soul.

Thus began the final ordeal of Four Bears, the thing that was worse than anything a Mandan had ever suffered in any Okeepa. Four Bears's people broke out in pustules and died in misery. At night there were brief thunderstorms when blinding forks of lightning played in the dark sky and rain fell in drowning gushes, but not even the beating of Thunderbird's wings could drown out the screams of the suffering and the wailing of the newly bereaved. Then messengers came from the Arikaras. Some of them had traded with a Mandan who had visited on the steamer and now the Arikaras, too, were dying of the smallpox. There were signs of Sioux, but the Mandans stayed prisoners in their lodges, infecting each other. They made no war parties. Chardon sent them some buffalo meat, asking for robes in return. He did not worry about the death sickness because there were marks on his arm whose magic was powerful enough to protect him from it. But Four Bears had no such medicine. Near the end of the Chokecherry Moon, July, the insanity and the fever came to him. He could not think. Wildly he staggered out of the village toward the meat-drying camp. When he got there the ground lurched up to him; he slept deliriously, as shouting and visions of O-ke-hee-de, the Evil One, crashed in his brain.

He did not know that a large body of Arikaras had presented themselves at Fort Clark. They said that all their people were dying. Francis Chardon wrote in his journal on July 28:

> Rain in the Morning—This day was very near being my last—a Young Mandan came to the Fort with his gun cocked, and secreted under his robe, with the intention of killing me, after hunting me in 3 or 4 of the houses he at last found me, the door being shut, he waited some time for me to come out. Just as I was in the act of going out, Mitchel caught him and gave him in the hands of two Indians who conducted him to the Village. Had Mitchel not perceived him the instant he did, I would not be at the Trouble of Makeing this statement! I am upon my guard. . . . I have got 100 guns ready and 1,000 lb. Powder, ready to hand out to them when the Fun commences—the War party of Rees . . . came back today—with five horses, that they stole from the Sioux—a lodge that was encamped at the little Misso.—They attacked it in the night, after fireing several shots they departed, takeing with them all the horses—they think to have killed 3 or 4. . . . The Mandans and Rees gave us two splendid dances, they say they dance, on account of their Not haveing a long time to live, as they expect to all die of the small pox—and as long as they are alive, they will take it out in dancing.[3]

On July 31 he noted, "Mandans are getting worse. Nothing will do them except Revenge. . . . Killed 61 rats this month."

The Mandans knew where their disease had come from. In the meat-drying camp, Four Bears roused himself. Suddenly his mind became keen as a knife's edge, and he dragged himself to the fort where the visiting Arikaras were camped and his own people were now dancing away their hours before the Lord of Life struck them all down with the white plague which outlasted any torture on earth. Four Bears shouted for silence. Steadying himself, he began his speech, his voice growing sonorous and rational in his own ears:

> My friends one and all, listen to what I have to say. . . . I have loved the Whites. I have lived with them . . . and to the best of

my knowledge I have always protected them from the insults of others, which they cannot deny. The Four Bears never saw a white man hungry but what he gave him to eat, drink, and a buffalo skin to sleep on, in time of need. I was always ready to die for them, which they cannot deny. I have done everything that a red skin could do for them, and how they have repaid it! With ingratitude! I have never called a white man a dog, but today, I do pronounce them to be a set of blackhearted dogs. They have deceived me, them that I always considered as brothers has turned out to be my worst enemies. I have been in many battles, and often wounded, but the wounds of my enemies I exult in. But today I am wounded, and by whom? By those same white dogs that I have always considered and treated as brothers. I do not fear Death, my friends. You know it. But to die with my face rotten, that even the wolves will shrink with horror at seeing me, and say to themselves, "That is Four Bears, the friend of the whites."

Listen well to what I have to say, as it will be the last time you will hear me. Think of your wives, children, brothers, sisters, friends, and in fact all you hold dear, who are all dead or dying, with their faces all rotten, caused by those dogs the whites. Think of all that, my friends, and rise all together and not leave one of them alive![4]

But it was too late for the red men to rise together. They were perishing at the rate of ten a day. "I keep no account . . . as they die so fast it is impossible," Chardon had to write. "One old fellow who has lost the whole of his family to the number of 14, harangued today, that it was time to begin to kill the whites." In his lodge, Four Bears experienced fresh pain and vivid dreams: he saw Sun and Moon and People Above and Wolf. Retching, in convulsions, Ma-to-toh-pe who had made the greatest Okeepas in Mandan history was being forced by the hands of the spirits from the nightmare life had become. He had experienced his Okeepas proudly, but not this disease. Drained, he lay limp in the final silence from which the Lord of Life would never again give him the medicine to rise.

The epidemic raged on in August. "Saturday 19," recorded

Chardon, "a Mandan and his wife killed themselves yesterday to not Out live their relations that are dead. . . . New cases daily . . . Where it will stop GOD only knows. . . . An old Mandan harangued from the opposite side, to the few that are remaining in the village, to Prepare themselves. . . ."

> Sunday 20 . . . The wife of a young Mandan that caught the disease was suffering from the pain. Her husband looked at her, and held down his head. He jumped up, and said to his wife, "When you was young, you was handsome, you are now ugly and going to leave me, but no, I will go with you." He took up his gun and shot her dead, and with his knife ripped open his own belly. . . . A young Ree that has been sick for some time with the small pox, and being alone in his lodge, thought that it was better to die than to be in so much pain. He began to rub the scabs until blood was running all over his body, he rolled himself in the ashes, which almost burnt the soul out of his body. . . .
>
> Thursday 22 . . . Two young Mandans shot themselves this morning.[5]

Some of the men tomahawked their wives and then cut their own throats. A visiting Arikara brave asked his mother to dig his grave; when she had finished, he wove toward it, fell in, and died, his corpse covered with rancid sores. A mother bludgeoned her children and then hanged herself "to complete the affair." The Mandans in his village would have mourned for Four Bears, but there were almost none left. When frost came and the fury of the plague abated, 80 percent of the Mandan Nation in their villages of Nupta and Mitutak had been extinguished. Litanies of the lost haunted the minds of the survivors: Four Bears and Two Hearts, Child Chief and Chief Blind, Wolf Chief and Bear Heart and Mad Bear and Plume and Crow Belt and Pheasant and Fur Robe and The Four Men, Old Buffalo and Returning Bear and Bull's Neck and Pine Lake and Buffalo Horn and Seven Hairs . . .

In Washington, D.C., officials in the Bureau of Indian Affairs were privately relieved that there was one less tribe which would have to be removed from the path of the country's expansion. In the removal of the Mandans not only the destination but the conductor had been Death.

And to the American Fur Company's St. Louis office, a subordinate of Francis Chardon wrote a summary:

I do not know how many Assiniboins have died as they have long since given up counting but I presume at least 800 and of the Blackfeet at least 700. . . . The Mandans have all died except 13 young and 19 old men. . . . The loss to the company by the introduction of this malady will be immense in fact incalculable as our most profitable Indians have died. . . . Please send some Vaccine.[6]

And the American Fur Company, alert as always for its own interests, did. Finally.

～ 10 ～

Apostle to the People of Fire

"Behold, I go forth to move around the earth.
Behold, I go forth to move around the earth.
I go forth as the black bear that is great in courage.
To move onward, I go forth. . . ."
—Osage *Warrior's Song*

"Shall not one line lament our forest race,
Struck out for you from wild creation's face?
Freedom—the selfsame freedom you adore—
Bade us defend our violated shore."
—Simon Pokagon, Potawatomi

FOUR BEARS STILL HAD TWO YEARS OF LIFE LEFT ON THE AUTUMN evening in 1835 when the city of Rennes, France, received a distinguished visitor. Simon Guillaume Gabriel Bruté de Remur, Roman Catholic bishop of Vincennes, Indiana, lectured on the subject of America's Indians to an enthralled city. For the bishop, this trip to Rennes was a homecoming. He had been born in the Breton city so cool and misty in summer when America's woodlands were sweltering and mosquito-ridden. In winter, gentle rains fell on Rennes almost incessantly, for Brittany jutted into the Atlantic.

Situated on the Ile and Vilaine rivers, the ancient metropolis had known the sackings of Norsemen and a contentious medieval parliament of Breton nobles. Bretons were Celts, who acknowledged their racial ties with Ireland and Scotland. The countryside was studded with monolithic Celtic stones once dedicated to forgotten gods, or perhaps to primitive astronomy. At nearby Carnac, nearly three thousand of these stones stretched out for more than a mile. Bretons might feel an instinctive kinship with anyone who lived in a pagan land. This was why Bishop Bruté had grown to respect the Potawatomis of his American diocese. People of Fire, the Potawatomis called themselves. They were savages, of course, but the bishop knew his own ancestors, in a remote past, had been savages too. They had loved their corner of French earth as the Potawatomis loved their Indiana and Michigan and Illinois forests, canopies of emerald arching over bright rivers and dark soil.

At the University of Rennes, the bishop gathered the townspeople together to tell them how the Potawatomis had been visited by Jesuits centuries before. The Black Robes, as the Indians had called them, had not been able to stay with their missions continuously but they had converted many Potawatomis, and Catholic Indians still begged for more Black Robes. Devout bronze-skinned families prayed morning and evening and made the sign of the cross. In the simple figures of Jesus and Mary many had found an alternative to the austerities of *manito*, the power residing in nature. Because the early French

Jesuits were kind men who dispensed unfailing charity, there were Potawatomis who became willing to replace visions of thunderbirds and eagles with those of a martyr who forgave humanity its weaknesses as Indian deities could not. Potawatomi sorcery was uniquely virulent and destructive among the tribes of North America. Conversion meant immunity from the malevolent magic of rivals. All these things Bishop Bruté explained to a moved audience which donated money for his Indiana labors. One of his hearers was a young lawyer who had recently graduated from the university and was starting on a brilliant courtroom career. But as Benjamin Marie Petit listened to the Most Reverend Father in God from Indiana, his mind strayed from courtrooms. He wondered if his destiny lay not in law but in a far wilderness where red men were begging for the sacraments. Petit was just twenty-four.

A few months later he abandoned his legal robes forever for those of a seminarian at St. Sulpice, in Paris. The two-hundred-year-old seminary had branches in Canada and the United States. Petit began training for the work he prayed would be granted him: the privilege of priesthood under Bishop Bruté and the opportunity of bringing his church's rites to the Potawatomis. Among them, he learned, lived a saintly French-woman, Mlle. Angelique Campeau, who knew their language and who had previously served her church in an Indian school at Detroit. He would not be alone.

In April 1836 he broke the news to his mother and brother that his parish would not be near Rennes. Bishop Bruté had invited him to come to Indiana, where he would be ordained first to the diaconate and then to the priesthood. There he would learn many things—among them, perhaps, why the government of the United States wished to strip the Potawatomis of their lands and claimed to be justified before God in doing so. Benjamin Petit as yet knew little of the ethics of enlarging nations.

Madame Petit was appalled, as was her son Paul. Both wrote stormy letters to Bruté telling him that Benjamin's health was too delicate for him to think of living on a desolate frontier.

The bishop answered that Benjamin seemed to know his own mind. This provoked another missive from Paul and two more from Madame Petit, but Benjamin's resolve remained firm. With other fledgling priests destined to serve Catholic Indians and whites in the New World, he sailed for New York, where he landed on a sultry afternoon in July. The people he encountered did not saunter or even walk; they ran. The journey in turbulent seas had been difficult and the sight of so much energy depressed him, but he had no time to rest. His job was to superintend the shipment of vestments, breviaries, crucifixes, and the paraphernalia of the Mass first to Pittsburgh and from there down the Ohio River to Indiana. He arrived weeks later than his comrades, exhausted and white-faced, but with the baggage intact.

Petit was often homesick during those first months in Vincennes with Bruté. He missed the fields of Brittany, its rock-bound coast, and the fortress-church of Mont St. Michel, the sturdy peasant women in their warm black woolen shawls and winged white caps and their farmer husbands in smocks who raised orchards of apples whose blossoms fell as white rain every spring. Petit missed the cries of onion sellers in cobbled streets, the familiar altar of his parish church, and the smell of newly turned fields and herds of dairy cattle. But his private regrets were nothing compared to the fierce joy he had increasingly begun to feel in the knowledge that he would soon be bringing salvation to native Americans. Just before Christmas 1836 he attained his minor orders. In September 1837, as the Mandans of North Dakota lay writhing in their final agony, he was ordained to the diaconate, the last step before priesthood. His eagerness—sometimes even impatience—to go to his charges moved Bishop Bruté. The boy was physically delicate, but spiritually he was resilient and tough and did not shrink from privation. Petit wanted to go to the Potawatomis "as soon as I am prepared for the priesthood"—which, he hinted, was now. Bruté yielded and Petit wrote to his mother, who had been reconciled to what she could not change, that he was happy and humble on the eve of his great work:

When I think that in two days I shall start from here all alone, going nearly three hundred miles to bestow sacraments—graces ratified in heaven—among people whom I do not know at all, but to whom God sends me—I tremble at the thought of my nothingness. You know how I often said I was born lucky. Well! I can still say it, and God has treated me on my first mission like a spoiled child! I had always longed for a mission among the savages . . . it is I whom the Potawatomis will call their "Father Black Robe."

In November, when bitter winds were stripping elms and maples and the mallards were flying south toward the sun, Benjamin Petit arrived on the Yellow River Indian Reservation in Northern Indiana. A Catholic predecessor who had died had built a log chapel. So small, serene, and kind was Petit as he greeted his charges beside a reservation lake, that the Catholic Potawatomis christened him the Little Duck. He did not tell his mother and brother this, but sent back to Rennes an otherwise vivid account of his experiences:

I have stayed twenty-one days among them. This is the life we led during that time: At sunrise the first bell rang, and you would have seen the savages come along the forest paths and the shores of the lakes. There are four adjoining each other, and the church is built on a hillock on the shore of the largest. When they arrived, the second bell rang. While waiting for the laggards to assemble, the catechist gave in an animated manner the substance of the . . . sermon. Then they recited a chapter of the catechism and the morning prayer, translated by a respectable French Demoiselle [Mademoiselle Campeau] of seventy-two years who has consecrated herself in the capacity of an interpreter in the work of the missions. Then they concluded with a *Pater* and an *Ave,* sang:

> *In thy protection do we trust,*
> *O Virgin, meek and mild,*

and left the chapel.

Then it was time for me to hear confessions until evening, sometimes even after supper. At sunset they came together

again for catechism, followed by an exhortation, evening prayer,
the hymn to the Virgin, and I gave them my blessing—poor
Benjamin's blessing!

God had already "done great things." Many of the Indians,
Petit found, had the habit of practicing spiritual communion.
Eighteen adults wished to be baptized, and the young missionary solemnized nine marriages. The piety of the Catholic
Potawatomis stunned him. Was it possible these were the warriors, the People of Fire, who had once terrified American settlers? "We were orphans," his flock told Petit, "and as if in
darkness, but you appeared among us like a great light, and we
live." One old Indian came forward: "Father, I do not hold the
hearts of others in my hand, but mine will never forget what
you have spoken." Petit saw tears in the Indian's eyes.

When the priest passed their wigwams, Indians would salute
him with "Good day, Father!" Men asked him to write down
the fast days for them when they departed on their fall hunt.
Repeatedly battered by the forces of white America, the old
Potawatomi ways were passing. Here, the Indians felt, was
something to replace them. Life—and death—might yet have
meaning. For if the Great Manito had not departed long ago,
surely there would be no Chemokemons to plague the Potawatomis. And so they prayed, and Benjamin Petit told his mother
that whenever he left them he felt as he had when leaving
Rennes—that he was saying good-bye to his family. Delighted
at being the Little Duck, Petit gave the name to his mission:
Chichipé Outipé.

The Little Duck had many problems which did not fit within
the conventional theology of Catholic France. Many of them
he confided in anxious letters to Bishop Bruté:

> What about a good man quite ready for baptism who does
> not want to be baptized because it will then be necessary to
> marry and his present Christian wife has too melancholy a
> temperament? He is waiting for her to change before he binds
> himself to her forever, and so at present refuses his baptism.

A woman's unfaithful, bigamous husband becomes converted. She has custody of the children. Is it necessary to require her to leave this husband, who supports her and her children? She was his first wife, a Christian woman sent away by an unfaithful husband, not married by the Church. Can she marry another, and vice versa? What if both are unfaithful?

Petit had not completely left his legal training behind him, for which he apologized to his superior. At other moments he was entirely the priest:

On Saturday evening a girl of eighteen or nineteen years comes to confession. We notice that she speaks with difficulty. She finishes her confession and goes away. Evening comes, very dark and rainy. Two little Indians arrive and consult me about this girl, who fell into convulsions on the way home. I take a woolen blanket, wrap myself in it like an Indian, and my guides and I go forth, each with a torch in his hands which spreads a dubious light on the way through the woods when he waves it. There are creeks to cross on treetrunks by this light. We arrive. . . . I give extreme unction by the light of the fire burning in the center of the Indian hut. I start to withdraw, but they appear to want me to stay. I sleep for a moment on a mat; then I remain awake in their midst. I have them sleep by turns. I speak to them with some Indian words . . . and many gestures learned from my mother, from France. The night passes, the moon looking down upon us from on high and revealed by the hole through which the smoke escapes.

The prayers of the dying, and absolution in a stately Latin no more alien to some of the older Indians than English . . . As Father Petit left to go back to his chapel and other confessions, he heard the report of a rifle. The young girl had died, he understood, and his task now was to pray for her in Purgatory.

On a gray autumn afternoon Petit wrote to his bishop:

The Indians, Monseigneur, are preparing to leave for Washington to protest against the unworthy manner with which they are treated. The treaty is indeed a thing as illegal as possible. . . .

It seems to me that if the government has not decided to be completely unjust, they will be listened to. . . . I just found out, however, that at the payment at which the savages were to receive the money necessary for their journey, the Catholics got nothing, or next to nothing.

For the Great Father in Washington knew that the Potawatomis now had among them a priest who had taken honors in law. When the Catholic Indians received money for their trip it was not from Martin Van Buren but Madame Chauvin Petit who had wanted her son Benjamin to be able to buy little luxuries for himself in the New World. Benjamin Petit soon found out more about the Potawatomis, treaties, and Old Kinderhook in the White House. One Indian informant was Leopold Pokagon, a man whose memories of treaties were particularly bitter.

Pokagon was a high-ranking civil chief, who could recall the time he had wept unashamedly in front of white men. It had happened in the windswept little frontier town of Chicago, on the River of the Wild Garlic, where the stars and stripes whipped in lakeshore gusts over the crude blockhouses of Fort Dearborn. There Leopold Pokagon had signed his world away: his high oak forests, the wide and hazy prairies over which the sun set like a huge copper gong in summer, the vastness of icy-blue Lake Michigan, and the white dunes that ringed it. Colonel Zachary Taylor, Old Rough and Ready, had represented the Chemokemons. Pokagon had no choice, Old Rough and Ready told him. White men would steal his land and leave him homeless; it would be better to accept government money and remove west of the Mississippi, where so many other tribes were happily bound to a land which would be theirs as long as green grass grows and water flows.

Pokagon hadn't believed what Taylor said about the West, but he knew Old Rough and Ready spoke the truth when he said the lands of the Potawatomis would be stolen. And so the old chief, wearing the multicolored turban of his office, had slowly walked to the treaty table in Chicago, taken up the

goose quill, and made his mark. He then turned to the Chemokemon officers from Fort Dearborn and the government agents
who had come to watch. He could feel tears running down his
cheeks and onto his buckskin jacket. "I would rather die than
do this," he said. "But it is better to endure a wrong than to
commit one." Love thy neighbor, the Black Robes had recited
long ago. Pokagon lived by the memory of their code. He took
Christianity literally. *Nossimaw wawking, kithiwa kiaik ano-
sowin,* he prayed each night: Our Father, Who art in Heaven.
And he honored the Savior's mother Mary, as his father and
grandfather had done before him.

Pokagon never understood why the white man who called
himself a Baptist, Isaac McCoy, was so displeased when Pokagon told him this. The Ottawas, McCoy said, were converting
to the True Religion as revealed in the Bible. But what good
was the Bible, Pokagon asked him, when you could not read it?
The Black Robes had taught easily remembered words and in
their ceremonies acted out a drama the Fire People could
understand. To Potawatomis schooled in the traditions of
French Jesuits, the cross was sacred and the Mother of God
was always ready to intercede for them so that they might
prosper in the hunt and in the growing of their crops, and
might be spared illness.

But the Catholic Potawatomis respected Isaac McCoy, even
if they could not believe in his God. While the treaty negotiations had been going forward, McCoy had taken several of the
chiefs aside. He wanted to build a Baptist school in Michigan,
and he wanted the Potawatomis to get the best terms for their
land. Together, McCoy and the chiefs laid their plans.

When the Great Father, after dispensing the usual delicious
food, presented his terms, the chiefs stood firm. "We will not
part with our land. We will not make a treaty." The Great
Father gave out presents and promised annuities; that part of
America that lay west of the broad, brown Mississippi became
idyllic on Chemokemon lips. "No," reiterated the chiefs. "We
do not want money. We will make no treaty. It is not money,
not lands, not earthly goods we crave. It is education, and the

Christian religion. Give us schools, and give us the Bible. Let our children be brought up in the light of the Gospel."

The Great Father had been moved. So had the Baptists of the United States. McCoy had gotten his school, and the Potawatomis received stacks of King James Bibles.

Mrs. John Kinzie, wife of a prosperous fur trader, had heard about the proceedings and had asked her friend Mukonse, the brother of old Shabbona, about them. Admiration and respect were mutual between Mrs. Kinzie and the Potawatomis, a nation that had not flocked to the banner of Black Hawk though they had been asked.

"Tell me about this, Mukonse," she said with a knowing smile.

"Well, you see, McCoy the preacher, he got us all down by the Oak Wood, down on the Lake Shore. 'Now,' says he, 'if you want to please the commissioners, and get good price for your lands, and plenty of presents, you must ask for schools and books. They are people who value such things, and the more you seem to value them, the more earnestly you beg for them, the better they will like you, and the greater price they will pay you. Stick to it, now—*no school, no treaty*—let them think you want to be civilized and Christian like the whites, and you can have it all your own way.' McCoy had an ox roasted whole and feasted all who would come. We had a good time, and we all did as McCoy told us. All we knew how to say was 'school' and 'bible'—and the treaty was made—and McCoy got his school established over at St. Joseph, in Michigan. McCoy was a good man—and that was the way he got his school."

"And what about the bibles the religious good gentlemen got together and presented to each of you?"

"Oh! We left them—we could not read in them. We walked along, and if we saw a window open we put our bible in there. Somebody that could read it would find it."[1]

The story was well known to the Potawatomi Nation; it was one of the few things that had been able to make Leopold Pokagon smile in the time of the treaty signing.

Shabbona. *Courtesy Illinois State Historical Library, Old State
Capitol, Springfield.*

After the signing, the Potawatomis had danced for their old customs and for their ancestors' might. It was a dance of death, and Chicago rocked with its convulsions. "A little mushroom town," travelers in the Old Northwest were fond of calling it. It had no harbor; the river flowed directly into Lake Michigan, and ships had to anchor in the open water. In storms the lake swelled treacherously. In December and January the lake front echoed for blocks with the slap and the roaring suck of waves on hard-packed sand. Year-round undertows churned beneath the lake's surface to claim unwary swimmers.

Fort Dearborn boasted two companies of infantry, though it had nearly been abandoned before the rising of Black Hawk. The "upstart village" lay on the river's right bank above the fort. To Anders Larsson, an immigrant Swedish writer, the place was "dirty and unhealthy. . . . Wherever I turned my eyes I could discern nothing but wretched wooden hovels a few feet high supposed to be human dwellings. . . . The whole area between Chicago Avenue and Kinzie Street was to a large extent only a cleared sodden woodland."[2]

Life was normally dull at the tawdry frontier outpost, but when the Potawatomis converged upon it, it suddenly swelled to bursting. Indians camped on every side—on the flat prairie beyond the village, in the woods near the lake, and on the dunes of the beach. The Indians, who told more than one white spectator that the Great Father in Washington must have seen a bad bird which had told him a lie since they did not want to move west, had to accept what they could not alter. And so they took out their frustration in war dancing, and "kept the eyes and ears of all open by running bawling about the village." The tourists who had been brave enough to come were agog. Old warriors sat under the trees smoking and regaling each other with reminiscences of battle. Leopold Pokagon, in his day, had seen action under Tecumtha. Besides the Potawatomis, observed Charles Latrobe, a young English traveler, there were "birds of passage . . . emigrants and land-speculators as numerous as the sand."

You will find horse-dealers and horse-stealers, rogues of every description, white, black, brown, and red half breeds, quarter breeds, and men of no breed at all; dealers in pigs, poultry, and potatoes:—men pursuing Indian claims, some for tracts of land, others . . . for pigs which the wolves had eaten:—creditors of the tribes, or of particular Indians . . . sharpers of every degree: pedlars, grog-sellers: Indian agents and Indian traders . . . and contractors to supply the Pottawattomies with food.[3]

Chicago was a chaos of "mud, rubbish, and confusion." Every night the Indians sang and chanted, the light of their campfires illuminating their gaily painted faces. Their clothes were vivid: blue and scarlet coats, green turbans, yellow sashes, vests covered with beads and plates of silver and tiny mirrors and embroidery. The women wore heavily embroidered petticoats and voluminous shawls.

The Indians raced their ponies and gossiped in their tents. "You peep into a wigwam [reported Latrobe] and see a domestic feud; the chief sitting in dogged silence on the mat while the women, of which there were commonly two or three in every dwelling, and who appeared every evening even more elevated with the fumes of whiskey than the males, read him a lecture."[4]

From another tent would echo laughter, and from another, weeping. Five thousand Potawatomis shouted in revelry born of futility. Pigs rolled and defecated in the mud of the streets. Every evening, the sun was a sinister, hazy bronze. One twilight eight hundred braves assembled at the Indian Council House on the north side of the river. Transient confidence men quartered in the little Sauganash Hotel nearby at Lake and Market streets knew there would be no sleep that night. A young lawyer, John Caton, saw a spectacle he would not forget:

These eight hundred men danced as they went, to the din of hideous noises produced by beating on hollow vessels and striking sticks and clubs together. They proceeded west, up and along the bank of the river on the north side, stopping in front of every house they passed to perform some of their grotesque movements. They finally crossed the north branch of the river and proceeded along the west side of the south branch to the vicinity of the present Lake Street, where they performed in front of the Sauganash Hotel.[5]

Although the music was hideous to Caton and the dancing grotesque, both were stirring to Leopold Pokagon, a Potawatomi who lacked John Caton's Victorian soul. The dance was mesmerizing to Pokagon. The braves were naked except for breechcloths, and their bodies were streaked with vermilion, lime, and indigo paint. Foreheads, cheeks, and noses were covered with curves of scarlet edged with black dots. They had gathered their hair into scalplocks on top of their heads, and the locks were decorated with eagle feathers; some of the feathers were strung together to reach down to the ground, in the western style of the Dakota Sioux. The braves, wanting to be remembered in full majesty, carried tomahawks and war clubs. The atmosphere was torrid; sweat poured from the Indians' bodies and filled the humid air with its honest rankness. The braves' eyes were bloodshot from whiskey, but their arms and legs were knotted with muscles still vigorous and hard. The dancers leaped and arched, shouted and whooped.

At the Sauganash they stared up at "windows full of Chemokemon squaws." They brandished their war clubs, and laughed uproariously when the ladies hastily withdrew. It was "a picture of hell itself before us," one of the women decided, "a carnival of damned spirits." What if the Potawatomi braves should attack in earnest? "They will massacre us all, and leave not a living soul to tell the story!" But the Potawatomis danced on, down Lake Street toward the Exchange Coffee House and then, at Lake and Dearborn streets, to the Tremont House Hotel, where Chemokemon ladies again appeared in the windows and the Indians merrily brandished their clubs, howling with delight. Just as the women decided murder was imminent, the column of warriors wove down to Fort Dearborn, where they danced for the men of the garrison.[6] The officers and their troops, more sophisticated than the women of the Sauganash and the Tremont, understood that they were watching a lavish farewell. But even they would have gaped at the report of one of the Sisters of Charity who had been working with Michigan Catholic Potawatomis: "I could not believe that such piety existed among them. On the contrary I had always believed them to be a very barbarous people that had neither laws nor religion; but I am now convinced of their sincerity and simplicity." For Sisters Magdalene and Lucina understood what Leopold Pokagon was helping Benjamin Petit to understand as he recalled his nation's *Totentanz*: that two souls warred in every red man, and two worlds. The heat of the contest either consumed him or forged in him a spirit of steel.

Some disturbing rumors had begun to drift in to Bishop Bruté in Vincennes from the environs of Chichipé Outipé. Was Father Petit telling the Potawatomis not to march west? "Monseigneur," Petit protested, "I have never said a word to them tending in the least to influence them to disobey in case they should not obtain justice and be forced to depart. . . . Nor have I ever had the least idea of asking your permission to accompany them in their emigration, and I am, thanks to God, wholly prepared to leave them when you say to me: 'Depart' (not, however, without some inner pangs, but that does not matter.)" Bishop Bruté knew the pangs would matter desperately. He loved the young priest who was too innocent for discretion, and he had heard about the things that happened to American Indians on their forced marches. How could he give Petit what he wanted? "Is it necessary to sacrifice the innocent to the guilty by keeping silent?" Petit asked him repeatedly. When Chief Menomini appeared in Washington, D.C., it was with a petition that was a very model of legal reason—the kind taught in Rennes, France. Wearily then Bruté advised his subordinate: "These people will not be successful in having the law repealed. Whatever may have been its origin—however faulty or dishonest even—if the fault lay in the documents upon which the law was based then above all we should . . . refrain from meddling in what is not in the line of our duties."

Slightly (and only temporarily) chastened, the Little Duck replied: "I am ashamed of myself, Monseigneur, and I fear you find me still too much a lawyer. I should perhaps have cast that spirit far from me, and yet it was at a time when the weak oppressed had no sure defense against the oppressor other than the priest's voice."

Bishop Bruté was also worried about Petit's delicacy. Not without guile, Petit regaled him with descriptions of his own strength.

> I am surprised, Monseigneur, at my health; one evening at sunset I left Bertrand in snow which was falling heavily to go twenty-four miles to administer to a sick woman at Pokagon's. I traveled all night through the forest; there were, in the sleigh, M. Benjamin Bertrand and I. We upset nine times on the way—superb!—we laughed like kings. . . . I remember the time when Benjamin would have coughed, grown pale, etc., but he was not a missionary then; that makes quite a difference. . . . I shall tell you that my boots are full of holes, and I should be glad to buy a pair of them, or even shoes, but that does not mean that I am suffering at all from the cold; I am like a prince. I have so well got into the habit of sleeping in a mat wrapped in blankets that I have one uninterrupted sleep that way from evening to morning, and today I was completely out of my element in the feather bed at M. Coquillard's house.

(Many of the people Petit served were descended from the French who had garrisoned Fort Vincennes.)

Petit was learning Potawatomi, even as he wrote his family in Rennes of his nightmare that his mission would be destroyed: "The government wants to transport the Indians to the other side of the Mississippi. I live between fear and hope, but I entrust my hope and fear to the hands of the Lord. . . . How little savage at heart they are, these Indians, whom the Americans with their hearts dry as cork and their whole thought 'land and money' fail to appreciate and treat with so much disdain and injustice."

By now Petit was prescribing his grandmother's poultices for ailing Indians. As they had already learned to look to him for spiritual help, they learned to bring him their sick. "As to France, let them marry, run about, dance, die (that is the world as I knew it when I was young and a Frenchman); I scarcely bother myself about it any longer, now that I am old and an Indian. Yet I still deeply desire that the Good Lord will bless them. *Nin Muckahtaokonia Chichipé Outipé angenickaso gatamikoa tchaiai Muckatahokonia Autchakpock Kick:* I, the Black Robe, called the Little Duck, I greet all. . . ." Was he to see his people exiled? Would he have to destroy his altar and his church, "lay low the cross . . . in order to spare the sacred articles from profanation . . . and never to see them again?" Would the Potawatomis languish under a strange sky where he could not follow them?

"I am sad, Father," an old Indian woman told him. "I think perhaps you will go away soon to the great Black Robe and we shall see you no more."

"If my chief desires it, I must obey; I am not my own master. But God will send you another French father in my place."

"Yes. He would be a Frenchman, but you are already a Potawatomi and soon will be nothing but a Potawatomi."

To Indiana's Protestants, Petit's absorption into the tribe smacked of "Catholic high treason." An Indian agent provoked Petit into telling him that the right to preach to the Potawatomis was a right guaranteed to him by the Constitution of the United States.

"I do not know, Father, why the Indians always believe we are lying."

"That is very simple, sir. During the last few years ten or twelve men have come who have so grossly lied to the Indians that today they naturally believe an agent is a man paid to deceive them."

When Chief Menomini returned from Washington, he told

Petit that Martin Van Buren had said about Indian removal, "I do not wish to speak of it." The Secretary of War had been more blunt: "Your lands are lost." Petit took his courage in his hands and petitioned Bishop Bruté:

> I know my presence would be a protection during the journey . . . until now they have been driven like dogs on these journeys, and they arrived broken-hearted and dispirited from mistreatment along the way. . . . The diocese would lose nothing by it; I should return perhaps within a year. . . . My Bishop could not refuse me this without reducing these poor children to the plight of exposed infants whom Providence, it is true, can save but who, humanly speaking, are completely destitute of aid. Because a good father would not do such a thing, and my Bishop is a good father . . . I suspect the promises to be fulfilled on the other side of the river; the slight dependability hitherto shown is a poor guarantee.

Unknown to Petit, Bruté had also written to Washington. He, too, had met with failure. And now he knew that he could not refuse his priest the journey into earthly hell.

At Chichipé Outipé, where troops rounded up the Potawatomis, blue-coated American soldiers dealt summarily with several rebellious headmen. They "immured them in a cage," reported Petit, where they were kept to await their trip and be the butt of military merriment. The cage would "directly follow the American flag." The day came when Petit said his last Mass at Chichipé Outipé. Afterward, he and his Potawatomis stripped the chapel of its appointments. The Indians sobbed as a white squatter marched in to claim the chapel for his house. Petit watched as the army prodded the Indians with bayonets. He himself felt feverish, but he willed away the fever to become strong for his ordeal. Horses' hooves beat tattoos on the forest floor as the soldiers came and went. General John Tipton, in charge of the removal, ordered several discharges of musketry. Indian women screamed with grief. One fled into the forest where she starved for several days. Then she ate a dead pheasant and, retching, returned. Petit squared his shoulders as the three-mile-long procession set out. "On the flanks of the line at equal distance from each other are the dragoons and volunteers, hastening the stragglers." As the march wound toward Logansport, the Indians, predictably, began falling sick. In Logansport many died of dysentery and lost hope. Out of eight hundred people, more than three hundred had turned overnight into invalids. From Logansport they were urged on to "the grand prairies of Illinois, under a burning sun and without shade from one camp to another." At night, the Indians gathered around Petit who led them in telling the rosary and singing hymns in their language. By day Petit harassed General Tipton for water for his charges until he was felled by fever on the banks of the Illinois River. But after he had rested in the home of a white Catholic couple who had discovered him shaking with chills, he was ready to proceed. At Quincy, Illinois, on the banks of the Mississippi, the Indians were visited by a citizen who advised Petit, "Make them better than they are." Quincy was troubled. Several of its leading inhabitants had "resolved to exterminate or at least expel certain sectarians called Mormons." As Benjamin Marie Petit marched toward St. Louis with the Potawatomis, Brigham Young was marching with his Latter Day Saints toward Utah. The paths of the two bands of pilgrims crossed briefly on the hot flood plain of the Mississippi.

Petit's fever returned. This time his eyes were inflamed and his throat was seared with pain. Huge running sores broke out over his body. Unchecked streptococcus ravaged him, while Indians died of the infection all the way to St. Louis. Petit rode proudly erect in the intervals between the funerals he conducted. Winter arrived early with sudden high winds and driving rains beating yellow fields of spent grass. When the Indians reached St. Louis, they were met by Catholic dignitaries, who took one look at Petit and carried him to their headquarters, replacing him on the march with another chaplain. Petit was too weak to protest. In a strange room in St. Louis, he drifted in and out of delirium for weeks. It was not of

Brittany that he had visions, though, but of the wooden chapel at Chichipé Outipé. He was, indeed, a Potawatomi.

By February it was plain that he was near death. One of the priests, Father Elet, came to pray with him.

"Are you suffering greatly?" asked Elet.

Slowly, Petit moved his eyes toward a crucifix on the wall.

"You mean to say that He suffered more for you?"

"Ah, yes!" Petit whispered.

Twenty minutes before midnight, on February 10, he died listening to the solemn spoken music of Catholic last rites. He was smiling still. His name suited him, reflected Father Elet; he had been "the Benjamin of all those who could appreciate his good qualities. By his modesty, his humility, he was *Petit* in his own eyes, although great in the eyes of God." In Vincennes, Bishop Bruté understood that he had given Bejamin Petit what he had most wanted, the crown of martyrdom.

In the decades that followed, the Indians were herded from Iowa into Kansas. The Potawatomis remembered Petit as Chichipé Outipé. They did not know that their priest's body had been brought back from Missouri to Indiana for its final rest at the site of the struggling young university, Notre Dame, on St. Mary's Lake. In the troubled waters of the New World, the Little Duck would swim no more.

White Bird's Last Stand

"In truth, our cause is your own. It is the cause of liberty and justice. It is based upon your own principle which we have learned from yourselves; for we have gloried to count your Washington and your Jefferson our great teachers. We have practiced their precepts with success and the result is manifest. The wilderness of forest has given place to comfortable dwellings and cultivated fields. . . . We have learned your religion also. We have read your sacred books. Hundreds of our people have embraced their doctrines, practiced the virtue they teach, cherished the hopes they awaken. We speak to the representatives of a Christian country; the friends of justice; the patrons of the oppressed; and our hopes revive, and our prospects brighten, as we indulge the thought. On your sentence our fate is suspended, on your kindness, on your humanity, on your compassion, on your benevolence, we rest our hopes."

    —MEMORIAL OF THE CHEROKEE NATION TO THE
UNITED STATES CONGRESS, DECEMBER 29, 1835

By the time Old Kinderhook succeeded Jacksa Chula Harjo in the White House, most of America had accepted the policy of Indian Removal. The country watched the tribes depart: Potawatomis, Weas, Piankeshaws, Ottawas, Miamis, Winnebagoes. Some newspapers carried morally outraged editorials, but the same papers also carried fascinating real estate advertisements for government land. When Americans had to choose between morals and their dreams of money, they invariably opted for money. Men like Daniel Webster, who defended the beleaguered Indians repeatedly in the Senate, were admired as a matter of form, and little heeded. When Webster's name was put forward by New England Whigs as a presidential candidate in the election of 1836, he received only the electoral vote of Massachusetts. But Webster continued to watch closely the seemingly eternal negotiations of the Cherokee Nation with the United States. The eloquent frock-coated parliamentarian with the intense eyes and high domed forehead knew that the power of his own oratory was matched by the quiet persuasiveness of John Ross, the Cherokees' chief.

Ross was seven-eighths white, but his wife Quatie was a full-blood, and his people trusted him. Cooweescoowee, they called him: the White Bird. Sometimes they spoke of him affectionately as Little John, for he was only five feet six. "It's too damned late, Mr. Ross," Jacksa Chula Harjo had told him of his homeland. "I will not go to war for you."[1] But White Bird continued to hope and to play for time. Memorial after memorial was sent to Washington, to the Americans whom the Cherokees called Unakas.

There was a sinister specificity to the Blood Law which had been passed by the Cherokees as far back as 1829:

> Whereas a law has been in existence for many years, but not committed to writing, that if any citizen or citizens of this nation should treat and dispose of any lands belonging to this nation without special permission from the national authorities, he or they shall suffer death;—therefore, resolved, by the Committee and the Council, in general Council convened, that any person

or persons who shall, contrary to the will and consent of the legislative council of this nation in General Council convened, enter into a treaty with any commissioner or commissioners of the United States, or any officers instructed for the purpose, and agree to sell or dispose of any part or portion of the national lands defined in the constitution of this nation, he or they so offending, upon conviction before any of the circuit judges of the Supreme Court, shall suffer death. . . . Any person or persons, who shall violate the provisions of this act, and shall refuse, by resistance, to appear at the place designated for trial, or abscond, are hereby declared to be outlaws; and any person or persons, citizens of this nation, may kill him or them so offending, in any manner most convenient, within the limits of this nation, and shall not be held accountable for the same.[2]

One important actor in the Cherokee drama had removed himself. Sam Houston, Blackbird, had addressed his own series of memorials to Washington. He had been ignored, until Andrew Jackson had decided to occupy the impetuous Houston, of whom he personally was fond, with the affairs of the Texas Comanches. Texas, a northern Mexican province chafing under the restraints of Mexico City, was filling with white Americans. Houston went to Texas to hold ceremonious conferences with the warlike Comanches. While he was there, the Americans of Texas decided to break with Mexico altogether. They made Sam Houston commander-in-chief of their army and declared Texas an independent republic. In February 1836 the Mexican General Santa Anna successfully besieged the Alamo and 182 Americans perished. Among them was Colonel David Crockett of Tennessee who, in his time, had also been a partisan of American Indians. Sam Houston now had something with which to incite his troops to revenge. "Remember the Alamo!" he roared triumphantly as he led them into battle at San Jacinto. Victory brought him the post of constitutional president of Texas. He no longer had time for the Cherokees in the United States. Now considered a dashing hero, he married a soft-spoken girl named Margaret Lea who managed to wean him from the whiskey bottle. Eliza Allen and Tiana Rogers were forgotten. So was Ootsetee Ardetahskee, the Big Drunk. So, even, was the name of Blackbird. General Sam Houston was the victor of San Jacinto, with a new country to keep him busy and a new love to heal the wounds that Eliza Allen had left festering in Tennessee.

With Houston out of the way, native Cherokee leaders in the West and East grew more prominent. John Ross was in his forties now. If his wife, Quatie, was his link with conservative-minded Cherokees, his ancestry was his tie to the Unakas. His grandfather, a Scotsman named John McDonald, had been a Tory agent among the Cherokees of Tennessee during the American Revolution. His father, Daniel Ross, had been a Scotsman who had married McDonald's part-Cherokee daughter Mary and had declared his royalist sympathies. He had raised his son like an aristocratic Scots highlander, so that there were now two sides to White Bird: one the flourishing southern planter who was the product of Unaka schools, and the other the Indian mystic whose sense of the blood tie with his mother's race was strong. When a man had the vision of harmony with his earth—and the vision came from being an Indian—he could not ignore it, White Bird believed. Such a man's duty was to use the Unaka education he had acquired in defending his people.

One of the most commanding presences among the Cherokees had long been Ka-nun-da-cla-geh, the Ridge. His son, John, was an intellectual, an alumnus of New England missionary schools. Sam Houston had once warned Congress, "These Indians are not inferior to white men. John Ridge is not inferior in point of genius to John Randolph. His father, in point of native intellect, is not inferior to any man." John Randolph of Roanoke, at that time minister to Russia, probably had not appreciated the comparison. But John Ridge was incontestably saner than John Randolph, who conducted nightly séances with Satan.

The Ridge had been born into the life of a warrior. He had listened to the prophecies of Cherokee medicine men in his nation's council houses; by then the Unakas, "elder brothers,"

The Ridge. Portrait by C.B. King. *Courtesy Smithsonian Institution, Washington, D.C.*

had already become the Cherokees' neighbors. "This is as our forefathers told us," droned the medicine men.

> They said, "Our feet are turned toward the West—they are never to turn around." Now mark what our forefathers told us. Your elder brother will settle around you—he will encroach upon your lands, and then ask you to sell them to him. When you give him a part of your country, he will not be satisfied, but ask for more. In process of time he will ask you to become like him. . . . He will tell you that your mode of life is not as good as his—whereupon you will be induced to make great roads through the nation, by which he can have free access to you. He will teach your women to spin and weave and make clothes, and teach you to cultivate the earth. He will even teach you his language, and to read and write. . . . But these are but means to destroy you, and to eject you from your habitations. He WILL POINT YOU TO THE WEST, but you will find no resting place there, for your elder brother will drive you from one place to another until you get to the western waters. These things will certainly happen, but it will be when we are dead and gone. We shall not live to see and feel the misery which will come upon you.[3]

The Ridge, named for the sprawling fir-clad mountains of his native country, listened to these things. He watched the red glow of the firelight play on wrinkled copper faces in the council house as blue-veined conjurors' hands fanned their ancient bodies with turkey wings. The sad music of the wise men's voices floated upward into the warm smoke heavy with hickory. Every evening, the Ridge's father taught him, he must bathe and pray the hunter's prayer: "Give me the wind. Give me the breeze. . . . O Great Earth Hunter, let your stomach, the ground, cover itself; let it be covered with leaves. And you, O Ancient Red Fire, may you hover about my breast while I sleep. Now let good dreams come."

During the Revolution, the Ridge had fought Americans and had taken many of their scalps. But then he had watched ferocious Chief Doublehead murder a family of unoffending

Unaka women and children at an isolated Tennessee block-house. Something in him had revolted. Doublehead was also rumored to practice cannibalism. When Doublehead made a secret treaty to lease some of his land to white men, the Ridge and several Cherokees appointed themselves his executioners under the Blood Law, as yet unwritten but in inexorable oper-ation. They ambushed him, shot him in the jaw, severed one of his thumbs, then shot bullets through his hips and plunged a tomahawk so deeply into his skull that it took two hands and a bracing foot to pry it loose. After this they smashed Double-head's brains to pulp.

Ambivalent in his conceptions of cruelty, the Ridge came to be ambivalent about the ancient Cherokee ways. He saw white men around him thriving as planters. Why could he, too, not learn to till the soil? He applied himself to farming with such industry that he was soon a substantial landowner. When he married a Cherokee princess, Sehoyah, the couple determined their children should have "a *great* education." The Ridge was no Christian, but he was not afraid of the new ways any longer. As a high Cherokee chief, honored as a slayer of the traitorous Doublehead, he wanted to do what he honestly thought best for his people.

He was firmly opposed to removal, and became a more fa-miliar figure than ever to the Cherokees as he rode about the nation making speeches to strengthen their determination to stay where they were. His massive jaw set sternly, his dark eyes sweeping his audiences, he appeared before them in an elegant frock coat trimmed with gold lace and in polished white boots. He now had slaves to till his fields.

He spoke in Cherokee saying,

We have noticed the ancient ground of complaint founded on the ignorance of our ancestors and their fondness for the chase, and for the purpose of agriculture as having in possession too much land for their numbers. What is the language of objection this time?

The case is reversed, and we are now assaulted with menaces

of expulsion because we have unexpectedly become civilized, and because we have formed and organized a constitutional government. . . . We hereby individually set our faces to the rising sun, and turn our backs to its setting. . . .

If the country to which we are directed to go is desirable and well-watered, why is it so long a wilderness and a waste, and uninhabited by all respectable white people, whose enterprise ere this would have induced them to monopolize it from the poor and unfortunate of their fellow-citizens as they have hitherto done?

John Ridge, as the Ridge's son was now known, grew to manhood in a series of Protestant schools, where he wrote moralistic verse:

> *Withers the rose, the blossom blasts,*
> *The flower fades, the morning hastes,*
> *The sun is set, shadows fly,*
> *The gourd consumes—so mortals die.*[4]

When the Ridge, on triumphal progresses in his planter's carriage, visited his son, he was "the nice big gentleman with the warlike step" to John's fellow pupils. John was more delicate than his father, but not too delicate to capture the heart of a missionary's white daughter, Sarah Northrup, whom he married to the accompaniment of Unaka cries of "Miscegenation!" The cries were even more indignant when John's cousin Elias Boudinot, also a mission school product, married Harriet Gold, who was white and had Protestant relatives. Harriet was hanged in effigy in her hometown of Cornwall, Connecticut, and her own brother set fire afterward to the mock corpse. But the Golds, like the Northrups, were finally reconciled to their daughter's marriage. When they went south to visit their Cherokee kinsmen they gaped in astonishment. The Ridge was daily growing richer. His orchards were graced with 1,141 peach trees, 418 apple trees, 11 quince bushes, 21 cherry trees, and scattered plum trees. "My father has plenty," John Ridge affirmed proudly. He traveled to eastern cities to raise money for the conversion of the Cherokees, and his light voice and tall, darkly slender smartness touched his listeners, who wanted to ensure their own salvation with a down payment to Cherokee missions. John knew how to appeal to them: "Can anyone convince me that the degraded Hottentot in Africa, or the wild Arab in the Sahara, whose head is exposed to the piercing rays of a meridian sun, entirely dependent upon his camel for safety, enjoys more real contentment of mind than the poorest peasant of England?" There had evidently been nothing in John's school textbooks about burnooses on Arab heads or swords in Arab scabbards.

> Will anyone compare the confined pleasures of the Hindoo, whose mind is burdened with the shackles of superstition and ignorance, who bows before the car of the juggernaut, or whose wretched ignorance compels him to invoke the river Ganges for his salvation—Will anyone, I say, compare his pleasures to the noble and well regulated pleasures of a Herschel or a Newton, who surveys the regions of the universe—views the wisdom of the Deity in forming the lights of heaven with all the planets and attending satellites revolving in their orbits, irradiating infinite space as they move around their common centres—and who demonstrates, with mathematical exactness, the rapid flights of the comet and its future visits to our solar system? . . . I have made this contrast to give you a general view of the wretched state of the Heathen, particularly of the aborigines of this country.[5]

The Ridge himself had to be numbered among the wretched heathen, but paganism was more palatable in a man who owned more than a thousand peach trees. The contrast between John Ridge and the Cherokees' chief, John Ross, was marked. Ross, too, had been moulded by Unaka civilization, but in marrying Quatie he had shown his will to be a Cherokee to the core. In the columns of Elias Boudinot's *Cherokee Phoenix* the utterances of Ross and Ridge ran side by side. John Ridge turned his back on what he had been taught to see as savagery; John Ross found in the full-blooded Cherokees a dignity and strength which, in his eyes, raised them above the

John Ridge. Portrait by C.B. King. *Courtesy Smithsonian Institution, Washington, D.C.*

Unaka level. John Ridge was also beginning to flirt with the advocacy of removal. While still in office Jacksa Chula Harjo was able to write to General John Coffee, with whom he had marched in the Creek War, about the Cherokees' status: "I believe John Ridge has expressed despair, and that it is better for them to treat and move."

What converted John Ridge to removal? Was it true that Ka-nun-da-cla-geh, the Ridge, was also reversing his stand? Under the state government of Wilson Lumpkin, whose words were compared by himself to gold and silver, Georgia established a lottery—with a simple purpose. Lumpkin put the plantations and farms of the Cherokees up for grabs. Unakas drawing lucky numbers as a great wooden state wheel spun around and around might simply evict any resident Indians and move in. Washington would not interfere because to do so would violate the sacred principle of states' rights.

After a trip to the nation's capital to plead with Congress, John Ross returned to his home to find Georgia militia encamped on its grounds. Outbuildings, corn cribs, orchards, fields, and livestock herds were being claimed by lottery winners. A weeping Quatic and two of John Ross's children were imprisoned in a bedroom by armed guards. Chief Joseph Vann's mansion was taken over because he had dared to employ a white overseer. A squatter with a rifle guarded the top floor of Vann's house while Vann and his family were shut up on the first. The Vanns managed to escape while Georgia agents opened fire on them. Ross and Vann were not alone. Chief after chief lost his holdings to Georgia crackers. Ross moved his family to Tennessee, to the site of modern Chattanooga. Vann built a Tennessee log cabin with a dirt floor.

The outrages made John Ross resolve to fight removal in the courts with the best attorneys he could hire. But for John Ridge and Elias Boudinot and Boudinot's brother, Stand Watie, removal was now the only reasonable alternative. They believed the Cherokees had to go where their property would be respected. When at last the Ridge himself assented, the Cherokee Treaty Party knew it had won a major victory. Cynics noted that Elias Boudinot's house was promptly withdrawn from the Georgia lottery. Rumors of a revival of the old Blood Law began to drift along the Georgia-Tennessee border along with the smoke from militia rifles. The Ridges, the Waties, and the Boudinots were now openly calling for a mass exodus westward. The Ridge had turned his back on the rising sun to dream of a sunset retreat. He wanted his people safely out of Georgia. The old warrior who had slain Doublehead was willing to fight no longer.

Trudging through Tennessee was a writer who wanted to gather material for a book on the American South. He had lived abroad for many years, and was anxious to reacquaint himself with his country. John Howard Payne had had a series of successes; he was most famous for his opera libretto *Clari, the Maid of Milan*, which had been performed on the London stage. The house had been brought down when the heroine finished one of her arias, "Home, Sweet Home." But success had not gone to Payne's head; he was still a working journalist willing to dig for his facts at first hand. He decided it would be interesting to visit John Ross, principal chief of the Cherokees, in his home in exile at Ross's Landing in Tennessee. Ross was supposed to have papers on tribal history, and Payne thought he could use them.

Ross welcomed him cordially. "I regret I have only a one-room log cabin," he told him. Payne copied the manuscripts and after conversations with Ross became a staunch partisan of the antitreaty Cherokees, who were about to hold a tribal convention in the corner of Tennessee to which they had had to flee after the Georgia lottery. Payne's pen scratched at night in the low light of an oil lamp:

With internal dissensions attempted to be fomented by the agents of the Government, and with incessant external attacks from Georgia, and not only undefended by their legitimate protector the United States but threatened by the chief magistrate of those states, the Cherokee nation now stands alone, moneyless, helpless, and almost hopeless; yet without a dream of yielding. With these clouds around them, in . . . Tennessee to which they have been driven from Georgia for shelter, their national council holds its regular convention tomorrow. I cannot imagine a spectacle of more moral grandeur than the assembly of such a people, under such circumstances.

This morning offered the first foretaste of what the next week is to present. The woods echoed with the trampling of many feet: a long and orderly procession emerged from among the trees, the gorgeous autumnal tints of whose departing foliage seemed in sad harmony with the noble spirit now beaming in this departing race. Most of the train was on foot. There were a few aged men, and some few women, on horseback. The train halted at the humble gate of the principal chief; he stood ready to receive them.

Everything was noiseless. The party, entering, loosened the blankets which were loosely rolled and flung over their backs and hung them, with their tin cups and other paraphernalia attached, upon the fence. The chief approached them. They formed diagonally in two lines and each, in silence, drew near to give his hand. Their dress was neat and picturesque: all wore turbans, except four or five with hats; many of them, tunics, with sashes; many long robes, and nearly all some drapery; so that they had the oriental air of the old scripture pictures of patriarchal processions.[6]

The old men remained near Ross; the rest withdrew to other parts of the yard. Some sat underneath the trees and smoked, some perched on fences. The eyes of all were on Ross as he spoke to them in Cherokee. Most had walked sixty miles or more to hear him. Afterward Ross explained to Payne that he would be leaving once more for Washington, to try to buy time for his people.

Before Ross had finished packing, twenty-five members of the Georgia guard crossed the Tennessee border and arrested not only Chief Ross but, for good measure, John Howard Payne. Payne thought the militia looked like *"banditti."* He and Ross were hauled off in a torrential rainstorm to a Georgia jail with no explanation of why they had been arrested. The militia

John Ross. Portrait by C.B. King. *Courtesy Smithsonian Institution, Washington, D.C.*

seized Ross's papers and Payne's notes, and were infuriated when they read of Payne's open partisanship with the Indian side. They conceived the plan of having both men lynched and rode through the countryside telling Georgia farmers that Payne was an abolitionist from the North who had come to stir up their slaves. White husbands would be slain in their beds and women raped by murderous black men. For thirteen days this rumor was spread in rural Georgia, but rural Georgians had too much sense to believe it. Where was the proof against Payne? The militia was finally forced to release both men, whereupon Payne began writing white-hot articles for America's newspapers. He was a long way from home, sweet home himself—for he was a Long Islander—but he was caught up in the cause of Cherokee resistance and tried to rouse the rest of the country.

The country, however, was weary of Indians in general. In the absence of ranking Cherokee chiefs, a treaty was drawn up and signed by members of the Ridge, Boudinot, and Watie families and their friends. The Reverend J.F. Schermerhorn, whose theological principles were flexible enough to permit him to license the proprietors of grog shops which were daily stupefying their Indian patrons, acted as agent for the U.S. Government. "Devil's horn," the Cherokees called him. To the adherents of White Bird, the signatures of the Ridges and Stand Watie and Elias Boudinot on the treaty were treasonous.

General John Ellis Wool was put in charge of keeping down Cherokee rebellion in the Indians' ceded territory. By this time Martin Van Buren was President. When he told General Wool to persuade the Cherokees to remove swiftly and to inform them that their cause was futile, the general replied with a few home truths:

> It is vain . . . to talk. . . . So determined are they in their opposition that not one of all those who were present and voted at the council held but a day or two since, however poor or destitute, would receive either rations or clothing from the United States lest they might compromise themselves in regard

to the treaty. These same people as well as those in the mountains of North Carolina, during the summer past, preferred living on the roots and sap of trees rather than receive provisions from the United States, and thousands, as I have been informed, had no other food for weeks. Many have said they will die before they will leave the country.[7]

Henry Clay, dean of the Senate Whigs, found the treaty "unjust, dishonest, cruel, and shortsighted in the extreme." Representative Henry Wise of Virginia thought the Cherokees were "more advanced in civilization" than the rest of Georgia. Clay had lost a bitterly contested presidential election to Jackson, and Wise was a patrician who regarded Georgia crackers as rabble. In the House, John Quincy Adams said the compact was "infamous . . . It brings with it eternal disgrace upon this country." In Georgia, the property of Elias Boudinot remained strangely immune to seizure.

When old Chief Junaluska heard about the Schermerhorn Treaty, the tears ran down his cheeks. At the side of Pushmataha of the Choctaws, Junaluska had been one of the Cherokees in the army of Jacksa Chula Harjo at Horseshoe Bend. His face upraised to the Master of Breath who resided somewhere in the cruelly brilliant southern sky, he lamented: "If I had known that Jackson would drive us from our homes, I would have killed him that day at the Horse Shoe." Like Pushmataha, he had trusted whites. Now in the Byronic, aquiline features of John Ridge, Junaluska saw a traitor.

As the lottery of Cherokee holdings proceeded apace, Georgians cheerfully sang the latest song:

> All I want in this creation
> Is a pretty little girl and a big plantation
> Way down yonder in the Cherokee nation.[8]

To Ka-nun-da-cla-geh, the Ridge, the enmity of his people was becoming unendurable. His broad face full of the pain which was racking it daily, he pleaded for understanding:

I am one of the native sons of these wild woods. I have hunted the deer and turkey here more than fifty years. . . . The Georgians have shown a grasping spirit lately; they have extended their laws, to which we are unaccustomed, which harass our braves and make the children suffer and cry. . . . I know the Indians have an older title than theirs. We obtained the land from the living God above. . . . Yet they are strong and we are weak. We are few, they are many. We cannot remain here in safety and comfort. I know we love the graves of our fathers. . . . We can never forget these homes, I know, but an unbending, iron necessity tells us we must leave them.[9]

The operative words, charged White Bird's men, were "safety and comfort." The Cherokees were prepared to sacrifice both, though the Ridge evidently was not. Now his tribesmen spat in his face when he walked among them. They refused to speak to him or to his family. By the beginning of 1837, a contented Wilson Lumpkin was observing: "A large company of the most wealthy and intelligent of the Cherokee people have availed themselves of that provision of the treaty which authorizes them to emigrate themselves and families." The criterion of intelligence was, naturally, agreement with the views of Wilson Lumpkin. Large sums of money, he noted parenthetically, "had been placed where it would be most effective."

The Ridge and his relatives and six hundred of his followers set out to cross the Father of Waters equipped handsomely with black slaves, sleek saddle horses, and droves of rotund oxen who plodded along at their own pace. There were no soldiers with bayonets standing by. The Ridge and his six hundred traveled in comfort, in spacious carriages and wagons, and when they reached Oklahoma they congratulated themselves that they had arrived in plenty of time to plant spring crops on the choicest lands—or, rather, to order the planting of such crops by their slaves. "Well-mounted, well-dressed, well-fed," remarked white observers of these Cherokees. Were these obvious aristocrats the Indians Henry Clay and John Quincy

Adams kept telling the country were downtrodden? Ridiculous!

But General Wool was not deceived by such splendors as the gold lace on the Ridge's cuffs. Daily he saw the rank and file of the nation who refused to leave the rolling, rhododendron-clad mountains they loved. When he tried to prohibit the sale of whiskey, Georgians howled in protest. States' rights were once again at stake. By the summer of 1837 Georgia was charging the general with "having usurped the powers of the civil tribunals, disturbed the peace of the community, and trampled upon the rights of the citizens."[10] Martin Van Buren listened, and that autumn a military court of inquiry was set up at Knoxville, Tennessee. When asked to produce definite evidence of Wool's subversion, the state of Georgia could not. But General Wool had had enough. He asked to be relieved of his command among the Cherokees "on moral grounds." He was replaced by General Winfield Scott, "Old Fuss and Feathers," who arrived with seven thousand men "to carry out the benevolent intentions of the United States Government." He established concentration camps, even while John Ross made trip after desperate trip to Cherokee sympathizers in Washington.

One of the Indians who was prodded toward a camp was Tsali, whom the whites called Charley. Tsali and his family were marching the first steps on the road to exile when one of Scott's soldiers prodded Tsali's wife with a bayonet for being too slow. Furious, Tsali watched and began laying plans for his escape. Deceived by his apparent meekness, the soldiers relaxed their vigilance that night. As noiselessly as a panther, Tsali crept through the dark, knifed the offending soldier, and then with his wife and children fled into the mountains of North Carolina. There, among evergreen laurels, azaleas, rhododendrons, and high pines, they found a cave where other families were hiding. By day the Indians stayed in the cave and listened to the slow dripping of a spring on eroding limestone rock. At night the men hunted and dug roots from stubbornly unyielding soil matted with the growth of its own richness.[11]

General Scott found his job as thankless as General Wool

had, but Scott was a master of compromise. He knew where the bands were hiding in Carolina, and considered them too few to bother about. What mattered was the main body of the tribe who stood defiantly on their home ground at the urgings of White Bird. Scott sent William Thomas—a Georgian who had been adopted by Yonaguska, old Drowning Bear—into Carolina to find Tsali and his sons and make them an offer. If they gave themselves up to be tried for the soldier's murder, Scott would ignore the rest of the Cherokees holed up in their mountain fastness. Thomas, long an intimate of Yonaguska, did not find it hard to locate the band of fugitives. When he made his offer Tsali listened; then, slowly, he nodded. He and his sons went with Thomas to Scott's headquarters. Because Tsali's youngest son was only a boy, Scott spared him. The other three sons and their father were shot by Scott's firing squad. They had proudly refused blindfolds. As one more humiliation, the firing squad consisted of Indians of the treaty party. But Scott was not without honor. He studiously ignored reports of Cherokees in North Carolina caves, while the half-starved Indians tenaciously clung to their rocky refuges in the Great Smokies. Because no white farmer wanted such steep land, they were allowed to remain. Gradually America forgot about them. The Indian menace was personified instead by John Ross.

In Georgia and northern Alabama, the spring of 1838 opened with rare beauty. Far away, in Indiana, the Little Duck was fighting for his Potawatomis. In the hills of the Southeast the sun shone brilliantly; there was no frost after March, and the robins returned early from Florida. Azaleas burned like golden fire in the hollows; the pale pink blooms of mountain laurels bobbed gently in soft winds. Warblers buzzed in the hickories and maples, and mockingbirds trilled. At night the world lay cradled in mist, and little screech owls hooted softly. Rivulets tumbled over stones, and waterfalls fell on banks of ferns. The forest floor was carpeted by wildflowers. Wild roses festooned the trees in white walls of fragrance. Cherokee children ran laughing in the squares of their villages as they chased each other in games. Men vied with each other in ball games.

Women spun and mended and washed while the men went into tribal fields to turn dark earth. "The Indians dance all night and are not preparing to move," reported a white farmer. "They say they prefer death to Arkansas." But in the midst of fertile mountains, Winfield Scott's soldiers were an unreal dream.

In Washington, John Ross, his brow damp with the sweat of anxiety, appeared before Congress to ask for a delayed removal. His people, he said, were neither physically nor emotionally ready. His requests were tabled. "Get the Indians out of Georgia, sir!" Martin Van Buren ordered Winfield Scott. It was a matter of chagrin that only two thousand Cherokees had moved into the Arkansas Territory. Fifteen thousand of them remained in the East. Everywhere in north Georgia and Alabama smoke wound upward from Cherokee chimneys as housewives baked bread and made soup. Bushes and briars were cleared from fence posts. William J. Cotter, who farmed near a Cherokee village, noted that the Indians were unusually industrious, and their corn was "planted better than ever," though the Cherokees had always been good farmers. Soldiers rode through the hills while red men planted the slopes with food. Stores of rations arrived at government warehouses in wooden crates, and Winfield Scott's men built twenty-three forts to be used in the work that lay ahead. All had stout pickets and blockhouses and were manned by militia standing stiffly at attention when they were not mopping wet foreheads with bandannas. In the lodges, ritual storytellers told and retold to dark-eyed children the old tales of earth's origin. Adawehis, the storytellers were called. "The earth is a great island floating in a sea of water," they said.

It is suspended at each of the four cardinal points by a cord hanging down from its sky vault, which is of solid rock. When all was water, the animals were above in *galun lati*, beyond the arch; but it was very much crowded, and they were wanting some more room. They wondered what was below the water, and at last Dayunisi, "Beaver's Grandchild," the little water-beetle, offered to go and see if he could learn. He darted in every direction over the surface of the water, but could find no place to rest. Then he dived to the bottom and came up with some soft mud, which began to grow and spread on every side until it became the island which we call the earth. It was afterwards fastened to the sky with four cords, but no one remembers who did this.

The world had been cold until the Thunders, who also lived in *galun lati*, sent their lightning and put fire into the bottom of a hollow sycamore tree that grew on an island. The animals knew it was there but were prevented from reaching it by the water. Raven tried to remove the fire but his feathers were scorched and turned black. Wa Huhu, the screech owl, got his eyes almost burned out. The eyes of Hooting Owl and Horned Owl became ringed with ashes they couldn't wipe away. Eventually the fire was captured by Water Spider, who from the secretions of her body spun a bowl in which to carry the fire. She brought a coal in the bowl which she balanced on her back while she swam. Ravens, owls, wolves, and water insects— everything in their universe had a place in Cherokee hearts. This was why they could not comprehend what Winfield Scott, the bushy-browed, six foot three giant in blue, had told their chiefs:

> The emigration must be commenced in haste. . . . The full moon of May is already on the wane, and before another shall have passed away every Cherokee man, woman and child must be in motion to join their brethren in the far West. . . . I come to carry out the determination. My troops already occupy many positions in the country that you are to abandon; thousands and thousands are approaching from every quarter, to make your residence and escape alike hopeless.
>
> Will you, then, by resistance compel us to resort to arms? . . . Will you . . . oblige us to hunt you down? . . . I am an old warrior, and have been present at many a scene of slaughter, but spare me . . . the horror of witnessing the destruction of the Cherokees.[12]

Since the tribe could read English, Scott had his speech printed on handbills with which his men marched into Cherokee farms. He instructed other soldiers in their forthcoming tasks: "Infants, superannuated persons, lunatics and women in a helpless condition will all, in the removal, require peculiar attention." He organized his men into squads, provided them with new rifles and sharpened bayonets, and ordered them to search out "every small cabin hidden away in the coves or by the sides of mountain streams, to seize and bring in as prisoners all the occupants." Doubtless the fugitives in North Carolina caves would die of starvation; there was no point in bothering about them. The Indians to be removed by force were those with long dinner tables and full larders. Officers instructed their men to wait until Cherokee families had gathered to dine and to surprise them by standing in the doorway with bayonets flashing in the setting sun. If the sight of the orange-gleaming bayonets didn't get immediate results, "oaths and blows" would.

When the capture of the Indians began, it took men from their fields, children from their play, and women from their kitchens. Two children fled into the woods ahead of the soldiers marching determinedly down red clay Georgia lanes. The troops seized the mother. She begged them to wait until she could find her children; she gave her word she would then come to the stockade. The soldiers ignored her. Other runaway children were herded into the removal camps without any of the authorities bothering to learn who their parents were. Families away on visits were not allowed to return home. A hunter, bringing home a deer, was seized and hauled into camp while the army of Winfield Scott distributed the venison among themselves. Occasionally, the soldiers whooped and roared as if they were driving cattle. Indians were pushed with bayonets into rivers with their shoes and stockings still on. The shoes were ruined, but no new ones were issued. Reporters from national newspapers could hardly believe the rumors that were filtering in from Georgia and went down to see for themselves.

"The scenes of distress at Ross's Landing," said *Niles' National Register*, "defy all description."

> On the arrival there of the Indians, the horses brought in by some of them were demanded by the commissioners of Indian property, to be given up for the purpose of being sold. The owners refusing to give them up—men, women, children *and horses* were driven promiscuously into one large pen, and the horses taken out by force and cried off to the highest bidder, *and sold for almost nothing.*

With unintentional irony, the government made John Ross superintendent of removal and subsistence. As superintendent of subsistence, let alone removal, he had his hands full. Some of his people refused to eat. Sometimes, turning back to look at their homes a last time, they saw their plantations and farm houses in flames, fired by Georgia citizens adept at pillage.[13] Sometimes the thieves and the soldiers clashed head-on as each sought to drive out his captives, animal and human. Women and children wept while silver pendants were pulled off their necks. The looters visited Cherokee graves and stripped exhumed corpses of the jewelry in which they had been buried.

The soldiers soon became adept at capture. They would surround a house, taking its inhabitants by surprise, and, if the Indians resisted, jab rifles and bayonets into their backs. One group of army regulars was indulgent; they permitted a family patriarch to pray with his relatives in Cherokee before dragging him to the stockade. A housewife begged for a few moments to feed her chickens for the last time; then she strapped her baby on her back and followed her husband with the soldiers. An Indian who struck a soldier he had seen stick a bayonet into a Cherokee woman was sentenced to a hundred lashes. General Scott explained that all the trouble came from the Indians' faith in John Ross, whom they had thought could save them. John Ridge, in exile in the West, said that Ross had lied to his people, which was why they were losing their property.

But the Cherokee Nation knew better; White Bird had tried until the end to save them, and they were unshaken now in their loyalty.

The *New York Observer* made daily reports: Indians were being "taken from their houses leaving their fields of corn, their cattle, horses, and most of their moveable property for any person who pleased to take it into possession." It was, said General Scott, "regrettable." Litanies of stolen goods read like household inventories: saddles, harnesses, rifles, hoes, ducks, geese, chickens, money, "grist mills, feather beds, blankets, quilts, pots, ovens, kettles, dishes, cups and saucers, knives and forks, pails, one set blue-edged plates . . . belonging to Elizabeth Cooper . . . bacons, potatoes, beans, salt, cabins, looms, shuttles, weavers' tools, spinning wheels, thread reel, bedstead, cherrywood table, chairs, cupboard, wooden spoons, ploughs, chains, baskets, a first-rate fiddle saw, shovel and carpenter tools."

The Reverend Evan Jones sent dispatches to the *Baptist Missionary Magazine* from Tennessee:

June 16. The Cherokees are nearly all prisoners. They had been dragged from their houses and encamped at the forts and military places, all over the nation. In Georgia especially, multitudes were allowed no time to take anything with them except the clothes they had on. . . . Females who have been habituated to comforts and comparative affluence are driven on foot before the bayonets of brutal men. Their feelings are mortified by vulgar and profane vociferations. It is a painful sight. The property of many has been taken and sold before their eyes for almost nothing—the sellers and buyers, in many cases, having combined to cheat the poor Indians. These things are done at the instant of arrest and consternation; the soldiers standing by, with their arms in hand, impatient to go on with their work, could give little time to transact business. The poor captive, in a state of distressing agitation, his weeping wife almost frantic with terror, surrounded by a group of crying, terrified children, without a friend to speak a consoling word, is in a poor condition to make a good disposition of his property, and in most

cases is stripped of the whole, at one blow. Many of the Cherokees who a few days ago were in comfortable circumstances are
now victims of abject poverty. . . . And this is not a description
of extreme cases. It is altogether a faint representation of the
work which has been perpetrated on the unoffending, unarmed,
and unresisting Cherokees. Our brother Bushyhead and his family . . . are here prisoners. . . . It is the work of war in time of
peace.[14]

The Reverend Jesse Bushyhead, a Baptist convert, led his flock
in prayer in the stockade into which they had been thrust.
Quatie, the ailing wife of John Ross, wept quietly but gathered
frightened children around her, trying to soothe them. One of
the Indians, William Shorey Coodey, found a pen and paper
and, as the Indians were being lined up and turned toward the
Arkansas Territory, wrote to his friend John Howard Payne:

At noon all was in readiness for moving. The teams were
stretched out in a line along a road through a heavy forest,
groups of persons formed about each wagon, others shaking the
hand of some sick friend or relative who would be left behind.
The temporary camp covered with boards and some of bark
that for three summer months had been their only shelter and
home, were crackling and falling under a blazing flame; the day
was bright and beautiful, but a gloomy thoughtfulness was de-
picted in the lineaments of every face. . . . At length the word
was given to move on. I glanced along the line and the form of
Going Snake, an aged and respected chief whose head eighty
summers had whitened, mounted on his favorite pony passed
before me and led the way in silence, followed by a number of
younger men on horseback. At this very moment a low sound of
distant thunder fell on my ear—in almost an exact western direction a dark spiral cloud was rising above the horizon and sent
forth a murmur I almost thought a voice of divine indignation
for the wrong of my poor and unhappy countrymen, driven by
brutal power from all they loved and cherished in the land of
their fathers to gratify the cravings of avarice. The sun was
unclouded—no rain fell—the thunder rolled away and seemed

hushed in the distance. The scene around and before me, and in the elements above, was peculiarly impressive and angular.[15]

Coodey estimated the number of his tribe that day at seventeen thousand. Now they began to move west, toward the setting sun, out of the pines and rocks and red clay of Georgia into a drought in Tennessee and Alabama where in hot, dried-out swamps the moss hung listlessly from high cypresses. From there they went into Kentucky and its grassy swards, the churning Ohio River, and more swamps, these swollen, in the southern tip of Illinois—then as now called Little Egypt because it contained the town of Cairo. Swamps bred fevers. The weakness bred by fevers bred in its turn measles, pleurisy, whooping cough, and biliousness. "They are dying like flies," reported white spectators who saw the weeping Cherokee Nation as it passed them. General Scott tried to contradict such news. "There is no more sickness among the Indians than might ordinarily take place amongst any other people under the same circumstances." He did not elaborate on what the "same circumstances" were.

In Georgia, General Charles Floyd, the militia officer assigned to supervise the removal in his state, wrote triumphantly to the governor who had succeeded Wilson Lumpkin:

> I have the pleasure to inform your excellency that I am now fully convinced there is not an Indian within the limits of my command, except a few in my possession who will be sent to Ross's Landing tomorrow. My scouting parties have scoured the whole country without seeing an Indian, or late Indian signs. If there are any stragglers in Georgia, they must be in Union and Gilmer counties, and near the Tennessee and North Carolina line, but none can escape the vigilance of our troops. Georgia is ultimately in possession of her rights in the Cherokee country.[16]

The idea that in a hundred and forty years Georgia would be begging her Cherokees to return—for the sake of tourism—on a "Trail of Cheers" occurred, naturally enough, to no one.

But not all the Indians had left Georgia. Many compassionate white families suddenly acquired relatives with what looked like deep suntans. Who would question a white man's word about his Auntie Nancy, recently come to live with her nephew?[17] Cherokees who escaped the rifle and bayonet of the United States Army under General Winfield Scott had to cease to exist as Cherokees. But, inwardly, spiritually and emotionally, they remembered. Their descendants remember still.

The drought of summer continued, corn crops were light, and the bellies of Cherokee children became distended with famine. The drought continued, except in isolated spots, into a torrid autumn; Indians and cattle died daily. Some of the men met death dressed in the turbans of their chieftaincy. Others, stripped by poverty and suffering, met it nearly naked. Rivers and streams dried up leaving the Indians thirsty. Jesse Bushyhead prayed each day for rain, but his prayers remained unanswered. Some oxen died from eating poisonous weeds.

It was November when one party of Cherokees reached the Mississippi. Another had still to cross the Tennessee and the Cumberland. "It was like the march of any army," a witness said. "Regiment after regiment, the wagons in the center, the officers along the line and the horsemen on the flanks and at the rear." Chief White Path was dying; Nocowee drank himself into oblivion, but not before "our police had to drive him along the road sometimes fettered." The grog shops had set up portable quarters. Indians complaining they had been robbed were informed of a recent federal appointment. The gentleman to whom to apply for redress, by correspondence from the West, would be the Honorable Wilson Lumpkin, of Georgia. The proprietors of toll bridges upped their prices and charged every Cherokee who crossed. Some demanded money for horses and pigs. "They fleeced us," said Jesse Bushyhead simply. "We have a large number of sick and very many extremely aged and infirm persons."[18]

Nashville, Tennessee, watched the Cherokees pass. So, perhaps, did Jacksa Chula Harjo, the elder statesman at the Hermitage. Did he see John Ross on his mount, a fading Quatie at his side? The winter set in as icy cold as the summer had been hot. Sleet stiffened bare trees while tubercular Indians died beneath them. A child, sick and a victim of pellagra, cried, begging for warmth. Quatie Ross gave the child her blanket, although she herself had a cold. The child survived; Quatie Ross's cold became pneumonia. She lasted until Little Rock, where John Ross saw her body dumped into a tiny cemetery grave. Now, he was alone. The White Bird would exist from henceforth as the leader of a displaced people, husband and lover no more.

Later the full-bloods told how it was: "Long time we travel on way to new land. People feel bad when they leave old nation. Womens cry and make sad wails. Children cry and many men cry, and all look sad like when friends die, but they say nothing and just put heads down and keep on go towards West. Many days pass and people die very much. We bury close by trail."[19]

The father of one such full-blood fell dead in the snow. A week later the mother collapsed. "She speak no more. We bury her and go on." All five of the full-blood's brothers and sisters fell sick and died. "One each day. Then all are gone." Wind swept high snows down from Canada. "Maybe we all be dead before we reach new country." Later, he told a historian: "People sometimes say I look like I never smile, never laugh in lifetime." A physician said he himself was living close to death. A traveler from Maine passed a camp of Cherokees many of whom "were in the last struggles of death." The wind keened, and snowclouds obscured a cold moon:

Aged females, apparently nearly ready to drop into the grave, were traveling with heavy burdens attached to the back—on the frozen ground . . . with no covering for the feet except what nature had given them. We learned from the inhabitants on the road where the Indians passed that they buried fourteen or fifteen at every stopping place. . . . When the Sabbath came, they must stop, and not merely stop—they must worship the Great Spirit too.

"Your country," said an old chief, "your country no do me justice now." A woman carried her sick three-month-old child until it died; she was allowed just enough time to bury it before she was prodded on. The man from Maine watched it all, unbelieving at first:

> When I passed the last detachment of those suffering exiles and thought that my native countrymen had thus expelled them from their native soil and their much loved homes, and that too in this inclement season of the year in all their suffering, I turned from the sight with feelings which language cannot express and "wept like childhood then." . . . When I read in the President's Message that he was happy to inform the Senate that the Cherokees were peaceably and without reluctance removed —and remember that it was on the third day of December when not one of the detachments had reached their destination, and that a large majority had not even made half their journey when he made that declaration, I thought I wished the President could have been there that very day in Kentucky with myself, and have seen the comfort and the willingness with which the Cherokees were making their journey.[20]

On this journey, a quarter of the Cherokee Nation died. In the Arkansas Territory at last, in the southeast part of modern Oklahoma, White Bird stood in solitude to survey what would be his new fields. Quatie slept in Little Rock. His people slept all along the road out of the green Southeast on what they called, simply, "The Trail Where We Cried." He would always hear the sound of their grief. He would also hear the stern rasp of Jacksa Chula Harjo: "I will not go to war for you, John Ross. It's too damned late."

John Ridge had already settled near Honey Creek, on the Cherokee line which defined the Missouri-Arkansas boundary. When he and the Ridge and their families had arrived, Honey Creek had been "an entire wilderness." But the creek flowed swiftly and transparently into the Neosho River, and its banks were laden with flowering Judas. Honey Creek was fertile.

Some of it was forest, full of persimmons, oaks, sassafras, and cedars; in the bottomlands elms and cottonwoods waved their leaves in the western winds. Hardest to break was the prairie sod, thick with the toughly matted roots of buffalo grass. But the Ridge family already had the beginnings of "a splendid farm." The $25,000 spent for equipment ordered from New York had helped; the Ridges' assets had not been plundered in Georgia.

The Ridge and his son were sensitive about their stand on the Schermerhorn Treaty. They believed they had acted in the best interests of the Cherokees. "You say John Ridge was prompted by a selfish ambition when he signed the treaty," John wrote a detractor.

It is not so. John Ridge signed his death warrant when he signed that treaty, and no one knows it better than he. . . . John Ridge may not die tomorrow . . . but sooner or later he will have to yield his life as the penalty for signing. John Ridge has not acted blindly, for he sees plainly that his people cannot hope to stand against the white man in their present situation. . . . Let it not be said that John Ridge acted from motives of ambition, for he acted for what he believed to be the best interests of his people.

For a cloud hung over Honey Creek. The Ridge and John had not forgotten the Cherokee Blood Law. To comfort themselves as they waited for reprisal they reread the letter to John from Wilson Lumpkin: "To comand a sufficient stock of reason, fortitude and energy to overcome not only the prepossessions of our minds in favor of our native land, but to be the leader and guide of a whole nation in making a similar sacrifice . . . requires the most lofty efforts of man. Sir, you have made this sacrifice. You have made this effort in the face of death."[21]

John Ridge was wary as he rode around his new property, or when he left home to visit old Cherokee friends like James Rogers, who had once lived on the Chattahoochee, but was well contented with his new acreage with its deep black topsoil. Other members of the Rogers family would also learn to love Oklahoma—especially, nearly a century later, Will.

The Cherokees who had gone west with Tahlonteskee years before—the Old Settlers—did not resent the Ridge and his son. They couldn't understand why Elias Boudinot was working with a missionary to translate the Bible into Cherokee, but that, they believed, was Boudinot's business. What the Old Settlers did mind was the coming of the Late Immigrants. They were mollified only when White Bird and his followers agreed to live under the government the Old Settlers had already established. At Double Springs, near present-day Tahlequah, more than six thousand Cherokees met to sign a compact. The Ridge, John Ridge, Boudinot, and his brother Stand Watie came to watch the proceedings. But when they appeared, both Old Settlers and Late Immigrants muttered uneasily and the Treaty Party quickly left. They did not hear White Bird vow to sue the United States for the spoliations it had committed, nor did they witness the arguments that erupted over who was now the Cherokees' principal chief. The meeting broke up before any agreement between the west and east factions was ever signed.

Later, some of White Bird's followers recalled that they had seen the Ridge, John Ridge, and Boudinot talking to the western chiefs. Was the Treaty Party going to make havoc in the West, too? White Bird pleaded with the Late Immigrants to forget the Treaty Party. But tempers ran high, even as grief over Cherokee deaths ran deep. Unknown to White Bird, some of his councillors gathered in a secret meeting. Before it was over they had invoked the Blood Law. John Ridge had committed the offense of an unsanctioned sale of his Georgia land—an offense which, ironically, he had originally defined. Therefore, John Ridge must die, and with him his father, Elias Boudinot, Stand Watie, and several others who had followed Treaty Party policies. Three men from the clan of each absent defendant were summoned to sit in judgment. His own Deer Clan condemned the Ridge. Numbers were placed in a hat by each man present. Twelve of the numbers had an X mark after the number, which indicated executioners. Each man was instructed to draw. Young Allen Ross, White Bird's son, was there, and agreed to keep his father busy enough "to keep him from finding out what was being done."[22]

In the still western darkness, the executioners mounted their horses. The occasional cry of a whippoorwill and the beat of hooves broke the heavy silence. When the sun rose red and low in a June morning mist, the murder party reached John Ridge's house and surrounded it. Three of the men forced the lock of the front door and crept inside. They heard the deep breathing of a family asleep as they passed the bedrooms noiselessly. They were interested in only one sleeper. When they found him, they swiftly fired a pistol at his head. The pistol failed to discharge. Then they grabbed John Ridge who woke in his death struggle. But he was a small-framed, slender man. His captors dragged him into the yard; two men held his arms, and others held his body. The murderers stabbed him until blood poured from twenty-five wounds. By this time his terrified family had gathered. The Indians cut his jugular vein, and when the body had fallen to the ground, each executioner stepped on it contemptuously. But John Ridge was not yet dead. When the assassins had departed, he raised himself on his elbow and tried to speak. What poured from his mouth was a stream not of words but of blood. After he fell back dead, his wife, Sarah, and his son, John Rollin, carried his body into the parlor. The Ridge's wife, John's mother, was staying in the house. When she saw the corpse she loosed her long white hair and tore at it, wailing the ancient lamentations of her race. In the yard a gloating crowd who listened to the old woman's grief unmoved began to assemble.

The second band of executioners hid in a thick cluster of trees near the house Elias Boudinot was building. When he arrived to begin work, the men told him that their families were sick and they needed medicine; Boudinot, who was in charge of "public medicines," did not suspect them. When he turned toward the house, one man stabbed him in the back. He screamed and fell, and another assailant split his head open with a tomahawk. Six times they struck his skull until his brains were running into the prairie grass.

A Choctaw who was clearing land nearby watched in horror. Then Boudinot's colleague, the missionary Samuel Worcester, ran toward him. Worcester told him to mount a horse the Choctaw would find in Worcester's barn and to go warn Stand Watie. The horse's name was Comet, and it streaked to the store Watie had opened. Inside, the Choctaw asked to talk to Watie about some sugar he needed. When they were together in a corner, the Choctaw poured out his tale. Watie pressed the Choctaw's hand and left to make his escape on Comet.

The third band of murderers visited the Ridge near the cabin of one of his slaves, who was sick. They waited until the Ridge came riding down a small path with a black boy in attendance. Twelve times they shot their rifles into him, until he fell to the dust and his horse began to rear and plunge over his corpse. Ka-nun-da-cla-geh's body was trampled into shaplelessness.

So began years of murders among the Cherokee factions. Killing raged across the land "like a Corsican vendetta."[23] Stand Watie had been put on his guard. His men slaughtered and were slaughtered in turn. Watie eluded the fate of the Ridges and Boudinot while the great Sequoyah counseled the Cherokees to declare an amnesty on both sides. White Bird watched in sorrow as his people refused. Ahead lay not only the Cherokees' but the American Civil War and Stand Watie's disastrous adherence to the Confederate Army, in which he became a brigadier general. White Bird remained loyal to the very Union that had betrayed him, and still begging for reparations, died in Washington. With his passing, the Cherokees realized they had lost a statesman. Grieving, they united at last under a full-blood chief named Louis Downing and began to restore to their shattered tribe the glory which had once belonged to it, before the vendettas and the Trail of Tears. Perhaps some of them remembered John Ridge's schoolboy poem written after the Ridge, dashing in gold lace and a polished carriage, had delivered him to his mission school in Connecticut:

> *Withers the rose, the blossom blasts,*
> *The flower fades, the morning hastes,*
> *The sun is set, shadows fly,*
> *The gourd consumes—so mortals die.*

All of the western Cherokees did not die, and many survived in North Carolina, but their Golden Age was at an end.

Asi-Yaholo Makes a Promise

"They are taking us beyond Miami,
They are taking us beyond the Calusa River,
They are taking us to the end of our tribe . . .
They are taking us to an old town in the west."
—SEMINOLE
Song of the Removal to Oklahoma

Among all the Indian nations of North America, the Seminoles of Florida were unique. They had never elected their identity as a tribe. History had elected their identity for them. When they emerged as a people at the close of the eighteenth century, it was as a response to white pressure. But white America was not long in learning what it had wrought in the Seminoles. By the time the beleaguered Cherokees were dying their way westward, the Seminoles were gathering in Florida's steaming swamps, from where they mounted successive attacks on the invading United States Army in the naïve belief that they could win a war with Behemoth. It was their turn to be rounded up and marched west, but they were not surrendering.

Florida's reputation in general was sinister. Mad John Randolph of Roanoke had told a congressional colleague sanely enough: "If I were given the choice of emigrating to Florida or to Hell, Sir, why then, Sir, I should choose Hell." Florida was malaria, cottonmouth moccasins, and huge rattlesnakes whose scales glittered in cruel sunlight; it was dengue fever, often symptomless until it struck its victim suddenly unconscious. It was long rainy seasons and the attendant mold that rotted food stores. It was trackless forests green with dark leaves and red with a sun like a giant bloodstone; it was the cacophony of panthers, and the glut of choking vines. But America meant to tame it and its inhabitants. The Seminoles, according to the Americans, had learned to live in Florida only during the past century, and had to be driven out.

It was true that the Seminoles were not the Florida peninsula's original inhabitants. Conquistadores early in the sixteenth century had found Apalachees in western Florida, Timucuas east of the Aucilla River down to Tampa Bay, and warlike Calusas in the Everglades. Smaller tribes like the Ais and Tequestas fought for their existence among the larger groups. It took the Spanish exactly two centuries virtually to extinguish Florida's aboriginal life. When Florida passed into the hands of the British in 1763, the remaining Indians fled with the retreating Spanish: 83 from St. Augustine, 80 families from southern Florida, and 108 converted Catholic Yamassee and Apalachees from the roistering port of Pensacola on the upper Gulf Coast. These Indians were all that remained of an original population of 25,000.

As the eighteenth century opened, Florida was on its way to becoming a no man's land except for scattered whites along its east coast. But venturesome Creeks were soon filling the vacuum; these *siminoli* (exiles, wanderers) moved in to hunt the deer and bears and wildcats that Apalachees and Timucuas had hunted before them. They planted patches of beans and corn and yellow-blossomed squash. Splinter groups joined them: Carolina Yamassees pursued by Cherokees, Oconees from central Georgia, Apalachicolas and Chiahas from the vast coastal oyster beds of the northern Gulf. These last two groups established a town in northern Florida they called Mikasuki; they became strong and prosperous, and of all the tribes of the peninsula they were easily the most formidable. They spoke Hitchiti, a Creek dialect related to the Muskogee dialect of the Upper Creeks but different enough from it so that a Hitchiti-speaking Indian could not understand his Muskogee kinsman.

After the middle of the eighteenth century, Muskogeans arrived in droves to join the Hitchiti-speakers. After them came Yuchis from Georgia and the Carolinas; these Indians spoke neither Muskogee nor Hitchiti, but shared the dominant culture of the Southeast: war towns and peace towns, descent reckoned through the female line, the religious beliefs most splendidly expressed in the annual Green Corn Ceremony with its sacred fire and measured dancing.

In the beginning the term "Seminole" was applied by whites to bands who roamed the pine forests and prairies of modern Alachua County in north central Florida. But the usage spread until Americans considered Seminoles any Indians found in Spanish Florida. After Red Eagle's defeat at Horseshoe Bend, the Americans lumped fleeing Creek Red Sticks with the Seminole Nation too. When Andrew Jackson came marauding into Florida to take it from Spain, he fought what later became known as the Seminole War. It kept the name until the middle of the 1830s, when it was changed to the First Seminole War to distinguish its scattered raids and counterraids from the gargantuan bloodletting of the second.

The Seminoles considered the roughly one hundred years of their occupancy of Florida enough to make Florida the land of their ancestors. "Here our navel strings were first cut," they said, "and the blood from them sunk into the earth to make the country dear to us." They knew how it came to be that the white man had schools and books and the Seminoles did not. Long ago the Great Spirit had created a blind old man and had put a book in his hands. The old man had called together the red man and the white and told them: "This book, and the learning it represents, shall go to the first people to kill a deer and bring it to me." The Indians and whites set forth. Deer were very scarce that season, and the Indians had to wander far in their search. The whites found a sheep close by and killed it. They quickly brought it back to the blind man, who could not see their deception, and gave the whites the book. As with most other things whites possessed, said the Seminoles, they had come by literacy through treachery. They valued possessions and used people; Indians valued people and used possessions.

The problems of the Seminoles in Florida were complicated by an additional element: blacks. Years before the American Revolution, slaves belonging to Indians and whites in Georgia and the Carolinas had fled their owners for the refuge of non-American land. They were joined by an ever-increasing stream of their fellows until, by the nineteenth century, Yankee abolitionists were calling them the "Exiles of Florida." The Seminoles, technically their new owners, held them in an easy captivity consisting only of close association and a tiny yearly tribute of food, cattle, and pelts. When America became a nation, the federal government tried to placate irate Georgia and Carolina slaveholders by demanding that the Seminoles yield up their Negroes.

Sometimes the Americans went on raids. On one occasion, more than three hundred terrified blacks, two hundred of them women and children, set up defenses on the Apalachicola

River. Carolina General Duncan Clinch bombarded them until a witness could write:

> The explosion was awful and the scene horrible beyond description. You cannot conceive, nor I describe, the horrors of the scene. In an instant hundreds of lifeless bodies were stretched upon the plain, buried in sand and rubbish, or suspended from the tops of the surrounding pines. Here lay an innocent babe, there a helpless mother; on the one side a sturdy warrior, on the other a bleeding squaw. Piles of bodies, large heaps of sand, broken guns, accoutrements, etc., covered the site of the fort.[1]

The carnage did not stop more blacks from escaping into Florida. When the United States gained its subtropic booty from a debilitated Spain, it decided it was high time to treat with its newest red men. Commissioners arrived at vine-banked Moultrie Creek, a few miles south of St. Augustine, where they were met by the same Neamathla whom Jacksa Chula Harjo had evicted from Tallahassee. The commissioners were businesslike. They demanded that the Seminoles yield up their blacks and vacate all lands on the fertile riverbottoms of north Florida for interior woodlands below Tampa Bay.

Neamathla protested reasonably at first: "We rely on your justice and humanity. We hope that you will not send us south to a country where neither the hickorynut, the acorn, nor the persimmon grows; we depend much on these productions of the forest for food; in the south they are not to be found." The Indians needed nuts to make oil. But Neamathla could not save at Moultrie Creek what he had not been able to save earlier in Tallahassee. When, under coercion, he touched the goose quill to paper, he promised to prevent runaway slaves from joining his people and to trek south to the pinewoods near Tampa Bay, on the shores of which Hernando de Soto had long ago landed and begun exterminating its earlier inhabitants. The United States gave the Seminoles six thousand dollars' worth of livestock and the principal chiefs—Neamathla, Tuski Harjo, Econchattemicco, Blount, Mulatto King, and Emathlochee—annual annuities of five thousand dollars.

The commissioners had never seen the land near Tampa Bay, and when William DuVal, the Seminole agent, went down to examine it he was "depressed."

> I suffered much from drinking water alive with insects, from mosquitoes, intolerable hot weather, and my horses were reduced by the journey. . . . I have never seen a more wretched tract. . . . I entered a low wet piney country spotted with numerous ponds; I had much difficulty to pass through them, although the season has been uncommonly dry. . . . No settlement can ever be made in this region, and there is no land in it worth cultivation . . . the most miserable and gloomy prospect I ever beheld.[2]

Most of the Indians refused to budge from north Florida and continued to welcome black fugitives. Whites poured into Florida to begin beating and killing the Seminoles, slaughtering their stock, and setting fire to their villages. The Indians retaliated with murderous raids of their own. By the time the Indian Removal Act was law, the Indians were scattered far and wide, living on roots and cabbage palm hearts that they hacked down in swamps impenetrable to all but themselves. Game was retreating before the white onslaught. An Indian agent reported to his superiors:

> There is not at this moment . . . a bushel of corn in the whole nation, or any adequate substitute for it. The coontie and briar root . . . are almost entirely consumed. . . . What they are to do another year I cannot imagine. They have not corn for this year's need nor can I procure it for them. . . . The situation of some of these people is wretched, almost beyond description, those particularly who . . . were robbed of their guns have been absolutely famishing.

Seminoles died of hunger as most of the tribes of eastern North America had before them. How could they go west if they were naked, chiefs asked when they were told about the wonders of the Indian Territory? By 1832, at Payne's Landing, near the broad Alachua Savannah, the United States was negotiating a fresh treaty: if the Seminoles wanted blankets to cover themselves, they would have to remove to Arkansas. If the chiefs refused, their annuities would be handed over to Georgia's Creeks. A delegation might go to far Fort Gibson by way of Little Rock. Then, said the treaty, if "they"—meaning the Seminole Indians as a people—were satisfied with the delegation's report, they would start leaving Florida. One of the authors of the treaty was none other than the Reverend Mr. Schermerhorn. He and his colleagues decided on a slight change in the wording: "should they be satisfied" was altered to "should this delegation be satisfied."

At one of the meetings between the Indians and the commissioners a new chief appeared. "The only treaty I will ever make is this!" he shouted as he hurled his knife into the table that separated him from the Americans. "I will make the white man red with blood. I will blacken him in the sun and the rain, where the wolf shall smell of his bones and the buzzard live upon his flesh."[3] This was no elderly Neamathla. Asi-Yaholo, "Cryer of the Black Drink," was a young mixed-blood—part Scottish, part Englishman, and part Creek. He had cast his lot with the Seminoles of Florida and already held a subordinate chieftainship. Beside him the present head chief, fat, rumsoaked old Micanopy, was a joke. Americans who saw Asi-Yaholo acknowledged the formidable presence of the young man they called Osceola.

Negotiations with the Seminoles were particularly tortuous because of their principal interpreters, two blacks named Abraham and King Cudjoe. Abraham, tall and courteous, the squint in his right eye the only outward sign of his skepticism of white overtures, had won his freedom from a Seminole owner by virtue of services to the tribe on a previous delegation to Washington. The black was, in fact, sufficiently pokerfaced to convince whites and Indians alike that he was looking after their respective interests, although he and Chief Micanopy were intimates.

Cudjoe was called King in derision by the whites; he had

Osceola. Portrait by George Catlin. *Courtesy Smithsonian Institution, Washington, D.C.*

suffered some paralysis on the right side of his body and as a result walked with a deliberate, regal step. Not only did the Americans not understand the Hitchiti and Muskogee dialects of the Seminole dignitaries, but they did not always understand Abraham and Cudjoe's plantation-African speech rich with deep accents from far-off tribal brethren: Ibos, Egbas, Ashantis, and Senegalese. Because it was foreign, Americans dismissed it as ignorant.

When the chiefs had spoken, one of the Americans asked: "What's he say, Cudjoe?"

"He say he no go, he like this country very well, he born here, he not like to leave in his old age. He say Micanopy sent him to say so, and he also say he thought when last war hatchet was buried, you promised him no more trouble to his children. . . . If he say 'Dig up de hatchet' he is ready, he fear not death, it is his duty to die for his people."

"Tell him, Cudjoe," said the agent, "if he breaks his word with us I shall be obliged to call upon the white warriors to force him."

When a semicomprehending Indian laughed outright, the negotiating agent begged in frustration: "What's he say, Cudjoe?"

"He say talk not to him of war! Is he a child that he fear it? No! He say when he bury the hatchet, he place it deep in the earth with a heavy stone over it, but he say he can soon unearth it for the protection of his people. When he look upon the white man's warriors, he sorry to injure them, but he cannot fear them, he has fought them before, he will do so again, if his people say fight."

"What's he say, Cudjoe? Abraham, what's he say?" was a plaintive echo from both sides as they moved ever closer toward confrontation. X's signed at Payne's Landing belonged to Indians who, as usual, did not understand what they were signing. Full of government food, they even prepared an entertainment for their defrauders: a war dance, under oaks laden with pale green Spanish moss that moved gently in the rippling heat generated by Indian council fires. The Seminoles appeared in what finery they had left. A single warrior sprang into the center of the dance with a shrill cry and began whirling round and round. A sudden whoop preceded a low ritual moan as the rest of the tribe began dancing the rhythmic steps of accompaniment and the warriors twisted and stamped. An Englishman present was startled by the war cries, which reminded him of "murder and bloody deeds—of Irish cries."[4]

The Englishman was moved by the speech of Jumper, Micanopy's austere brother-in-law. His nation, Jumper said, was like a tree of the forest. The branches were children; the leaves, the hair on the head; the sap, the blood; and the bark, the clothing.

> If you then spoil the tree of its bark, will it not die? There is nothing to carry the nourishing sap to support the branches. And if you lop off the branches, will they not die also? Such then is the case with my people. Take them from their forests and woods, where from childhood they have wandered, will they not pine and die also? If you sow the seeds of disaffection among them, will they not devour each other? If by force you separate them, obliging them to go to the distant land, will they not long to be again with their friends and fathers?

Florida itself, the terrible and poetry-laden country of dreaming, treacherous morasses, heightened the drama of the Seminole gatherings. Firelight played on high pines and massive oaks, leopard frogs called at night, and by day the rain crows lamented. Alligators lumbered over decaying logs into sulphurous depths. And red men stood before it all implacable, their voices charged with lyric tragedy as they spoke of its holiness.

The party of Indians who explored the proposed Seminole reservation in the Arkansas Territory was composed of Jumper, a chief named Tsali Emathla who was old and inclined to favor removal because it meant peace, Coee Harjo and Tsali Emathla's brother, Holata Emathla, Yaharjo and John Hicks and

Nehathloco. With them went "their faithful interpreter, Abraham." John Hicks, an immense Mikasuki chief, was grudgingly described by an American as "one of nature's noblemen."

The delegation reached Little Rock by steamboat in the autumn of 1832. There government representatives gave them horses and they proceeded across low hills and bare oak thickets to Fort Gibson. The government had been thoughtful: their friend the Reverend Mr. Schermerhorn was waiting for them at the fort, where he presented them with a piece of paper to be signed as a mere formality.[5] The tired explorers signed, not knowing it was a report on the new country, which they had not even seen. But they found out about some of that country's features soon enough. A party of resident Creeks took them on a buffalo hunt across the straw-brown plains and showed them the "marauding Indians of the prairies"—Kiowas, Comanches, Sioux, Osages, Wichitas. The Creeks might be willing to share the austere grasslands with these death-dealing nomads; the Seminoles were not. These people stole horses, Jumper protested; did the government think his people, too, were thieves? The country was not bad, but its denizens were impossible. When Mr. Schermerhorn amiably pointed out to the Seminole delegates that they had just signed the Treaty of Fort Gibson, they were dumbfounded. Schermerhorn told them that the Treaty of Payne's Landing was formally in effect because the delegation had said it approved of the western land. The Seminoles had to leave Florida.

The Seminoles in Florida flared up in protest when they heard the news. Their tempers did not improve when it was discovered that their agent, John Phagan, had absconded with some tribal funds. How could the swindle of a few chiefs at Fort Gibson bind a nation? Osceola's voice rang louder and louder in musty fort council rooms, his shoulders squared and his mouth contemptuous. His warnings were explicit. "When I make up my mind," he said, "I act. If I speak, what I say I will do. If the hail rattles, let the flowers be crushed. The oak of the forest will lift up its head to the sky and the storm, towering and unscathed." Now the oak stood ready. Between it and the coming storm stood only one man, Phagan's successor, General Wiley Thompson. The first mistake he made at the tiny post of Fort King in central Florida cost his country years of an unjust and desperate war that deeply drained its resources. When Osceola threw a laughing insult at Thompson during a conference, the hot-tempered Thompson ordered him thrown in irons in the fort stockade. Osceola at first railed in humiliation and spleen, then was silent. Some older chiefs visited Thompson and persuaded him to release Osceola. Smiling blandly, Osceola said his heart had changed and he was sorry. Thompson, who was not only impetuous but slow-witted said, "I now have no doubt of his sincerity." With regard to Seminole emigration, the "greatest difficulties have been surmounted." Did Osceola's smile not grow broader and broader every time he came to call?

Wiley Thompson was a career officer who had been born in Virginia and had emigrated to Georgia. He knew the subtropics and their heat, the ruthless mosquitoes that stung perspiring faces, the mildew that ate military boots and saddles, the sickly odor of the broad lagoons. He had emerged from the War of 1812 as a major, and had subsequently served Georgia in Congress. In his fifty-second year he was gray-haired and weakened from repeated bouts of malaria, but he was a man of honor who wanted to serve his country and his God. He would treat the Seminoles in as "fair and Christian" a fashion as possible. He did not yet understand the principles of Christian treaty making as well as Mr. Schermerhorn, nor did he understand Christian removal as well as the leaders of the Choctaws and Senecas, but he found himself drawn to the vigor and physical presence of Osceola, whose head was decked in egret plumes and whose wide shoulders carried their buckskins well.

The second mistake General Wiley Thompson made at remote Fort King was to be lonely and to want a friend. Incredibly, he picked Osceola and even ordered a hand-carved rifle for the young chieftain from merchants in Savannah. He told them not to stint on its workmanship, for he was willing to pay. When the rifle arrived, he sent for Osceola and presented him with it.

Osceola stared. He fingered the darkly shining rifle stock, his features motionless. Thompson was smiling. When at last Osceola's eyes met the agent's, he said levelly: "Thank you. I will use it well." And General Wiley Thompson congratulated himself for having won a worthy friend at the same time that he had served his country. It merely remained to persuade Osceola and the rest of the Seminole chiefs that the treaties of Moultrie Creek, Payne's Landing, and Fort Gibson were all binding, and that the nation must vanish across the broad, silted Mississippi into the country of the Comanches and Kiowas—as unwanted guests of the western Creeks.

Along the southern frontier of the United States, the news that the Seminoles were about to emigrate spread like a tidal wave. Florida was soon to be "relieved of Indians" forever. Crowds of speculators and would-be squatters gathered along the Suwannee Valley, waiting to rush into Seminole strongholds. Some couldn't wait.

One afternoon a party of six Seminoles set out for Deadman's Pond, at the edge of the Alachua Savannah. Along the way they had slaughtered one of the tribe's own cows and in camp were preparing to cook it over a slow hickory fire. While the beef was being turned on the spit, a gang of whites burst into the thicket, seized the Indians' rifles, tore open their traveling packs, and began beating the Indians until huge welts were raised on their backs and blood poured from open flesh. At this juncture four Seminoles arrived to join their fellows for the barbecue; when they saw what was happening they fired their own rifles; the whites shot one of them and severely wounded another. The whites made their escape with all the guns, the ammunition, and the Indians' baggage in hand. This incident was condemned as another bloody Seminole raid, and a party of Florida militia hastened into the field. The general feeling was the more the Seminoles were hounded, the quicker they would leave. But the persecution did not have quite the anticipated effect. The Indians did not start loading baggage wagons for a journey to Oklahoma. Instead, they smouldered with resentment. Wiley Thompson merely noted that Osceola, as usual, was very polite whenever he came to Fort King.[6]

To the southwest, on Tampa Bay, stood the larger barracks of Fort Brooke, named for the United States officer who had originally seized its buildings from the legal owner, a man named Hackley, who had fondly believed he might keep his newly built plantation house even when the army wanted it. He had been wrong, though he continued to sue. Fort Brooke officers drilled where the Hackley family had planted fields of cotton and corn, and maintained a careful correspondence with Fort King. Fort Brooke was also making orderly preparations to remove the Seminole tribe in the near future by steamboats bound for New Orleans, the first stage of the journey to the West. The military were gathering sacks of weevily flour, barrels of mildewed grain, and sides of dried meat for the travelers. The state of the provisions shocked no one, for the men of Fort Brooke were not used to much better. Florida's climate was not conducive to the preservation of food. Fort Brooke did, however, have stern principles of hygiene when they could be enforced. The post doctor had specified that no more than fourteen men were to use the same toothbrush.

One of the soldiers enjoying such medical supervision was Private Kinsley Dalton, a slight youngster fond of making jokes, who often said he preferred the rough life of the Florida wilds to that of the barracks. Kinsley Dalton's job was to carry the mail back and forth between Fort Brooke and Fort King. On a sultry August afternoon, in a cypress swamp along the military road up from Tampa Bay, Dalton found himself surrounded by a party of Indians. One of them roughly grasped his mule's bridle while another shot him from his saddle. The rest tore at his uniform, lifted his scalp deftly with keen knives, and ripped open his belly. When his corpse was found several days later, it was so bloated identification was difficult. Fort Brooke friends who had often laughed at his camp sallies buried him in the Florida woods, covering his grave with debris to protect his body from further violation by wolves. When Wiley

Thompson heard of the murder, he was hopeful that one of the rifles involved had not been a finely carved present for a young Seminole chief.

When Washington pressed him for a report on Seminole strength, he tried to reassure them. The entire nation, including its Negroes, certainly numbered no more than three thousand, he said, and over half were females; he doubted if the Seminoles could muster more than a thousand warriors. And then a band of Seminole braves killed old Tsali Emathla, who had favored removal, on his way to beg rations at Fort Brooke. He was shot down in the presence of his daughters, no more to wonder sadly what he could, and could not, take with him to the West. The old man's last sight was of Osceola, his dark head raised proudly against a burning sky, his carved rifle smoking in his hand. Osceola let the girls escape. They were soon sobbing out that he had killed their father. He did not care. A reputation as a killer would, he thought, be useful.

When Wiley Thompson heard the news, he did not at first believe it. But the girls had seen Osceola and described the rifle; Thompson had to believe it. Bitterly he wrote to Washington: "The consiquences [sic] resulting from this murder leave no doubt that actual force must be resorted to for the purpose of effecting removal, as it has produced a general defection." Wiley Thompson was awakening to the knowledge that the Seminoles had actually refused to leave. He began to fear as well that Osceola's carved rifle might find another victim at Fort King. He scribbled out a hasty request to the commandant at Fort Brooke for reinforcements. His little stockade, mosquito-ridden and tangled with brush, was not well manned. If "the natural propensities of the savages" made the Indians attack, the defenders—himself among them—would be killed in an hour or two.

Leading the expedition along the Fort Brooke–Fort King Road was handsome Major Francis Langhorne Dade, astride his horse, Richard III. In quieter times, Dade had raced the horse in camp contests. Dade's men found their major a stirring figure. His fair hair shone in the sun; at his side the scabbard of his sword glistened. Major Dade, whose kinsmen were among the First Families of Virginia, was confident that no savage could outsmart him. He would have four rivers to cross on the way to Fort King: the Big Hillsborough, the Little Hillsborough, and the north and south branches of the Withlacoochee which the Seminoles called We-wa-thlock-o. His path led along the edge of one of the most formidable wildernesses in North America, the Green Swamp—thick with cypresses, water oaks, and pines; leathery green vines festooned the treetops as Major Dade stared upward. In the palmettos, wild orchids spilled racemes of creamy blooms. How many Seminoles waited for him in the Green Swamp, it was only natural for him and his men to wonder.

Osceola knew that December as *hailing ci*, the Moon of Birds and Fish Frozen. In winter there were usually some nights when chill winds swept down to Florida from continental America; the birds and fish did not really freeze, but the mockingbirds sought shelter from the cold in evergreen magnolias and oaks, and the redfish and sea trout of the Gulf swam up coastal rivers to the warmth of inland waters. Days were usually balmy; it was rare in Florida that the sun did not shine with authority. This year the Moon of Birds and Fish Frozen would be memorable not for its weather but for the rise of the Seminoles against American aggressors; the lesson that had been taught to Tsali Emathla would also be taught to Francis Dade and Wiley Thompson. Whenever Osceola thought about Thompson a slight smile played over his lips. Did the agent think him so lacking in manhood and honor that he would ever forget having been put in irons? Had Thompson believed that the bribe of a rifle was enough to make a chief forget his compromised dignity?

There were other grudges Osceola had against America. By a supreme irony of history, he was a descendant of the Scottish trader James McQueen who had lived among the Creeks and taken one of them as his woman. Osceola had begun life in southern Georgia. His mother, McQueen's granddaughter, a mixed-blood born Polly Copinger, had been living at the time with a trader named Powell. Whites called the child Billy Powell, but Osceola did not think Powell was his real father. What he did know was that he had been close to his mother's cousin Peter McQueen. And it was Peter McQueen who had led a party of Creeks from their Alabama village to Pensacola in the summer of 1813 to trade. On the way back, they had rested at Burnt Corn Creek, where the whites had attacked them, beginning the Red Stick uprising under Red Eagle. After the carnage at Horseshoe Bend, Polly and Peter McQueen had taken Polly's son south to Florida with McQueen's Tallassee band of Creeks. Osceola's boyhood had been a prolonged flight from America, and now, feeling himself to be Red Eagle's spiritual heir, he was determined to succeed where Red Eagle had failed. He, too, would lead a red war, but he would win his; on his side were the shaded swamps of Florida, vaster and more sinister to whites than those of Alabama or Georgia had been. Between the Alabama and Georgia swamps had lain cultivated fields. There were as yet few fields in Florida except in the northern part.

Osceola had not been born to chieftaincy among the Seminoles; his physical magnificence, his courage, and his talent for speechmaking had brought him to prominence. Young braves listened raptly when he declaimed, sure-voiced after the stutterings of old Micanopy. Because he believed himself fitted to be the leader of the Seminole nation in their fight for Florida, he became that leader. Both Seminoles and Americans took him at his own evaluation.

Osceola left Major Dade and his contingent to the care of Jumper and his band. While the Major toiled his way up to Fort King, Osceola and a group of hand-picked warriors surrounded the fort and waited for Wiley Thompson to take a stroll, as Osceola knew was his habit after meals. December 28 dawned in a drizzling rain, but in the middle of the morning the cloud cover broke and golden sun played on the leaves of the liveoaks and the needles of the pines. After dinner, Thompson and an assistant emerged from the agency to smoke Cuban cigars under the trees. Swiftly Osceola accosted Thompson with the carved rifle, and peppered the agent and his colleague with bullets. But the shooting was not enough. When Thompson lay sprawled on the moist ground, Osceola dug a knife into his heart. Then his warriors cut pieces of skin from his scalp to use as trophies. Osceola delivered the final blow by slashing his knife through Thompson's neck. Taking the still-bleeding talisman of the general's head in his hand, he led his band back toward Wahoo Swamp, on the edge of the Green, where he would rendezvous with Jumper.

When he reached Wahoo he was not disappointed. Jumper was exultant as he proudly told Osceola how he and his men had watched Dade and his command spend two days crossing the Hillsborough River. The Indians could have shot them then, but it had been more entertaining to play cat and mouse. There was hardly a Seminole in Florida whose Creek kinsmen had not been involved in the desperate wars with Jacksa Chula Harjo. Remembering what had been done to them and to their parent tribe, the Seminoles wanted a revenge proportionate to the offenses of the whites. Jumper had almost hated to bring a end to the game, but on the morning of the twenty-eighth, while Osceola waited at Fort King to kill Wiley Thompson, Major Dade led his men unflanked into open pinewoods. "Soon," he had shouted back to his soldiers, "we shall keep Christmas at Fort King." Within minutes he and his force had been gunned to extinction. Some of the whites were plucky; Jumper remembered one little fellow who had kept shouting "God *damn!*" to urge his men on. But of the entire expedition, only one soldier survived, though Jumper did not know it. It was this battered man, more dead than alive, who half-crawled, half-staggered back to Fort Brooke to tell of the Dade Massacre.[7]

Osceola and Jumper were jubilant that night in Wahoo Swamp. High on a pole, the severed head of Wiley Thompson dangled its sparse gray locks. The Indians lit a fire below and circled the pole singing victory songs. After their dancing they drank. One of them climbed on a tree stump and imitated

Thompson's Georgia drawl: "The Indians who do not go peaceably, the Great Father will remove by force!" The joke became
bigger as the whiskey canteens became lighter. Osceola did not
interfere in his people's triumph. Later there would be time
enough for sobriety.

Before the news of Thompson's murder and the obliteration
of Dade's command had traveled farther than Florida, American troops were massing on the Withlacoochee. General Clinch,
late of Carolina and now of Florida, feared for his plantation
at nearby Fort Drane. He was joined there by Richard Keith
Call, a former territorial governor of Florida. Call was a pep-
pery little man whose troops adored him. When he told them he
meant to attack the Indians on the Withlacoochee, an Irish
private joked: "Begorra, the Battle of Waterloo will be a cock-
fight to it!"[8]

The Seminoles waited until the army of Clinch and Call
were concentrated in a horseshoe-shaped forest opening surrounded on all sides by dense hammock land. The horseshoe
was a fateful symbol in the annals of Creeks and Seminoles.
While the Americans were resting, the Seminoles opened fire.
Bullets sang in the mild winter wind, and over the Withlacoochee hung a haze of battle smoke that stung throats and eyes.
While their officers roared commands at them, the troops
charged with their bayonets. Call yelled at his volunteers on
the north bank of the river to cross and join the regulars who
were fighting in the bend. Unfortunately, most of the volunteers held terms of enlistment which were due to expire on the
following day. Between thirty and sixty volunteers reluctantly
made it to the opposite shore, but not before Clinch had been
enraged at their slowness.

Osceola, who led the Seminoles wearing an old army coat,
did not emerge unscathed; a bullet grazed his arm. But the
Battle of the Withlacoochee was a victory for him all the
same. General Clinch had been prevented from attacking Seminole settlements, and Osceola watched with satisfaction as the
Americans retreated to Fort Drane. The Indians were now

thoroughly convinced that Osceola was their savior. His daring could repulse any white forces that tried to drive them out of Florida.

The Second Seminole War began with extravagant massacres; as it continued, it turned into a duel between Osceola and successive American generals, each of whom believed he could rout the red men in short order. While generals came and went, Osceola continued to smile. What history had begun in the making of the Seminole Nation, his regal daring had completed. There were Americans who watched his defense of his homeland in admiration, although most of the admirers, to be sure, lived in Boston or Philadelphia, and certainly nowhere near Florida. The United States was involved in a war that many of her own people did not want, and into the conduct of which she began pouring dollars in a futile stream to save north Florida from a "desperate danger." Most of the ardor for the war came from young, hotheaded southern bucks in splendid uniforms. "Never," declaimed the scion of a family in Charleston, South Carolina, "did Rome or Greece in days of yore—nor France, for England in modern times—pour forth a nobler soldiery than the Volunteers from Georgia, Alabama, Louisiana, and South Carolina." The self-styled bluebloods had strong notions about honor and the sacredness of land.[9] What the young men from America's southeastern states forgot was that Osceola was also a bluehood of his people, and he thoroughly shared white southern ideas about inviolate honor and land. In the sordidness of the war there was an archaic splendor. Great knights rode forth to battle. On the American side they were called Winfield Scott and Zachary Taylor and Thomas Jesup; on the Seminole, their names were Jumper, Alligator, Tigertail, Coacoochee, the Wildcat, and above all, Asi-Yaholo, who had started life in a Creek trading post carrying in his veins the blood of adventurous Scotsmen as well as that of the Creeks of Red Eagle. Osceola knew he fought not only for Seminoles, but for every red man in America. If his tactics were terrible, so be it. Exile was a thing of terror too.

13

Pascofa Takes the Cup

"I had hopes I should be killed in battle,
but a bullet never touched me."
—COACOOCHEE, SEMINOLE

As Florida was cherished by the Seminoles, it was almost universally hated by the fighting forces of the United States. They found it "swampy, hammocky, low, excessively hot, sickly, and repulsive in all its features." The men were terrified of the alligators, which never attacked them, and yellow fever, which did. Rattlesnakes, they had heard, could turn life into a hell that preceded a welcome death for which the victim screamed in agony. It is strange that no commander ever recorded any snakebite deaths in his reports to Washington. Wolves keened and panthers screeched. "I have offered," said a volunteer ruefully, "to do duty in Hades."

Into Hades, Washington sent fifty-year-old General Winfield Scott, an iron disciplinarian. He was six feet four inches tall, broad-shouldered and massive-jawed, and fond of fine raiment. He arrived in Florida with a military band, "marquees of furniture," and cases of French wines. His men had christened him Old Fuss and Feathers because of these expensive tastes. Old Fuss and Feathers, who had impressed recalcitrant Cherokees in Georgia, conducted military inspections in Florida dressed in his heaviest uniform coat, while lesser men were having heat strokes. Scott's strategy was to drive the Indians back into North Florida where there was more open land than in the Green Swamp. The citizens of Tallahassee did not appreciate the scheme, but they needn't have worried; the Seminoles were nearly impregnable in their natural fortress at the Cove of the Withlacoochee, today Lake Tsala Apopka.

Scott's arch-rival was Major General Edmund Pendleton Gaines; Old Fuss and Feathers despised Gaines as much as had Black Hawk during the Wisconsin rebellion. Gaines had a terrible temper which was probably not improved by the state of the Florida troops. In one nine-month period, 15,794 soldiers were listed on sick rosters, and all the men drank like fish.

Gaines's strategy was to concentrate the Indians into a small area and then to pump them full of lead. The difficulty was that the Indians were already concentrated in one place, but there was not enough lead to go around. At this point Osceola,

Jumper, and Alligator sent a proposal to Gaines: if he would let the tribe stay where they were, the war might end. Gaines answered that the matter would be taken under advisement and presented to the proper authorities. The proper authorities relieved him of his Florida command and put their money on General Clinch, but not before Gaines had announced that he had ended the Second Seminole War. Clinch and Scott shouted with mirth. The Seminoles were daily raiding frontier settlements.

A "grand campaign" mounted by the two generals resulted in the deaths of less than sixty Indians. The American armies periodically had to journey to Fort Brooke, on Tampa Bay, for food. Floridians were derisive. One said Scott was trying to "apply the shreds and patches of the obsolete system of European tactics where they could not possibly work," and was full of "incapacity, presumption and ignorance." Scott was soon forced to turn over his command to Richard Call. And while the brass danced their military minuets, tales of Osceola's bravery spread across the country. It was said that he "used his authority to prevent war on women and children." At a banquet in St. Augustine at which General Clinch was present, a visitor from the North offered a toast "to the great untaken and still unconquered red man." For if the red men were inferior to the white, how was it that they had kept Florida?

A fresh general entered the fray: forty-eight-year-old Thomas Sidney Jesup, veteran of the promotion-making War of 1812 and now quartermaster general with the rank of brigadier. The austerity of Jesup's high forehead was matched by the almost unnerving directness of his gaze. But that directness was deceptive, for Thomas Jesup could be devious indeed. He was also firmly on the side of progress, equipping his men with Colt's new revolvers and Cochran's repeater rifle. Osceola immediately recognized in him a formidable opponent. Jesup knew that Gaines had not ended the war, and thought that privilege would be reserved for himself. He was pleased when Seminole leaders consented to parley, but he was clever enough to recognize the reason. The parleys took place during the harvest season, while the women and children tended the cornfields undisturbed; after harvest, the parleying ceased.

But there were Seminoles who could stand their precarious existence no longer. In straggling, hungry little bands they made their way to Fort Brooke; most of them were ancient, undernourished, or women and children. For these people the Trail of Tears began on Egmont Key, an island in Tampa Bay where they were kept in a stockade, like refractory cattle, to await the steamers bound for New Orleans. On one journey from Fort King to Fort Brooke, 55 out of 512 Indians died of malaria and dysentery; on Egmont the Seminoles died faster. The lieutenant in charge noted that he had a surplus of food "because of sick Indians—and dead Indians." On the way to Oklahoma, both by sea and land, four deaths a day were common among Seminole bands of a few hundred people.

In October 1837 several chiefs, among them Coacoochee, the Wildcat, unwisely made a journey to an old Seminole stronghold near St. Augustine. Under Thomas Sidney Jesup, the United States Army had sharpened its eyes and ears. The chiefs were captured, and Jesup sent a message to Osceola that he wished to talk, although Jesup himself decided to remain aloof. He sent Brigadier General Joseph Hernandez to the conference as his deputy. Hernandez stationed himself near Moultrie Creek where the Seminoles had once signed a capitulation and waited until Osceola and Coee Harjo emerged from the woods carrying a flag of truce. Hernandez had his orders. He ignored the flag and captured the two chiefs. Osceola was so bitter at this treachery that he said to Coee Harjo, "Speak for me."

General Hernandez looked every inch the Spanish Floridian that he was. His hair was dark, his nose slender and aquiline, and his mouth as proudly disdainful as a grandee's. "I wish you all well," he told the chiefs in slightly accented English, "but we have been deceived so often that it is necessary for you to come with me. You will all see the good treatment that you experience. You will be glad that you fell into my hands."[1]

For a moment, Coee Harjo looked him in the eyes. Then the Indian answered tersely, "We will see about that." The first "good treatment" Osceola received at the huge, sprawling stone Castillo de San Marcos, built by the Spanish at St. Augustine, was to be thrown into chains. From there he was shipped to high-security Fort Moultrie on Sullivan's Island off Charleston harbor. He was accompanied by a physician, Dr. Frederick Weedon, who had examined him in St. Augustine and had diagnosed him as suffering from malaria. As Osceola weakened from anguish and the malaria's fresh attacks, his chains were removed. He was even taken by a party of officers to a Charleston theater to see *The Honeymoon*, a comedy of American domestic manners. At his entrance, splendid in his egret plumes and silver jewelry, the audience gasped. He sat utterly still during the performance, making himself a legend. Exposing him to public view had been a mistake, the well-meaning officers decided when the nation's reporters began publishing stories about the chief. Americans also read the words of one of the aged Seminoles incarcerated on Egmont Key waiting to be shipped west: "If suddenly we tear our hearts from the homes around which they are twined, our heart strings will snap. This was our home when the game was plenty and the corn was high. If the deer have departed and the corn tassels not, it is still our home."[2] Everyone remembered Osceola's declaration: "When I make up my mind, I act. If I speak, what I say I will do. If the hail rattles, let the flowers be crushed. The oak of the forest will lift up its head to the sky and the storm, towering and unscathed."

His spirit towered still, but his body was weakening rapidly. He contracted a quinsy sore throat—acute tonsillitis—which did not improve when he learned that Mary Weedon, the sister of his attending physician, Dr. Weedon, had been the wife of Wiley Thompson. When Weedon offered Osceola medicine, he steadfastly refused it. "Probably he will not live through the winter," Weedon decided, and conscientiously tried to persuade the embattled chief to forsake his medicine men. Their

chants echoed low in the stony corridors of the fort all through
that autumn and winter. Osceola's wives had been summoned,
and they wept. By January 1838, the Moon of the Little Moon,
Osceola was calling for his war costume.

When his wives brought it, he put it on slowly, for he was
exhausted. He thrust his arms into the calico shirt and eased
his legs into their deerskins. Silently he chained the ornaments
around his neck. He had his war belt, and his bone powder
horn, and his turban waving its tall plumes. Those plumes were
reminders of another world—the green stillness of the swamps
where prothonotary warblers had buzzed and the ivory-billed
woodpeckers the whites called Lord Gods had flashed their red
and white and black feathers in the sun as they cried. Seminole
canoes had moved through those languid waters undisturbed.
Seminole spirits inhabited every rock and tree. At night the
moon had ridden over the blackness like a giant silver gorget,
as perfectly round as the one Osceola now wore for the occasion of his dying. His egret plumes brought back to him the
faint scent of jasmine, visions of high epidendrum orchids in
the trees, and little turtles sunning themselves on fallen logs.
The Chief streaked his face with red ochre, then his neck and
aching throat, his wrists, and the backs of his hands. He was a
warrior, and he would go as one. Laboriously, he rose from his
bed and shook Dr. Weedon's hand. Then, one by one, he shook
hands with watching officers. He smiled impassively, as he had
once smiled for Wiley Thompson. When the soldiers had
helped him into his bed again, he pulled the scalping knife
from his belt and laid it across his chest. Then he breathed a
last long breath which sounded hollowly from his tired chest.
Osceola of the Seminoles was dead, and the soldiers who had
seen him die found themselves moist-eyed.

Afterward they left, but Dr. Weedon stayed. He wanted a
trophy. Skillfully he severed Osceola's head from his neck, then
transferred both head and body into a coffin and tied a scarf
around the neck. Immediately before the funeral, Weedon removed the head and shut the coffin tight. It was not long be-

fore the head of Osceola hung in the house of Dr. Weedon in St. Augustine as the head of Wiley Thompson had bobbed on its pole over the Wahoo Swamp. As a doctor, Weedon had done the best he could for a patient dying of heartbreak, but as Mary Weedon Thompson's brother he had taken a revenge his fellow southerners found natural. Whenever his boys misbehaved, he hung Osceola's head on the bedpost in their nursery. When the boys were older he presented the head to his daughter's new husband. Possibly the young man found the wedding present a little too unusual, for he gave it in turn to a New York physician named Valentine Mott, head of the New York university medical school. "I am aware," Weedon's son-in-law wrote Dr. Mott, "that the classic lands of Greece and Rome, the isles of the sea, and many a well-fought field of Europe, have alike given up their evidences of life, and in your cabinet of heads we travel into the distant past and hold communion with those times that were."

The head, replied Dr. Mott, would be "deposited in the collection and preserved in my library at home, for I fear almost to place it in my museum at the University—temptation will be so strong for someone to take it. Your letter will be attached to the head."[3] The separate existence of Osceola's head ended when Dr. Mott's museum caught fire; he hadn't been able to resist displaying it at the university after all. Museum and head were destroyed in the fire.

In death, Osceola captured the minds and hearts of Americans as he had begun to do in life. He had been the incarnation, to many, of the utter injustice of the war of extermination waged upon his tribe. At Lake Okeechobee, where several bands unwisely stood their ground instead of melting into the Everglades, there was another slaughter of Indians. After the battle, on the shores of Tampa Bay, weeping Seminole captives boarded steamers for deportation. The sight was so commonplace, the citizens of Tampa hardly noticed it, but when such scenes were covered by the national press, readers had second thoughts about the issue of removal. Was it really for the Indians' good? Reports of the Seminole Trail of Tears were matching those of the Cherokee Trail. Conductors were writing the familiar accounts to Washington: "From one, two, and three deaths a day we now have four. The effluvia and pestilential atmosphere of the wagons, where some twenty sick or dying lay in their own filth, and even the tainted air of the camps is unsupportable." The Seminoles who had already reached Oklahoma had complaints of their own. "I have no gun to kill squirrels and birds for my children," a chief pleaded. "No axe to cut my firewood. No plows or hoes with which to till the soil for my bread." The government was being slow in sending weapons and tools. "We are *very hungry* and do not expect to make much corn. . . . All the promises made to us have not been fulfilled."[4]

Oddly enough, General Jesup protested along with the Seminoles. He browbeat Washington into sending west the rakes and hoes and cauldrons the Indians needed, and from his own pocket bought one of the chiefs a rifle so that the man might hunt the game with which to feed his family. Jesup had violated a flag of truce and killed Seminoles in Florida. But when Seminoles began to die in Oklahoma, he felt he could not stand by. What had his betrayal of Osceola been for, if not to ensure the Indians' safe removal west?

He knew, of course. Perhaps he had always known. He was an American, and America was straining at its boundaries. The continent had to be conquered, as God had intended from the start. But Thomas Sidney Jesup now regretted bitterly the betrayal to which he had unwittingly contributed. He hounded officialdom until, grudgingly, the government began fulfilling its treaty promises. Meanwhile more Seminoles perished because they had no weapons with which to shoot the plentiful buffalo.

In the war in Florida, U.S. Army commanders entered and exited as usual. In May 1838, Jesup retired in disgust and Zachary Taylor took over. The tenure of Old Rough and Ready was unusually long—two years. As he began it, his subordinate Richard Keith Call had the bright idea of using bloodhounds to

track down the Indians in the swamps. The current governor of
Florida, Robert Reid, was in enthusiastic agreement:

> The efforts of the general and territorial governments to quell
> the Indian disturbances, which have prevailed through four
> long years, have been unavailing. . . . The close of the fifth year
> will find us still struggling in a contest, remarkable for mag-
> nanimity, forbearance and credulity on one side, and ferocity
> and bad faith on the other. We are waging a war with beasts of
> prey; the tactics that belong to civilized nations are but shackles
> and fetters in its prosecution; we must fight fire with fire; the
> white man must, in a great measure, adopt the mode of warfare
> pursued by the red man, and we can only hope for success by
> continually harassing and pursuing the enemy. If we drive him
> from hammock to hammock, from swamp to swamp, and pene-
> trate the recesses where his women and children are hidden; if,
> in self defense, we show him as little mercy as he has shown to
> us, the anxiety and surprise produced by such operations will
> not, it is believed, fail to produce prosperous results. It is high
> time that sickly sentimentality should cease. "Lo! The poor In-
> dian!" is the exclamation of the fanatic pseudo-philanthropist.
> "Lo! The poor white man!" is the ejaculation which all will utter
> who have witnessed the inhuman butchery of women and chil-
> dren and the massacres that have drenched the territory in
> blood.[5]

Exactly why killing women of one color and cherishing those
of lighter hue was permissible the governor did not specify.

Call sent to Cuba for his bloodhounds; the island made a
specialty of raising them for the hunting down of escaped
slaves. The Cubans wanted the "exorbitant" price of $151.72
per dog, but Call paid it when Cuba threw in five Spanish
specialists in tracking. The specialists carefully explained their
technique. First the dogs were to be fed bloody meat, then
they were to be muzzled and leashed, and made to smell the
footprint of the individual to be followed. The dogs, along with
the calves they would eat, were attached to columns of troops.

Henry Wise, a member of the House of Representatives from

Virginia, was horrified. He introduced a resolution of inquiry and found he was not alone in his indignation. Feisty old John Quincy Adams, the former President who was now a congressman, submitted a recommendation of his own:

> That the Secretary of War be directed to report to this House, the natural, political, and martial history of the bloodhounds, showing the peculiar fitness of that class of warriors to be the associates of the gallant army of the United States, specifying the nice discrimination of his scent between the blood of the freeman and the blood of the slave . . . between the blood of savage Seminoles and that of the Anglo-Saxon pious Christian. . . . Also, whether a further importation of the same heroic race into the state of Maine, to await the contingency of a contested Northeastern Boundary question is contemplated. . . . whether measures have been taken to secure to ourselves exclusively the employment of this auxiliary force, and whether he deems it expedient to extend the said bloodhounds and their posterity the benefits of the pension laws.

The *Tallahassee Floridian* took a different view; they only regretted the use of muzzles since the dogs would thus be prevented from "tearing the red devils to pieces."[6]

Joel Poinsett, the Secretary of War, was forced to pay attention to things other than poinsettias. "I am decidedly in favor of the measure," he said, "and beg leave to urge it as the only means of ridding the country of the Indians, who are now broken up into small parties that take shelter in swamps and hammocks as the army approaches, making it impossible for us to follow or overtake them without the aid of such auxiliaries." Bloodhounds might have saved Major Dade, he added. The Seminoles, moreover, had actually dared to "mortally wound an officer of distinguished merit" who had happened to be chasing them at the time.

The dogs, however, were dense. John Quincy Adams had been only too right when he had wondered how a dog could discriminate between an Indian and a Christian. The dogs couldn't. They tracked everything in sight, including soldiers. The Territory of Florida did not help matters when it billed the army $2,429.52 for the wayward canines. Old Rough and Ready flatly refused to pay; those dogs, he said, were simply "no damn good."

Though its people had their crudities, Florida was not without its cultural refinements. A traveling Shakespearean company visited the territory's citizens, but when they left their baggage unattended, a band of Seminoles made off with it into the swamps. Soon afterward, Coacoochee, the Wildcat, now the leading war spirit of the Seminoles, sent a message that he wanted to talk about a peace treaty. His people were hungry. As Coacoochee approached the military camp, the soldiers gaped in astonishment. On his brow he wore the ostrich feathers of Hamlet, Prince of Denmark. In the rear was Richard III, "judging from his royal purple and ermine." Beside him was "a faithful friend wound up in the simple garb of Horatio." In the spangles, crimson vests, and paste necklaces, the soldiers were seeing the beginning of the modern Seminole costume; the cloak of Richard III became the Seminole woman's cape, and the headgear of Hamlet the badge of the tribe's medicine men. The soldiers found nothing touching in the Indians' love of their finery, but against their wills they were moved when Coacoochee spoke to them.

The land I was upon I loved; my body is made of its sands. The Great Spirit gave me legs to walk over it; hands to aid myself; eyes to see its ponds, rivers, forests, and game; then a head with which I think. The sun . . . shines to warm us and bring forth our crops, and the moon brings back the spirits of our warriors, our fathers, wives, and children. The white man comes; he grows pale and sick. Why cannot we live here in peace? I have said I am the enemy to the white man. I could live in peace with him, but they first steal our cattle and horses, cheat us, and take our lands. The white men are as thick as the leaves in the hammock;

they come upon us thicker every year. They may shoot us, drive our women and children night and day; they may chain our hands and feet, but the red man's heart will always be free.[7]

He promised to round up his band after the year's Green Corn Dance. Because they must eat, they would consent to go west. Coacoochee was yet unaware of the state of affairs in the Indian Territory.

By this time Old Rough and Ready had retired from the Florida command to be followed by General Armistead, who didn't much care for Florida himself. Armistead was succeeded by square-jawed William Jenkins Worth. One of Worth's lieutenants was William Tecumseh Sherman, who set out to bring Coacoochee into the south Florida post of Fort Pierce. Sherman didn't trust Coacoochee's good faith. When Sherman found him—Coacoochee was too hungry to hide—the chief insisted on making a ceremonial surrender in his Shakespearean regalia. He marched into the fort and assured the troops that in thirty days he would deliver his people. When the thirty days were over, Sherman put Coacoochee in irons, and to save him his band surrendered.

On July 3, 1841, Coacoochee and his people arrived in Tampa to board a prison ship. "Coacoochee and his warriors came slowly to the quarterdeck," reported a soldier on duty, "their feet irons hardly enabling them to step four inches, and arranged themselves according to rank. As they laid their manacled hands on their knees before them, in the presence of so many whom they had long hunted as foes, they hung their heads in silence." When General Worth came aboard to see his prisoner, the chief's dark eyes bored into his own. "I am here," said Coacoochee, "and I feel the irons in my heart."

Finally, the Seminoles were surrendering. But one of the wiliest of their chiefs was old Arpeika, whose white name was Sam Jones, an octogenarian captured several times only to escape. Private Theophilus Rodenbough of the Second Dragoons wrote verses about him:

Ever since the creation
By the best calculation
The Florida War has been raging,
And 'tis our expectation
That the last conflagration
Will find us the same contest waging.

And yet 'tis not an endless war
As facts will plainly show,
Having been "ended" forty times
In twenty months or so.

Sam Jones! Sam Jones! Thou great unwhipped,
Thou makest a world of bother.
Indeed we quite expect thou art
One Davy Jones's brother.

"The war is ended," comes the news,
"We've caught them in our gin;
The war is ended past a doubt—
Sam Jones has just come in!"

But, hark! Next day the tune we change
And sing a counter strain,
"The war's not ended," for behold!
Sam Jones is out again.

And ever and anon we hear
Proclaimed in cheering tones
"Our General's had a battle?" No,
A "talk with Samuel Jones."

For aught we see while ocean rolls
(As though those crafty Seminoles
Were doubly nerved and sinewed)
Nor art nor force can e'er avail
But, like some modern premium tale,
The war's "to be continued."[8]

Halleck Tustenuggee was captured by the proven strategy of a
violated flag of truce. When he accepted an army bribe of a
thousand dollars, some of his followers were contemptuous. He

immediately turned on the men; after he had knocked down two warriors, he kicked a third in the chest with both feet, jumped on him, pummeled him, and tore one ear from his head with his teeth. "I am your chief!" he screamed. "Whether prisoner or not, remember I am your chief!"

Billy Bowlegs was one warrior who refused to surrender. Instead, he led the Seminoles so deep into the mangrove labyrinths of the Everglades no white man could pursue them. There were now two processions of Indians: one starving, bound for Tampa Bay and thence to Oklahoma; and the other in the Glades starving but vowing to raise corn once more, this time in hammocks no one but themselves could discover. The United States watched the second procession with weary indifference; since no white man could ever tame the Everglades, why not leave them to the red men? What America didn't want it could easily ignore. What was defeating the Seminoles north of the Glades was their inability to settle permanently in villages where they could raise food.

The country had spent close to forty million dollars on a conflict that had consumed more than a thousand young lives; the fatality rate in the army was 14 percent. In the early stages of the war, Americans outside the South had not realized what they had since learned: the war to hunt down Indians was also the war to hunt down escaped southern slaves. Now northerners of conscience protested more loudly than ever, and southerners in their turn perceived in the Second Seminole War the lineaments, as yet only vaguely defined, of a greater disaster to come. The Civil War was years away, but most of the seeds of its conflicts had already been sown.

By March 1842 a scant three thousand Seminoles had been removed west. One of the principal groups still at large was that of Pascofa, chief of the Ochlockonee band on the Apalachicola River in northern Florida. He was found there by that veteran of removal Major Ethan Allen Hitchcock, once the champion of Oklahoma Chickasaws who had been sent rotten rations. He despised the Seminole War and sympathized

wholeheartedly with the Indians, but felt he had to perform his
military duty as a soldier of the United States.

"As I am the last chief to give up I will do something special," Pascofa told him quietly, holding back tears. Even Sam
Jones had been taken. At three o'clock on December 17 his
warriors appeared in a long file singing a Seminole war song,
their scalp locks adorned with egret feathers. When they were
two hundred yards from their chief, they discharged their rifles,
and filed past Major Hitchcock and his officers. Hitchcock
gave the chief his respects in a speech. Pascofa solemnly returned them. Then Hitchcock's aide, Lieutenant Henry,
brought in the liquor. He handed Hitchcock a tin cup "filled
with the most abominable stuff." Hitchcock took it, debated
whether to say grace and decided not to, drank, and then gave
the cup to Pascofa.

"Iste linus tcha,"[9] Pascofa intoned; it was a Seminole toast.
The cup was passed from warrior to warrior like a communion
chalice. "Iste linus tcha!" The echoes resounded in the virgin
Apalachicola River forest; when the echoes died, the spirits of
the Ochlockonee Seminoles had died with them.

Hitchcock put the Indians on board a boat and traveled with
them toward the market town of Port Leon, on the St. Mark's
River south of Tallahassee. At Port Leon, Pascofa and his warriors gave a ceremonial war yell to watching spectators. Soon
afterward, Hitchcock noted, "a revulsion of feeling" overtook
the Indians. The men became silent, and the women clutched
their army blankets tighter about their bodies—some had been
nearly naked when they had surrendered. Then the women
began weeping, and Hitchcock saw that Pascofa's lips were
trembling uncontrollably.

"Soon you will be happier than you have been," Hitchcock
told them all through an interpreter. "You have lived more like
wild animals than human creatures, but now you will begin to
have houses and make gardens. You can bring up your children
to something besides war." At this, one old woman moaned
because so few of the band's children had survived hunger and

being hunted. If the land in the West were alien, it would still support young life. The Seminoles wept for the dead, but some of them wept also in relief.

When America's newspapers announced that Major Ethan Allen Hitchcock had singlehandedly ended a war in which few white Americans now had any belief, the nation turned its attention to other tribes who had no swamps to hide in and no tropical heat with which to kill white soldiers. Pascofa had drunk from the cup of defeat, but some stragglers remained east of the Mississippi.

In the Everglades, the Seminoles wept too. They wept for northern Florida, whose broad fertility had once been theirs. But they were thankful for their dusky refuge. These Seminoles never emerged to sign a formal peace treaty with speechmaking bluecoats. They have not signed one yet. Dogged in their historic retreat, they are still there.

14

Prayers for the White Chief

"The deer and the turkey will go next,
and with them the sons of the forest."
—SENACHWINE, POTAWATOMI

SANDUSKY, OHIO, WAS FAR FROM THE SHADOWS OF THE EVER-
glades. Once it had been full of the heartiness of Wyandot
men, the muted speech of Wyandot women, and the laughter
of their children. Its high hickories and oaks, ironwoods and
elms had formed so dense a canopy that the heat of the sun
never scorched, and the gray fury of the rain was always miti-
gated. Wigwams had stood in orderly rows. Beyond the village
the game had roamed, bear and deer and bison. But everything
was changing now. Sandusky, once an Indian city as Saukenuk
had been, was turning into a small midwestern town full of
hardware salesmen, preachers, and shopkeepers. They had cut
down the forest with its sugar-maple trees which had once
given the Wyandots a yearly harvest.

Yet America had not swept Ohio quite clean. In 1836 Washington sent agents to negotiate a treaty with the Wyandots that
lopped off more of their lands than had been lopped off already, but the tribe still held over a hundred thousand acres,
too much for Ohioans to stomach. William H. Hunter, a United
States Representative living in Sandusky, was by the early
1840s working actively for the complete banishment of the red
men. Already, he could note with satisfaction, the Ottawas
were out, as were the Senecas. Then the government decided
to send a new agent to Ohio, John Johnston, a man who believed it was his duty to his country to press a fresh treaty on
the Wyandots but who also felt for them in their plight. The
dilemma was becoming a familiar one in the Bureau of Indian
Affairs.

In March 1842, the year in which Pascofa of the Seminoles
would surrender to Ethan Allen Hitchcock in Florida, John
Johnston presented the Wyandots with their terms of their
capitulation.[1] Outnumbered and debilitated, they signed.
Then they waited for government appraisers to tell them what
the United States thought the improvements on their lands
were worth. The appraisers were careful and tried to be as fair
as they could. The figure they came up with was $125,937.24,
which Washington promptly told them was ridiculous. The
Great Father said he had exactly $20,000 to spend on keeping

the Wyandots calm, and agent Johnston was given the job of explaining to them that they could not bankrupt the United States. The Wyandots had built a new blacksmith shop; now they learned they would have to pay for a blacksmith with whatever money they already had. Without a blacksmith to help them prepare their wagons, how could they leave? They had also exhausted their supply of iron, coal, and steel. When they asked for $400 to get more, they were tersely told the limit was $200.

In Sandusky, they prepared for their trek. They met frequently to pray in their small mission church; they also had work to do in the churchyard. The bodies of Summendewat, a chief murdered the year before by whites, and John Stewart, a black missionary they had loved, were moved to rest in the little building's shadow. The Wyandots deeded the church land to the Methodists, who could be trusted as the Indian Bureau could not.

In the last council ever held at Sandusky, Chief Squire John Grey Eyes delivered a speech in Wyandot. He bade farewell to the Sandusky River, where Wyandots had paddled their long war canoes, to the cranberry marshes, to the felled forests, to old trails, to the animals, and to the people he had loved who lay buried in Wyandot ground. The Wyandots could not fight as the Seminoles had and were exhibiting, said a subagent with satisfaction, "the most perfect resignation."

In that spring of 1842 there appeared a stranger in Sandusky. He was handsome, frock-coated, and English, his throat fashionably muffled by an enormous dark cravat. He had a mane of flowing hair, and his eyes missed nothing as he surveyed the scene before him. His name was Charles Dickens.

Almost anywhere else in America outside of Sandusky and other Indian villages he was famous. The city of Hartford, Connecticut, had lionized him with a banquet featuring seventy dishes, among them cod's head in oyster sauce and ham in champagne. American women had gazed on him in delight as he read his works to them from platforms draped in Union Jacks. But one of the things that had most fascinated him on his triumphal progress was the American Indian. On the steamboat *Pike* on the Ohio River, Dickens was given the calling card of "one Pitchlynn, a chief of the Choctaw tribe." He was astonished to hear Pitchlynn's good English. The two earnestly discussed the novels of Sir Walter Scott, Dickens afterward reported,

> On my telling him that I regretted not to see him in his own attire, he threw up his right arm for a moment as though he were brandishing some heavy weapon, and answered, as he let it fall again, that his race were losing many things besides their dress and would soon be seen upon the earth no more. He told me that he had been away from his home, west of the Mississippi, seventeen months, and was now returning. He had been chiefly at Washington on some negotiations pending between his tribe and the Government: which were not settled yet (he said in a melancholy way) and he feared never would be; for what could a few poor Indians do against such well-skilled men of business as the whites? He had no love for Washington; tired of towns and cities very soon; and longed for the forest and the prairie.

When Pitchlynn told Dickens he would like to see England, Dickens promised that if he came to England he would show Pitchlynn the British Museum.

"Ah!" Pitchlynn smiled. "The English used to be very fond of the red men when they wanted their help, but haven't cared much for them since." He was teasing—partly—but then he seriously asked Dickens to visit him in the western Choctaw territory and hunt buffalo.

"I fear I shouldn't damage the buffaloes much," Dickens told him. Pitchlynn roared with laughter. Then he "took his leave; as stately and complete a gentleman of Nature's making as ever I beheld; and moved among the people in the boat, another kind of being."[2]

Dickens thought more of Pitchlynn than he did of most Americans. He was also amused by what he considered the primitive little towns, among them Sandusky where rooting pigs roamed the streets and mosquitoes swarmed, and where he couldn't get a drink. Liquor was illegal in Sandusky because of the presence of the Wyandots, though the Indians managed to get overpriced bootleg moonshine from itinerant salesmen.

At breakfast in his hotel, Dickens met John Johnston, the Wyandot agent, and the two men fell into conversation. Johnston told him about the Wyandot treaty:

> He gave me a moving account of their strong attachment to the familiar scenes of their infancy, and in particular to the burial places of their kindred; and of their great reluctance to leave them. He had witnessed many such removals, and always with pain, though he knew that they departed for their own good. The question whether this tribe should go or stay had been discussed among them a day or two before, in a hut erected for the purpose, the logs of which still lay on the ground before the inn.[3]

As the Wyandots passed from Ohio, Charles Dickens watched them riding their shaggy ponies; they looked to him like gypsies. Sandusky, except for them, was "sluggish and uninteresting . . . something like the back of an English watering-place out of the season."

The newspaper editors also watched the Wyandots as they left. The Logan *Gazette* was astonished to see only one of them drunk; the Xenia *Torchlight* and the Lebanon *Western Star* found the spectacle solemn. The Indians were bearing "exposure to the heat and dust" with stout hearts, but they were "melancholy . . . Just civilized enough to have lost their savage courage they go forth on the broad prairies of the West like sheep among wolves." Along the Ohio River, they passed the tomb of William Henry Harrison, whom the rigors of a presidential campaign had killed in 1841. Old Tippecanoe had once pitted himself against Tecumtha and won; Wyandots, who had always hated their neighbors, the Shawnees, had helped Harrison, and they remembered him as a beloved commander. Near the tomb they asked the captain of their steamboat to salute, and when the cannon boomed they gathered on the hurricane roof. The engine was stopped, and the boat drifted in the current. The Indians uncovered their heads and gently waved their hats in silence. When the boat had passed and the guns were still, Chief Squire John Grey Eyes stepped forward to deliver a sonorous valediction. "Farewell, Ohio, and her brave!"[4] The Wyandots prayed for the dead white chief. Before the party of 630 had finished their first year along the Kansas River in Missouri, 100 of them would be mourned as well.

At first, the Wyandots were busy in their new home. One of them, William Walker, educated in mission schools, wrote back to a friend in Columbus:

> We have landed. . . . I have been employed busily in collecting and getting under shelter my household goods and in getting a house to live in temporarily. . . . My company are all about two miles above this place, some in tents, some in houses, and some under the expanded branches of the tall cottonwood trees. You cannot imagine my feelings on landing . . . and hunting a shelter for the family—faces all strange—we felt truly like *strangers in a strange land.*

They were befriended by a band of Delawares living nearby, who eventually sold them some of their reservation. The transaction was not legal until the Bureau of Indian Affairs had approved it. President Tyler wondered if he himself had any power to act on the affair, but he submitted the Delaware-Wyandot Treaty to Congress which stalled ratification for four years. Meanwhile, the emigrants were dying of starvation, and their survivors were afraid to build on land that might be taken from them as Ohio had been. In the spring of 1844 the tribe planted corn only to lose it to spring floods on the swollen Kansas. Stony-eyed, they drank, while a new Methodist missionary busied himself in the "correction of their morals . . . *whiskey* is the red man's curse." The observation was not, of course, new, nor were the conditions which had prompted it.

When Congress finally acted on the Delaware-Wyandot Treaty, it was the summer of 1848. The Wyandots waited in suspense to learn what would happen to their new land. When word of the treaty's ratification came at last, they amazed white observers by stopping their drinking and setting busily to work planting corn, potatoes, beans, and other crops. They even started a Temperance Society. It was in the following year that they learned the new land was in the path of a mass migration to the gold fields of California. All Indians in Kansas and Missouri stood in the way and must be shunted into the hinterlands. But by this time both sides understood that the glittering discovery at Sutter's Mill had made all hinterlands obsolete. It was just that some were as yet less obsolete than others.

⤙ 15 ⤚

The Munificent Mr. Manypenny

"The sound is fading away . . .
Freedom:
The sound is fading away."
—CHIPPEWA SONG

FREEDOM WAS OF FIVE SOUNDS, POETS OF THE WISCONSIN AND
Minnesota Chippewas had long intoned. The Chippewas too
had by now been pushed back from their fir forests in northern
Michigan and had reached western Minnesota. Ahead lay the
Plains. The five sounds were to them, perhaps, the keening
breath of wind in dark needles, the rushing of falls in woodland
glades, the crying of lynxes in the night, ghostly choruses of
braves who had taken the warpath and perished, and the soft
birth and death songs of the women who worked and, always,
waited. The Chippewas, who wrote some of the most moving
songs of exile, joined the other tribes passing westward: Wyandots and Senecas and Seminoles, Potawatomis and Me-
nominis and Mascoutens, Weas, Piankeshaws, Winnebagoes,
Cherokees, Shawnees, Munsees, Catawbas, and Caddoes.

Sometimes, in the twilight of their unity, the tribes were
gripped by religious fervor, messianic creeds that sought to
save them from European ways and bring them fresh faith in
themselves. Among the Kickapoos, once of southern Illinois
and Michigan and now of many places from Mexico to Nebraska, arose the Prophet Kannekuk, who promised his followers that they would one day be able to return to Michigan and
Illinois. Soon they would be able to cast off the burden of
drink, for they would have new ideals to live for. Kannekuk
made five prayer sticks, one for the heart, the second for the
flesh, the third for life, the fourth for one's own name, and the
fifth for kindred. "O our Father," he taught his charges to pray,
"make our hearts like Thy heart, our flesh like Thy flesh," In
sermons he exhorted them: "Where are your thoughts today?
Where were they yesterday? Were they fixed upon doing
good? Or were you drunk and tattling, or did anger rest in your
hearts? If you have done any of these things, your Great Father in Heaven knows it. . . ." Missionaries who listened to
Kannekuk from time to time decided that he had "some good
morals." But this did not protect him from the missionaries'
constant attempts to proselytize one or another of a bewildering array of theologies. It was not easy for Kickapoos to understand why some of the preachers equated the Pope with the

Devil and others said His Holiness could do no wrong, but few of the Kickapoos cared. The sound of freedom was, for Kickapoos as well as Chippewas, fading away.

"On my arrival here," reported a commissioner from Washington at one of the Kickapoos' villages,

I found a female preacher who claims to have received a communication from Heaven to dwell among the Kickapoos. Her name is *Miss Livermore*. She is the same person who, last year, thought she was directed to sojourn with the Osages. . . . She now evidently appears more deranged, and I was sorry to find her thus far among the Indian tribes N. West. It is true, her visit to the Kickapoos is by consent of the Superintendent of Indian Affairs at St. Louis, but I do not believe [he] is acquainted with her present principles. With the kindest feelings as a Gentleman to a Lady, I am decidedly of opinion that her residence among the Indians can do no good and may do much harm. . . . Lest she might deem my opinion a matter of persecution, I beg to mention what she publicly professes to believe and teaches here:

1. That Bonaparte is *not* dead but will soon reign as antiChrist and rule over the white man and Indian.

2. She pretends to receive direct communications from Heaven, and believes that the Kickapoo Prophet receives communications also from Heaven in an *audible* voice.

3. That immediately after the reign of *this* president a military despotism will be established in this country.

4. She believes that she is to be translated by Elijah to Heaven from Kickapoo ground and that all the Kickapoos are going up with her, and she is very anxious to get settled on Kickapoo ground before the 4th of Sept. when some great event is to occur, and she has informed a few Kickapoos of their speedy translation in company with herself.[1]

When Miss Livermore was interviewed, officials explained to her that they did not want to encourage "dreamers" (Black Hawk had been led astray by dreamers, they said). Furthermore, they did not want her telling the Kickapoo tribe it was about to ascend because then the Indians would not raise food for their families. She departed, to the relief of Kickapoo agents.

By 1853 the commissioner of Indian Affairs under President Franklin Pierce was George W. Manypenny. And as Mr. Manypenny reviewed the treaties it was his business to know about, he became increasingly disturbed.[2] Some of the wording was uncomfortable; he underlined key words. "The lands ceded to the Cherokee nation," he read of their trans-Mississippi exile, "shall *in no future time, without their consent*, be included within the territorial limits or jurisdiction of any state or territory." The Cherokees were to govern themselves *"eternally."* In the Creek treaties the phrasing was also explicit: the new lands west of the Mississippi "shall be solemnly guaranteed to the Creek Indians, *nor shall any state or territory ever have a right to pass laws for the government of such Indians*, but they shall be allowed to govern themselves. . . ." As he read, Commissioner Manypenny knitted his brows. The Choctaws had been assured that "no territory or state shall ever have a right to pass laws for the government of the Choctaw nation." The Seminoles had gotten their corner of the Indian country as "a future residence *forever*." The Delaware reservation also belonged to its inhabitants "forever" as did that of the Shawnees, the Miamis, and various others. But now that the gold rush was on, things were different, as they had been different for the Cherokees in Georgia after the gold rush of Dahlonega. President Pierce ordered Manypenny west to confer with the tribes who stood in the way of the glory trail to California. They would have to be governed by the United States, Pierce said, not themselves. When Manypenny arrived he saw white squatters on every side. The Indians had heard that hordes of whites were on the way. Some said they were for "lighting up the old fires Indian fashion" and confederating for defense. Bitterly the older warriors wondered if the Trail of Tears was to be enacted over again, until every red man in America had walked out into the Pacific to drown.

Several of the tribes had already banded together in an informal confederation. The Wyandots, Delawares, Potawatomis,

Shawnees, Ottawas, Kickapoos, Miamis, Kansas, Peorias, Weas, Piankeshaws, and Foxes had costumed themselves in their most splendid dress and had gathered to dance and affirm the compact. The western Plains had echoed with eastern songs, and woodland scalp roaches had bobbed in prairie winds. On paper, the confederation looked good. In reality, it meant nothing. The immigrant Indians in what was to become Kansas and Nebraska realized exactly how tenuous was their hold on the refuge they occupied. When George Manypenny came to them, they knew they had heard his message before. So had their fathers, grandfathers, and great-grandfathers. They would have to move. Manypenny reported to President Pierce that they were demoralized, though he had seen "noble specimens." Mission schoolteachers, he added, had astonishingly told him that Indian children were as teachable as white. Little Piankeshaw girls were doing needlework, religious samplers, and mottoes from the poetry of Alexander Pope: "Order is Heaven's First Law." Their brothers were learning how to milk cows and slop hogs. It was the old people who could remember camping out in the forests at night and, by day, pursuing game with the wind. They told their descendants romances of braves who had carried medicine pipes into battle, and of councils where the red people had danced unafraid. But now, again, the white man was coming. Commissioner Manypenny decided it was unwise to make treaties that year with the tribes. They looked like the despairing people they were, and he pitied them. They needed time to accept the inevitable.

But in 1854 he went west again to begin his work under the prodding of Franklin Pierce, the charming New Hampshireman whom even southerners liked. On May 30 the territories of Kansas and Nebraska were officially created. The Indians were now to occupy something called "diminished reserves"—diminished by white settlers who took a fancy to Indian land. Manypenny's job was to bilk the Indians of 18,000,000 acres, leaving them little more then 1,000,000. The system, said Manypenny, was not "wholly free from abuses." But what could be done? America was civilized; Indians were barbarians; a Christian

God had decreed that the hands which held the plows that broke tough prairie sod should be white. Besides, there were to be monies "in trust" for the evicted. But there was no trust on earth that could stop incoming whites from hacking down the timber in Indian woods and setting up as whiskey peddlers in Indian fields.

"The rage for speculation and the wonderful desire to obtain choice land," said Manypenny ambivalently,

> cause those who go into our new Territories to lose sight of and entirely overlook the rights of the aboriginal inhabitants. The most dishonorable expedients have, in many cases, been made use of to dispossess the Indian; demoralizing means employed to obtain his property. . . . In Kansas, particularly, trespasses and depredations of every conceivable kind have been committed on the Indians. They have been personally maltreated, their property stolen, their timber destroyed, their possessions encroached upon, and divers other wrongs and injuries done them.

Nevertheless, Manypenny began his prescribed negotiations with the Omahas, the Otos, Missouris, Sacs and Foxes, Iowas, Kickapoos, Delawares, Shawnees, Kaskaskias, Peorias, Weas, Piankeshaws, and Miamis. The Indians were persuaded by him to send deputations to Washington where the government presented the delegates with what became known as the "Manypenny treaties."[3] They sounded generous to white ears; the money paid by the government for western Shawnee lands, for instance, was to be invested in 6 percent bonds which would yield nearly fifty thousand dollars' annual interest. This, plus the crops of their farms "if properly cultivated," and the profits from their bison hunting, would put the Shawnees in "an independent position." Perhaps even George Manypenny believed this. The Indians didn't; they were listening to white speculators professing to be their friends who told them to ask for a lump sum. The friends, in many cases, were railroad lawyers.

"The locomotive engine built by our townsman M.W. Baldwin," the *Philadelphia Chronicle* had pontificated as long ago as 1832, "has proved highly successful . . . working with great ease and uniformity." Farmers in the East who first saw the giant machines said they "caused the eyes to bung out" and that they ran "faster than ever deer can run." It was not long before the railroads got into the business of buying western land. In 1852 the first tracks reached Chicago; a year before, the state of Illinois had granted a charter to a new corporation, the Illinois Central Railroad Company, which advertised its newly acquired prairies on impressive posters: "The attention of the enterprising and industrious is directed to the Garden Spot of the West. There is no portion of the world where all the conditions of climate and soil so admirably combine."

American tycoons began thinking in terms of transcontinental railroads stretching their shining tracks from Manhattan to Sacramento. On the plains of Illinois, the nighttime howling of sleek timber wolves was swiftly giving way to the haunting wail of engine whistles. In the 1840s an impetuous explorer named John Charles Frémont, who had previously eloped with Jessie Benton, the daughter of Missouri Senator Thomas Hart Benton, made his way to surf-washed Oregon and the dark redwood vaults of the Sierra Nevada in California, where he advised the resident Americans to revolt against Mexico. Eventually Frémont became one of California's first United States senators. By 1853 Congress had had long enough to think about the implications of the Frémont expeditions to pass a series of bills, the first of them introduced by Ohio Senator Salmon P. Chase. Chase, stern of profile and eloquent of speech, called for the construction of a railroad between the 32nd and 49th parallels, which included everything from the Red River in the south to the Canadian border on the north. Mississippi Congressman Jefferson Davis favored a southern route; after all, the Indians in *his* part of the country had already been cleared out. But a twenty-one-year-old fledgling engineer named Grenville Dodge had already hired himself out in Iowa to Peter Day, chief engineer for the Rock Island Railroad which now bisected the lands of the Sacs and Foxes. Dodge was soon writing his father: "When the various railroads under construction are complete, we will have direct communication by rail with Iowa and the far West, for this is the true Pacific road and will be built to Council Bluffs, where a good road from St. Louis will meet it, and then to San Francisco, this being the shortest and most feasible route."[4]

It was feasible to everybody except the tribes who had been shunted into the coveted territory. What Grenville Dodge was already thinking of as the Great Platte Valley Route, he called the "natural" one to the Pacific. Along the 42nd parallel were laced the paths of buffalo, Indians, trappers, migrating Mormons, and the first wave of emigrants from poverty-stricken Scandinavia. At Council Bluffs the councils now were not held among feathered braves gathering to treat with William Clark, who had been dead for fifteen years; they were made up of surveyors and representatives from the Baldwin Locomotive Works.

The idea of a Pacific railway had first found printed expression in a manifesto written by John Plumbe, a civil engineer from Dubuque. But Salmon P. Chase's bill did something concrete by granting appropriations for explorations of the Pacific railway's possible routes. Chase's bill was the first of a series. One set aside the staggering sum of $96,000,000 for the construction of roadbeds and tracks. The Mississippi and Missouri Railroad Company came into being in 1852 for the purpose of building a line westward across Iowa as an extension of the Rock Island. By 1853 Grenville Dodge and Peter Day were busily surveying. Day sent Dodge to the valleys of the Missouri and the Platte in autumn. The leaves of high cottonwoods were beginning to brown and drift slowly down to the water when the flatboats of Dodge's party crossed the Missouri. Technically, the land belonged to the Omaha Indians. From the site of the future city of Omaha, Dodge led an exploring party overland. When they reached the Platte Valley, Dodge went surveying on his own. Growing tired at one point, he tied his horse to a tree and lay down, using his saddle as a pillow and placing his rifle under it. His sound sleep was broken by the neighing of the horse. When Dodge looked up he saw an Indian leading the horse away; the Indian was "pulling with all his might," and the horse was holding back. Dodge grabbed his rifle and shouted at the Indian until the red man let the horse go. Then Dodge saddled up and made his way back to the explorers' main camp. He found it full of Omahas, who stood around glowering while a frightened party of whites cooked food for them in an effort to placate them. Dodge was aghast. His men were using their rations. Since they were all armed, he called them together and told them to show their rifles. "I know only one Indian word," Dodge said. "It's *puckechee,* and it means 'get out.'" When the explorers advanced on the sullen Omahas brandishing their weapons and shouting "Puckechee!" the Omahas got the idea and left. Dodge afterward wrote a memorandum about the incident; engineers and surveyors were advised not to let Indians into their camps if they wished to preserve their livestock, their food, and their lives.

By 1854 Dodge and his assistants in Nebraska were busily obtaining "all valuable information" for railway companies wishing to expand. The companies named their projects grandly: the line along the 42nd parallel became the Pacific Railroad; along the 49th parallel, the North Route. The Buffalo Trail, named by Missouri Senator Benton, would run along the 38th and 39th parallels. Along the 35th and 34th the South Route was projected. The Union Pacific Railway wasn't named until America had erupted into civil war, but in the 1850s, when white men conquered the Great Plains, it was already a powerful impetus to national growth. The diplomatic skills of George W. Manypenny, whose job it was to present Indians on the coveted parallels with treaties, were crucial to its success. But Manypenny was not a happy man, as his annual report in 1854 bore witness:

I am constrained to submit a few suggestions in relation to the emigrated tribes in Kansas Territory, who, by the policy of the government adopted nearly thirty years ago, and reluctantly acquiesced in by them, were removed to, and became inhabitants of, the country now embraced in this territory. Already many of them have ceded, and it is expected that others will cede, the larger portions of their lands to the United States, for the use and occupation of our citizens. The faith of the nation was pledged in the most solemn form, before these tribes were removed to the west of the Mississippi, that they should have the undisputed possession and control of the country, and that the tracts assigned to them should be their permanent homes. It was called "the Indian Territory" and the intercourse act made it unlawful for white men to go into it, except on a license obtained and for special purposes; and in this secluded home, it was believed that the efforts of the government and the philanthropist to civilize the red man would be more successful than ever before. Such, however, was not the case. Our population advanced rapidly to the line which was to be the barrier. . . .

In the recent negotiations for their lands the Indians dwelt upon the former pledges and promises made to them, and were averse generally to the surrender of any portion of their country. They said that they were to have the land "as long as green grass grew or water ran," and they feared the result if they should consent to yield any part of their possessions. When they did consent to sell, it was only on the condition that each tribe should retain a portion of their tract as a permanent home. All were unitedly and firmly opposed to another removal.

The opposition, said Mr. Manypenny, was hardly surprising.

He made his peace with his uneasy conscience as best he could. The immigrant Indians in Kansas were there to stay.

What a spectacle for the view of the statesman, philanthropist, Christian! . . . There they stand, the representatives and remnants of tribes once as powerful and dreaded as they are now weak and dispirited. . . . They can go no further. . . . Extermination may be their fate, but not of necessity. By a union of good influences, and a proper effort, I believe they may and will be saved, and their complete civilization effected.

In other words, once the Indians were confined to their "diminished reserves," the answer to their troubles would be missionaries and more missionaries.

Kansas itself was in ferment over the issue of slavery. Its abolitionists, the Indians noted wryly, were interested in "the condition of the African race" but not of the red. Red men owned land as black men did not, and it was easier to want to emancipate people who had no property than to deal fairly with those who did.

Comforting himself with the thought of a tidal wave of preachers of the gospel who would "save" the Indians who had been removed west, Manypenny presented the Indians with government treaties. In 1854 he concluded negotiations with the Omahas, Otos, Missouris, Sacs and Foxes, Iowas, Kickapoos, Delawares, Shawnees, Kaskaskias, Peorias, Weas, Piankeshaws, and Miamis—the tribes with whom he had already begun his work. Progress was swift; on March 15, 1854, the Otos and Missouris surrendered, and the next day the Delawares followed suit. Article No. 3 of the Delaware Treaty was particularly illuminating:

The Delaware tribe of Indians, entertaining the belief that the value of their lands will be enhanced by having a railroad passing through their present reservation, and being of opinion that the Leavenworth, Pawnee, and Western Railroad Incorporated by an act of the legislative assembly of Kansas Territory, will have the advantage of travel and general transportation over every other company proposed to be formed, which will run through their lands, have expressed a desire that the said Leavenworth, Pawnee and Western Railroad Company shall have the preference of purchasing the remainder of their lands after the tracts in severalty and those for the special objects herein named shall have been selected and set apart, upon the payment into the United States Treasury, which payment shall be made in six months after the quantity shall have been ascertained, in gold or silver coin, of such a sum as three commissioners, to be appointed by the Secretary of the Interior, shall appraise to be the value of the said land.[5]

Of course, every Delaware was burning with the desire to ride the rails of the Leavenworth, Pawnee and Western. An accommodating United States Government was only too ready to make him happy by granting him his wish.

The Manypenny treaties had many similarities. All tribes expressed the hope that a specific railroad should come through their lands. Two preferred the Leavenworth, Pawnee and Western, while another group opted for the projected Atlantic and Pike's Peak Company. The Potawatomis were made to express the wish that their surplus farm products should be carried to market by the L, P & W. Not that they had enough to sustain more than marginal life among themselves, but a truly progressive Potawatomi should attune his mind to the future. Maybe there would be a surplus someday. A common sale price for Indian land to the railroads was a thrifty dollar and a quarter an acre. The esteem of Indians for railroads was, evidently, boundless.

Westward, in the hills of Oklahoma, the Five Civilized Tribes could see what was coming. First the red refugees from Kansas and Nebraska would be dumped on them, then it would be their turn to develop a passionate desire for the coming of Iron Horses of various lineages. Following its war with Mexico, the United States had fallen heir to new tribes. Old Rough and Ready had moved on from the Sacs, Foxes, and Seminoles to subdue relatives of the mysterious Aztecs. The newest red Americans were quick to understand their own plight, as gold seekers plunged into their midst. White America also had its methods on the Pacific, Commissioner Manypenny learned:

A party started up the coast from San Francisco on a gold hunting expedition. They had a vessel loaded with supplies, tools, etc., sufficient for a substantial outfit. After sailing up to near the southern boundary of Oregon, they landed, when a portion of them immediately set out on a tour of exploration, leaving the remainder to discharge the cargo and in due time follow their comrades. About thirty Indians came to the beach, and at the request of the Americans proceeded to help unload the vessel. The Indians labored faithfully for the newcomers. There were on the vessel two pieces of cannon and a supply of guns and pistols. In the bay near the landing and close to the vessel, there was a large rock, the top surface of which was above the water, and of sufficient area to accommodate many persons. The cannon, when removed from the vessel, were placed upon the rock and in proper position. When the work was completed, the Indians were requested to come on the rock to receive pay for their labor. As they passed up in Indian file, at the proper moment, the guns were brought to bear upon them, and all but two were killed.

How long, wondered Commissioner Manypenny, would the Indians have to wait before missionaries arrived in force to deliver them from all evil?

By the end of his life, he knew the answer. George W. Manypenny went to his death haunted by words which had begun as a whisper but which had long since become a deafening roar: "as long as the green grass grows and the water flows. Forever."

16

Sir St. George Gore Goes Hunting

"I go to kill the buffalo.
The Great Spirit sent the buffalo
On hills, in plains and woods,
So give me my bow, give me my bow:
I go to kill the buffalo."
— SIOUX HUNTING SONG

A SATISFIED UNITED STATES HAD NOW SENT MOST OF ITS EASTERN Indians to what it called the Great American Desert. Early expeditions had described those windy reaches vividly:

> This portion of the country [said an army observer] . . . has an average width of five or six hundred miles, extending along the base of the Rocky Mountains from north to south. . . . I do not hesitate in giving the opinion that it is almost wholly unfit for cultivation, and of course uninhabitable by a people depending on agriculture for their subsistence. Although tracts of fertile land considerably extensive are occasionally to be met with, yet the scarcity of wood and water almost uniformly prevalent will prove an insuperable obstacle in the way of settling the country. . . . The whole of this region seems peculiarly adapted as a range for buffaloes, wild goats, and other game.[1]

No human being was expected to survive in the Great American Desert—except displaced Indians.

Zebulon Montgomery Pike had found the western prairies and plains

> likely to become in time as celebrated as the sandy deserts of Africa, for I saw in my route in various places tracts of many leagues where the wind had thrown up the sand in all the fanciful form of the ocean's rolling wave, and on which not a speck of vegetable matter existed. . . . Our citizens being so prone to rambling and extending themselves on the frontiers will, through necessity, be constrained to limit their extent on the west to the borders of the Missouri and Mississippi, while they leave the prairies incapable of cultivation to the wandering and uncivilized aborigines of our country.[2]

The red natives of the plains rode small strong horses with wild eyes, said Pike, descendants of the horses of Spanish Conquistadores. By 1854 the eastern Indians were learning to ride them too on "diminished reserves" in Indian Territory not yet diminished to nothing.

And always there were gales, intensely hot and dry in summer, Arctic in winter. White Americans read explorers' ac-

counts of the trans-Mississippi West with wonder, little caring
that they were demanding of woodland Indians an unprece-
dented adjustment from humid forests to arid expanses. Methods of travel, weapons, techniques of tilling the soil, tools,
food—all changed west of a line from central Texas north to
Illinois. Where in the East there had been earth, water, and
timber for the tribes to rely on, on the prairies in many places
there was only earth. But the refugees learned from plains Indians until their solutions were being coveted by the whites
who had ejected them from their original homelands.

The newcomers became daring horsemen and hunted bison,
raising range cattle when they could afford to invest in stock.
Jesse Chisholm, a half-breed Cherokee, established a trail
which led from Texas up to Kansas slaughterhouses. Creeks
and Choctaws and Miamis had seen nothing like western Nebraska and Kansas and Oklahoma and the Staked Plains of
Texas. Everywhere was a wide, crackling blue sky and brown-
ish-green grass bending perpetually in the wind. Between the
sky and the ground in summer, the horizon danced up and
down in waves of heat, as did the outlines of occasional hills.
When the winds abated, the plains became eerily soundless,
without the stir of leaves or the hum of insects; they could
embody life and death in a transition of a few short seconds.
Infrequently dark skies roared during thunderstorms but more
often, under a cloudless sun, fires erupted sending jackrabbits
dashing in horror from the clamor of the flames only to suffo-
cate in their heat. After the prairie fires, the ground was strewn
with the corpses of coyotes and badgers; ignited piles of buffalo dung smoldered for hours, a crematorium for insects.
Buffalo which had barely outrun the holocaust staggered
blindly over the charred earth. No one who ever saw the mingled majesty and horror of the American West remained un-
marked by the experience. It was, wrote a traveler into Indian
Territory,

> a world almost without a feature, an empty sky, an empty earth,
> front and back. . . . The green plain ran till it touched the skirts
> of heaven. . . . Even my own body or my own head seemed a

great thing in that emptiness. . . . This spacious vacancy, this greatness of the air, this discovery of the whole arch of heaven, this straight, unbroken prison-line of the horizon . . . The eye must embrace at every glance the concave of the visible world, the universe laid bare in all its gauntness.[3]

If the prairies sometimes looked lifeless to white observers, to the Indians who first inhabited them and to those who were sent to live on them in exile, they were teeming. Every spring was full of the booming of prairie chickens, the chatter of waterfowl on infrequent shallow rivers like the Platte, the calling of meadowlarks. Tiny pipistrelle bats flitted in twilit summer skies before the stars erupted overhead. August was the Moon of Ripe Wild Plums; the prairies had fruits for those who learned to gather them. But most of all they provided the gigantic buffalo herds which wandered from grassland to grassland in search of forage. To lure the buffalo, the Indians of the Plains had fashioned their ceremonies and sung their songs. Now the Indians of the East also began to pray for buffalo, and watched with awe tribes like the Pawnees who hunted down the humped, matchstick-legged beasts in surrounds and stampedes, summer and winter.

The Pawnees too had become nomads, evicted from their Kansas villages to make room for the Delawares. A succession of missionaries had come to them to preach farming and peace, but the Pawnees knew they were at the mercy of the Sioux on the north and of the incoming tribes on the south. Under such conditions, who could plant? To get swift results in Christianity and agriculture, a group of missionaries from Oberlin, Ohio, took to beating their pagan charges. The word "Oberlinism" became a synonym for enslaving Indians. The strongest defense of all the tribes against such enslavement was the American bison. As long as the numberless herds existed, there would be freedom and food. From buffalo came housing, meat, clothing, and the sinew ropes which bound the possessions of hunting camps. Buffalo skulls were powerful medicine. The Creeks,

Cherokees, and Delawares learned rapidly from the Pawnees, Crows, and Blackfeet.

By the mid–nineteenth century, newspapers in Kansas were reporting a new phenomenon: "To shoot buffalo seems a mania. Men come from London—cockneys, fops, and nobles—and from all parts of the Republic to enjoy what they call sport. Sport! Where no danger is incurred and no skill required." No skill was required, that is, if one could buy a good rifle, against which a slow-witted bison had little chance. Americans were hunting buffalo commercially for hides and tongues, and it was not long before the western Indians, natives and immigrants alike, understood that they faced a white menace other than land-stealing. By the time Scottish baronet Sir William Drummond Stewart led a hunting force of eighty into the tallgrass Plains, his guides were admonishing their subordinates: "Half of you are ordered to stay sober, on account of the hostility of the Indians."[4] Sir William watched in fascination as his insect-ridden prey rolled in prairie wallows to rub themselves free of vermin. The number of tiny calves nursing from huge mothers seemed infinite. But in reality the grazing lands of the buffalo herds had already been decreased by half since the turn of the century. The herds were being steadily crowded out of Kansas and Nebraska and Oklahoma into the heart of the Plains at the foot of the Rockies. Their dependent Indian hunters followed them there.

As the range grew smaller, white sportsmen grew more formidable. Sir William's total of dead buffalo was modest compared to that of his successor, an Irish baronet from Sligo named Sir St. George Gore.[5] Sir St. George, whose family motto admonished that man's sole salvation was to serve God, was not concerned for his salvation but for his reputation. He was out to break records and to fill his trophy room. A stout bachelor, he was forty-three in 1854, the possessor of a luxuriant crop of sandy side-whiskers. It was the displaced Pawnees in particular who watched the triumphal progress of deer-stalker-hatted Sir St. George. He prodigiously enjoyed killing things, and the grouse and stags of his native Britain had begun to pall. The West was his oyster.

Sir St. George burst upon the American frontier in all his glory at St. Louis one hot, dusty summer and had the natives gaping. In the center of town were lined up his men and equipment: 21 two-horse charettes (in the West they were called Red River carts), 112 thoroughbred horses, 3 milk cows, 18 oxen, 4 six-mule wagons, 2 three-yoke wagons, and a magnificent canopied brass bed for the nightly use of Sir St. George. Forty men were in his retinue; the majority hired in Mound City, Missouri, where Sir St. George had also bought his transportation and provisions. One wagon was for firearms alone. An immense green-and-white-striped tent, ten by eighteen feet (it came with a carpet), had been brought from Britain by Sir St. George as a shelter against the western winds. In case of wet weather, a spring wagon had been equipped as living quarters. Sir St. George had also crossed the ocean with solid silver drinking cups embossed with the family crest, a tiger rampant. These were kept in a locked box to which his valet had the key. There was an iron dining table to put them on. There were also a marble washstand and a big wooden bathtub. Sir St. George traveled with a full set of Shakespeare, which he quoted nightly to his minions.

When the expedition passed through Leavenworth, Kansas, it was seen by an astonished youngster named William Frederick Cody, not yet famous as Buffalo Bill. He marveled especially at the telescope in one of the wagons, presided over by Sir St. George's great friend, Sir William Thomas Spencer-Wentworth-Fitzwilliam. Sir William intended to make astronomical observations on the Plains and in the Rocky Mountains. The expedition's chief guide was a canny frontiersman named Henry Chatillon, who knew the Rockies as few men did. He had sense enough to keep his mouth shut on the subject of his employer's luxuries.

He arrived at Fort Laramie, on the north fork of the Platte, at the end of June. There a fledgling newspaper duly noted his arrival: "Between forty and fifty dogs, mostly greyhounds and staghounds of the most beautiful breeds, compose part of the expedition. Sir St. George has a large carriage. The dogs are the most magnificent pack ever seen in this country." All belonged to the "resolute-looking" baronet, who began making the acquaintance of maverick hunters, trappers, traders, and a motley crew of adventurers on the frontier. He also struck up acquaintances with several Indians of the tribes on whose lands he was about to intrude. From Fort Laramie the expedition headed into what is now Colorado; the guide for this part of the trip was Henry Chatillon's brother Joe.

Sir St. George hunted mule deer with his dogs, and buffalo from a shooting stand; his scouts steadily stampeded the animals into his range, while his gun bearers were kept busy loading rifles for him. After he had vanquished a herd, his custom was to stroll the ground picking out the shaggy corpses he thought would look best in his trophy room. There were several taxidermists along who were kept as busy as the gun bearers.

When autumn came and purple and yellow and white asters bloomed in fields of grass, Sir St. George retired to Fort Laramie again. Here he spent a winter full of blizzards listening to camp fables and planning his wanderings for the following spring. When the first spring flowers unfolded, he decided to go fishing at Pike's Peak. The only trouble was that there was no road to it. This didn't bother Sir St. George; he hired an entire tribe of Blackfoot Indians to hack one out, and soon he was decimating the trout population in mountain streams.

One day one of his scouts came to him with a nugget of gold.

"It's only mica," said Sir St. George. The scout threw the gold away. Later Sir St. George loftily explained to Joe Chatillon, "That was gold, but I did not come here to seek it. I don't need gold. This is a pleasure hunt." By this time the camp had been moved, and Joe knew it would be useless to tell the scout what he had lost.

When Sir St. George had had his fill of fishing, the party headed back to Fort Laramie. Here he met a mountaineer named Jim Bridger. Bridger had been the first white man to see the geysers of Yellowstone, and he mapped out new routes for Sir St. George, who listened to his buckskinned companion with reverent attention. Bridger, who had started life in Richmond, Virginia, was now a grizzled fifty. When he was still a boy he had cut out for St. Louis, where he had run the ferry for a while. He had seen the eastern Indians as they crossed the Mississippi to their prairie prison, tribe after tribe of them, and the austere figure of William Clark, whose West he meant to explore. It was not long before he got a job as a trapper for the Rocky Mountain Fur Company. The track he had begun as the Overland Trail had since become the Oregon Trail. He had had three wives: the first a Flathead, the second a Ute, and for four years he had been married to a Snake woman. His daughter by the Ute was being raised on buffalo milk. He never strayed long or far from the Rockies. He loved the mountains with inarticulate passion. He was unimpressed with the treasures of Sir St. George Gore, whom he refused to address by his title. "Mister Gore" was good enough he said, and Sir St. George meekly assented. When the baronet found that Bridger was illiterate, he began reading him *As You Like It*.

"I reckon it's high-falutin'," Bridger said. Of *King Henry the Fourth* he remarked, "That Dutch man Mr. Full-Stuff must of been a little too fond of lager beer. He'd of done better on good Kentucky bourbon."

When Sir St. George recited the tales of Baron Münchhausen, Bridger exclaimed: "That there baron is a damned liar!" His own adventures with the Blackfeet had been as exciting. One evening Sir St. George favored him with Sir Walter Scott's description of the Battle of Waterloo.

"Well, now Mister Gore, that there must of been considerable of a scrimmage, doggone my skin if it mustn't. Them Britishers must of fit better there than they did down to Horleans where Old Hickory gin um the forkedest sort of chain lightning

you ever see in your born days. You can jist go yer pile on it,
Mister Gore, you can sure as yer born."⁰ The "exotic pair" of
Bridger and Gore arrived in a large village of Crow Indians,
where vagabond whites attached to the camp interpreted for
Sir St. George as he questioned the Indians about the way they
lived. The Indians were monosyllabic and impassive, even at
the sight of the expedition.

For a year Sir St. George wandered in the Yellowstone country; in the winter of 1855–56 he built a fort to winter in. The
Piegan band of Blackfeet were less impassive than the Crows
had been, and one night raided his horses, making off with
twenty-one of the best. Sir St. George angrily sent pursuers
after them, but a blizzard intervened. A month later the Blood
band of Blackfeet had their turn with his horses. This time he
was prepared. Without hesitation he shot the chief, Big Plume.
He had no intention of losing his best mount, aptly named
Steel Trap. Sir St. George himself was a walking trap for anything on four legs. In the spring he began shooting again.
When the Blackfeet observed him in action they sent a protest
to Washington via an agent of the American Fur Company.
The food supply of the Indians of the West was being systematically killed off, they said. Washington, as was usual in such
cases, did nothing.

In the Dakotas, one of Sir St. George's scouts again brought
him a nugget of gold.

"No, Jerry, that's mica," said Sir St. George. He did not want
the Black Hills invaded by riffraff; the hills were, temporarily,
his.

In the autumn of 1856 he decided he wanted to live with the
Hidatsas and with what was left of the Mandans for a while.
Crow's Breast, a Hidatsa chief, hospitably moved out of his
lodge, and Sir St. George's brass bedstead was carried in. At
first Sir St. George bought his beef from traders at fifty dollars
a head. When the traders raised the price by half, he shifted his
business to a competitor and, to teach the culprits a moral
lesson, bought fifty head of cattle to give to the Indians. After

that the Hidatsas cared little about what was happening to the buffalo as Sir St. George returned each night with his kill. He would shoot at the rushing herds until the scene around him under the vibrating sky was the desolate haunt of coyotes and buzzards. Everywhere lay dead bulls, cows, and calves, and in places the grass was red with their blood. A stench hung over the hills and plains. All this was too much for Jim Bridger, who believed in killing for necessity. He left his employer to his own devices and headed back to the Rockies and seclusion. From the Dakotas Sir St. George moved into Nebraska, where refugee Winnebagoes, Pawnees, and Miamis watched helplessly as Sir St. George's men rounded up buffalo herds while he fired avidly from his shooting stand. When the ground thundered with hooves and the buffalo were a solid mass, Sir St. George could shoot at random. It was virtually impossible to miss.

When he had ranged over a total of six thousand miles, and had spent three years' worth of income from his Irish estates, he decided to return to Britain, where he intended to save up for an expedition into the Seminoles' Everglades. He had, as yet, no alligators or egrets in his study. At the American Fur Company agency in Fort Union, he offered to sell the company what was left of his expedition for less than a third of the cost. The agent offered him a tenth, whereupon Sir St. George stalked out of the office and ordered his retinue to haul his wagons to the top of a bluff. Then he distributed presents to the Hidatsas encamped nearby: priceless rifles, staghounds, Arabian horses, the cornmeal on which his mount Steel Trap had been fed, and provisions enough to feed every Hidatsa for a year. After this, carrying a large stick coated with tar, he set fire to the half-million dollars' worth of equipment on the bluff. The helpless employees of the American Fur Company watched. Then he ordered his men to built two flatboats for his trophies. On these decks the tons of booty meat went to St. Louis, while he himself rode overland into history with a modest escort of twelve. Today, on State Highway 84, high in Colorado, there is a sign:

GORE PASS
Altitude 9,000 Feet

Here in 1855 crossed Sir St. George Gore, an Irish
baronet bent on slaughter of game and guided by Jim
Bridger. For three years he scoured Colorado, Montana, and Wyoming, accompanied usually by forty
men, many carts, wagons, hounds, and unexampled
camp luxuries. More than 2,000 buffalo, 1,600 deer and
elk, and 100 bears were massacred for sport.

There was barely a generation left for the American bison.
But as the second half of the nineteenth century began, the
diminished herds still moved on prairies where warm winds
came blowing and singing up from the Indian Territory and
the Staked Plains of Texas. The animals marched from grassland to grassland in a brown mass, the front of the herd's column white with horns. In winter they braved the icy winds and
in spring the calves were born. The bulls still circled clumsily
to protect their herd from wolves; the oldest bulls, outcast,
roamed alone in search of pasture. Sometimes, when an alarm
was raised, the buffalo would hurl themselves forward, strong
in terrible thousands, to wither the grass. The grass would
grow back; the bison, pursued by white hunters, would not. As
the bison galloped along, their mouths foamed in fear and
gunsmoke stung their eyes. "Where the Indian kills one buffalo," said the Sioux, "the hide and tongue hunters kill fifty."
They said, "A cold wind is blowing across the prairie when the
last buffalo fall—a death-wind for our people."

The death wind was blowing in Indian Territory and Texas,
in Colorado mountains and hills, and over rugged Montana
buttes. The last pageantries of the tribes who hunted for sustenance—Plains Indians resident from time immemorial and
transplants from the East—passed with the buffalo. The grand
spectacle was doomed: the motley colors of horses' trappings,
the sacred paint on rawhide pouches, eagle feathers and flowing fringes, the rough teasing of youths and the dignity of
mothers who bore their babies on their backs, the wrinkled old

men with skin like leather, patriarchs struggling to remain erect on willful horses, shamans who rode in front of their tribes chanting of hunts long gone, the whims of spirits, and of the holiness of the rare white buffalo they had seen in dreams and on the hoof. A human as well as an animal world was dying.

In the East, America had stolen the lands of her original discoverers and shipped those discoverers out like so many cattle. In the West, she permitted the extermination of their food in the new land. In the decade from 1840 to 1850 the country acquired approximately 20,000,000 acres from the Indians at a cost close to $3,000,000, roughly fifteen cents an acre. In exchange, the Indians had gotten 4,000,000 acres of land that was considered unfit for human life unless that life belonged to people with red skins.[7] Every treaty left the Indian tribes of the nation poorer, while the nation itself grew richer as it moved inexorably toward the Civil War which would rend but not destroy it. The Trail of Tears had had its start where the sun rose. Finally, in the West of vast skies, thrusting grasses, painted sunsets, and dwindling buffalo, that trail became the road to Wounded Knee.

References

"The vitality of our race still persists. We have not lived for naught. We are the original discoverers of this continent, and the conquerors of it from the animal kingdom, and on it first taught the arts of peace and war, and first planted the institutions of virtue, truth, and liberty. The European nations found us here and were made aware that it was possible for man to exist and subsist here. We have given to the European people on this continent our thought forces—the best blood of our ancestors having intermingled with their best statesmen and leading citizens. We have made ourselves an indestructible element in their national history. We have shown that what they believed were arid and desert places were habitable and capable of sustaining millions of people. We have led the vanguard of civilization in our conflicts with them for tribal existence from ocean to ocean. The race that has rendered this service to the other nations of mankind cannot utterly perish."[1]

—PLEASANT PORTER, CREEK

Notes

INTRODUCTION

1. Grant Foreman, *The Five Civilized Tribes* (Norman: University of Oklahoma, 1934), passim.
2. Angie Debo, *The Road to Disappearance* (Norman: University of Oklahoma, 1941), p. 43.
3. Albert J. Pickett, *A History of Alabama* (Birmingham: Webb Book Co., 1900), p. 531.
4. Wild men: this is traditional Creek usage.
5. Marquis James, *Andrew Jackson: The Border Captain* (New York: Literary Guild, 1933), pp. i, 149.
6. Pickett, *A History of Alabama*, p. 525.
7. Ibid., pp. 524ff.
8. Ibid., pp. 528ff.
9. Ibid., pp. 538ff.
10. David R. Wrone and Russell S. Nelson, Jr., *Who's the Savage?* (Greenwich, Conn.: Fawcett Publications, 1973), p. 230.
11. James, *Andrew Jackson: The Border Captain*, pp. i, 183.

CHAPTER 1

1. Annie Heloise Abel, "Proposals for an Indian State 1738–1878," American Historical Association, Annual Reports, 1907 (Washington, D.C.: Government Printing Office, 1908), pp. 89ff.
2. Gloria Jahoda, *The Other Florida* (New York: Scribner's, 1967), p. 62.
3. Council on Interracial Books for Children, *Chronicles of American Indian Protest* (New York: The Council, 1971), p. 59.
4. Henry R. Schoolcraft, *The American Indians: Their History, Conditions, and Prospects* (Rochester, N.Y.: Wanzer Foot and Co., 1851), p. 389.
5. Grant Foreman, *Indians and Pioneers* (Norman: University of Oklahoma, 1936), p. 43.
6. John J. Mathews, *The Osages* (Norman: University of Oklahoma, 1961), p. 416.
7. Foreman, *Indians and Pioneers*, p. 49.
8. Grant Foreman, *The Last Trek of the Indians* (Chicago: University of Chicago, 1946), pp. 48–51.
9. Foreman, *Indians and Pioneers*, p. 74n.
10. James D. Richardson, *Messages of the Presidents* (Washington, D.C.: Government Printing Office, 1899), vol. 2, p. 282.

11. Alice Fletcher, *The Hako, A Pawnee Ceremony*, Bureau of American Ethnology, 22nd Annual Report (Washington, D.C.: Government Printing Office, 1904).
12. Foreman, *The Last Trek of the Indians*, pp. 16, 51; Foreman, *Indians and Pioneers*, p. 197.
13. Foreman, *The Last Trek of the Indians*, p. 16; Foreman, *Indians and Pioneers*, p. 197.
14. Reverend Jedediah Morse, *Report to the Secretary of War of the United States on Indian Affairs* (New Haven: S. Converse, 1822), p. 67.
15. Morse, *Report to the Secretary of War of the United States on Indian Affairs*, p. 212.
16. George Schultz, *An Indian Canaan* (Norman: University of Oklahoma, 1972), p. 103.
17. United States Congress, 23rd, 1st session, Senate Document 512, vol. 2, p. 290.

CHAPTER 2

1. Reverend Jedediah Morse, *Report to the Secretary of War of the United States on Indian Affairs* (New Haven: S. Converse, 1822), p. 83.
2. W.L.G. Smith, *The Life and Times of Lewis Cass* (New York: Derby and Jackson, 1856), pp. 200ff.
3. James D. Horan, *The McKenney-Hall Portrait Gallery of American Indians* (New York: Crown Publishers, 1972), p. 104.
4. David R. Wrone and Russell S. Nelson, Jr., *Who's the Savage?* (Greenwich, Conn.: Fawcett Publications, 1973), pp. 232–33.
5. Wilson Lumpkin, *The Removal of the Cherokee Indians from Georgia* (New York: Dodd Mead, 1907), p. 49.
6. Margaret L. Coit, "The Presidency of Andrew Jackson" (unpublished, manuscript courtesy of the author).
7. Marquis James, *The Raven: A Biography of Sam Houston* (New York: Paperback Library, 1962), p. 67.
8. Ibid., pp. 106ff.
9. Lumpkin, *The Removal of the Cherokee Indians from Georgia*, pp. 54ff.
10. James, *The Raven: A Biography of Sam Houston*, pp. 77ff.
11. John Q. Adams, *Diary*, Allen Nevins, ed. (New York: Longmans Green, 1929), pp. 526ff.
12. Washington Irving, *A Tour on the Prairies* (New York: Pantheon, 1967), pp. 12ff.

CHAPTER 3

1. United States Congress, 23rd, 1st session, Senate Document 512, vol. 2, p. 597.
2. Lewis H. Morgan, *League of the Ho-de-no-sau-nee* (New York: Corinth Books, 1962), pp. 149ff.
3. James A. Shackford, *David Crockett: The Man and the Legend* (Chapel Hill: University of North Carolina, 1956), pp. 117ff.
4. United States Congress, 23rd, 1st session, Senate Document 512, vol. 1, p. 732.
5. Ibid., p. 399.
6. Ibid.

CHAPTER 4

1. United States Congress, 23rd, 1st session, Senate Document 512, vol. 1, p. 240.
2. Migration of Choctaws: Creek and Choctaw tradition agree on the main points of the march.
3. C.J. Kappler, ed., *Indian Affairs, Laws, and Treaties* (Washington, D.C.: Government Printing Office, 1892–1913), vol. 2, p. 221.
4. United States Congress, 23rd, 1st session, Senate Document 512, vol. 2, p. 42.
5. Angie Debo, *The Rise and Fall of the Choctaw Republic* (Norman: University of Oklahoma, 1934), p. 50.
6. Ibid., p. 51.
7. Ibid., p. 52; United States Congress, 23rd, 1st session, Senate Document 512, vols. 2 and 3, pp. 75, 240.
8. Debo, *The Rise and Fall of the Choctaw Republic*, p. 54; Jackson, Tennessee, *Gazette*, August 4 and October 9, 1830.
9. Debo, *The Rise and Fall of the Choctaw Republic*, pp. 54–55; United States Congress, 23rd, 1st session, Senate Document 512, vol. 2, p. 252.
10. United States Congress, 23rd, 1st session, Senate Document 512, vol. 1, pp. 591ff, vol. 2, pp. 393, 418.
11. Grant Foreman, *Indian Removal* (Norman: University of Oklahoma, 1953), p. 36.
12. United States Congress, 23rd, 1st session, Senate Document 512, vol. 1, pp. 369ff.
13. Ibid., p. 719.
14. Foreman, *Indian Removal*, p. 84.
15. United States Congress, 23rd, 1st session, Senate Document 512, vol. 1, pp. 387ff.
16. Ibid., vol. 1, p. 411.

CHAPTER 5

1. General A. G. Ellis, "Some Account of the Advent of the New York Indians into Wisconsin," *Wisconsin Historical Collections,* vol. 2 (1855), pp. 415ff; Grant Foreman, *The Last Trek of the Indians* (Chicago: University of Chicago, 1946), pp. 330ff.
2. William Fenton, *Parker on the Iroquois* (Syracuse, N.Y.: Syracuse University, 1968), pp. 9ff.
3. General A. G. Ellis, "Recollections of Rev. Eleazer Williams," *Wisconsin Historical Collections,* vol. 8 (1877–79), pp. 322ff.
4. Ellis, "Some Account of the Advent of the New York Indians into Wisconsin," pp. 415ff.
5. Ellis, "Recollections of Rev. Eleazer Williams," p. 365.
6. Hon. John Y. Smith, "Eleazer Williams and the Lost Prince," *Wisconsin Historical Collections,* vol. 6 (1872), pp. 313ff.
7. Ibid., pp. 330ff.

CHAPTER 6

1. William T. Hagan, *The Sac and Fox Indians* (Norman: University of Oklahoma, 1958), pp. 5ff.
2. Hagan, *The Sac and Fox Indians,* pp. 5ff.
3. Ibid., p. 16.
4. Ibid., pp. 23ff.
5. Black Hawk's remarks and viewpoint of the war, are, of course, to be found in his *Autobiography.*
6. Cecil Eby, *That Disgraceful Affair, The Black Hawk War* (New York: Norton, 1973), pp. 71ff.
7. Ibid., pp. 101–5.
8. Ibid., p. 97.
9. Ibid., pp. 122ff.
10. Ibid., p. 123.
11. N. Matson, *Memories of Shaubena* (Chicago: D. E. Cook and Co., 1878), pp. 415ff.
12. Eby, *That Disgraceful Affair, The Black Hawk War,* p. 132.
13. Ibid., p. 234.
14. Ibid., p. 256.

CHAPTER 7

1. C.J. Kappler, ed., *Indian Affairs, Laws, and Treaties* (Washington, D.C.: Government Printing Office, 1892–1913), pp. 2, 247; United States Congress, 23rd, 1st session, Senate Document 512, vol. 4, pp. 293–94.

2. United States Congress, 23rd, 1st session, Senate Document 512, vol. 2, p. 305; *Niles' Weekly Register*, July 16, 1831.
3. United States Congress, 23rd, 1st session, Senate Document 512, vol. 3, p. 485; Grant Foreman, *Indian Removal* (Norman: University of Oklahoma, 1941), p. 115.
4. *American State Papers* (Gales and Seaton), (Washington, D.C.: Gales and Seaton, 1832–1860), "Military Affairs," vol. 2, p. 68.
5. Albert J. Pickett, *History of Alabama* (Birmingham: Webb Book Co., 1900), pp. 510–14.
6. United States Congress, 23rd, 1st session, Senate Document 512, vol. 4, p. 423.
7. Foreman, *Indian Removal* (Norman: University of Oklahoma, 1953), p. 121.
8. Ibid., p. 128. This interpretation of the dust clouds is a Creek tradition.
9. Ibid., p. 133.
10. Ibid., p. 147.
11. Ibid., p. 151.
12. *American State Papers*, "Military Affairs," vol. 1, p. 953.
13. Foreman, *Indian Removal*, p. 154.
14. Ibid., p. 164.
15. Ibid., p. 176.
16. Creeks remembering: information from Sakim, Medicine Man to the Creeks, Tallahassee, Florida, and from Chief Neal McCormick, Bainbridge, Georgia.

CHAPTER 8

1. Arrell M. Gibson, *The Chickasaws* (Norman: University of Oklahoma, 1972), p. 53.
2. Ibid., p. 104.
3. Grant Foreman, *Indian Removal* (Norman: University of Oklahoma, 1953), p. 307.
4. Ibid., pp. 204ff.
5. Ibid., pp. 210ff.
6. John Parsons, ed., "Letters on the Chickasaw Removal of 1837," *New York Historical Society Quarterly*, vol. 37 (1953), pp. 273ff.
7. Foreman, *Indian Removal*, pp. 204ff.
8. Ibid., p. 222.
9. Ibid., pp. 223ff.
10. Ibid., p. 225.

CHAPTER 9

1. George Catlin, *Letters and Notes on the Manners, Customs, and Conditions of the North American Indians* (Minneapolis: Ross and Haines, 1965), vol. 1, pp. 45ff.
2. George Catlin, *O-Kee-Pa: A Religious Ceremony and Other Customs of the Mandan, Hidatsa, and Crow Indians* (New Haven: Yale University, 1967), pp. 39ff.
3. Annie H. Abel, ed., *Chardon's Journal at Fort Clark 1834–1839* (Pierre, South Dakota: Department of History of the State of South Dakota, 1932), p. 123.
4. Ibid., pp. 124–25.
5. Ibid., p. 124.
6. Ibid., p. 395.

CHAPTER 10

1. Juliette A. Kinzie, "Chicago Indian Chiefs," *Bulletin of the Chicago Historical Society,* vol. 1 (1935), pp. 105ff.
2. Ulf Beijbom, "Anders Larsson—Immigrant Pioneer in Chicago," reprint from *Swedish Pioneer Historical Society Quarterly,* n.p., n.d., Courtesy Chicago Historical Society.
3. Charles J. Latrobe, *The Rambler in North America* (London: R. B. Seeley and V. Burnside, 1935), vol. 1, pp. 149ff.
4. Ibid., vol. 1, p. 155.
5. John D. Caton, *The Last of the Illinois and a Sketch of the Pottawattomies* (Chicago: Rand McNally, 1870), pp. 5ff.
6. Ibid., p. 7.

CHAPTER 11

1. Margaret L. Coit, "The Presidency of Andrew Jackson" (manuscript courtesy of the author), p. 2.
2. Thurman Wilkins, *Cherokee Tragedy* (New York: Macmillan, 1970), p. 201.
3. Ibid., p. 7.
4. Ibid., p. 124.
5. Ibid., p. 136.
6. Grant Foreman, *Indian Removal* (Norman: University of Oklahoma, 1953), pp. 266–67.
7. Ibid., pp. 271–72.
8. This is traditional in the author's family.
9. Wilkins, *Cherokee Tragedy,* pp. 276–77.
10. *American State Papers,* "Military Affairs," vol. 7, p. 534.

11. This is traditional among the North Carolina Cherokees and, of course, their tourist pageant "Unto These Hills" is based on it.
12. Foreman, *Indian Removal*, pp. 286–87.
13. James Mooney, *Myths of the Cherokees*, Bureau of American Ethnology, 19th Annual Report (Washington, D.C.: Government Printing Office, 1900), p. 131.
14. Foreman, *Indian Removal*, pp. 289ff.
15. Ibid.
16. *Army and Navy Chronicle*, vol. 7, p. 57.
17. Many Creeks and Cherokees have ancestors who passed in this fashion. For stories of ancestors who witnessed the removal, I am indebted to Mr. E. E. Callaway, Bristol, Florida, and Dr. Henry Grady Young, Thomasville, Georgia.
18. Foreman, *Indian Removal*, pp. 286ff.
19. Wilkins, *Cherokee Tragedy*, pp. 304ff.
20. Foreman, *Indian Removal*, pp. 305–7.
21. Wilkins, *Cherokee Tragedy*, p. 295.
22. Ibid., pp. 316ff.
23. Ibid.

CHAPTER 12

1. Joshua Giddings, *The Exiles of Florida* (Columbus, Ohio: Follett Foster and Co., 1858), pp. 35ff. See also United States Congress, 25th, 1st session, Senate Executive Document 119, passim.
2. Gloria Jahoda, *River of the Golden Ibis* (New York: Holt, Rinehart and Winston, 1973), pp. 110–11.
3. Ibid., p. 117.
4. John K. Mahon, *Reminiscences of the Second Seminole War by John Bemrose* (Gainesville: University of Florida, 1966), pp. 17ff.
5. Grant Foreman, *Indian Removal* (Norman: University of Oklahoma, 1953), p. 321.
6. John K. Mahon, *The History of the Second Seminole War* (Gainesville: University of Florida, 1967), pp. 96ff.
7. Frank Laumer, *Massacre!* (Gainesville: University of Florida, 1968), pp. 9ff. A marvelously vivid and accurate account. He was Ransome Clarke, and he ended up on the lecture circuit before he finally died in weakened health from his wounds.
8. Mahon, *Reminiscences of the Second Seminole War by John Bemrose*, pp. 108ff.
9. Mahon, *The History of the Second Seminole War*, pp. 135–36.

CHAPTER 13

1. John K. Mahon, *The History of the Second Seminole War* (Gainesville: University of Florida, 1967), pp. 214ff.
2. Gloria Jahoda, *River of the Golden Ibis* (New York: Holt, Rinehart and Winston, 1973), p. 139.
3. Ibid., pp. 140–41. The story is repeated in legion sources.
4. Ibid., p. 139.
5. Mahon, *The History of the Second Seminole War*, pp. 265ff.
6. Ibid., p. 267.
7. John T. Sprague, *The Origin, Progress, and Conclusions of the Florida War* (New York: D. Appleton, 1848), p. 260, as also the Shakespeare costumes.
8. Mahon, *The History of the Second Seminole War*, p. 304.
9. Iste linus tcha: Greetings, I drink your health. Grant Foreman, *Indian Removal* (Norman: University of Oklahoma, 1953), pp. 381ff. "Iste" may have been incorrectly heard; the traditional Muskogee greeting sounds more like "Ixchay," and at least among the Creeks it is still very much in use.

CHAPTER 14

1. John Johnston, *Recollections of Sixty Years* (Dayton: J. H. Patterson, 1915), p. 47.
2. Charles Dickens, *American Notes* (London: Oxford University Press, 1957), pp. 145ff.
3. Ibid., pp. 145ff.
4. Grant Foreman, *The Last Trek of the Indians* (Chicago: University of Chicago, 1946), p. 97.

CHAPTER 15

1. John Treat Irving, Jr., *Indian Sketches Taken During an Expedition to the Pawnee Tribes (1833)* (Norman: University of Oklahoma, 1955), p. xxvii.
2. George Manypenny, *Our Indian Wards* (Cincinnati: Robert Clarke and Co., 1880), passim., as also his reports.
3. Grant Foreman, *The Last Trek of the Indians* (Chicago: University of Chicago, 1946), pp. 232ff.
4. Grenville M. Dodge, *How We Built the Union Pacific Railway* (Denver: Sage Books, 1965), pp. 5ff.
5. Foreman, *The Last Trek of the Indians*, pp. 233–34.

CHAPTER 16

1. Walter P. Webb, *The Great Plains* (New York: Grosset and Dunlap, 1931), pp. 155ff.
2. Ibid., p. 315.
3. The traveler was Robert Louis Stevenson, in Webb, *The Great Plains*, pp. 155ff.
4. William C. Kennerly, *Primrose Hill* (Norman: University of Oklahoma, 1949), pp. 143ff.
5. Colin Rickards, *Bowler Hats and Stetsons: Stories of Englishmen in the Wild West* (New York: Bonanza, 1965), pp. 77ff; George F. Heldt, "Narrative of Sir George [sic] Gore's Expedition 1854–56," Historical Society of Montana, *Contributions*, vol. 1 (1876), pp. 128–31.
6. Rickards, *Bowler Hats and Stetsons*, p. 81.
7. George D. Harmon, *Sixty Years of Indian Affairs* (Chapel Hill: University of North Carolina, 1941), passim.

REFERENCES

1. Angie Debo, *The Road to Disappearance* (Norman: University of Oklahoma, 1941), p. 377.

Bibliography

Neither the general bibliography nor the chapter bibliographies cover everything I read. Over the years, my reading on the subject of Indian Removal has been wide, and an inclusive bibliography would be unmanageable. But I have listed the principal sources, usually those cited, and I have given a list of pertinent government documents in an appendix. Congressional speeches have seldom been annotated; their source is obvious, namely government records of the Senate and House. Some items—for instance, the speeches of Osceola and John Ross—are reported in so many places that a specific footnote seemed unnecessary.

GENERAL BIBLIOGRAPHY

Alexander, Hartley. *North America*. The Mythology of All Races Series. New York, Cooper Square Publishers, 1964.

Alford, Thomas Wildcat. *Civilization*. Norman, University of Oklahoma, 1936.

American State Papers (Gales and Seaton). Washington, D.C., Gales and Seaton, 1832–1860: "Indian Affairs," 2 vols., 1832–1834; "Military Affairs," 7 vols., 1832–1860; "Public Lands," 8 vols., 1832–1860.

Brady, Cyrus Townsend. *Indian Fights and Fighters*. New York, McClure Phillips, 1908.

Debo, Angie. *A History of the Indians of the United States*. Norman, University of Oklahoma, 1970.

Guttman, Alan. *States' Rights and Indian Removal*. Boston, D.C. Heath, 1965.

Hill, Edward E. *Records of the Bureau of Indian Affairs*. 2 vols. Washington, D.C.: National Archives and Records Service, 1965.

Hilliard, Sam B. *Indian Land Cessions*. Washington, D.C., Association of American Geographers, 1972.

Hodge, Frederick W., ed. *Handbook of American Indians North of Mexico*. Bureau of American Ethnology, Bulletin 30. 2 vols. Washington, D.C., Government Printing Office, 1910.

Horan, James D., ed. *The McKenney-Hall Portrait Gallery of American Indians*. New York, Crown Publishers, 1972.

Jackson, Helen Hunt. *A Century of Dishonor*. Boston, Roberts Brothers, 1888.

Josephy, Alvin M., Jr., ed. *The American Heritage Book of Indians*. New York, American Heritage Publishing Co., 1961.

———. *The Patriot Chiefs*. New York, Viking Press, 1961.

McKenney, Thomas, and Hall, James. *The Indian Tribes of North America*. 3 vols. Edinburgh, John Grant, 1934.

Martin, John N. *List of Documents Concerning the Negotiation of Indian Treaties 1801–1869*. National Archives Special List, no. 6. Washington, D.C., Government Printing Office, 1949.

Moquin, Wayne, and Van Doren, Charles. *Great Documents in American Indian History*. New York, Praeger, 1973.

Paxon, Fred L. *History of the American Frontier*. Cambridge, Eng., Cambridge University Press, 1924.

Royce, Charles C., ed. *Indian Land Cessions in the United States*. Bureau of American Ethnology, 18th Annual Report. Washington, D.C., Government Printing Office, 1899.

Swanton, John R. *The Indians of the Southeastern United States*. Bureau of American Ethnology, Bulletin 137. Washington, D.C., Government Printing Office, 1946.

————. *The Indian Tribes of North America*. Bureau of American Ethnology, Bulletin 145. Washington, D.C., Government Printing Office, 1922.

United States Board of Indian Commissioners. *Annual Reports*, 1838–1839. Washington, D.C., Government Printing Office, 1839.

United States Commissioner of Indian Affairs. *Annual Reports*, 1824–1863. Reprinted Washington, D.C., Microcard Editions, 1968.

Utley, Robert N. *Frontiersmen in Blue: The U.S. Army and the Indian 1848–1865*. New York, Macmillan, 1967.

Washburn, Wilcomb E., ed. *The Indian and the White Man*. New York, Doubleday Anchor Books, 1964.

Wise, Jennings C., and Deloria, Vine, Jr. *The Red Man in the New World Drama*. New York, Macmillan, 1971.

Wissler, Clark. *Indians of the United States*. New York, Doubleday Anchor Books, 1966.

Woodford, Frank B. *Lewis Cass: The Last Jeffersonian*. New Brunswick, Rutgers University Press, 1950.

Wright, Muriel H. *A Guide to the Indian Tribes of Oklahoma*. Norman, University of Oklahoma, 1951.

Zeisberger, David. "David Zeisberger's History of North American Indians." *Ohio Archaeological and Historical Quarterly*, vol. 19 (1910).

INTRODUCTION

Coit, Margaret L. *Andrew Jackson*. Boston, Houghton Mifflin, 1965.

Cotterill, R. S. *The Southern Indians*. Norman, University of Oklahoma, 1954.

Debo, Angie. *The Road to Disappearance.* Norman, University of Oklahoma, 1941.

Densmore, Frances. "The Alabama Indians and Their Music." *Publications of the Texas Folklore Society,* vol. 8 (1937), pp. 270–93.

Drake, Benjamin. *Life of Tecumseh . . . with a Historical Sketch of the Shawnee Indians.* Cincinnati, Anderson, Gates and Wright, 1858.

Foreman, Grant. *The Five Civilized Tribes.* Norman, University of Oklahoma, 1934.

———. *Indian Removal.* Norman, University of Oklahoma, 1953.

James, Marquis. *Andrew Jackson: The Border Captain.* New York, Literary Guild, 1933.

———. *Andrew Jackson: Portrait of a President.* New York, Grosset and Dunlap, 1937.

Meek, Alexander R. *The Red Eagle.* Montgomery, Ala., Paragon Press, 1914.

Parton, James. *Life of Andrew Jackson.* 3 vols. New York, Mason Brothers, 1861.

Pickett, Albert James. *A History of Alabama.* Birmingham, Webb Book Co., 1900.

Richardson, James D., ed. *Messages of the Presidents.* Washington, D.C., Government Printing Office, 1899.

Shackford, James Atkins. *David Crockett: The Man and the Legend.* Chapel Hill, University of North Carolina, 1956.

Stewart, George R. *American Place Names.* New York, Oxford University Press, 1970.

Trowbridge, C.C. *Shauwanoa Traditions.* Occasional Contributions from the Museum of Anthropology of the University of Michigan, no. 9. Ann Arbor, University of Michigan, 1939.

Wrone, David R., and Nelson, Russell S., Jr., eds. *Who's the Savage?* Greenwich, Conn., Fawcett Publications, 1973.

Wroth, Lawrence C. "The Indian Treaty as Literature." *Yale Review,* vol. 17 (1928), pp. 749–66.

CHAPTER 1

Abel, Annie Heloise. "Proposals for an Indian State 1738–1878." *American Historical Association Annual Reports,* vol. 1 (1907). Washington, D.C., Government Printing Office, 1908.

American State Papers (Gales and Seaton), Washington, D.C., Gales and Seaton, 1832–1860. "Indian Affairs," 2 vols., 1832–34.

Army and Navy Chronicle, vols. 1–10, 1835–1840. B. Homans, ed. Washington, D.C., B. Homans, 1835–1840.

Brinton, Daniel G. *The Lenape and their Legends*. New York, AMS Press, 1969.

Coit, Margaret L. *Andrew Jackson*. Boston, Houghton Mifflin, 1965.

————. *John C. Calhoun: American Portrait*. Boston, Houghton Mifflin, 1950.

————. "The Presidency of Andrew Jackson," ms. courtesy of the author.

Council on Interracial Books for Children. *Chronicles of American Indian Protest*. New York, the Council, 1971.

Fletcher, Alice. *The Hako, A Pawnee Ceremony*. Bureau of American Ethnology, 22nd Annual Report. Washington, D.C., Government Printing Office, 1904.

Foreman, Grant. *Indians and Pioneers*. Norman, University of Oklahoma, 1936.

————. *The Last Trek of the Indians*. Chicago, University of Chicago, 1946.

Harrington, M.R. *Religion and Ceremonies of the Lenape*. New York, Museum of the American Indian, Heye Foundation, 1921.

Jahoda, Gloria. *The Other Florida*. New York, Scribner's, 1967.

James, Marquis. *Andrew Jackson: Portrait of a President*. New York, Grosset and Dunlap, 1937.

————. *The Raven: A Biography of Sam Houston*. New York, Paperback Library, 1962.

La Flesche, Francis. *The Osage Tribe*. Bureau of American Ethnology, 39th Annual Report. Washington, D.C., Government Printing Office, 1925.

————. *The War Ceremony and Peace Ceremony of the Osage Indians*. Bureau of American Ethnology, Bulletin 101. Washington, D.C., Government Printing Office, 1939.

Lumpkin, Wilson. *The Removal of the Cherokee Indians from Georgia*. 2 vols. New York, Dodd Mead, 1907.

McCoy, Isaac. *History of Baptist Indian Missions*. New York, H. and S. Raynor, 1840.

McDermott, John Francis. *Tixier's Travels on the Osage Prairies*. Norman, University of Oklahoma, 1940.

McReynolds, Edwin C. *Oklahoma: A History of the Sooner State*. Norman, University of Oklahoma, 1954.

Mathews, John Joseph. *The Osages*. Norman, University of Oklahoma, 1961.

————. *Wah-kon-tah: The Osage and the White Man's Road*. Norman, University of Oklahoma, 1932.

Morse, Reverend Jedediah. *Report to the Secretary of War of the United States on Indian Affairs*. New Haven, S. Converse, 1822.

Nuttall, Thomas. "Journal of Travels into the Arkansa [sic] Territory." In

R.G. Thwaites, ed. *Early Western Travels*. Vol. 13. Cleveland, Ohio, Arthur H. Clark, 1905.

Parton, James. *Life of Andrew Jackson*. 3 vols. New York, Mason Brothers, 1861.

Pourtales, Count Albert-Alexandre. *On the Western Tour with Washington Irving*. Norman, University of Oklahoma, 1968.

Richardson, James D., ed. *Messages of the Presidents*, Washington, D.C., Government Printing Office, 1899.

Sandoz, Mari. *The Buffalo Hunters*. New York, Hastings House, 1954.

————. *Love Song to the Plains*. New York, Harper and Row, 1961.

Schmeckebier, Laurence F. *The Office of Indian Affairs*. Institute for Government Research Service, Monographs of the U.S. Government, no. 48. Baltimore, Johns Hopkins University, 1927.

Schoolcraft, Henry R. *The American Indians: Their History, Conditions, and Prospects*. Rochester, N.Y., Wanzer Foot and Co., 1851.

Schultz, George. *An Indian Canaan*. Norman, University of Oklahoma, 1972.

Turner, Katherine C. *Red Men Calling on the Great White Father*. Norman, University of Oklahoma, 1951.

United States Congress. 23rd. 1st session. Senate Document 512. 5 vols.

Wislizenus, F.A. *A Journey to the Rocky Mountains in the Year 1839*. Glorieta, N.M., Rio Grande Press, 1969.

CHAPTER 2

Adams, John Quincy. *Diary. Allen Nevins*, ed. New York, Longmans Green, 1929.

Blackbird, Andrew J. *History of the Ottawa and Chippewa Indians of Michigan*. Ypsilanti, Ypsilanti Job Printing House, 1887.

Blair, Emma H. *The Indian Tribes of the Upper Mississippi Valley and the Great Lakes*. Cleveland, Ohio, Arthur H. Clark, 1911.

British Museum. Miscellaneous pamphlets: A Courtier, an Esquire, a Clergyman, and a Farmer, *The Reign of Felicity, being a plea for Civilizing the Indians of North America without Infringing on their Individual or National Independence*. London, 1796. *Missions to the North American Indians*. London, 1848. *The Removal of the Indians: An article from the American Monthly Magazine; and an examination of an article in the North American Review; and an exhibit of the advancement of the Southern tribes in civilization and Christianity*. Boston, 1830.

Cass, Lewis. *Considerations on the Present State of Indians*. N.p., n.d. In Florida State University Library.

Coit, Margaret L. *Andrew Jackson*. Boston, Houghton Mifflin, 1965.

———. *John C. Calhoun: American Portrait*. Boston, Houghton Mifflin, 1950.

———. "The Presidency of Andrew Jackson," ms. courtesy of the author.

Evarts, Jeremiah, ed. *Speeches on the Passage of the Bill for the Removal of the Indians*. Boston, Perkins and Marvin, 1830.

Foreman, Grant. *The Last Trek of the Indians*. Chicago, University of Chicago, 1946.

Frothingham, Paul Revere. *Edward Everett, Orator and Statesman*. Boston, Houghton Mifflin, 1925.

Horan, James D. *The McKenney-Hall Portrait Gallery of American Indians*. New York, Crown Publishers, 1972.

Irving, Washington. *A Tour on the Prairies*. New York, Pantheon, 1967.

James, Marquis. *Andrew Jackson: Portrait of a President*. New York, Grosset and Dunlap, 1937.

———. *The Raven: A Biography of Sam Houston*. New York, Paperback Library, 1962.

Lee, Francis Bazley. *New Jersey as a Colony and as a State*. Vol. 3. New York, Publishing Society of New Jersey, 1902.

Lumpkin, Wilson. *The Removal of the Cherokee Indians from Georgia*. New York, Dodd Mead, 1907.

McReynolds, Edwin C. *Oklahoma: A History of the Sooner State*. Norman, University of Oklahoma, 1954.

Malin, James C. *Indian Policy and Westward Expansion*. Bulletin of the University of Kansas, Humanistic Studies, vol. 2, no. 3. Lawrence, Kans., University of Kansas, 1921.

Morse, Reverend Jedediah. *Report to the Secretary of War of the United States on Indian Affairs*. New Haven, S. Converse, 1822.

Schmeckebier, Laurence F. *The Office of Indian Affairs*. Institute for Government Research Service, Monographs of the U.S. Government, no. 48. Baltimore, Johns Hopkins University, 1927.

Schoolcraft, Henry R. *The American Indians: Their History, Conditions, and Prospects*. Rochester, N.Y., Wanzer Foot and Co., 1851.

Schultz, George A. *An Indian Canaan: Isaac McCoy and the Vision of an Indian State*. Norman, University of Oklahoma, 1972.

Smith, W.L.G. *The Life and Times of Lewis Cass*. New York, Derby and Jackson, 1856.

United States Supreme Court. *Cases Argued and Decided in the Supreme Court of the United States* . . . 1790—. Lawyers' edition. Rochester, N.Y., Lawyers' Cooperative Publishing Co., 1926—. 100 vols. as of 1975.

Wrone, David R., and Nelson, Russell S., Jr., eds. *Who's the Savage?* Greenwich, Conn., Fawcett Publications, 1973.

CHAPTER 3

Unless otherwise indicated, all material quoted in this chapter appears in
Klopfenstein, Carl Grover. *The Removal of the Indians from Ohio
1820–1843*. Ph.D. Dissertation, Western Reserve University, 1955.
Other sources are:
Klopfenstein, Carl Grover. "Westward Ho: Removal of the Ohio Shaw-
nees 1832–33." *Bulletin of the Historical and Philosophical Society of
Ohio*, vol. 15 (1957), pp. 3–31.
Morgan, Lewis Henry. *League of the Ho-de-no-sau-nee*. New York,
Corinth Books, 1962. Reprint of 1851 edition.
Parker, Arthur C. *An Analytical History of the Seneca Indians*. Researches
and Transactions of the New York State Archaeological Association.
Rochester, N.Y., Lewis H. Morgan Chapter, 1926.
Shackford, James Atkins. *David Crockett: The Man and the Legend*.
Chapel Hill, University of North Carolina, 1956.
Stone, William L. *The Life and Times of Sa-go-Ya-Wat-ha*. Albany, N.Y.,
J. Munsell, 1886.
United States Congress. 23rd. 1st session. Senate Document 512. 5 vols.

CHAPTER 4

Burt, Jesse, and Ferguson, Robert B. *Indians of the Southeast: Then and
Now*. Nashville and New York, Abingdon, 1973.
Cotterill, R.S. *The Southern Indians*. Norman, University of Oklahoma,
1954.
Debo, Angie. *The Rise and Fall of the Choctaw Republic*. Norman, Uni-
versity of Oklahoma, 1934.
DeRosier, Arthur H., Jr., *The Removal of the Choctaw Indians*. Knox-
ville, University of Tennessee, 1970.
Forman, Grant. *Indian Removal*. Norman, University of Oklahoma, 1953.
Gibson, Arrell M. *The Chickasaws*. Norman, University of Oklahoma,
1972.
Jackson, Tennessee, *Gazette*, Aug. 4 and Oct. 9, 1830.
Kappler, C.J., ed. *Indian Affairs, Laws and Treaties*. Washington, D.C.,
Government Printing Office, 1892–1913. (Published as Senate Docu-
ment 452, 57th Congress, 1st session, 2 vols.; also as Senate Document
319, 58th Congress, 2nd session, 3 vols.)
Lafferty, R.A. *Okla-Hannali*. New York, Pocket Books, 1973.
Lewis, Anna. *Chief Pushmataha*. New York, Exposition, 1959.
Nammack, Georgiana C. *Fraud, Politics, and the Dispossession of the
Indians*. Norman, University of Oklahoma, 1969.

Ridaught, Horace. *Hell's Branch Office*. Citra, Fla., n.p., n.d.
United States Congress. 23rd. 1st session. Senate Document 512. 5 vols.

CHAPTER 5

Addison, James Thayer. *The Episcopal Church in the United States 1789–1931*. New York, Scribner's, 1951.
Ellis, General A.G. "Recollections of Rev. Eleazer Williams." *Wisconsin Historical Collections*, vol. 8 (1877–79), pp. 322–69.
———. "Some Account of the Advent of the New York Indians into Wisconsin." *Wisconsin Historical Collections*, vol. 2 (1855), pp. 415–49.
Fenton, William, ed. *Parker on the Iroquois*. Syracuse, N.Y., Syracuse University, 1968.
Foreman, Grant. *The Last Trek of the Indians*. Chicago, University of Chicago, 1946.
Smith, Honorable John Y. "Eleazer Williams and the Lost Prince." *Wisconsin Historical Collections*, vol. 6 (1872), pp. 308–42.
Trowbridge, C.C. "Notes on Eleazer Williams." *Wisconsin Historical Collections*, vol. 7 (1876), pp. 413–14.
University of Michigan Alumni Quarterly Review, vol. 49 (1942).
Wilson, Edmund. *Apologies to the Iroquois*. New York, Random House, 1960.

CHAPTER 6

Armstrong, Honorable Percy. *The Sauks and the Black Hawk War*. Springfield, Ill., H.W. Rokker, 1887.
Black Hawk. *Autobiography*. Donald H. Jackson, ed. Urbana, University of Illinois, 1965.
Bracken, Charles. *Further Strictures on Governor Ford's History of the Black Hawk War*. Madison, Wisconsin Historical Society, 1855.
——— and Parkison, Peter. "Pekatonica [sic] Battle Controversy." *Wisconsin Historical Collections*, vol. 2 (1855), pp. 365–92.
Britt, Albert. *Great Indian Chiefs*. New York, Whittlesey House, 1938.
Brunson, Reverend Alford. "Memoir of Hon. Thomas Pendleton Burnett." *Wisconsin Historical Collections*, vol. 2 (1855), pp. 233–325.
Davis, Jefferson. "Indian Policy of the United States." *North American Review*, vol. 43 (1886), pp. 436–46.
Downey, Fairfax D. *Indian Wars of the United States Army 1776–1865*. New York, Doubleday, 1963.
Eby, Cecil. *That Disgraceful Affair, The Black Hawk War*. New York, Norton, 1973.

Fulton, Alexander. *The Red Men of Iowa*. Des Moines, Mills and Co., 1882.

Hagan, William T. *The Sac and Fox Indians*. Norman, University of Oklahoma, 1958.

Hauberg, John H. "The Black Hawk War." *Illinois State Historical Society Transactions* (1932), pp. 91–134.

Josephy, Alvin M., Jr. *The Patriot Chiefs*. New York, Viking, 1961.

Kellogg, Louise P. "The Removal of the Winnebago." *Transactions of the Wisconsin Academy of Sciences, Arts, and Letters*, vol. 21 (1924).

Kubiak, William J. *Great Lakes Indians*. Grand Rapids, Mich., Baker Book House, 1970.

Lockwood, James H. "Early Times and Events in Wisconsin." *Wisconsin Historical Collections*, vol. 2 (1855), pp. 98–232.

Matson, N. *Memories of Shaubena*. Chicago, D.E. Cook and Co., 1878.

———. "Sketch of Shaubena, A Pottawattamie Chief." *Wisconsin Historical Collections*, vol. 7 (1876), pp. 415–21.

Meeker, Dr. Moses. "History of the Wisconsin Lead Region." *Wisconsin Historical Collections*, vol. 6 (1872), pp. 271–96.

Merrell, Henry. "Pioneer Life in Wisconsin." *Wisconsin Historical Collections*, vol. 7 (1876), pp. 366–401.

Parkison, Daniel. "Pioneer Life in Wisconsin." *Wisconsin Historical Collections*, vol. 2 (1855), pp. 326–64.

Parkison, Peter, Jr. "Strictures upon Governor Ford's History of the Black Hawk War." *Wisconsin Historical Collections*, vol. 2 (1855), pp. 393–401.

Rennick, Percival. "The Peoria and Galena Trail and Coach Road." *Illinois State Historical Society Journal*, vol. 27 (1935), pp. 403–5.

Strong, Moses M. "Indian Wars of Wisconsin." *Wisconsin Historical Collections*, vol. 8 (1877–79), pp. 241–86.

Whitney, Ellen M., ed. *The Black Hawk War 1831–32*. Vol. 1. Springfield, Ill., Illinois State Historical Society, 1970.

CHAPTER 7

American State Papers (Gales and Seaton). Washington, D.C., Gales and Seaton, 1832–1860. "Military Affairs," vols. 1 and 2.

Burt, Jesse, and Ferguson, Robert B. *Indians of the Southeast: Then and Now*. Nashville and New York, Abingdon, 1973.

Cotterill, R.S. *The Southern Indians*. Norman, University of Oklahoma, 1954.

Creek Nation East of the Mississippi, Inc. *The Creek Nation East of the Mississippi*. Poarch-Switch, Ala., Creek Nation East of the Mississippi, Inc., 1972.

Debo, Angie. *The Road to Disappearance*. Norman, University of Oklahoma, 1941.

Foreman, Grant. *Indian Removal*. Norman, University of Oklahoma, 1953.

Gatschet, Albert S. *A Migration Legend of the Creek Indians*. Philadelphia, D.G. Brinton, 1884.

Kappler, C.J., ed. *Indian Affairs, Laws, and Treaties*. Washington, D.C., Government Printing Office, 1892–1913. (Published as Senate Document 452, 57th Congress, 1st session, 2 vols.; also as Senate Document 319, 58th Congress, 2nd session, 3 vols.)

Kilpatrick, Jack F., and Gibbs, Anna. *Muskogean Charm Songs Among the Oklahoma Cherokees*. Smithsonian Institution Contributions to Anthropology, vol. 2, no. 3. Washington, D.C., Government Printing Office, 1967.

Nammack, Georgiana C. *Fraud, Politics, and the Dispossession of the Indians*. Norman, University of Oklahoma, 1969.

Niles' Weekly Register, July 16, 1831.

Pickett, Albert James. *History of Alabama*. Birmingham, Webb Book Co., 1900.

Posey, Alexander Lawrence. *Poems*. Okmulgee, Okla., Oklahoma Cultural Foundation, 1968.

Speck, Frank G., and Sapir, J.D. *Ceremonial Songs of the Creek and Yuchi Indians*. Philadelphia, University of Pennsylvania Anthropological Publications 1, 1911.

Swanton, John R. *Early History of the Creek Indians and their Neighbors*. Bureau of American Ethnology, Bulletin 73. Washington, D.C., Government Printing Office, 1922.

United States Congress. 23rd. 1st session. Senate Document 512. 5 vols.

Woodward, Thomas S. *Reminiscences of the Creek or Muscogee Indians*. Montgomery, Ala., Barrett and Wimbish, 1859.

CHAPTER 8

Burt, Jesse, and Ferguson, Robert B. *Indians of the Southeast: Then and Now*. Nashville and New York, Abingdon, 1973.

Cotterill, R.S. *The Southern Indians*. Norman, University of Oklahoma, 1954.

Foreman, Grant. *Indian Removal*. Norman, University of Oklahoma, 1953.

———. *Indians and Pioneers*. Norman, University of Oklahoma, 1936.

Fundaburk, Emma Lila. *Southeastern Indians*. Luverne, Ala., E.L. Fundaburk, 1958.

Gibson, Arrell M. *The Chickasaws*. Norman, University of Oklahoma, 1972.

New York Observer, August 5, 1837.

Parsons, John, ed. "Letters on the Chickasaw Removal of 1837." *New York Historical Society Quarterly*, vol. 37 (1953), pp. 273–83.

CHAPTER 9

Abel, Annie Heloise, ed. *Chardon's Journal at Fort Clark 1834–1839.* Pierre, S.D., Department of History of the State of South Dakota, 1932.

Bannon, John Francis. *Bolton and the Spanish Borderlands.* Norman, University of Oklahoma, 1964.

Beckwith, Martha Warren. *Mandan-Hidatsa Myths and Ceremonies.* New York, J.J. Augustin, 1937.

Bowers, Alfred W. *Mandan Social and Ceremonial Organization.* Chicago, University of Chicago, 1950.

Catlin, George. *Letters and Notes on the Manners, Customs, and Conditions of the North American Indians.* 2 vols. Reprint. Minneapolis, Ross and Haines, 1965.

————. *O-Kee-Pa: A Religious Ceremony and Other Customs of the Mandans.* New Haven, Yale University, 1967.

Chouteau, Frederick. "Reminiscences." *Kansas Historical Society Collections*, vol. 8 (1903–04), pp. 423–34.

Densmore, Frances. *Mandan and Hidatsa Music.* Bureau of American Ethnology, Bulletin 80. Washington, D.C., Government Printing Office, 1923.

Federal Writers' Project—WPA. *North Dakota: A Guide to the Prairie State.* New York, Oxford University Press, 1950.

Lowie, Robert H. "Notes on the Social Organization and Customs of the Mandan, Hidatsa, and Crow Indians." *Anthropological Papers of the American Museum of Natural History*, vol. 21 (1924), part I.

Mails, Thomas E. *The Mystic Warriors of the Plains.* New York, Doubleday, 1972.

Maximilian, Prince of Wied-Neuwied. *Travels in the Interior of North America 1832–1834.* In R.G. Thwaites, ed. *Early Western Travels*, vol. 24. Cleveland, Arthur H. Clark, 1906.

Will, G.F., and Spinden, H.J. "The Mandans." *Peabody Museum Papers*, vol. 3 (1906).

CHAPTER 10

Unless otherwise stated, all material quoted in this chapter and all references to Father Petit are from: McKee, Irving, ed. *The Trail of Death: Letters of Benjamin Marie Petit.* Indianapolis, Indiana Historical Society, 1941.

Other sources are:

Anson, Bert. "Chief Francis LaFontaine and the Miami Emigration from Indiana." *Indiana Magazine of History* 60 (1964), 241–68.

Beijbom, Ulf. "Anders Larsson—Immigrant Pioneer in Chicago." Reprint from *Swedish Pioneer Historical Society Quarterly*, n.p., n.d., courtesy Chicago Historical Society.

Buechner, Cecilia. *The Pokagons*. Indianapolis, Indiana Historical Society, 1933.

Buley, R. Carlyle. *The Old Northwest*. Bloomington, University of Illinois, 1964.

Caton, John Dean. *The Last of the Illinois and a Sketch of the Pottawattomies*. Chicago, Rand McNally, 1870.

Faber, W.W. "Indians of the Tri-State Area—the Potowattamis." *Northwest Ohio Quarterly* 30 (1957–58), 49–53.

Gordon, Leon M. "The Red Man's Retreat from Northern Indiana." *Indiana Magazine of History* 66 (1950), 39–60.

"Journal of an Emigrating Party of Potawatomi Indians." *Indiana Magazine of History* 18 (1922) and 21 (1926).

Hill, Mabel. "Paul Hill, Removal of the Pottawatomie." *Nebraska Historical Magazine*, Sept. 1917. Reprint.

Kinzie, Juliette A. "Chicago Indian Chiefs." *Bulletin of the Chicago Historical Society* 1 (1935), 105–16.

Kubiak, William J. *Great Lakes Indians*. Grand Rapids, Mich., Baker Book House, 1970.

Landes, Ruth. *The Prairie Potawatomi*. Madison, University of Wisconsin, 1970.

Larsson, Anders. "Minnen af en Svensk som vistäts 28 år i Amerika." Chicago, *Nya Werlden*, 1873–74.

Latrobe, Charles J. *The Rambler in North America*. 2 vols. London, R.B. Seeley and V. Burnside, 1835.

Luckenbach, Abraham. "The Moravian Indian Mission on White River." *Indiana Historical Collections* 23 (1938).

Matson, N. *Memories of Shaubena*. Chicago, D.E. Cooke and Co., 1878.

——. "Sketch of Shaubena, a Pottawattamie Chief." *Wisconsin Historical Collections* 7 (1876), 415–21.

Schultz, George A. *An Indian Canaan*. Norman, University of Oklahoma, 1972.

Stewart, Benjamin F. "The Deportation of Menominee and his Tribe of Potawatomi Indians." *Indiana Magazine of History* 18 (1922), 255–65.

Strong, William Duncan. *The Indian Tribes of the Chicago Region*. Chicago, Field Museum of Natural History, 1938.

CHAPTER 11

American State Papers (Gales and Seaton). Washington, D.C., Gales and Seaton, 1832–1860. "Military Affairs," vol. 7.
Army and Navy Chronicle, vols. 1–10, 1835–1840. B. Homans, ed. Washington, D.C., B. Homans, 1835–1840.
Bird, Traveller. *Tell Them They Lie*. Los Angeles, Westernlore Publications, 1971.
Burt, Jesse, and Ferguson, Robert B. *Indians of the Southeast*. Nashville and New York, Abingdon, 1973.
Coit, Margaret L. *Andrew Jackson*. Boston, Houghton Mifflin, 1965.
———. *John C. Calhoun: American Portrait*. Boston, Houghton Mifflin, 1920.
———. "The Presidency of Andrew Jackson," ms., courtesy of the author.
Cotterill, R.S. *The Southern Indians*. Norman, University of Oklahoma, 1954.
Filler, Louis, and Guttman, Allen, eds. *Removal of the Cherokee Nation*. Boston, D.C. Heath, 1962.
Foreman, Grant. *Indian Removal*. Norman, University of Oklahoma, 1953.
———. *Sequoyah*. Norman, University of Oklahoma, 1938.
Gabriel, Ralph Henry. *Elias Boudinot, Cherokee*. Norman, University of Oklahoma, 1941.
Goulding, F.R. *Sa-Lo-Quah*. Macon, Ga., J.W. Burke, 1880.
Guttman, Allen. *States' Rights and Indian Removal*. Boston, D.C. Heath, 1965.
Lumpkin, Wilson. *The Removal of the Cherokee Indians from Georgia*. 2 vols. New York, Dodd Mead, 1907.
Mooney, James. *Myths of the Cherokees*. Bureau of American Ethnology, 19th Annual Report. Washington, D.C., Government Printing Office, 1900.
———. *Sacred Formulas of the Cherokees*. Bureau of American Ethnology, 7th Annual Report. Washington, D.C., Government Printing Office, 1888.
Parton, James. *Life of Andrew Jackson*. 3 vols. New York, Mason Bros., 1861.
Underwood, T.B., and Sandlin, M.S. *Legends of the Ancient Cherokees*. Asheville, N.C., Stephens Press, 1956.
United States Supreme Court. *Cases Argued and Decided in the Supreme Court of the United States . . .* 1790—. Lawyers' edition. Rochester, N.Y., Lawyers' Cooperative Publishing Co., 1926—. 100 vols. as of 1975.
Wilkins, Thurman. *Cherokee Tragedy*. New York, Macmillan, 1970.

Woodward, Grace Steele. *The Cherokees.* Norman, University of Oklahoma, 1963.

Young, Mary Elizabeth. *Redskins, Ruffleshirts, and Rednecks.* Norman, University of Oklahoma, 1961.

CHAPTER 12

Burt, Jesse, and Ferguson, Robert B. *Indians of the Southeast.* Nashville and New York, Abingdon, 1973.

Cohen, Myer M. *Notices of Florida and the Campaigns.* Quadricentennial Edition. Gainesville, University of Florida, 1964.

Cotterill, R.S. *The Southern Indians.* Norman, University of Oklahoma, 1954.

Densmore, Frances. *Seminole Music.* New York, Da Capo Press, 1972.

Foreman, Grant. *Indian Removal.* Norman, University of Oklahoma, 1953.

Giddings, Joshua. *The Exiles of Florida.* Columbus, Ohio, Follett Foster and Co., 1858.

Hartley, William, and Hartley, Ellen. *Osceola: The Unconquered Indian.* New York, Hawthorn Books, 1973.

Jahoda, Gloria. *River of the Golden Ibis.* New York, Holt, Rinehart and Winston, 1973.

Laumer, Frank. *Massacre!* Gainesville, University of Florida, 1968.

Mahon, John K. *The History of the Second Seminole War.* Gainesville, University of Florida, 1967.

————— ed., *Reminiscences of the Second Seminole War by John Bemrose.* Gainesville, University of Florida, 1966.

McReynolds, Edwin C. *The Seminoles.* Norman, University of Oklahoma, 1957.

Porter, Kenneth W. "The Seminoles in Mexico 1850–61." *Hispanic-American Historical Review,* vol. 31 (1952), pp. 1–36.

—————. "Seminoles in Mexico." *Chronicles of Oklahoma,* vol. 29 (1951), pp. 153–68.

Sprague, John T. *The Origin, Progress and Conclusion of the Florida War.* New York, D. Appleton, 1848.

United States Congress. 25th. 1st session. Senate Executive Document 119.

CHAPTER 13

The bibliography for this chapter is identical to that of Chapter 12.

CHAPTER 14

Bauman, Robert F. "Kansas, Canada or Starvation." *Michigan History,* vol. 36 (1952), pp. 287–99.

—————. "The Removal of the Indians from the Maumee Valley." Reprint, *Northwest Ohio Quarterly,* vol. 30 (1957–58), pp. 10–25.

Dickens, Charles. *American Notes*. London, Oxford University Press, 1957.

Foreman, Grant. *The Last Trek of the Indians*. Chicago, University of Chicago, 1946.

Hoffman, Walter J. *The Midewiwin*. Bureau of American Ethnology, 7th Annual Report. Washington, D.C., Government Printing Office, 1891.

Johnson, Edgar. *Charles Dickens: His Tragedy and Triumph*. New York, Simon and Schuster, 1952.

Johnston, John. *Recollections of Sixty Years*. Dayton, J.H. Patterson, 1915.

Klopfenstein, Carl Grover. *The Removal of the Indians from Ohio 1820–1843*. Ph.D. Dissertation, Western Reserve University, 1955.

———. "Westward Ho! Removal of the Ohio Shawnees 1832–33." *Bulletin of the Historical and Philosophical Society of Ohio*, vol. 15 (1957), pp. 3–31.

Oliphant, J.O., ed. "The Report of the Wyandot Exploring Delegation, 1831." *Kansas Historical Quarterly*, vol. 15 (1947), pp. 248–62.

Smith, Dwight L. "An Unsuccessful Negotiation for Removal of the Wyandot Indians from Ohio, 1834." *Ohio State Archaeological and Historical Quarterly*, vol. 58 (1949), pp. 305–31.

CHAPTER 15

Custer, Milo. "Kawnekuk the Kickapoo Prophet." *Illinois State Historical Society Journal*, vol. 11 (1918), pp. 48–56.

Densmore, Frances. *Chippewa Music*. New York, Da Capo Press, 1972.

Dodge, Grenville M. *How We Built the Union Pacific Railway*. Denver, Sage Books, 1965.

Fabila, Alfonso. "La Triba Kickapoo." *Biblioteca Enciclopedica Popular*, no. 50. Mexico, D.F., 1945.

Foreman, Grant. *The Last Trek of the Indians*. Chicago, University of Chicago, 1946.

Gibson, Arrell M. *The Kickapoos*. Norman, University of Oklahoma, 1963.

Holbrook, Stewart H. *The Story of American Railroads*. New York, Bonanza, 1947.

Irving, John Treat, Jr. *Indian Sketches Taken During an Expedition to the Pawnee Tribes (1833)*. Norman, University of Oklahoma, 1955.

King, Joseph B. "The Ottawa Indians in Kansas and Oklahoma." *Kansas Historical Collections*, vol. 13 (1915), pp. 373–78.

Malin, James C. "Indian Policy and Westward Expansion." *Bulletin of the University of Kansas*, Humanistic Studies, vol. 2, no. 3. Lawrence, University of Kansas, 1921.

Manypenny, George W. *Our Indian Wards*. Cincinnati, Robert Clarke and Co., 1880.

Stover, John F. *American Railroads*. Chicago, University of Chicago, 1961.

Wright, Robert M. "Personal Reminiscences of Frontier Life in Southwest Kansas." *Kansas Historical Collections*, vol. 7 (1901–2), pp. 79–80.

CHAPTER 16

Allen, Joel. *History of the American Bison*. Washington, D.C., Government Printing Office, 1877.

Boyd, Mark F. "Occurrence of the American Bison in Alabama and Florida." *Science* (new series), vol. 84 (1936), p. 203.

Bryan, Park. "Man and the American Bison." *National Wildlife*, vol. 2 (1964), p. 1.

Burnett, Wesley R. "Buffalo Killer—Sharps." *Field and Stream*, vol. 61 (1956), p. 59.

Dacy, David A. *The Buffalo Book*. Chicago, Swallow Press–Sage Books, 1974.

Debo, Angie. *The Road to Disappearance*. Norman, University of Oklahoma, 1941.

Dodge, Richard Irving. *The Plains of the Great West*. New York, Archer House, 1959.

Gard, Wayne. *The Great Buffalo Hunt*. New York, Knopf, 1959.

Haines, Francis. *The Buffalo*. New York, Crowell, 1970.

Harmon, George Dewey. *Sixty Years of Indian Affairs*. Chapel Hill, University of North Carolina, 1941.

Heldt, George F. "Narrative of Sir George [sic] Gore's Expedition 1854–56." *Contributions*, Historical Society of Montana, vol. 1 (1876), pp. 128–31.

Hornaday, William T. *Extermination of the American Bison*. Washington, D.C., Annual Report of the United States National Museum, 1899.

Kennerly, William Clark. *Primrose Hill*. Norman, University of Oklahoma, 1949.

Martin, Cy. *The Saga of the Buffalo*. New York, Hart, 1973.

Park, Ed. *The World of the Bison*. Philadelphia, Lippincott, 1969.

Prucha, Francis Paul. "Indian Removal and the Great American Desert." *Indiana Magazine of History*, vol. 59 (1963), pp. 295–322.

Rickards, Colin. *Bowler Hats and Stetsons: Stories of Englishmen in the Wild West*. New York, Bonanza, 1966.

Sandoz, Mari. *The Buffalo Hunters*. New York, Hastings House, 1954.

———. *Love Song to the Plains*. New York, Harper and Row, 1961.

Smith, Winston O. *The Sharps Rifle*. New York, Morrow, 1943.

Webb, Walter Prescott. *The Great Plains*. New York, Grosset and Dunlap, 1931.

Appendix:
Selected Government Documents
on Indian Removal

United States Congress. 16th. 1st session. House Document 46.
————. 17th. 1st session. House Document 59.
————. 18th. 2nd session. Senate Document 64.
————. 19th. 1st session. House Executive Document 102.
————. 19th. 1st session. House Document 124.
————. 19th. 1st session. House Document 146.
————. 20th. 2nd session. House Report 87.
————. 20th. 2nd session. House Executive Document 117.
————. 21st. 1st session. Senate Document 110.
————. 22nd. 1st session. House Executive Document 38.
————. 22nd. 1st session. House Document 56.
————. 22nd. 1st session. House Executive Document 116.
————. 22nd. 1st session. House Executive Document 171.
————. 22nd. 1st session. House Report 502.
————. 23rd. 1st session. House Document 2.
————. 23rd. 1st session. House Document 149.
————. 23rd. 1st session. House Document 474.
————. 23rd. 1st session. Senate Executive Document 386.
————. 23rd. 1st session. Senate Document 512. 5 vols.
————. 24th. 1st session. House Document 2.
————. 24th. 1st session. House Document 286.
————. 25th. 1st session. House Document 27.
————. 25th. 1st session. House Document 46.
————. 25th. 1st session. Senate Executive Document 119.
————. 25th. 2nd session. House Document 285.
————. 25th. 2nd session. House Document 327.
————. 25th. 2nd session. House Document 453.
————. 25th. 2nd session. Senate Document 120.
————. 25th. 2nd session. Senate Document 426.
————. 25th. 2nd session. Senate Executive Document 453.
————. 25th. 3rd session. House Executive Document 238.
————. 26th. 1st session. House Executive Document 2.
————. 26th. 1st session. House Document 129.
————. 27th. 2nd session. House Report 1098.
————. 27th. 3rd session. House Report 271.
————. 28th. 1st session. House Executive Document 234.
————. 28th. 2nd session. Senate Document 107.
————. 29th. 1st session. Senate Document 331.

————. 29th. 1st session. Senate Document 461.

————. 29th. 1st session. Senate Executive Document 1.

————. 29th. 2nd session. House Executive Document 76.

————. 30th. 1st session. House Report 736.

————. 30th. 1st session. Senate Report 171.

————. 31st. 2nd session. House Executive Document 25.

————. 32nd. 1st session. House Document 2.

————. 32nd. 1st session. Senate Document 14.

————. 32nd. 2nd session. Senate Executive Document 54.

————. 33rd. 1st session. House Executive Document 129.

————. 33rd. 1st session. House Report 133.

————. 33rd. 1st session. Senate Report 379.

————. 36th. 1st session. Senate Executive Document 56, vol. 12.

————. 36th. 2nd session. Senate Executive Document 1.

————. 41st. 2nd session. Senate Report 131.

————. 45th. 3rd session. House Report 188.

————. 48th. 2nd session. Senate Executive Document 95.

————. 59th. 2nd session. Senate Report 5013.

United States National Archives. Microfilm M243, *Indian Wars and Disturbances.*

United States Supreme Court. *Cases Argued and Decided in the Supreme Court of the United States* . . . 1790—. Lawyers' edition. Rochester, N.Y., Lawyers' Cooperative Publishing Co., 1926—. 100 vols. as of 1975.

Index

Abert, Col. John J., 71–72, 147–149
abolitionists, 44, 297
Abraham (black interpreter), 249–253
Adams, John, 165
Adams, John Quincy: Congressman, 53–54, 224, 225–226, 272; President, 36, 38, 39
agents, Indian, 20, 22, 24, 31, 46, 49, 52, 68, 99, 115, 120, 130, 139, 145, 147, 149, 150, 153, 165, 205, 248, 253, 280–281, 290
Ai Indians, 244
Alabama, Indians in, 2–3, 42, 55, 144–151, 153, 155, 159, 162, 163, 165, 166, 168, 169, 170, 227–228, 234, 259
Alabama River, 3–7, 15, 155
Alachua, Fla., 249, 255
Alamo, San Antonio, Tex., 211
Albany, N. Y., 91, 95
Allegany, N. Y., 92
Allen, Col., 50
Allen, Eliza, see Houston, Eliza Allen
Alligator (Seminole chief), 262, 265
Altamaha River, Ga., 20
American Fur Co., 93, 113, 181, 182, 187, 309, 310
annuities, government, 25, 82, 99, 150, 197, 247, 249
Apalachee Bay, Fla., 27
Apalachee Indians, 4, 244–245
Apalachicola Indians, 245
Apalachicola River, Fla., 246–247, 276–277
Appalachian Mts., 5, 23, 24, 31
Apukshunnubbee (Choctaw chief), 75, 77
Arbuthnot, Alexander, 27

Arikara Indians, 174, 176, 178, 182, 183, 184, 186
Arkansas, 78, 86; Indians in, 26, 27, 31–34, 49–54, 59, 168, 227, 228, 233, 237, 249, 252–253
Arkansas River, 18, 23, 25–26, 80, 87, 88, 149, 150, 167, 170
Armistead, Gen. Lewis Addison, 274
Armstrong, Mjr., 87, 88
Army, U. S., 14, 168, 171–172, 235, 244, 266, 270; see also militia; War Dept.; wars
Arpeika, see Jones, Sam
Artussee, Ala., 14, 15
Asi-Yaholo, see Osceola
Asshewequa, see Singing Bird
Assiniboin Indians, 174, 178, 187
Astor, John Jacob, 93
Astor family, 115
Atkinson, Gen. Henry, 122, 123, 128, 130, 132–140
Atlantic and Pike's Peak Co., 298
Atwater, Phineas, 105
Aucilla River, Fla., 244
Aztec Indians, 298

Bad Axe River, Wis., 135, 137; Battle of, 137–139
Bailey, Dixon, 6
Bailey, Mjr. David, 126, 127
Baldwin, M. W., 292–293
Baldwin Locomotive Works, 294
Baptist Missionary Magazine, 232–233
Baptists, 34, 96, 165, 197–198
Bartram, William, 162
Bear Heart (Mandan), 186
Beasley, Mjr. Daniel, 8, 9, 11
Benton, Jessie, see Frémont, Jessie Benton
Benton, Sen. Thomas Hart, 33, 293, 295

Bertrand, Benjamin, 204
Bienville, Jean Baptiste LeMoyne de, 164
Big Plume (Blackfoot chief), 309
Blackbird, *see* Houston, Sam
Blackfoot Indians, 23, 174, 187, 305, 307–309
Black Hawk War, 121, 128–140
Black Hills, S. D., 309
blacks, 246–249, 296; *see also* slaves, black
Black (Sparrow) Hawk (Sac chief), 112–113, 115, 117–136, 138–142, 144, 198, 200, 264, 289
Black Warrior River, Ala., 13
Black Warriors' Town, Ala., 13
Blanchard's Fork, Ohio, 68
Blood Blackfeet, 309
bloodhounds, 270–273
Blood Law, Cherokee, 210–211, 215, 220, 238, 239
Blount (Seminole chief), 247
Blue Jacket, Widow (Seneca), 60
Boudinot, Elias (Cherokee), 216, 217, 219–220, 223, 224, 239–241
Boudinot, Harriet Gold, 216
Bowlegs, Billy (Seminole chief), 276
Bowles, William Augustus, 21
Bread, Daniel (Oneida chief), 102
Bridger, Jim, 308–311
Brish, Henry, 59–68
British and Indians, 2, 4–5, 8, 26, 38, 112–113, 117, 118, 120–121, 130, 164, 244; *see also* Revolution, American; War of 1812
Brotherton Indians, 96, 101
Bruté de Remur, Bishop Simon Guillaume Gabriel, 190–192, 194–196, 203–206, 208
Buchanan, James, 46
Buffalo, N. Y., 91, 92
Buffalo Horn (Mandan), 186

buffalo hunts, 24, 174, 304–305, 307, 309–312
Buffalo Trail, 295
Bull's Neck (Mandan), 186
Burnt Corn Creek, Ala., 6, 12; Battle of, 7–9, 45, 259
Burr, Aaron, 132
Bushyhead, Rev. Jesse (Cherokee), 233, 235

Caddo Indians, 288
Cairo, Ill., 234
Calabee Creek, Ala., 14
Calhoun, John C., 26, 30, 31–32, 34, 43, 50
Calhoun, Tenn., 26
California, 38, 285, 290, 293
Call, Richard Keith, 261, 265, 270–271
Caller, Col. James, 5–7
Calusa Indians, 4, 244
Campeau, Angelique, 191, 193
Canada, 61, 93, 113, 119, 293
Canadian River, 77, 80
Captain Pipe (Delaware chief), 64
Carolinas, Indians in, 20, 22, 226–227, 230, 245
Cass, War Secy. Lewis, 32, 41–42, 66, 70, 71, 84, 102, 104, 142, 146, 148, 149, 151, 153
Castillo de San Marcos, 267
Catawba Indians, 288
Catholics, 94, 105, 190–191, 193–197, 203, 244
Catlin, George, 181–182
Caton, John, 201–202
Cattaraugus, N. Y., 92
Caughnawaga, Can., 104, 105
Cayuga Indians, 91
Cayuga, Jim (Seneca), 64
Chardon, Francis, 181–187
Charleston, S. C., 267
Chase, Salmon P., 293, 294

Chatillon, Henry, 306, 307
Chatillon, Joe, 307
Chattahoochee River, 2, 150, 151, 153, 154, 238
Cherokee Indians, 16; constitution, 35; in East, 26, 27, 29, 41–43, 46–49, 112–113, 151, 163, 210–234, 242, 245, 264; emigration, 32, 50, 53, 225–237, 244, 288; language, 25, 30, 238; treaties, 20, 26, 48, 210–211, 215, 219, 223–225, 237; in West, 23–30, 34, 51–53, 58, 72, 77, 225, 228, 237–242, 290, 303, 305
Cheyenne Indians, 182
Chiaha Indians, 245
Chicago, Ill., 196–202
Chicago River, Ill., 125, 196
Chichipé Outipé, see Petit, Father Benjamin Marie
Chichipé Outipé Mission, Ind., 194, 203, 206, 208
Chickasaw Indians: in East, 162–166, 168; emigration, 166–172; treaties, 166; in West, 170–172, 276
Chief Blind (Mandan), 186
Child Chief (Mandan), 186
Chillicothe, Ohio, 58
Chippewa Indians: in East, 92–93, 96–98, 110, 288–289; emigration, 36, 288; treaties, 36
Chippionnock, Ill., 112, 142
Chisholm, Jesse (Cherokee), 303
Chisholm, John D., 26
Chisholm Trail, 303
Choctaw Indians, 6, 13, 14, 16, 22–23; in East, 39, 74–85, 88, 120, 162, 163, 166, 224; emigration, 74, 85–88, 91, 254; language, 18, 162, 245, 251; treaties, 75–77, 80, 82, 165, 166, 290; in West, 167, 241, 282, 290, 303
Chouteau family (Osages), 33

Christians, 67, 84, 117; see also Baptists; Catholics; Episcopalians; Methodists; missionaries; Mormons; Presbyterians; Quakers
Cincinnati, Ohio, 62
Civil War, U. S., 41, 241, 276, 312
Clark, William, 20, 23, 24, 29–30, 32, 38, 62–64, 68, 110, 115, 119–121, 294, 308
Clay, Henry, 224, 225
Clear Boggy River, Okla., 170, 172
Clermont (Osage chief), 25
Clinch, Gen. Duncan, 247, 261, 265
Coacoochee (Seminole chief), 262, 266, 273–274
Cody, William Frederick, 306
Coffee, Gen. John, 13–14, 82, 219
Colbert, James Logan, 164
Colbert, Levi (Chickasaw High Minko), 166
Colbert family (Chickasaws), 165
Colorado, 307, 310, 311
Columbia, Mo., 71
Columbus, Ga., 145, 150
Comanche Indians, 170, 211, 253, 255
Congress, U. S., 13, 293; and Indians, 20, 27, 44–48, 80, 171, 210, 219, 224, 271–272, 284–285
Constitution, U. S., 35–36
Coodey, William Shorey (Cherokee), 233, 234
Cooper, Elizabeth (Cherokee), 232
Cooper, James Fenimore, 36, 42
Coosa River, 3, 16, 151
Cooseescoowee, see Ross, John
Copinger, Polly (Creek), 258–259
Cornstalk (Seneca chief), 59
Cotter, William J., 228
Council Bluffs, Iowa, 294
councils, Indian, 2, 4, 8–9, 14, 27–30, 33, 75, 80, 97, 98, 112, 127, 150, 210, 212, 291
Crane Dance (Sac/Fox), 118

creation myths, 63, 74, 176, 228–229

Creek Indians, 2–17, 21, 79; in East, 43, 45–46, 48, 144–154, 159, 163, 165, 166, 245, 249, 259, 261, 262; emigration, 53, 148–151, 154–159, 168; language, 245; treaties, 144–147, 165, 290; in West, 146, 159, 253, 255, 290, 303, 304

Creek Wars, 7, 9–16, 22, 46, 49–50, 99, 153–155, 219, 260

Crockett, David, 13–14, 65–66, 211

Crow Belt (Mandan), 186

Crowell, John, 145, 147

Crow Indians, 174, 176, 305, 309

Crow's Breast (Hidatsa chief), 309

Cryer of the Black Drink, *see* Osceola

Cudjoe, King (black interpreter), 249–251

Cuivre River, Mo., 64–66

Cumberland River, Tenn., 235

Cusseta, Ala., 150

Dade, Mjr. Francis Langhorne, 257–261, 272

Dahlonega, Ga., 41–43, 53, 290

Dakotas, 309–310; Indians in, 174–187, 192

Dakota Sioux, 36, 138, 174, 202

Dalton, Pvt. Kinsley, 256

dances, Indian, 97, 118, 178–179, 199–202, 245, 273; war, 4, 251–252

Dancing Lakes Religion, 3–5, 14, 16

Dancing Rabbit Creek, Miss., 84

Davenport (trader), 113–115, 120, 123

Davis, Jefferson, 125, 135, 139, 293

Day, Peter, 293, 294

Dayton, Ohio, 61

dead, Indian treatment of, 67, 69–70, 112, 117, 142, 177–178

Deadman's Pond, Fla., 255

Deer-in-the-Water (Cherokee), 48

Delaware Indians: in East, 20, 45, 58; emigration, 32, 36, 62, 64–68, 85; treaties, 20, 284–285, 290, 297–298; in West, 29, 58, 59, 284, 290, 292, 297, 304–305

Dement, Mjr., 131

de Soto, Hernando, 74, 162, 164, 247

Dickens, Charles, 281–283

diseases: during emigration, 72, 86–88, 156–158, 168, 207, 234–237, 266, 270; among transplanted Indians, 33–34, 170–171; *see also* epidemics

Dixon's Ferry, Ill., 131

Doak's Stand, 77, 166

Dodge, Col. Henry, 132

Dodge, Grenville, 293–295

Doublehead (Cherokee chief), 214–215, 220

Double Springs, Okla., 239

Downing, Louis (Cherokee chief), 241

Drowning Bear (Cherokee), 227

DuVal, William, 248

Eads, Capt. Abner, 128

Eames, Charles, 96

Eastman, Col. H. E., 106

Econchattemicco (Seminole chief), 247

Ecunchate, Ala., 15, 18

Eel River Indians, 32

Egmont Key, Fla., 266, 267

Elet, Father, 208

Elk River, Okla., 67

Ellis, A. G., 97

Emathla, Holata (Seminole), 252

Emathla, Tsali (Seminole chief), 252, 257, 258

Emathlochee (Seminole chief), 247

English, Dr., 64

epidemics, Indian, 170–171, 183–187; during migrations, 64, 71, 88

Episcopalians, 61, 94, 102

Everett, Edward, 45

Everglades, Fla., 244, 269, 276–278, 280, 310

farmers, Indian, 25, 26, 29–30, 39, 45, 74–75, 113, 147, 176, 215, 216, 284, 285

Farnham (trader), 113–115

Feast of Death, 69–70

Fish Pond Town, 16

Flathead Indians, 308

Flint River, Ga., 2

Florida: Indians in, 55, 144, 154, 159, 244–278, 280; Spaniards in, 3, 26–27, 244, 245

Floyd, Gen. Charles, 234

Follett, Burley, 106

Folsom, David (Choctaw chief), 80

Folsom family (Choctaws), 77, 82

Fonda, John, 138

Forsyth, Thomas, 119–121, 130

Fort Armstrong, Ill., 117, 123

Fort Brooke, Fla., 256, 257, 260, 265, 266

Fort Clark, N. D., 181–184

Fort Coffee, 167, 170

Fort Crawford, Wis., 125, 139

Fort Dearborn, Ill., 125, 196, 197, 200, 203

Fort Drane, Fla., 261

Fort Gibson, Okla., 158, 249, 253

Fort King, Fla., 254–258, 259, 260, 266

Fort Laramie, Wyo., 306–308

Fort Malden, Can., 113, 120, 122, 124, 127, 130

Fort Mims, Ala., 7–9, 11–12, 14, 22, 45

Fort Mitchell, Ala., 154

Fort Monroe, Va., 140

Fort Moultrie, S. C., 267

Fort Pierce, Fla., 274

Fort St. Marks, Fla., 27

Fort Towson, Okla., 167, 168

Fort Union, N. Mex., 310

Fort Vincennes, Ind., 204

Fort Washita, Okla., 170, 172

Four Bears (Mandan chief), 174–186, 190

Four Men, the (Mandan), 186

Fox Indians: in East, 92, 110–123, 132, 144, 298; emigration, 36, 119; treaties, 36, 297; in West, 291–293, 297

Fox River, 98, 100; Valley, 132

Franklin, Tenn., 80

Frelinghuysen, Sen. Theodore, 44–45

Frémont, Jessie Benton, 293

Frémont, John Charles, 293

French, in America, 4, 38, 75, 110, 112, 163–164, 190–191, 204

Fur Robe (Mandan), 186

Gaines, Gen. Edmund Pendleton, 119, 121, 122, 264–265

Gaines, George, 82, 85, 119

Galena, Ill., 130, 133, 134

Gardiner, James B., 59, 60, 68–71

Garland, John (Choctaw chief), 80, 82

Garrison, William Lloyd, 44

George III of England, 112

Georgia, Indians in, 2–3, 20, 22, 35–36, 38, 41–44, 46–49, 52–55, 144–146, 151, 159, 168, 219–224, 226–228, 230, 231, 234–235, 238, 245, 258–259, 264, 290

Gold, Harriet, see Boudinot, Harriet

gold on Indian land, 41, 43, 290

Good Boy (Mandan chief), 177

Good Fur Robe (Mandan ancestor), 176, 179

Gore, Sir St. George, 305–311

Grand Medicine Societies, 92
Grand River, Mo., 66
Grant, Ulysses S., 125
Grayson, Sampson, 148
Great Lakes, 34, 92, 96, 110, 196, 200
Great Plains, 18, 288, 295, 305, 306
Great Platte Valley, Neb., 294
Great Sac Trail, 120
Great Smoky Mts., N. C., 227
Green Bay, Wis., 91, 92, 96–99, 101, 106, 110
Green Corn Ceremony (Seminole), 245, 274
Green Swamp, Fla., 258, 260, 264
Grey Eyes, John (Wyandot chief), 281, 284
Grizzly Bear (Menominee), 99

Hackley (farmer), 256
Haley, 80
Hamilton, Alexander, 125
Hamilton, "Uncle Billy," 125, 132
Hamilton, Ohio, 62
Handsome Lake (Seneca sachem), 93–94
Hanson, Rev. John H., 103, 104, 105–106
Hard Hickory (Seneca chief), 59
Harjo, Coee (Seminole), 252, 266, 267
Harjo, Eufaula (Creek chief), 148–149
Harjo, Tuski (Seminole chief), 247
Harrison, William Henry, 283
Hashequarhiqua (Sac chief), 115, 117
Hawkes, Rev. Dr., 103
Henry, Jim (Creek chief), 155
Hernandez, Gen. Joseph, 266
Herring, Elbert, 66, 68
Hickory Creek, Ill., 127
Hicks, John (Seminole), 252–253

Hidatsa Indians, 23, 178, 309, 310
Hillsborough River, Fla., 257–258, 260
History of the North American Indians (McKenney), 43
Hitchcock, Mjr. Ethan Allen, 171–172, 276–278, 280
Hitchiti Town, Ala., 154
Hitichi dialect, 245, 251
Hobart, Rt. Rev. Dr. John Henry, 94–96, 102
Hog Creek, Ohio, 68
Honey Creek, 237, 238
honor, codes of, 177–182
Horseshoe Bend, Ala., Battle of, 15–17, 22–23, 27, 42, 48, 75, 80, 100, 144, 224, 245, 259
Houma (Chickasaw High Minko), 164
Houston, Eliza Allen, 50–52, 211, 212
Houston, Margaret Lea, 211
Houston, Sam, 50–52, 211–212; and Indians, 29, 49–50, 52–54
Hunter, William H., 280
hunters: Indian, 21, 25, 30, 39, 59, 112, 113, 118, 145; white, 24, 304–312
Hutchechubbee River, Ala., 154

Iberville, Pierre Lemoyne d', 164
Illini Indians, 32
Illiniwek Indians, 110
Illinois, 38, 71, 234, 293; Indians in, 32, 93, 110–123, 127–142, 190, 196–202, 207, 288
Illinois Central Railroad, 293
Illinois River, 126, 207
Independence, Mo., 72
Indiana, 64, 71; Indians in, 29, 32, 33, 190, 193–195, 203–206
Indian Affairs, Bureau of, 35, 43, 63, 66, 68, 186–187, 280, 281, 284, 290; commissioners, 26,

Indian Affairs, Bureau of *(cont'd)* 82–84, 98, 247, 248; superintendents, 23; *see also* agents, Indian

Indian Affairs, Congressional Committee on, 46

Indianapolis, Ind., 71

Indian Removal Act, 48, 58, 248; as bill, 39–41, 43–48; and Jackson, 18, 26, 38–39, 44, 45, 55, 210; and Monroe, 26, 31–32; and Van Buren, 206

inspection tours, Indian, 23–24, 85, 165–166, 252–253

interpreters, Indian, 64–65, 84, 101, 138–140, 158, 181, 249–253, 277

Iowa, 294; Indians in, 122, 208

Iowa Indians, 292, 297

Iowa River, 119

Iroquois Indians, 42, 95, 98, 110; Six Nations, 63, 91

Irving, Washington, 54, 140

Ishtehopa (Chickasaw High Minko), 169

Jacksa Chula Harjo, *see* Jackson, Andrew

Jackson, Andrew, 5–6, 66, 235; and British, 120, 308; in Creek War, 12–17, 23, 46, 50, 75, 144, 224, 260; and Indian Removal, 17–18, 26–27, 38–39, 41–42, 44, 45, 47–48, 55, 61, 69, 80, 82, 147, 237, 247; and Indians, 26, 84, 123; as President, 52–53, 87, 91, 98–100, 110, 112, 120–122, 140, 142, 144–145, 147, 150, 158–159, 165, 183, 210, 219, 224; in Seminole War, 26–27, 245

Jackson, Ala., 5

Jefferson, Thomas, 21, 115, 116, 164–165

Jenkins, Rev., 95

Jesuits, 93, 190

Jesup, Gen. Thomas Sidney, 153–

154, 158, 262, 265, 266, 270

Johnson v. McIntosh, 27

Johnston, Albert Sidney, 125, 135

Johnston, John, 280–281, 283

Johnston family (Chickasaws), 165

Jolly, John (Cherokee chief), 29, 30, 49, 51, 72, 77

Jones, Rev. Evan, 232–233

Jones, Sam (Seminole chief), 274–277

Jumper (Seminole chief), 252, 253, 259, 260, 262, 265

Junaluska (Cherokee chief), 224

Kannekuk (Kickapoo prophet), 288–289

Kansa Indians, 31, 33, 36, 291

Kansas, 303, 305; Indians in, 33, 208, 285, 291, 295, 296–298, 303, 304

Kansas River, 33, 284

Ka-nun-da-cla-geh, *see* Ridge, the

Kaskaskia, Ill., 30

Kaskaskia Indians, 297

Kaukaulin, Wis., 101–102

Kaush-kaw-no-niew, *see* Grizzly Bear

Kellogg's Grove, Ill., 131

Kemper, Bishop Jackson, 102

Kenewatsenri, Marie Anne (Mohawk), 104

Kentucky, 234

Keokuk (Sac chief), 115, 118–119, 121, 122

Kerr, Joseph, 86

Kickapoo Indians: in East, 2, 132, 288; emigration, 32; treaties, 297; in West, 29, 170, 288–292, 297

Kinzie, Mrs. John, 198

Kiowa Indians, 170, 253, 255

Kishwaukee River, Ill., 127–130

Knoxville, Tenn., 226

Konope, Coolly (Chickasaw), 168

Koshkonong Lake, Wis., 132
Kunsha Choctaws, 75

Lake George, N. Y., 103
Lake Michigan, 92, 196, 200
Lake Superior, 110
Lane, Martin, 64–65
languages, Indian, 18, 25, 30, 94, 97, 162, 204–205, 238, 245, 251
Larsson, Anders, 200
La Salle, Robert Cavelier de, 164
Latrobe, Charles, 200–201
Lea, Margaret, *see* Houston, Margaret Lea
Leavenworth, Kans., 306
Leavenworth, Pawnee, and Western Railroad, 297–298
Lebanon, Ohio, 283
Leclair, Antoine, 142
LeFlore (Choctaw, nephew of Greenwood), 86
LeFlore, Greenwood (Choctaw chief), 80, 82, 85, 88
LeFlore, Louis, 77
LcFlore, Michael, 77
LeFlore family (Choctaws), 82
legends, Indian, 63, 74, 118, 176, 228–229
Lewis, Meriwether, 20, 30, 38, 110, 115
Lewis and Clark Expedition, 20
Lewistown, Ohio, 68
Lincoln, Abraham, 124, 126
Little Duck, *see* Petit, Father Benjamin Marie
Little Rock, Ark., 235, 237, 249
Livermore, Miss, 289
Logan, Ohio, 283
Logansport, Ind., 207
Lost Prince, The (Hanson), 103
Lot, Arthur, 45
Louisiana, 78, 86; Indians in, 163–164; Purchase, 20, 21
"Louis XVII of France," 102–107

Love family (Chickasaws), 165
Lovely, Mjr. William, 25–26
Lucina, Sister, 203
Lumhe Chati, *see* Red Eagle
Lumpkin, Wilson: Congressman, 45–48, 52; Ga. Governor, 52, 219, 225, 234, 235, 238

Mabila, Ala., *see* Mobile, Ala.
Mabila Indians, 4
McCoy, Isaac, 34–35, 96, 197–198
McDonald, John 212
McGillivray, Alexander, 20
McGilvery family (Chickasaws), 165
McIntosh, Roley (Creek chief), 156
McIntosh, William (Creek chief), 36, 146, 156
McIntosh Creeks, 149
McIntosh family (Chickasaws), 164, 165
McKenney, Thomas, 43–44
McNac (Creek), 9
McQueen, James, 258
McQueen, Peter (Creek), 5, 6, 8, 259
Mad Bear (Mandan), 186
Madison, James, 21–22, 165
Magdalene, Sister, 203
Maine, Indians in, 42
Ma-ka-tai-me-she-kia-kiak, *see* Black Hawk
Mandan Indians, 23, 174–187, 192, 309
Manypenny, George W., 290–292, 295–299
Ma-to-toh-pe, *see* Four Bears
Marais des Cygnes, Mo., 66–67
Marshall, John, 27, 36, 52
Mascouten Indians, 288
Massachusetts, Indians in, 45, 92
Maximilian of Neuwied, 181
medicine bags, 131, 136, 139
medicine bundles, 162, 177

medicine men, 74, 87, 113, 159, 179, 212–214, 266
Medicine Rock, N. D., 174, 182
Memphis, Tenn., 156
Menawa (Creek chief), 156
Menominee Indians: in East, 92–93, 96–99, 138; emigration, 288; treaties, 98–100
Menomini (Potawatomi chief), 203, 205
Methodists, 60, 79, 80, 165, 281, 284
Mexico, 150, 211, 288, 293, 298
Miami Indians: in East, 2, 30; emigration, 32, 36, 210; treaties, 36, 290, 297; in West, 290–292, 297, 303, 310
Miami River, Ohio, 62
Micanopy (Seminole chief), 249, 251, 252, 259
Micco, Eneah (Creek chief), 145, 150, 154
Micco, Yahola (Creek chief), 3
Michigan, 131; Indians in, 41, 58, 110, 120, 190, 203, 288
migrations, Indian, 24, 31, 55, 58, 60–68, 70–72, 74, 85–88, 91, 119, 122, 148–151, 154–159, 166–172, 203–207, 210, 225, 237, 244, 266, 269, 276–277, 283–284, 288
Mikasuki, Fla., 243, 253
militia: Ala., 5–7, 12; Ark., 156; Ga., 49, 151, 219–223, 228; Ill., 121, 124–127, 129, 135, 136, 137, 138; Mich., 125, 132
Millard, John M., 167–168
Milwaukee, Wis., 127
Mims, Samuel, 7, 11
Minetaree Indians, 176
Mingo Indians, 32
Minnesota, Indians in, 288
Misha Sipokni, see Mississippi
missionaries, 33–34, 49, 79–80, 81, 94, 95, 101–102, 165, 191–196, 203–208, 217, 238, 241, 281, 284, 288, 297, 299, 304
Mississippi, 120; Indians in, 39, 74, 77–79, 82, 85, 162, 163, 165, 166, 168, 169, 170
Miss. and Mo. Railroad, 294
Mississippi River, 23, 25, 30, 32, 74, 93, 110, 111, 113, 118, 122, 135–137, 142, 156–158, 167, 207, 235, 278, 302
Missouri, 72, 101; Indians in, 32, 284, 285
Missouri Indians, 292, 297
Missouri River, 29, 64, 66, 72, 174, 176–177, 302; Valley, 174, 294
Mitutak, 178, 186
Mobile, Ala., 4
Mohawk Indians, 91, 93, 94, 103; language, 94
Mohegan Indians, 169
Monroe, James, 21, 26, 31, 35, 36, 165
Montana, 311
Montgomery, Ala., 155
Mordecai, Abraham, 14–15
Mormons, 207, 294
Morris, Lt. Gouverneur, 168
Morse, Rev. Jedidiah, 33, 34, 38
Moshulatubbee (Choctaw chief), 75–79, 82, 84, 87, 88
Mott, Dr. Valentine, 269
Moultrie Creek, Fla., 247, 255, 266
Mound City, Mo., 306
Muk-a-ta-quet (Sac ancestor), 131
Mukonse (Potawatomi), 198
Mulatto King (Seminole chief), 247
Muncietown, Ind., 64–66
Munsee Indians, 96, 101, 288
Muskogee Creeks, 21, 245
Muskogee dialect, 162, 245, 251

Na-na-ma-kee (Sac ancestor), 131
Nanih Waya, 74–75, 78, 85, 88

Nashville, Tenn., 12, 75, 23, 123
Natchez, Miss., 75
Natchez Indians, 4, 163–164
Neamathla (Creek chief), 144, 154–156, 247, 249
Neapope (Sac), 120–122, 127, 130, 134, 140
Nebraska, 295, 305, 310; Indians in, 288, 291, 303, 310
Nehathloco (Seminole), 253
Neosho River, 59, 237
New Echota, Ga., 48
New Jersey, Indians in, 45
New Salem, Ill., 124
newspapers: Indian, 38, 217; white, 62, 65, 71, 79, 96, 133, 144–145, 153, 155–158, 169, 231–232, 269, 272, 283, 293, 305
New York City, Indian visitors to, 118, 140
New York State, Indians in, 29, 42, 61, 91–92, 95, 97–100, 102
Nitakechi (Choctaw chief), 82
Nocowee (Cherokee), 235
North Carolina, Indians in, 226–227, 230, 242
North Dakota, Indians in, 174–187, 192
Northrup, Sarah, *see* Ridge, Sarah Northrup
Nupta, 178, 186

Ochlocknee Seminoles, 276–277
Ocmulgee River, Ga., 2
Oconee Indians, 245
Oconee River, Ga., 20
Ocooch Mts., Wis., 135, 136
Offutt, Denton, 124
Ogden, David A., 91–92, 99, 100
Ogden Land Co., 96, 99
Ohio, Indians in, 2, 27, 29–30, 32, 33, 42, 54–55, 58–62, 68–71, 91, 147, 280–284
Ohio River, 234, 282, 283

Okeechobee Lake, Fla., 269
Okeepa ceremony (Mandans), 178–183, 185
Oklahoma, 78, 88, 305; Indians in, 18, 33, 67, 150, 159, 170, 171, 225, 237, 238, 256, 266, 270, 276, 298, 303
Old Buffalo (Mandan), 186
Old Rough and Ready, *see* Taylor, Zachary
Omaha Indians, 292, 294–295, 297
Onderdonk, Rt. Rev. Henry, 102
Oneida Indians: in East, 32, 91, 93–101, 106; language, 94; treaties, 98–100
Onondaga Indians, 91
Ontario Indians, 32
Ootsetee Ardeetahskee, *see* Houston, Sam
Opothleyaholo (Creek chief), 150, 151, 153, 154, 158
Oquanoxa, Ohio, 68
Oregon, 38, 293; Indians in, 298
Oregon Trail, 308
Osage Indians, 23–26, 30, 31, 33, 34, 58, 59, 62, 85, 112–113, 253, 289; treaties, 23–24, 36
Osceola (Seminole chief), 249, 253–262, 264–270
Oshkosh (Menominee chief), 98–100
Oto Indians, 292, 297
Ottawa Indians: in East, 2, 30, 34, 35, 58, 68, 70, 117, 139, 197; emigration, 36, 71–72, 210, 280; treaties, 36; in West, 291
Outchequa (Sac chief), 115, 117
Overland Trail, 308
Owen, Hardiman, 148
Ozark Mts., 23

Pacific Railroad, 295
Page, Capt. John, 148, 155
Pahuska (Osage chief), 24

Panther, the (Sac chief), 115, 117
Panton Leslie and Co., 3, 4, 6, 11, 21
Pascofa (Seminole chief), 276–278, 280
Pawnee Indians, 31–32, 304–305, 310
Payamataha (Chickasaw High Minko), 164
Payne, John Howard, 220–223, 233
Payne's Landing, Fla., 248, 251
Pecatonica River, 131, 132
Penn, William, 65
Penobscot Indians, 42
Pennsylvania, 38
Pensacola, Fla., 3–6, 8, 27, 245, 259
People of Fire, see Potawatomi Indians
Peoria Indians, 29, 291–292, 297
Petit, Father Benjamin Marie, 191–196, 203–208, 227
Petit, Mme. Chauvin, 191–193, 196
Petit, Paul, 191–193
Phagan, John, 253, 254
Pheasant (Mandan), 186
Pheasant People, see Mandan Indians
Philadelphia Chronicle, 293
Philleo, Dr. Addison, 133–134, 137
Piankeshaw Indians: emigration, 32, 210, 288; treaties, 297; in West, 29, 291–292, 297
Piegan Blackfeet, 309
Piegan Indians, 23
Pierce, Pres. Franklin, 290–291
Pike, Zebulon Montgomery, 302
Pike's Peak, Colo., 307
Pilgrims, 38
Pine Lake (Mandan), 186
Piomingo (Chickasaw High Minko), 164
Piqua, Ohio, 58
Pitchlynn (Choctaw chief), 282

Pitchlynn, John, 77
Pitchlynn, Peter (Choctaw), 84
Pitchlynn family (Choctaws), 77, 82
Plains Indians, 18, 24, 25, 311
Planting Festival (Oneidas), 93
Platte River, 294, 304, 306
Plumbe, John, 294
Plume (Mandan), 186
Poinsett, War Secy. Joel, 205, 271–272
Pokagon, Leopold (Potawatomi chief), 196–199, 202, 203
Pontotoc, Miss., 166, 169
Port Leon, Fla., 277
Potawatomi Indians: in East, 2, 117, 123, 127–128, 190–206, 227; emigration, 36, 206–208, 210, 288; language, 204–205; treaties, 36, 195–197, 298; in West, 290, 298
Powell, Billy, see Osceola
Powell (trader), 258
Powhatan (Algonquin), 21
Prairie du Chien, Wis., 25, 125, 133, 135, 139
Presbyterians, 82, 95, 165
prophets, Indian, 2, 11, 93–94, 113, 288–289
prospectors, white, 42–43
Pushmataha (Choctaw chief), 13, 75, 77–78, 82, 224
Putnam's Magazine, 102–104, 106

Quakers, 44, 47, 71
Quashquame (Sac chief), 115, 117
Quincy, Ill., 207
Quitewepea (Shawnee chief), 27, 29–30, 32, 33, 35, 58

railroads, 292–294, 297–298
rainmakers, 178
Randolph, John, 212, 244
rapes, by soldiers, 137–138, 140

Red Eagle (Creek chief), 4, 8–9, 11–17, 22, 42, 48, 79, 100, 144, 245, 259, 262
Red Jacket (Seneca chief), 65
Red River, 18, 24, 77, 80, 85, 88, 167, 293
Red Stick warriors, 4, 5, 9, 11–17, 245, 259
Ree Indians, 184, 186
Reid, Robert, 271
religions, Indians, 3–5, 9, 14, 16, 34, 63, 67, 69, 92–93, 117, 163–164, 176–177, 214, 217, 245; *see also* Christians; creation myths; sacred ground, Indian
Returning Bear (Mandan), 186
Revolution, American, 20, 164, 212, 214
Reynolds, Gov. John of Ill., 119–124, 126
Ridge, the (Cherokee chief), 212–217, 219–220, 223–225, 237–241
Ridge, John (Cherokee), 212, 216–217, 219–220, 223, 224, 231, 237–242
Ridge, John Rollin (Cherokee), 240
Ridge, Sarah Northrup, 216, 240
rights of Indians, 41, 44, 78–79
Robinson, Mr., 106
Rock Island, Ill., 110, 115, 117, 119, 121–123, 127, 130–131, 142
Rock Island Railroad, 293, 294
Rock River, Ill., 110–111, 113, 122, 126, 142; Valley, 123, 132
Rocky Mts., 302, 305–306, 308, 310
Rocky Mt. Fur Co., 308
Rodenbough, Pvt. Theophilus, 274–275
Rogers, James (Cherokee), 239
Rogers, Tiana (Cherokee), 52, 53, 211
Rogers, Will, 239
Ross, Allen (Cherokee), 240

Ross, Daniel, 212
Ross, John (Cherokee chief), 48, 53, 210, 212, 217, 219–223, 226–228, 231, 233, 235–237, 239, 241
Ross, Mary McDonald, 212
Ross, Quatie (Cherokee), 210, 212, 217, 219, 234–237
Ross's Landing, Tenn., 220, 230, 234
Rousseau, Jean-Jacques, 42

Sacajawea (Shoshone), 20, 30, 68, 181
Sac Indians: in East, 92, 110–123, 127–142, 144, 298; emigration, 36, 119, 136; treaties, 36, 116–117, 119, 297; in West, 122, 202, 203, 207
sacred ground, Indian, 14–16, 31, 74–75, 78, 85, 88, 134, 174
St. Augustine, Fla., 244, 247, 266, 267, 269
St. Charles, Mo., 64
St. Joseph, Mich., 198
St. Louis, Mo., 33, 62–63, 66, 71, 207, 306
St. Mark's River, Fla., 277
St. Mary's, Ind., 64
St. Mary's Lake, Ind., 208
Sandusky, Ohio, 58, 280–283
Sandusky River, Ohio, 281
Sanford, Gen., 150
San Jacinto, Tex., Battle of, 211–212
Sanota (Creek), 12
Santa Anna, Gen. Antonio López de, 211
Saukenuk, Ill., 110–112, 117–119, 122, 123, 142, 280
Schermerhorn, Rev. J. F., 223, 249, 253, 254
Schermerhorn Treaty, 223–224, 238
schools: mission, 78, 86, 91, 92, 197–198, 212, 216, 242, 248, 284, 291

Scott, Gen. Winfield, 226–232, 234, 235, 262, 264–265

Sehoyah (Cherokee), 215, 240

Seminole Indians: in East, 5, 26–27, 154, 165, 244–262, 264–277, 280; emigration, 266, 269–270, 276–278, 288; treaties, 165, 247, 249–253, 255, 277, 290; in West, 253, 269, 270, 290

Seminole Wars, 26–27, 245–246, 254, 256–262, 264–266, 269–277, 281, 298

Seneca Indians: in East, 58, 59, 91, 93; emigration, 32, 60–68, 70, 71, 85, 147, 254, 280, 288; treaties, 59

Seneca Steel (Seneca chief), 59

Sequoyah (Cherokee chief), 25, 30, 241

Setelechee, Ala., 150

settlers, white, 2, 17, 21–22, 31, 98, 119–120, 122, 132, 153, 165, 290, 291

Seven Hairs (Mandan), 186

Shabbona (Potawatomi chief), 127–128, 132, 198

Shawnee Indians, 2, 3, 27; in East, 29, 30, 36, 58, 68–70, 283; emigration, 32, 55, 70–72, 85, 147, 288; treaties, 290, 297; in West, 54, 85, 170, 290–292, 297

Sherman, William Tecumseh, 274

Siminoli, see Seminole Indians

Singing Bird (Sac), 113, 133

Sioux Indians, 36, 112–113, 138, 174, 176, 178, 181–184, 202, 253, 304, 311; languages, 97

Sisemore's Ferry, Ala., 5

slaves, black, 8–11; escaped, 246–247; of Indians, 84, 148, 154, 225, 246

Sleeping Rabbit (Cherokee), 48

Slim Fellow (Cherokee), 48

Small Cloud Spicer (Seneca chief), 59

Snake Indians, 308

Soskonharowane, Charles (Mohawk), 104

Spaniards, in America, 3, 26–27, 75, 116, 164, 302; and Indians, 4–5, 8, 244

Spencer, John, 123

Spencer-Westworth-Fitzwilliam, Sir William Thomas, 306

Sprague, Sen., 45

Squanto (Pawtuxet), 38

Staked Plains, Tex., 303, 311

Stambaugh, Thomas, 99, 100

Stewart, John, 281

Stewart, Sir William Drummond, 305

Stidham, Widow, 148

Stillman, Mjr. Isaiah, 126–128, 129

"Stillman's Run," 129–130, 134

Stockbridge Indians, 92, 96, 100–101

Stuart family (Chickasaws), 164

Summendewat (Wyandot chief), 281

Sundown, John, 101

Supreme Court, U. S., 27, 36, 42, 52

Suwannee Valley, Fla., 255

Tahlequah, Okla., 239

Tahlonteskee (Cherokee chief), 23–24, 29, 49, 50, 53, 239

Taino Indians, 3

Tait, David, 9

Takotoka (Cherokee chief), 29, 30, 50, 53

Talladega, Ala., 14

Tallahassee, Fla., 144, 154, 247, 264, 277

Tallai (Osage chief), 25

Tallapoosa River, Ala., 3, 14–17

Tallassee Creeks, 5, 259
Talley, Rev., 80
Tallussahatchee, Ala., 13–14
Tampa Bay, Fla., 244, 247–248, 256, 265, 266, 269, 274, 276
Taylor, Zachary, 124–125, 138, 139, 196, 262, 270, 273, 274, 298
Tecumtha (Shawnee chief), 2–4, 16, 27, 32, 48, 54, 55, 85, 128, 200, 283
Ten Islands, Ala., 13
Tennessee, Indians in, 50, 162, 219–220, 223, 232–234
Tennessee River, 235
Tensaw Lake, Ala., 7
Tenskwatawa (Shawnee), 2, 33
Tequesta Indians, 244
territories, Indian, 20–24, 30–31, 35, 58, 67, 72, 88, 170, 225, 228, 237–241, 252–253, 269–270, 284–285, 290, 295–296, 302, 303, 311
Texas, 150, 211, 303, 311
Thomas, William, 227
Thompson, Gen. Wiley, 254–261, 267, 269
Thompson, Mary Weedon, 267, 269
Throckmorton, Capt. Joseph, 136, 138
Tigertail (Seminole), 262
Timucua Indians, 4, 244, 245
Tipton, Gen. John, 206, 207
Tombigbee River, Ala., 3–5, 75, 77
Tonawanda, N. Y., 92
traders, white, 3, 4, 14, 20, 23, 34, 52, 68, 70, 82, 98, 113–115, 120, 123, 146, 164, 181, 182, 198, 259
treaties: Indian–Indian, 23–24, 98–100, 166, 284–285; Indian–U. S., 17, 26, 35–36, 39, 44, 48, 59, 68, 75–77, 80, 82, 116–117, 119, 144–147, 165, 166, 195–196, 210–211, 215, 219, 223–225, 247, 249–253, 255, 278, 280, 290–292, 295, 297–298
Trembling Lands, Wis., 132, 136
Troy, Mo., 64
Tsala Apopka Lake, Fla., 264
Tsali (Cherokee), 226–227
Tuckabatchee, 4–5
Tulsa, Okla., 149
Tuscaloosa, Ala., 148
Tuscarora, N. Y., 92
Tuscarora Indians, 30, 91
Tuskalusa (Chocktaw chief), 74–75
Tuskegee, Ala., 153
Tustenuggee, Hallek (Seminole chief), 275–276
Two Hearts (Mandan), 186
Tyler, John, 284

Union Pacific Railway, 295
Upshaw, A. M. M., 168, 171
Ute Indians, 308

Van Buren, Martin, 159, 183, 196, 206, 210, 223, 226, 228
Vandalia, Ill., 120
Vandruff, Joshua, 119–121
Van Horne, Lt. Jefferson, 86–87
Vann, Joseph (Cherokee chief), 48, 219
Verdigris River, 18, 25, 149, 150
Vincennes, Ind., 190, 192, 203

Wabash River, Ind., 71
Wabokeshiek, *see* White Cloud
Wahoo Swamp, Fla., 260, 269
Walker, William (Wyandot), 284
Wapakoneta, Ohio, 30, 32, 36, 58, 68
War Dept., U. S., 32, 33, 35, 43, 59, 92, 96, 171, 172
War of 1812, 2, 32, 117–118, 124, 254, 265
warriors, Indian, 4, 5, 9, 11–17, 23, 162–163, 177–182

wars: Indian–Indian, 9, 13, 14, 82, 174, 241; Indian–U. S., 5, 121, 128–140; *see also* Civil War, U. S.; Creek Wars; Revolution, American; Seminole Wars; War of 1812

Washington, D. C., Indian visitors to, 32, 48, 77–78, 99, 118–119, 195–196, 203, 205, 219, 226

Washita Valley, Okla., 170

Watie, Stand (Cherokee), 219–220, 223, 239–241

Waubonsee (Potawatomi chief), 127–128

Wea Indians, 29, 32, 210, 288, 291, 292, 297

Weatherford, Bill, *see* Red Eagle

Weatherford, John, 8

Webster, Daniel, 27, 36, 210

Weedon, Dr. Frederick, 267–269

Weedon, Mary, *see* Thompson, Mary Weedon

West Indies, 3

West Point, N. Y., 119

We-wa-thlock-o, *see* Withlacoochee

Whippingstick (Seneca), 64

Whirling Thunder (Sac), 123, 140

whiskey and Indians, 3, 23, 29, 34, 36, 42, 70–72, 79, 88, 119, 120, 146, 158, 164–166, 201, 226, 235, 250, 261, 284

Whistler, Mjr. William, 125

White Beaver, *see* Atkinson, Gen. Henry

White Bird, *see* Ross, John

White Cloud (Sac-Winnebago), 113, 121–123, 127, 130, 139–140

White Hair, *see* Pahuska

White Path (Cherokee chief), 48, 235

White Rock, Ill., 127, 128

Whiteside, Gen., 126

Wichita Indians, 253

Wilkinson, Gen. James, 116, 132

Williams, Eleazer (Mohawk), 91–107

Williams, Mary Ann (Mohawk), 105

Winnebago Indians: in East, 2, 92–93, 96–98, 113, 117, 123, 127, 130, 133, 135, 136, 139; emigration, 36, 210, 288; treaties, 36; in West, 310

Wisconsin, Indians in, 92–101, 110, 132–134, 264, 288

Wisconsin Heights, Wis., Battle of, 135

Wisconsin River, 133–134, 135

Wise, Henry, 224, 271–272

Withlacoochee River, Fla., 258, 261; Battle of, 261; Cove, 264

Wolf Chief (Mandan), 186

Wool, Gen. John Ellis, 223–226

Woolfolk, Dr., 64

Worchester, Samuel, 241

Worth, Gen. William Jenkins, 274

Wounded Knee, S. D., 312

Wright, Allen (Choctaw), 18

Wyandot Indians: in East, 30, 58, 60, 280–284; emigration, 32, 238–284, 288; treaties, 280; in West, 284–285, 290

Wyoming, 311

Xenia, Ohio, 283

Yaharjo (Seminole), 252

Yamassee Indians, 244, 245

Yellow River, Ind., 193

Yellowstone, Wyo./Mont., 308, 309

Yonaguska, *see* Drowning Bear

Young, Brigham, 207

Yuchi Indians, 245

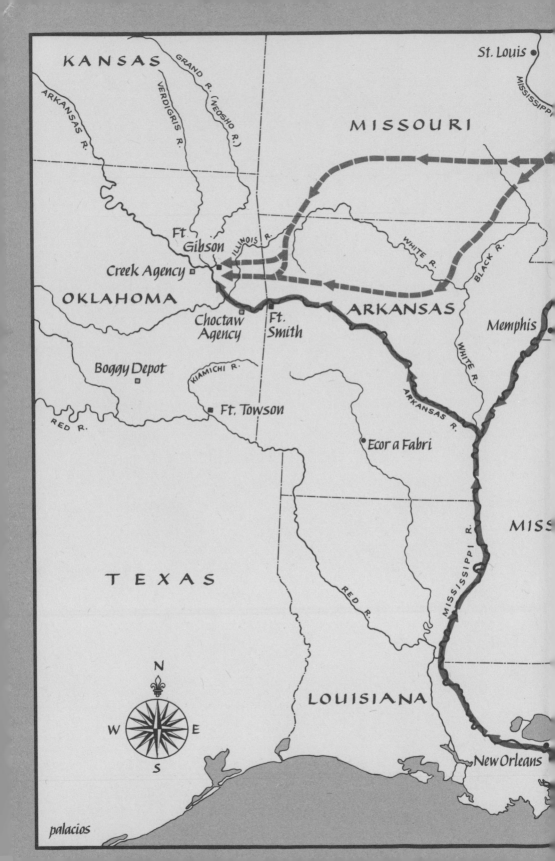